CANADA
THE TWENTIETH CENTURY

Fred McFadden

Don Quinlan

Rick Life

Fitzhenry & Whiteside

Contents

EDITOR-IN-CHIEF: Robert Read
EDITORS: Ian Gillen, Steven Rauchman,
Elizabeth Reid, Rosalind Sharpe
DESIGNER: Susan Budd
CARTOGRAPHER: Susan Wilkinson
COVER ARTIST: Brent Armstrong
PROJECT COORDINATOR: Elizabeth Reid

My contribution to this book is dedicated
to my parents in gratitude for their
inspiration and encouragement. D.Q.

Canadian Cataloguing in Publication Data

McFadden, Fred, 1928-
  Canada, the twentieth century

Includes index.
For use in schools.
ISBN 0-88902-198-8

1. Canada — History — 20th century. I. Quinlan, Don, 1947 —
  II. Life, Rick, 1953 —   III. Title.

C600.M32   971.06   C82-094334-7
F1034.2.M32

ISBN 0-88902-198-8

Here is a key to the images that appear on the cover of this book. Some faces are well known. Others represent Canadians active in a variety of fields during the twentieth century.

1. Longliner and fishermen, Newfoundland.
2. J.S. Woodsworth, 1874-1942, CCF leader.
3. Wilfred Grenfell, 1865-1940, medical missionary.
4. Marshall McLuhan, 1911-1980, writer and teacher.
5. Gabrielle Roy, born 1909, novelist.
6. Anne Murray, born 1945, singer.
7. Charlotte Whitton, 1896-1975, Ottawa mayor.
8. Frank Augustyn, born 1953, dancer.
9. Karen Kain, born 1951, dancer.
10. Norman Bethune, 1890-1939, surgeon.
11. William Aberhart, 1878-1943, Alberta premier.
12. Oscar Peterson, born 1926, jazz pianist.
13. Lionel Conacher, 1900-1954, athlete.
14. Henry Larsen, 1899-1964, navigator.
15. Mackenzie King, 1874-1950, prime minister.
16. Price-rise protester, 1950.
17. René Lévesque, born 1922, Quebec premier.
18. Car in Ontario mud, 1915.
19. Cora Hind, 1862-1942, journalist.
20. Forestry worker, British Columbia.
21. Marion Hilliard, 1902-1958, doctor.
22. Barbara Ann Scott, born 1926, skater.
23. Joe Clark, born 1939, prime minister.
24. Abby Hoffman, born 1947, athlete.
25. Canadian pavilion, Expo 67.
26. Maurice Richard, born 1921, hockey player.
27. Joey Smallwood, born 1901, Newfoundland premier.
28. Lucy Maud Montgomery, 1874-1942, author.
29. Railway workers, Manitoba.
30. Pierre Trudeau, born 1921, prime minister.
31. Foundry worker, Alberta.
32. Frederick Banting, 1891-1941, doctor.
33. Flora MacDonald, born 1926, politician.
34. David Suzuki, born 1936, scientist.
35. Mary Pickford, 1893-1979, actress.
36. Billy Bishop, 1894-1956, flyer.
37. Marie, Yvonne, Cécile, Annette, and Emilie Dionne, quintuplets, born 1934.
38. Reginald Fessenden, 1866-1932, inventor.
39. Paul-Emile Léger, born 1904, missionary.
40. John Diefenbaker, 1895-1979, prime minister.
41. Lord Beaverbrook, 1879-1964, statesman.
42. Nancy Greene, born 1943, skier.
43. Dan George, 1899-1981, actor.
44. Oil workers, Saskatchewan.

An advertising poster at the turn of the century. Fire hoses are now made of rubber and cotton. Before rubber and modern synthetics such as vinyl became common, leather was used for its strength and flexibility.

"October, a thousand shades of orange and yellow," by Clarence Gagnon. This is one of a series of illustrations that the artist painted between 1928 and 1933 for the famous French-Canadian novel *Maria Chapdelaine*. While ploughs like this were still used on small long-established farms, in the early years of the century machinery was making life easier for farmers all over Canada.

"New Canadians at Gonor, Manitoba," a woodcut by Valentine Fanshawe. Immigrants like this group of Ukrainian Orthodox churchgoers brought their ways of life and religious beliefs to their new country.

The cities grow. *Left:* the Union Bank building under construction at King and Bay Streets, Toronto, 1915, by Owen Staples.
Below: this was the scene a block east at the corner of King and Yonge Streets as seen by Dorothy Stevens in 1916.

The Canadian National Exhibition in the
well-established East.

The Dominion Exhibition in the still-growing West.

The Second Battle of Ypres, 22 April to 25 May 1915, by Richard Jack. Canadian soldiers face the first poison gas attack.

"WHY DON'T THEY COME?"

WHY BE
A MERE SPECTATOR HERE
WHEN YOU SHOULD PLAY A MANS PART
IN THE REAL GAME OVERSEAS?

JOIN
THE
148TH Battalion.
A.A.MAGEE,
LT COL.
Headquarters
197, PEEL ST.
MONTREAL.

OVERSEAS · BATTALION · CANADA
148
GRAND ESCVNT · AVCTA LABORE

AFFILIATED WITH
MᶜGILL UNIVERSITY CONTINGENT
CANADIAN OFFICERS TRAINING
CORPS.

J.J. GIBSONS LIMITED, MONTREAL-TORONTO.

If You
Gave Every
Dollar
You Own

how little would the sacrifice be compared to theirs.
We are not asked to give. We are asked only to *lend*. To
lend at good interest secured by the best collateral on earth.

Victory Bonds

THIS SPACE DONATED BY

FASHION CRAFT MFRS.
LIMITED
MONTREAL

If interested tear out this page and place with letters to be answered.

Above: an advertisement in *Men's Wear Review,* November, 1918. During the war, advertisers often gave up their space to promote the war effort.

Left: A World War I recruiting poster. By this time, hockey was already known as a "spectator sport."

"Launching the Seaplane," 1918, by Arthur Lismer. This plane was being launched from a United States naval air station at Eastern Passage, Nova Scotia. "Pusher" propellers were common in this period and are still used on some types of aircraft today.

An inspirational poster advertising an art exhibition to aid the war effort, 1914, by J.E.H. MacDonald. People in all walks of life, including artists, wanted to do their part.

In peacetime a Canadian Pacific poster invites Canadians to explore the splendour of their country.

An advertisement in *Mayfair Magazine*, October 1929, emphasizes the importance of public transportation.

An advertisement in *Canadian Automotive Trade*, October 1926, points out the advantages of buying Canadian.

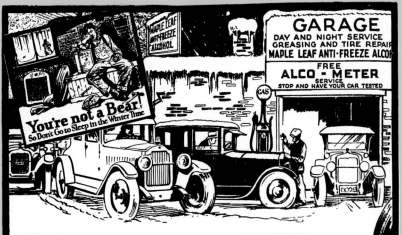

Brisk Business all Winter

Start your customers with "Maple Leaf" Anti-Freeze and "Alco-Meter" Service, and they will keep coming back all Winter.

To keep the slump out of your Winter business you must plan to keep your customers interested in your Winter service. Tell them about "Maple Leaf" Anti-Freeze and "Alco-Meter" Service, and invite them to leave their car with you for a few hours to put it in condition for Winter driving.

Make your customer a flat rate for this work, including the "Maple Leaf" Anti-Freeze, and tell him to come back as often as he wishes, but not less than once a week,

for an "Alco-Meter" test. **This will make a busy place of your garage or service station all winter, and your customers will appreciate the interest you take in their cars.**

Don't stock Anti-Freeze mixtures of unknown ingredients. Beware of Anti-Freeze compounds that are "Chemically Treated," they usually contain Calcium Chloride or other chemicals **that are injurious.** You are not looking after your customer's interest if you ask him to take chances with his car.

MAPLE LEAF
ANTI-FREEZE
ALCOHOL

FOR SALE BY ALL LEADING WHOLESALERS

If your wholesaler doesn't list MAPLE LEAF, write us direct

Canadian Industrial Alcohol Co., Limited, Montreal

Distributing Warehouses—Montreal, Toronto, Winnipeg, Vancouver

Another advertisement in the same issue of *Canadian Automotive Trade* offers service station operators useful tips on how to keep their business active in winter.

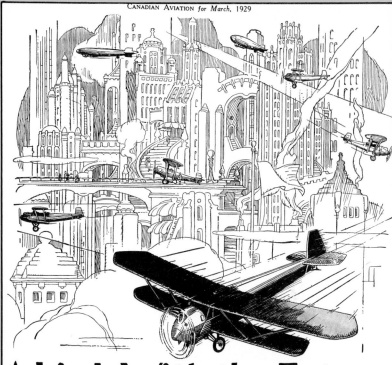

A Link With the Future

THE Great Cities of the Future! Lofty towers piercing the clouds . . . the heavens filled with commerce . . . the earth a lowly pedestal from which vast masses of masonry reach up to dim heights . . . stupendous monuments to man's conquest of the air!

And today, as if in anticipation, man is becoming air-minded.

Have you ever thought of all that the aeroplane has done! Have you ever thought that man's dominion of the air is an accomplished fact? Do you realize that the pioneer phase of aviation has passed . . . that the great doors of the Future are flung open to YOU?

The Reid Rambler is a link with the future. Already its Cirrus engine has won world-wide

acclamation by flights from London to Capetown– and back; from England to Australia; by winning the King's Air Cup in 1926 and 1927.

Its great strength is assured by wings and fuselage constructed of metal throughout. Its ease of control, its simplicity of construction, its economy of operation and maintenance . . . these qualities combine to make it the ideal plane for use by Flying Schools, Forest Patrols, Training Schools and . . . by the Private Owner.

The Reid Rambler is everywhere welcomed by men with forward-looking minds—men who bring distant markets infinitely nearer—who accelerate all their business activities by using this perfect expression of sane, swift, safe transportation. With its simplified dual control, you may quickly learn to fly the Rambler or, if you prefer, employ a pilot. Be in the vanguard of progress. Link up with the Future.

Write today for descriptive literature and prices.

A certificate of Airworthiness by the Director of Civil Aviation, Ottawa, is supplied with every Rambler.

RAMBLER
The Only All-metal Light Aeroplane

Curtiss-Reid Aircraft Company, Limited, Montreal

Airpark · · St. Laurent, Que.

An advertisement for a Canadian-built aircraft in *Canadian Aviation*, March 1929, offers the artist's impression of the world of the future.

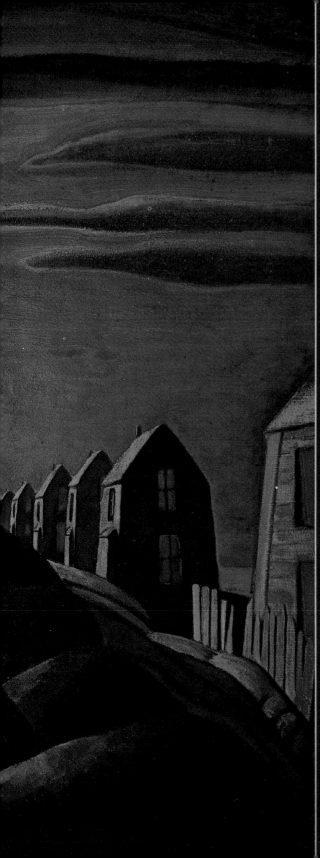

Sing a Song of Sixpence

Sing a song of sixpence,
 A pocketful of dough;
What? The timbers weren't safe?
 The inspector didn't know.

Sing a song of sixpence,
 Of dividends to sign,
Families need food you see,
 And that's why miners mine.

Sing a song of sixpence,
 Machines displacing men;
Songs of wealth and poverty,
 "They cut our pay again."

Sing a song of sixpence,
 A paycheck lean and thin,
"Judge, the children needed shoes —
 I took them." "Lock him in!"

Sing a song of labour,
 You men who dig the coal;
Only men who are organized
 Dare say each owns his soul.

Mildred Gaimes in The Nova Scotia Miner,
Glace Bay, Nova Scotia, 10 May 1930.

"Miners' Houses, Glace Bay," 1921,
 by Lawren S. Harris.

Mining

*Transportation and
Communication*

Refining

Agriculture

Oil

*Engineering and
Construction*

*Pulp and
Paper*

Smelting

Sketches for murals at the Toronto Stock Exchange, 1936, by Charles Fraser Comfort.

Above: "Bombs Away," 1943, by Paul Goranson showing action on a Halifax bomber. Goranson was an official war artist. At the right are some sketches by Goranson. He made notes on each sketch to remind himself of the colours in case he decided to turn it into a finished painting. *Top:* "Flight engineer;" *Lower Left:* "Plotting the course;" *Lower right:* "Dorsal gunner."

"Tank Advance," 1943, by Lawren P. Harris (son of Lawren S. Harris who painted "Miners' Houses" on pages 16 and 17). Harris was an official war artist sent to cover the Italian campaign. High on a hill above the camouflaged tanks are the ruins of the abbey of Monte Cassino. The monastery had been heavily bombed by the Allies in their attempt to take the hill.

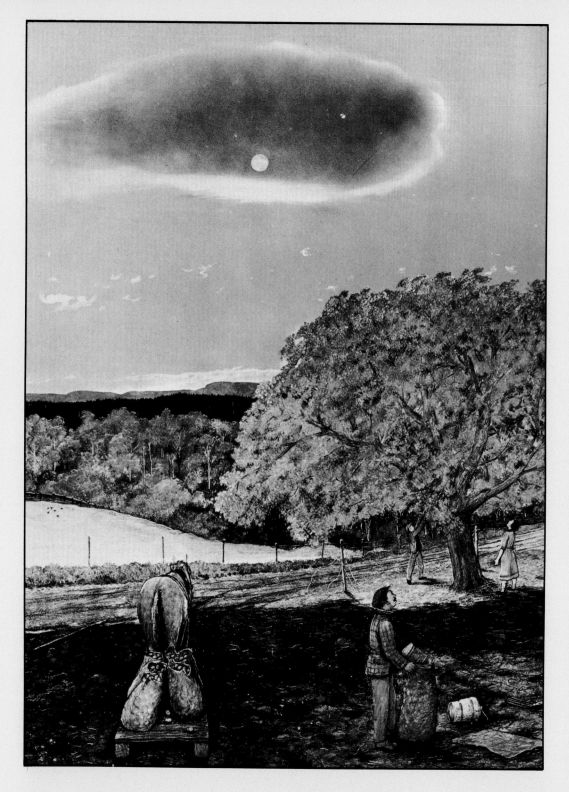

Hockey Hassles

William dreaded arguments, and there always seemed to be arguments in hockey games. A common cause was the lack of a net. For goal posts, two oak poles had been driven into the ground before flooding, but without a net it was often difficult to tell which side of the post the puck had gone. William was a poor skater and preferred not to play on skates, so he was made goalie. This put him right in the center of the arguments. All the boys joined in. Sometimes, one side pretended to be generous and give in on a goal. But usually the side that shouted the loudest and longest won the point.

William made his own shin pads by cutting off old trouser legs and sewing them up and down at regular, spaced intervals. Into these narrow pockets he slipped thin slats from apple boxes and then attached the pads to his legs with rubber sealing rings from his mother's preserve jars.

The goalie's stick was easier to make than those of the offensive players. William had only to nail two layers of support slats on the side of a board. But other boys spent days examining branches and small trees on their way home from school in the hope of finding one suitable for a hockey stick. Some simply nailed two thin boards together neatly at the right angle, and hoped they would not come apart at a crucial moment during the game. A lucky few got real hockey sticks for Christmas. Jesse, the star player, was among the lucky and it was often he who argued with William over which side of the post the puck went.

William Kurelek looking back from 1973 to his prairie childhood during the Depression and World War II.

Left: "New Brunswick Potato Diggers Admiring Autumn Colour," from *Kurelek's Canada* by William Kurelek published in 1978 by Pagurian Press.

Right: "Hockey Hassles," from *A Prairie Boy's Winter* by William Kurelek published in 1973 by Tundra Books.

"Reflections," 1947, by Robert Hurley. A familiar western landscape under a dramatic prairie sky.

"Winter Sun," 1961, by A.J. Casson. In 1982 Casson, one of the artists who joined the Group of Seven, was still living and painting at the age of 84 in Kleinburg, Ontario.

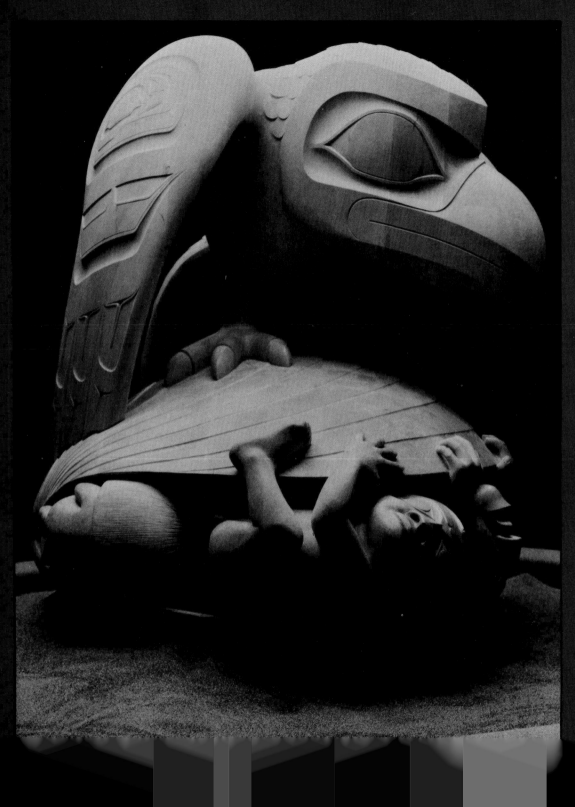

A Haida Legend

One day soon after the great flood the Raven walked upon the beach. The mischievous Raven was bored. In frustration he complained to the empty sky. To his delight, he heard an answering muffled squeak.

Right at his feet was a huge clamshell. He looked more closely and saw that it was full of little creatures.

Well, here was something to break the monotony of his day. But it wasn't much fun as long as the silly things stayed in their shell. So he leaned his great head close, and used his bell-like crooning voice to coax them to come out and play in the wonderful new shining world. First one, then another of the shell dwellers clambered out as curiosity overcame caution. Very strange creatures they were: two legged like the Raven, but there the resemblance ended. No glossy feathers, no thrusting beak; instead of strong wings, thin sticklike arms — these were the original Haidas, the first humans.

For a long time the Raven amused himself with his new playthings. He watched as they explored their new world. Sometimes they helped each other in new discoveries. As often they squabbled over some novelty they found on the beach. He taught them clever tricks at which they were very adept.

The descendents of these children of the coast grew to challenge the stormy North Pacific and wrest from it a rich livelihood. They built the strong, beautiful homes of the Haidas. They decorated them with powerful carvings that told the stories of the great families and the gallant beasts and monsters that shaped their world. For many generations they grew and flourished, built and created, fought and destroyed, and lived according to the changing seasons and the unchanging rituals.

It's nearly over now. Most of the villages are in ruins. The people who remain are changed. The sea has lost much of its richness. Great areas of the land itself lie in waste. Perhaps it's time the Raven found a way to start again.

as retold by Bill Reid

"Mother Earth and her Children." Cree artist Carl Ray has illustrated a legend common to many native peoples in North America as far west as the prairies.

An Iroquois Legend

Once long ago a Sky Woman fell through a hole in the sky to the wide waste of waters below. Two swans saw her falling and caught her on their backs.

"What shall we do with this Sky Woman?" asked one of the swans. "We cannot hold her up forever."

"We must call a meeting," said the other.

The water animals came together to decide what to do. Big Turtle said, "If someone will dive down and bring up some earth from below, I will hold the earth on my back. Then we shall have land for the Sky Woman to live on."

So the water animals took turns in diving. First the muskrat tried. When he came up, Big Turtle looked into his mouth but could find no earth. Then the beaver made a deep dive and came up. He too, had no earth in his mouth. Others tried, but none brought up any earth.

Finally, Little Toad tried. He stayed under the water a long time. When at last he came up his mouth was full of earth. The animals spread the earth over Big Turtle's back.

Then a strange thing happened. The amount of earth began to grow until Big Turtle was holding a whole island on his back. The Sky Woman stepped off the swans' backs and started to make it her home.

The island continued to grow until it was as large as all of North America. Sometimes, they say, Big Turtle grows weary and moves his back to shift the load. Then the earth shakes. People cry: "Big Turtle is moving!"

as retold by Marius Barbeau

Left: "Trans-Canada, No. 1," by Arthur Horsfall. This dreamlike vision is inspired by the idea of the highway crossing all obstacles in its path.

Above: "Light House and Schooners," by Joseph Norris. In this vivid yet "primitive" approach to art, the frame is part of the picture.

"The Migration," 1964, by Joe Talirunili,
an Inuit artist from Povungnituk in northern
Quebec. The sculpture is in stone and ivory.

A nation's postage stamps reflect the ideas, places, and stories important to its people. Canada's first stamp, the "threepenny beaver" was designed by Sandford Fleming. Since that time the post office has worked with Canadian artists to produce some of the world's most interesting stamps.

Canadians are well known for fine work in the motion picture field. They have won international recognition, especially in documentary films and in animation. This cartoon storyboard by Kaj Pindal illustrates themes in Canadian life.

A New Century
ADVANCE ORGANIZER

1

At the turn of the century Canada was mainly a rural society. Most people lived by farming, logging, or working in construction. The local community was the centre of most activities. Baseball and hockey games, songfests and church get-togethers were major social events.

Although the horse and buggy was still the most common method of transportation, the automobile was slowly becoming known as a new, freakish alternative. No one suspected the effects that this strange invention was to have on the new century.

2

In 1896 the minister of immigration put out a call for settlers to break new land in the Canadian West. This attracted, for the first time, many immigrants from the southern and eastern countries of Europe. Many of these pioneer families became wheat farmers. Farming methods were changing: horse-drawn and steam-powered machinery was slowly replacing the rake and sickle.

3

Industry was finding new uses for Canada's natural resources. New methods of processing them were also being developed. Timber supplied building materials and pulp and paper. Minerals such as copper, iron and nickel were used in construction and in machine equipment. Minerals and timber both found wide use in the railway building boom. Railway expansion continued until the coming of World War I in 1914.

Word List

alliance   immigrant   province
compromise   industry   reciprocity
economy   merger   resource
empire   pioneer   union

4 Factories and stores were thriving. Cities grew. People found jobs in construction and manufacturing. These jobs were usually poorly paid. Most cities became places of startling contrast. Factory and store owners lived in large comfortable houses. Their employees were usually forced to live in slum districts. To protect themselves from poor wages and working conditions, the workers banded together to form and strengthen their unions.

5 Most French Canadians were opposed to involvement in the Boer War, and were against helping to strengthen Britain's navy. English Canadians sided with Britain. The country was divided. Prime Minister Laurier sought compromises to both issues.

6 Many Canadians wanted freer trade with the United States. Competition would lower prices. Big business was against this. The Liberals wanted freer trade; opposition leader Robert Borden sided with business. The Conservatives defeated Laurier in the 1911 election.

7 Women were pressing for the right to vote. The most active groups were on the Prairies, where they were supported by farmers' organizations. Nellie McClung was a key figure in the struggle in both Manitoba and Alberta. In 1916 Manitoba granted the vote to women. Other provinces soon followed. Only Quebec refused women the vote until 1940.

Canadians at the Turn of the Century

A visit to Toronto Island might include a game at the stadium and stroll past the hotels to picnic on the beach.

What was life like in 1900? Try to place yourself back in time. Your life would have been quite different.

Many young people left school early. In the country, they were needed on the farm. In the city, their wages helped to pay for the family's food and rent. The work was heavy and the working hours long.

A Rural Society

Most people in Canada lived on farms. Halifax, Montreal, and Toronto were major cities, but much smaller than today. The railway made Winnipeg the gateway to the west. Vancouver was the boomtown of the West Coast. Regina, Calgary, and Edmonton were still pioneer cities.

Most still earned their living by the sweat of their brows. Farming was the main industry. Others worked in logging camps to provide lumber for the growing cities, the railways, and the treeless prairies. Still others worked in construction—on the rapidly expanding railways or on the roads, sewers, and buildings of the new cities. Women worked in factories, as servants for the rich, as teachers and store clerks, and on their own farms and homes.

Living close to home

The automobile was a strange sight on the roads of 1900. Most people depended on the horse and buggy for travel. Long journeys were made by train. People spent their lives close to home and their interest was centred on the local community. Life revolved round the town band, or the local baseball or hockey team.

The age of paid professional singers, comedians, or sports stars was still to come. There was no radio or television to tell of the outside world. Even newspapers were not common in many homes. The church played a great part in people's lives. They looked forward to Sunday, the day of rest. In rural areas, going to church gave an opportunity to meet neighbours and catch up on local news and gossip. Most people provided their own entertainment. A singsong round the family piano or dancing to a treasured violin brought from the old country—this was the high point of a family gathering. A night out meant watching local talent in a play or a concert at the church hall.

Boy Scout parade, Calgary, 1910. Boy Scouts were organized throughout the British Empire in 1908. Girl Guides started two years later.

FOCUS List at least 10 ways in which living in Canada in 1900 was different from today.
Select 3 ways in which life was better in 1900 and 3 ways in which it is better today. Explain your reasons.

Pick-up hockey, Saskatchewan.

A New Century

The 1800s had been a peaceful period—a period of gradual change. In 1900 most Canadians expected that the twentieth century would continue in that way. But the years ahead would be stormy and fast-changing.

Prime Minister Wilfrid Laurier said: "The nineteenth century was the century of the United States. The twentieth century belongs to Canada." Perhaps this century has not developed quite as he expected. Canada has taken part in two world wars. At other times Canadian statesmen have helped to keep world peace. There have been periods of prosperity but also times of hardship. The English and French cultures Laurier knew have grown and changed. Sometimes they have worked together. Sometimes they have seemed to be at each other's throats. Native Indians and Inuit have spoken up for their rights in their own land. Immigrants from all over the world have brought new cultures and traditions. Most Canadians lived in the country in 1900. Now most live in cities. Canada at the end of the twentieth century is a very different place from the Canada Laurier knew.

Tom Longboat (Cogwagee, Cyclone Jack)

1887 — born on the Six Nations Reserve, Brantford, Ontario.
1900 — ran away from school. Started to work. Raced at local town field days.
1905 — came second in Victoria Day 8-km race at Caledonia. Decided to train seriously for distance running.
1906 — ran and won 4 spectacular races. Toronto *Globe* headline: "Longboat Always Wins."
1907 — won 40-km Boston Marathon in record time.
Became Canadian hero, especially in southern Ontario.
1908 — ran in Olympics in London but collapsed after 32 km. Turned professional. Within 2 months ran and won 3 pro marathons. Was famous world-wide, and an inspiration for other Indian kids.
1909 — his contract sold twice "like a racehorse to make money." Lost some races. Papers blamed "Indian laziness" and said he was drinking too much. Was actually training at his own pace and had the odd friendly drink but was upset by contract problems.
1911 — bought contract and organized races himself.
1912 — broke his own record for 25.8 km twice.
1916 — served in army in France as dispatch runner.
1917 — competed and won in regimental games in France.
1919 — won 5-km race in "Grand Army of Canada Sports Show" at Toronto Island Stadium.
Public had lost interest in pro running. Got farm work in Alberta. Wanted to raise family near home. Worked in factories in Toronto, Hamilton, and Buffalo.
1926 — got job with Toronto streets department.
1927 — at age 40, won 6.5-km race at Hamilton.
1945 — retired from streets dept. to Six Nations Reserve.
1949 — died and buried there according to longhouse tradition.

Settling the West

Until 1896 most immigrants to Canada had come from France or the British Isles. In Quebec, most of the people were descendants of French settlers who had come to Canada 300 years before. In the other provinces, most were English, Scottish, or Irish. There were a few German settlements such as Lunenburg, Nova Scotia, and Berlin, Ontario (now Kitchener). The original native peoples were scattered across the country. Some were in reserves or in the distant lands of the North. Others had moved into the cities.

During the 1800s many people had emigrated from Europe. Most of them had gone to "the great melting pot," the United States. The United States was an independent country. It had no ties to Britain. People from other parts of Europe could feel welcome.

Not having a yoke of oxen to break the heavy soil, Doukhobor women pull the plough in this pioneer community near Yorkton, Saskatchewan.

"Without animals, nothing can be done. We are starting a new village over there. We must let the people for the new village have horses to haul logs to build homes and barns before winter. That means no rest for the animals — poor things. So to give them some rest, we humans hitch ourselves to the ploughs."

Adapted from Salt of the Earth *by Heather Robinson*

Where did most immigrants come from before the 1890s?
What was Sifton's new immigration policy? How did it change the
Canadian population and culture?
Compare immigration policy today with the policy in 1900.

1900 1910 1920 1930 1940 1950 1960 1970 1980 1990 2000

Immigration could be a lonely and frightening experience. This family waits outside the CPR station in Winnipeg.

Free Land

But now the free land in the United States had been filled. In Canada, the government wanted settlers to open up the Prairies. Clifford Sifton became the minister in charge of immigration in 1896. He advertised Canadian free land throughout the United States. He also encouraged settlers to come from all over Europe. He knew that only strong, healthy people could survive in the West. There they would have to break new soil, put up farm buildings, and make it through the tough Canadian winter.

Sifton's policies started a flood of immigration to the Canadian West. The outbreak of World War I brought this to an abrupt halt. Yet Canada had been changed forever. Along side the Bourassas, Cartiers, and Lafleurs; the O'Keefes, Carrs, and Macdonalds; people with names like Richler, Diefenbaker, Konihowski, Schreyer, and Steinberg would take their places as citizens and leaders of Canada.

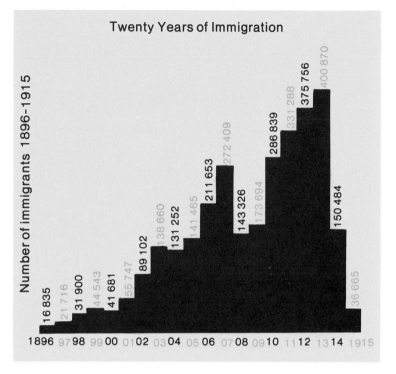

Twenty Years of Immigration

Number of immigrants 1896–1915

Year	Number
1896	16 835
97	21 716
98	31 900
99	44 543
00	41 681
01	55 747
02	89 102
03	138 660
04	131 252
05	141 465
06	211 653
07	272 409
08	143 326
09	173 694
10	286 839
11	331 288
12	375 756
13	400 870
14	150 484
1915	36 665

Settlers and their goods leave Edmonton for Lloydminster.

The New Immigrants

I think a sturdy peasant in a sheepskin coat, born on the soil, whose forefathers have been farmers for ten generations, with a stout wife and a half-dozen children is good quality.

Clifford Sifton

An English Immigrant

When I left school I went to Oxford University, but I had no training for a job. So I decided to emigrate to Canada. My uncle gave me $200 to help get me started.

I worked on a farm near Regina, and then another near Saskatoon. After 18 months, I had saved $1500. I was a wealthy young man.

I bought a horse and buggy and spent a month driving around looking for land. I found a good farm of 128 ha. The land company wanted $12.50 a hectare. I put $500 down. I hired a man to help me with the ploughing. As he turned that land over, those furrows rolled out like the waves of the sea.

I had about 60 ha broken and ready for spring. That winter I worked for a lumber yard in Regina. In spring I moved onto my farm with a seeder and four good horses. I brought some lumber, a keg of nails, and tarpaper, to build a shack. By this time I was pretty deep in debt but I knew what I was doing. I got that new Marquis wheat that everyone was talking about. That was the finest wheat I've ever seen. Hard and wonderful for milling and it made the finest bread in the world.

When I harvested that crop in October, I had enough money to pay off the land company, enough to buy my farm implements, enough to build a decent house and a barn, and enough to think that I was king of the world. And I was.

Adapted from The Pioneer Years *by Barry Broadfoot*

Students at Plum Ridge School, Manitoba, were mainly the children of Ukrainian settlers. Schools tried to teach good citizenship and loyalty to the British Empire. For many immigrant children, learning the customs and language of their new homeland was difficult and confusing.

Russian Jewish immigrants at Quebec City, 1911. Many groups of immigrants came to Canada to practise their religion freely.

By 1905 there were enough settlers in the West that two new provinces — Saskatchewan and Alberta — were created.

While immigrants from Europe were breaking new soil on the Prairies, Chinese, Japanese, and Indians were coming across the Pacific to work in the fisheries, mines, and lumber camps of British Columbia. The Asians were often resented by white Canadians. The government developed immigration rules that would make it difficult for Asians to enter Canada.

Imagine you are an immigrant to Canada in 1900 and write a letter to your parents describing life in your new homeland. Compare the problems faced by immigrants in 1900 to the problems faced by immigrants today.

Polish Immigrants

About 1905 the first Polish immigrants came to Manitoba. Up until then we'd had people from Ontario, and from the States, England, Germany, and Scandinavia.

At the immigration hall in Winnipeg they'd send them out to look at the land that was left. This was usually swampy or covered with poplar, but they usually took it. 64 ha of free land looked pretty good when all you needed was $10.00 for the registration fee. A peasant had about 2 ha in Poland or Russia if he had anything at all. But they worked hard and they learned. If you could get one for a hired hand, you were lucky.

At first they lived with their animals. This used to shock some of the oldtimers. The houses were small. They cut poles out of the bush and laid them one on top of the other for the walls. They laid smaller poles side by side for the roof. They plastered the walls with a guck of straw and mud and lime. The roof had straw on it and then a thick layer of dirt. You'd be surprised how cozy they were.

They liked music. They made their own violins. You could buy a violin at Eaton's for $2-5 but they'd spend a whole winter working on one. When they started coming to our dances, they could sure make the night lively.

When they started coming to our July 1 picnics, their children were the best behaved kids on the lot. One word from mother, and that was it.

Many of the Polish kids never went to school. A whole generation of those kids must have grown up never knowing how to read or write or do their sums. That's about all education was in those days anyway — the three Rs with some history and geography thrown in. If you could find Africa on the map you passed geography.

However, they finally realized the importance of education. One of us could still leave school at grade 8 and go into the city and make good. But if you had a "ski" or a "chuck" on the end of your name and you went to the city, you were on the end of a pick and shovel for the rest of your days. So they wanted the best school, the best teacher, the best of everything for their children.

Adapted from The Pioneer Years *by Barry Broadfoot*

Dr. Barnardo's orphans, Saint John, N.B. Between 1870 and 1935 over 80 000 children came to Canada from orphanages in England. They were sent to work in people's homes and on farms. In return for their labour they were to receive room and board and religious and moral instruction. Inspectors were supposed to check the conditions the children lived in. But it was often a long time between inspections, and some children were overworked and badly treated. On the other hand, others remember their Canadian "families" with affection and gratitude.

Within the past ten years, a nation has been born. We used to describe ourselves as English, Irish, Scotch, and French. Today our children boast they are Canadians, and the latest arrivals from Austria and Russia help to swell the chorus, "The Maple Leaf Forever."

Adapted from Strangers Within our Gates *by J.S. Woodsworth, 1909*

The Land

Most people in Canada lived on farms. Farming families tried to raise as much of their own food as possible. This meant they had a cow or two, some chickens, and perhaps a pig. They grew their own vegetables. But most of the farm was used to make money.

On the Prairies, the "cash crop" was wheat. In Ontario and Quebec, dairy farming was most common. Prince Edward Island farmers found their clay soil grew good potatoes. Fruit orchards did well in sheltered areas—the Annapolis Valley in Nova Scotia, the Niagara region of Ontario, and the Okanagan Valley in British Columbia. When the cash crop was sold, farmers could buy things they could not grow.

A new grain elevator at Estevan, Saskatchewan.

Manpower, horsepower, and steampower bring in the harvest, Alberta, 1907.

Mechanized Farming

By 1900 modern inventions were making farm work easier. Horse-drawn mowers and binders were replacing sickles and rakes. There were even steam-powered tractors to break up the soil and plough the land. Many farmers could not afford to own these machines. They rented them instead. Sometimes they hired a crew of workers with the machines. Sometimes groups of neighbours got together. They used the machines on each farmer's fields in turn.

There was still plenty of physical work to be done. Animals had to be cared for, eggs gathered, water hauled, firewood chopped and split.

Farming, especially wheat farming, was a booming business for Canada. The country advertised the Prairies as "the bread basket of the world" and "the granary of the empire."

How were modern inventions changing farming in the 1900s?
Compare the life of a farm boy in 1900 to the life of most young Canadians today.
Why was the Women's Institute useful and important?

Art Gallery page 5

Adelaide Hunter Hoodless

1857 — born on farm in Brant County, Ontario.

1881 — married John Hoodless. They had 5 children.

1889 — youngest child died from drinking impure milk. As a result, she decided to help women learn proper sanitation, child care, and home management.

1890s — persuaded school boards to start courses in "domestic science" for girls and "manual training" for boys. Helped found a national YWCA, the National Council of Women, the Victorian Order of Nurses.

1897 — Made a speech to Farmers' Institute at Stoney Creek, Ont. Suggested rural women needed an organization to encourage good home management. The first Women's Institute was formed. The idea soon spread to other rural communities across the country.

1903 — Persuaded William Macdonald, a tobacco millionaire, to found the Macdonald Institute (now part of University of Guelph) to teach domestic science.

1905 — Macdonald founded Macdonald College (now part of McGill University, Montreal).

1910 — Hoodless died while lecturing in Toronto.

1915 — Margaret Watt who had worked in Women's Institutes in B.C. started one at her new home in England.

1933 — Watt elected first president of Federated Countrywomen of the World in Stockholm, Sweden. Today there are Women's Institutes in 108 countries. In Canada there are 3350 branches with 72 000 members.

We sure knew how to work. We were doing things around the yard before we were 5 or 6. I hunted up brooding hens and got them back to the henhouse. I went for the cows. I handed dad things when he was fixing a piece of machinery, oiling it, or replacing a part he'd fixed. In the summer I'd load up my wagon with a jar of water and one of lemonade, and sandwiches and cookies. I'd take afternoon lunch to the field where the men were working.

When I was 7, I milked my one cow, and then it got to be two cows. By the time I was 9, I was doing a man's job with the cows.

When I was 11, I handled the team of four horses for ploughing. Other times, I helped load the hay on the wagon.

If you were a boy, by the time you were twelve, you'd pretty well given up the business of school. There didn't seem to be much sense to going any more. Each year you stayed away, the harder it got to go. What fifteen-year-old fellow wanted to sit with a bunch of eleven-year-olds? I don't think that there were any laws about when a fellow had to go to school or when he didn't. A lot of fellows never went beyond the third or fourth grade. I got to the sixth and I could read and write and do arithmetic. Usually a fellow married a girl who had gone through school. If it came to doing figures, she could do it. A lot of those farm wives did all the figuring, and books in those days.

Adapted from The Pioneer Years *by Barry Broadfoot*

BUY THIS EATON DISC DRILL 63⁰⁰

Forests and Mines

As wagons with wheels could not move freely in the forests, logs were usually brought out on sleds during the winter. Four horses were needed for a load like this.

When Europeans first came to Canada, Quebec, Ontario, and the Maritimes were covered with white pine forests. Lumbering was big business. Timber was needed in Europe. By 1900 people in the United States wanted to buy Canadian timber as their own forests were largely used up. Canadian cities and towns also needed more and more timber. Farmers on the Prairies needed timber to build their homes and barns. The railway building boom created a demand for wooden trestles and ties. The spread of electricity and the telephone required utility poles. Being a lumberjack was a good way to make a living.

As time went on, it became harder to find the big trees that produced the best timber. They had already been cut. Lumberjacks began to move west to the cedar and Douglas fir forests of British Columbia. The timber they cut was sold to the Prairie provinces, the United States, and Asia.

In the East, the end of the big trees was not the end of the forest industry. The trees that were left were ideal for making pulp and paper. Newspapers all over the world were requiring more and more paper. Canadian forest companies moved in to supply this need.

Unfortunately, little was done to conserve the forests. When trees were cut, new ones were not planted. Waste branches and cuttings were left in the bush where they created a fire hazard.

Forest products are Canada's largest industry. Only later did Canadians realize that forests have to be looked after if this valuable resource is to survive.

Mining

When people thought of the "new world" 400 years ago, they thought of new sources of gold and riches. The lure of gold led to two gold rushes in Canada. In

A paper mill, Ottawa, 1908.

FOCUS Why was *a)* pulp and paper in eastern Canada, *b)* gold on the Cariboo and Klondike, *c)* oil at Turner Valley important to the growth and development of Canada? How important are pulp and paper, gold, and oil to Canada today?

1900 1910 1920 1930 1940 1950 1960 1970 1980 1990 2000

Frontier College provided evening classes to help mining, railway, and lumber workers get an education. This class in "civics" was for immigrant miners from Scandinavia working in a newly opened nickel mine near Sudbury.

Alberta's first oil well, Turner Valley, 1914. The first oil discoveries in Canada were made at Petrolia and Oil Springs, Ontario, in the 1850s.

the 1860s the Cariboo gold rush took place in British Columbia. In 1898 would-be miners swarmed into the Klondike in the Yukon.

Coal, copper, iron, and nickel were less glamorous than gold, but they were far more useful. By 1900 industries all over the world needed minerals. New ways of processing minerals were being developed, and new uses found for them.

The rocky Canadian Shield north of the settled areas of the country proved to hold new wealth. In earlier days *coureurs de bois* had ranged the forests of the shield for furs. Lumberjacks felled its mighty trees. Now prospectors looked under the forest floor for minerals. New mining towns sprang up overnight, especially in northern Ontario. In other parts of the country too — Nova Scotia, and southern British Columbia — the development of our mineral wealth increased.

City Life

Today Canada is an urban society. Over three quarters of Canadians live in cities. In 1900 things were very different. More than half the people lived on farms. One quarter lived in small villages and towns. Less than a quarter lived in cities.

Immigrants were pouring into Canada. Most wanted to go to the rich farmlands of the West. Many never got there. They were too poor to buy the equipment and supplies they would need to set up a farm. They found jobs in the lumber camps and the mines. They helped build the new railways. They also came to the cities looking for work in the factories.

Population Statistics				1901	1911
	1901	1911	Hamilton	53 000	82 000
Halifax	40 000	47 000	Winnipeg	42 000	140 000
Saint John	41 000	43 000	Regina	2 200	30 000
Quebec	70 000	80 000	Saskatoon	113	12 000
Montreal	330 000	490 000	Edmonton	4 200	30 000
Ottawa	60 000	87 000	Calgary	4 400	44 000
Toronto	210 000	380 000	Vancouver	30 000	120 000

Children follow the ice wagon on a hot summer day hoping for a chip of ice to suck — a turn-of-the-century popsicle!

The Cities Grow

Canadian manufacturers were doing well. They made tractors and threshing machines for the new farms. They built buggies, bicycles, and automobiles. Steel mills turned out nails, wire, pots and pans, railway tracks, locomotives. Flour, canned meats and vegetables, brooms, stoves—all the things people needed for everyday life—came out of the factories.

There were plenty of jobs. As well as immigrants, people who had grown up on farms and in small towns moved to the cities to make some money.

Cities across the country grew by leaps and bounds. Still more jobs were created: digging sewers, paving streets, building streetcar lines. Even people with few skills and little knowledge of English or French could usually find some sort of work.

The grocery store.

How did Canadian cities change in the early 1900s?
Why did some cities grow faster than others?
List at least 5 differences between the lives of middle class people and working class people in the early 1900s?

Canada THE TWENTIETH CENTURY **Art Gallery page 7**

Two kinds of homes.

Contrasts

Factory and store owners lived in large beautiful houses on tree-lined streets. The houses and grounds were kept clean and tidy by armies of servants. Most city dwellers weren't so fortunate.

The supply of housing did not keep up with the numbers of people coming into the cities. Most people were very poorly paid. They could not afford decent homes even if they were available. Many downtown areas became "instant slums." Immigrant families of ten lived in one run-down room. Water was not always safe to drink. There was nowhere for children to play except the street.

City councils and concerned citizens knew these conditions were bad, but they didn't know what to do about it. The idea of planning the growth of cities to avoid problems was still very new. They did their best. They provided electric lights and a clean water supply. Then established public health clinics. They improved public transportation. They set up parks and playgrounds so people could relax and play in pleasant surroundings.

The Toronto Playground System

29 soccer fields	8 bowling greens
9 rugby fields	2 croquet grounds
98 tennis courts	2 quoit grounds
3 lacrosse fields	33 hockey cushions
10 cricket creases	39 skating rinks and toboggan slides

Choosing sides for hockey, Sarnia, Ontario. Immigrant children found that where you came from didn't matter on the playground. What counted was how well you played the game.

Industry and Unions

In the first 10 years of the twentieth century the output of Canadian industry more than doubled. In some areas, such as iron and steel, Canadians were producing 5 times as much in 1910 as they had in 1900.

Value of Production (in thousands of dollars)	1900	1910
Tobacco	8 000	13 000
Boots and shoes	7 500	16 000
Clothes	20 000	44 000
Furniture	4 300	8 000
Farm machinery	5 000	11 000
Iron and steel	3 100	15 000
Automobiles	—	2 500
Electric light and power	2 000	13 000

Electricity

One of the things that made this growth possible was electricity. From 1880 Canadian rivers and waterfalls were dammed to produce electric power. Electric motors replaced the horses that used to draw city streetcars. Electric lights made streets and homes brighter. Electric appliances — vacuum cleaners, irons — soon appeared, making life easier for the homemaker. The greatest changes were in factories. Electricity brought in new and faster ways to make pulp and paper, sew clothes, and grind wheat into flour.

Mergers and Take-overs

The bigger the factory, the more efficiently it could produce. Gradually large companies started to dominate the scene. Sometimes several small companies came together and "merged" into one. At other times one company would "buy out" its competitors.

Small local producers found they were losing business. Rural brewers found people preferred to buy from Molson in Montreal, O'Keefe in Toronto or Labatt in London. Instead of selling flour ground in the local mill the storekeeper stocked Ogilvie's, Five

This factory in Winnipeg in 1904 had electric light, but the sewing machines were probably still operated by foot treadles.

What will electricity do for you? To encourage the installation of electricity, Ontario Hydro loaded this truck with electric equipment. Among the items on display are a circular saw and a washing machine. This helped both manufacturers and the electric company sell their products.

How did electricity change life for many Canadians? Why would most farmers and loggers not be able to share these benefits? If you worked in a factory in the early 1900s, why might you have wanted to join a trade union?

Roses, or Robin Hood flour. Companies like Burns of Calgary, Swift, and Canada Packers took over the meat-packing business. Small town stores could not carry the variety of goods that people could buy from Eaton's catalogue.

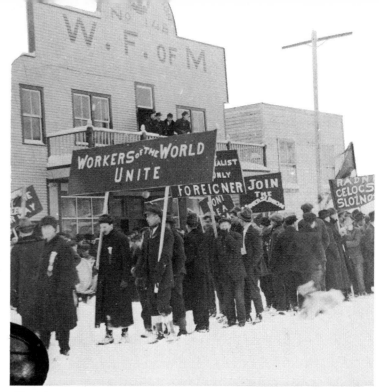

World Federation of Miners' strike, South Porcupine, Ontario, about 1912.

The Growth of Unions

Industry was changing fast. Profits were growing. The last thing on the minds of many mill owners and factory bosses was the life of the workers. Machinery was designed for efficiency, not safety. Work places were dark, uncomfortable, and poorly ventilated. Hours were long and wages low.

Workers had started to organize unions to demand better wages and working conditions in the 1830s. By 1900 many advances had been made. Some laws protecting workers and unions had been passed. But employers did not like dealing with unions. Many battles were still to be fought between management and labour.

A broom factory in 1896. Employers found they could pay children far less than adults for doing many tedious and unpleasant jobs. Unions fought to have laws passed to stop children working. They wanted to protect the children. They also wanted to make sure children did not take jobs away from adults. The first child labour law was passed in Ontario in 1908. Other provinces followed. By 1914 scenes like this were rare in Canada.

Big business did not take over completely. Many small companies survived, and others started up. Some people wanted a more independent way of life than working for others gave them. They scraped and saved until they had enough to open their own restaurants, barber shops, laundries, clothing stores, bakeries, or fruit stalls. Immigrants followed trades they had learned in the old country and worked as tailors, jewellers, music teachers, or shoemakers. Often they worked as hard or even harder than they would have in a factory. Their reward was that the profit, however small, was theirs and theirs alone.

Railways and Automobiles

The Canadian Pacific Railway was a great success. It carried settlers to the West. It brought the wheat crops to the ports of Vancouver, Montreal, and Quebec. New towns were growing along its tracks.

However, the CPR did not have enough railway cars to ship grain at harvest time. Settlers were moving into new areas of the West and North where the railway did not reach. Many western farmers thought the CPR should have some competition. This might bring down the freight rates they had to pay to ship their grain.

New Railways

In the early 1900s railway-building fever again swept Canada. Investors saw an opportunity to make a fortune by putting money into new railways.

The Grand Trunk Railway in eastern Canada decided to build a western extension. It would be called the Grand Trunk Pacific. The Manitoba government supported the Canadian Northern Railway as a western alternative to the CPR. Common sense said the two groups should co-operate. Greed got in the way.

Both groups had friends in Ottawa. They asked the government for financial help. Instead of deciding which plan was better, the government gave money to both. Prime Minister Laurier believed more railways were necessary.

The railway-building boom continued until 1914. World War I changed things. The government could no longer afford to provide money.

Then, economic reality burst the investors' dreams. There was not enough grain or other freight to support three transcontinental railway systems. Some of the new railways went bankrupt. The federal government was forced to take them over. In 1922 they were combined with other railways that were losing money to form Canadian National Railways. The CNR has been owned and operated by the federal government ever since.

Railway building, 1902-1914
Grand Trunk Pacific
Canadian Northern
Great Northern (B.C.)
National Transcontinental
Timiskaming and
    Northern (Ont.)
Hudson Bay
    (Sask. and Man.)
Canadian Pacific
    (branch lines)

Number of Telephones

Year	Number
1900	52 000
1902	71 000
1904	95 000
1909	239 000
1911	354 000
1914	542 000

Figures are not available for the years 1905 to 1908.

Telegraph and telephone wires were installed alongside the railway. Alexander Graham Bell's invention was changing Canadian life, especially in the country. People on isolated farms found the telephone was vital to keeping in touch. Many city people did not feel the need for a telephone in their homes until much later in the century.

Why was there a second railway-building boom in the 1900s? Why were the new railways combined to form the CNR in 1922? Describe the role of Sam McLaughlin in the early Canadian automobile industry.

Four means of transport: Grand Trunk Pacific train, Model T Ford, ox cart, and electric streetcar. Edmonton, 1912.

The Automobile

The railway was the fastest and most comfortable way of travelling. Rich and poor all used the train. But some Canadians were thinking about a new form of transport—the automobile.

Driving the new invention was not always easy. A Russell car on Yonge Street, Toronto, 1913.

Sam McLaughlin worked for his father at the McLaughlin Carriage Company at Oshawa, Ontario. Sam had seen Russell cars built by the Canada Cycle and Motor Company in Toronto. He decided it was time for the McLaughlins to start making cars.

Sam thought it would be too expensive to design his own engine. He arranged a deal with the Buick Company in Michigan. Buick supplied the engines and McLaughlin built the bodies. The tie with the Americans proved to be good business. In 1907 the

McLaughlin tries an alternate energy source, early 1900s.

McLaughlin Carriage Company produced 193 cars. In 1915 the carriage-making business was sold in order to make room to build Chevrolets. In 1918 General Motors bought the entire company. Sam McLaughlin became president of the new Canadian branch plant.

Canada and the British Empire

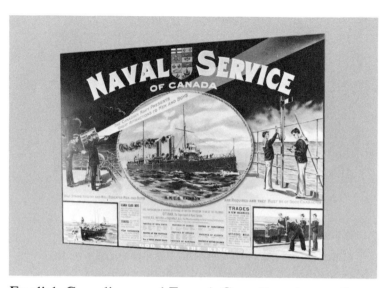

English Canadians and French Canadians have often differed. In 1900 most English Canadians were descendants of people from the British Isles. The idea of loyalty to the crown and to the British Empire remained strong. French Canadians did not share this feeling. Why should they be loyal to the British Empire? New France had been taken over by the English. To French Canadians, Britain was a foreign, conquering power. Why should they take part in British wars?

The Boer War, 1899-1902

These questions came up during the Boer War. Gold had been discovered in South Africa and the British wanted control of it. The area had been settled by the Boers. The Boers were Dutch pioneers and did not want to be ruled by Britain. Many English Canadians wanted to send soldiers to help the British.

Many French Canadians felt they should be on the side of the Boers. The British were conquering the Boers just as they had conquered New France. Most believed the Boer War had nothing to do with Canada. They were completely opposed to sending soldiers.

Prime Minister Laurier thought of a compromise. Canadians could volunteer to fight with the British in South Africa. Nobody would be forced to go. The volunteers would be paid by the British government. Yet neither side was satisfied. English Canadians felt Canada had not done enough. French Canadians felt that even the token force was too much.

The Naval Question

In Europe, Britain and Germany were competing for power. For hundreds of years Britain had had the most powerful navy. "Britannia ruled the waves." The British wanted to keep it that way. By 1900 Germany was

---

We French Canadians belong to one country, Canada. Canada is for us the whole world. The English Canadians have two countries, one here and one across the seas.

Wilfrid Laurier, quoted in Montreal La Presse

Those who cut your fathers to pieces on the Plains of Abraham are asking you today to go and get killed for them.

Quebec politician, 1911

There is Ontario patriotism, Quebec patriotism, and western patriotism. Each hopes it may swallow up the others. But there is no Canadian patriotism. We can have no Canadian nation when we have no Canadian patriotism.

Henri Bourassa, 1907

British Canadians will find a way, through the ballot box or otherwise, to rid themselves of the influence of this inferior and disloyal race.

Toronto News

One Fleet,
One Flag,
One Throne.

Slogan of the Conservative party in Election 1911 designed to appeal to feelings of loyalty to Britain.

I am branded in Quebec as a traitor to the French, and in Ontario as a traitor to the English. In Quebec I am attacked as an imperialist, in Ontario as a separatist. I am neither. I am a Canadian.

Wilfrid Laurier, 1911

Why did French and English Canadians have different views about the British Empire in the early 1900s?
Explain the different viewpoints of French and English Canadians to a) the Boer War, b) a Canadian navy.

1900 1910 1920 1930 1940 1950 1960 1970 1980 1990 2000

catching up. The British asked Canada, Australia, and the other countries of the Empire for help to keep the British navy strong. English Canadians thought this was the right thing to do. Canada should give money to Britain to buy a dreadnought (a new super-battleship).

Most French Canadians could not support this. Henri Bourassa was the editor of a Montreal newspaper, *Le Devoir*. He had left the Liberal party because he disagreed with Laurier over the Boer War. He said Canada should not give money to Britain in this way. It would only involve Canada in future British wars. French Canadians wanted to stay out of wars in Europe. Canada would gain nothing from them.

Once again, Laurier tried to compromise. He suggested that Canada should have a navy of its own. Some small ships would be built to protect Canadian shores. In case of war, this "Canadian navy" would fight alongside the British navy.

The leader of the Conservative party, Robert Borden, wanted to give money directly to the British navy. A small Canadian navy would be just silly—a

"tin-pot" navy. Most English Canadians sided with Borden and the Conservatives. French Canadians felt that once again the English Canadian majority had given in to Britain.

The new Canadian prime minister, Robert Borden, and the young British first lord of the admiralty, Winston Churchill, in London, 1912.

The naval question was a major issue in the election of 1911. Laurier and the Liberals lost this election. Laurier was never prime minister again. His policy of compromise seemed to have failed.

Henri Bourassa

1868 — born in Montreal, grandson of Louis-Joseph Papineau, leader of 1837 rebellion.
1890 — at age 22, elected mayor of Montebello. Also owned *L'Interprète,* a local newspaper supporting the Liberal party.
1892 — won interest of Laurier, leader of the opposition.
1896-1907 — elected as Liberal, but split with Laurier over Boer War. Continued to support all other Liberal policies. Fought for more balanced immigration so French Canada would not be swamped by English-speaking immigrants, and for equal status for French and English languages.
1908-12—sat in Quebec legislature.
1910—founded *Le Devoir,* to become one of Canada's most outspoken newspapers. Its first battle was over reciprocity which Bourassa claimed would lead to U.S. interference.
1911—attacked Laurier's naval policy. Did not want Canada involved in foreign wars, though supported ties with Britain.
1917—campaigned against conscription. Labelled a traitor by most English Canadians. Invited to speak in Ottawa, a riot broke out and he had to leave without speaking.
1918—feeling his vision of Canada was impossible, went into semi-retirement. *Le Devoir* became less controversial.
1925-35—returned to Commons as Independent. Devoted himself to local issues. Defeated in 1935 election.
1935 — advocated support of the CCF. Was a friend and admirer of J.S. Woodsworth
1952 — died in Montreal.

Reciprocity

In the 1800s Canada was still a colony of pioneer farmers. The United States was already an industrial country. This meant that American manufacturers had a headstart. They had bigger factories. They had a larger market for the goods they made, because there were more people in the United States. Therefore, they could sell things more cheaply.

The National Policy

John A. Macdonald and the Conservatives wanted to encourage Canadian industry. If people bought Canadian goods, money would stay in the country. Canadian manufacturers would make profits. There would be jobs for Canadians. The Conservatives developed a plan they called the National Policy. Goods coming into the country would have to pay a tariff or duty. This meant people would buy Canadian products because they would be cheaper than imported ones. The National Policy helped the Conservatives get elected in 1878.

How the tariff protected Canadian industries:

Cost of imported stove	$40	Cost of Canadian stove	$46
Import duty or tariff	$12		—
Total price in Canada	$52	Total price	$46

High or Low Tariffs?

The tariff policy was popular in industrial areas— Quebec, Ontario, and Nova Scotia. But the settlers in western Canada saw things differently. They wanted to buy cheaper manufactured goods from the United States. Because of the tariff, they had to buy more expensive goods made in eastern Canada. Many farmers in eastern Canada also objected to the tariff.

By the 1890s the country was split on the tariff. The factory owners and workers of eastern Canada supported the tariff—its protected profits and jobs.

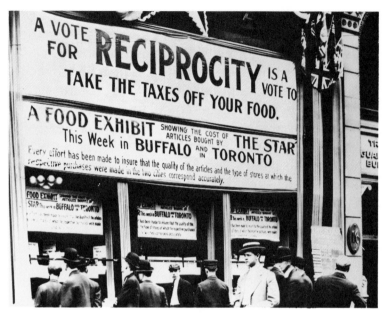

The *Toronto Star* supported the idea of reciprocity.

Farmers and people in the West opposed the tariff. They wanted a free trade policy which would let them buy goods at the cheapest world price.

The Conservatives supported the tariff policy. The Liberals wanted freer trade. However, when they were first elected, Laurier and the Liberals kept the tariff. In the early 1900s many farmers and consumers urged them to change the policy. Then in 1910 the Americans offered a deal. They would let more Canadian wheat and other products enter the States. Canada would lower the tariff on many American goods. This is called *reciprocity*. In a reciprocity agreement each side gives something to the other.

The Election of 1911

In 1911 Laurier called an election on the reciprocity issue. The Liberals campaigned for lower tariffs with the United States. They hoped to win support from the

What is *a)* a "protective tariff," *b)* "free trade"? Why did Canadians from different regions disagree on tariff policy? What is the attitude of people in your province today about tariffs? Explain why they feel this way.

 Art Gallery page 4

farmers and workers in the East as well as the settlers on the prairies.

The Conservatives under Robert Borden were strongly opposed to reciprocity. They argued that it would lead to cheaper American goods flooding the Canadian market. This would be the end of many Canadian industries. It would lead to unemployment in the cities. More than that, Canada would fall more and more under American control. In the end, Canada might have to join the United States.

Big business interests in Canada did not want reciprocity. They threw their support behind the Conservatives. They bought advertisements in newspapers across the country. They appealed to people's feelings of loyalty to the king and empire. They claimed Canada would soon become totally American if there were freer trade.

Laurier was an impressive speaker in both English and French, but even his active campaign style could not win the election of 1911 for the Liberals.

These tactics made a great impression in Ontario, Manitoba, and British Columbia—areas which had been settled largely by British immigrants. In Quebec the battle had little to do with reciprocity. The naval question was the big issue there. Henri Bourassa joined the fight against the Liberals because he thought Laurier's "pro-British" policy betrayed Quebec's interests.

Robert Borden at the meeting that planned the Conservative campaign to win the election of 1911.

The result of the election of 1911 was Conservatives 133, Liberals 86. Where the elected members came from was more significant. Some regions had voted heavily Conservative, others heavily Liberal. The split caused anger and resentment. Similar splits would cause problems in the future.

Results of the election of 1911		
	Con.	Lib.
B.C.	7	0
Alta.	1	6
Sask.	1	9
Man.	7	2
Ont.	73	13
Que.	27	37
N.B.	5	8
P.E.I.	2	2
N.S.	9	9
Yukon	1	0
TOTAL	133	86

Votes for Women

At the turn of the century more than half of Canadian adults had no vote. Women were not recognized as responsible human beings. Their fathers or husbands looked after them and controlled their property.

Some people, both men and women, were beginning to realize that this was unfair. It was also dangerous, because a woman had no legal protection. If her husband abused her, her property, or her children, the law could do nothing. Thus the matter of votes for women was tied in with other social issues.

Temperance and Women's Rights

One social problem that worried many people in the 1800s was the abuse of alcohol. Societies were set up to promote temperance, or moderation in the use of liquor.

Their concern was justified. Pay envelopes were often handed out in the local tavern. Workers would stay for a friendly drink. A man with a drinking problem would have more than one — he might have drunk most of his wages before starting home. If his wife also worked, he could legally demand her wages to spend as well. Because of the "demon drink," some families went without food, heat, and clothing.

Many people felt that the only answer was prohibition, or banning the sale of alcohol completely. The Women's Christian Temperance Union became the leader in the battle for prohibition. In 1878 a federal act allowed local areas to vote on the issue.

Temperance workers were usually concerned with promoting good family life. So it is not surprising that many of the same people were involved in the struggle for laws to give women a fairer say in marriage. By the turn of the century nearly all provinces had passed Married Women's Property Acts to allow women at least some control over their own property.

Many politicians thought this was enough. But the reformers wanted more: they wanted the abuse of alcohol to be stopped by total prohibition, and they wanted votes for women.

The Vote

It was on the Prairies that the movement for votes for women really got underway. There, farmers knew the importance of women's work and felt it should be properly recognized.

Manitoba was the scene of the most active struggle. In the early 1900s, the campaign for votes for women was led by an author, mother, and temperance worker named Nellie McClung. In 1912 McClung joined a group of Manitoba women in the Political Equality League. Her keen mind and quick tongue soon made her the league's chief spokesperson.

McClung: The hand that rocks the cradle does not rule the world. If it did, the world would be a sweeter, cleaner, safer place than it is now.

Male heckler at a meeting: Don't you wish you were a man right now, Nellie?
McClung: Don't you wish *you* were?

McClung: Woman's duty lies not only in rearing children but also in the world those children must one day enter.

Premier Roblin: I don't want a hyena in petticoats talking politics at me. I want a nice gentle creature to bring me my slippers.

McClung: You'll hear from me again and you may not like it!
Premier Roblin: Is this a threat?
McClung: No, it's a prophecy!

Man voting for the first time in 15 years: You bet I came out today to vote against giving these fool women a vote. What's the good of it? They wouldn't use it!

McClung: The time will come when women will be independent enough to refuse to have their food paid for by men. When women will receive equal pay for equal work. When all avenues of activity will be open to them.

Why were many men and women concerned about "temperance"?
How did Nellie McClung help bring about better conditions for women?
Today women still struggle for equality. Name some issues.

1900 1910 1920 1930 1940 1950 1960 1970 1980 1990 2000

In 1915 the new Liberal government said it would give women the vote if people really wanted it. 40 000 Manitobans signed a petition supporting the idea. Seated at the right is Amelia Burritt. Aged 94, she alone gathered 4250 signatures.

Premier Rodmond Roblin was determined that women should not get the vote. On 27 January 1914 he told the legislature the idea was "illogical and absurd. Making women equal to men would cause strife. It would break up the home. Women are too emotional."

The next night the Political Equality League held a "mock parliament" in a local theatre. All the members were women. They debated giving the vote to men. "Premier" Nellie McClung was against it: "If men start to vote, they will vote too much. Politics unsettles men. If men get into the habit of voting, who knows what might happen?".

Everyone thought it was a great joke. But it would take two more years and a change of government before Manitoba gave women the vote. Nellie's "bonny fight, knock-down fight, drag-out fight, uniting the women of Manitoba in a great cause," was finally over. Unfortunately, the McClungs had moved to Alberta, so she was not there to enjoy her triumph. Three months later, women got the vote in Alberta too.

McClung became a member of the Alberta legislature. She worked for the social issues which had convinced her that women were needed in politics.

Nellie McClung

1873 — born on a farm in Chatsworth, Ont.
1880 — family moved west to Manitoba.
1889 — taught grades 1-8 in one-room school.
1894 — became active in WCTU.
1896 — married Wes McClung. They had 5 children.
1908 — wrote 1st novel, about temperance
1911 — McClungs moved to Winnipeg. Nellie joined Canadian Women's Press Club, campaigned for laws to improve conditions for women factory workers.
1912 — helped found the Political Equality League. Worked for votes for women in Manitoba until Wes McClung was transferred to Alberta in 1914.
1916 — women granted the vote in some provinces.
1921 — elected as Liberal member of Alberta Legislature. Supported such measures as old age pensions, mothers' allowances, better conditions in factories, a minimum wage, prohibition, birth control, easier divorce, public health nurses, no matter which party introduced them.
1924 — referendum ends prohibition in Alberta.
1926 — defeated in election by 60 votes, probably because of prohibition stand.
1927 — joined Emily Murphy and 3 other Alberta women in court case to establish that women were "persons" and could be appointed to the Senate.
1936 — appointed to first board of governors of CBC.
1939 — on Canadian delegation to League of Nations.
1951 — dies at Victoria, B.C.

Women get the vote:
1916 Manitoba
     Saskatchewan
     Alberta
1917 British Columbia
     Ontario
     Canada (some women only)
1918 Nova Scotia
     Canada (all women)
1919 New Brunswick
1922 Prince Edward Island
1925 Dominion of Newfoundland
1940 Quebec

Support for votes for women came from farmers' organizations, labour unions, the Methodist church, and many newspapers across the country, as well as from women's organizations such as the WCTU, Women's Institutes, and the Canadian Women's Press Club.

Questions and Activities

Match the people in column A with the descriptions in column B.

A	B
1. Tom Longboat	a) founded the first Women's Institute.
2. Wilfrid Laurier	b) changed the family carriage factory
3. Clifford Sifton	into an automobile-making business.
4. Adelaide Hunter	c) fought for women's right to vote.
Hoodless	d) was a world champion marathon
5. Robert Borden	runner.
6. Nellie McClung	e) was the minister in charge of
7. Sam McLaughlin	immigration in the early 1900s.
	f) wanted a separate Canadian navy.
	g) opposed the policy of reciprocity.

Ideas for Discussion

1. What sorts of problems did immigrants to Canada face in the early 1900s? Which of these problems do immigrants still face today? What different sorts of problems do they face today?
   Discuss what the government should do to help immigrants. What can immigrants themselves do to help them adjust to life in their new country?
2. What problems did women face in the early 1900s? Which of these problems have been solved or reduced? Which still exist today?
   Select one problem that women still face in today's society. How would you solve or reduce that problem?
3. Why did workers join trade unions in the early 1900s? Why do they join trade unions today?
   Hold a debate on the topic: Resolved that trade unions are as necessary today as they were in the early 1900s.

Do Some Research

1. In the early 1900s many immigrants settled in the same area as others of their national group or religious background. In this way they often formed their own communities. Do some research on one of the following groups.
   a) Chinese   e) Mennonite
   b) Doukhobor   f) Mormon
   c) German   g) Polish
   d) Jewish   h) Ukrainian
   Divide your report into two sections: Origins in the Old Country, and Development in Canada.

2. Find out more about one of the following people. Write a brief biography, explaining his or her achievements and importance.
   a) Clifford Sifton   d) Nellie McClung
   b) Henri Bourassa   e) Tom Longboat
   c) Sam McLaughlin
3. a) Interview a local businessperson or farmer. Find out what his or her views are on high or low tariffs today.
   b) Interview a local trade union member. Find out why he or she thinks unions are still necessary.
4. Do some research on the history of a railway in or near your community. Your report might use the following headings.
   a) Plan for a Railway
   b) Building the Railway
   c) How the Railway Changed the Community
   d) State of the Railway Today
   If there is no railway near your community, find out about the alternate means of transportation the community has used in the past and is using today.

Be Creative

1. With a small group of other students, prepare a folder about settlement on the Prairies. Your folder should include:
   a) a *map* of Canada showing the ports where settlers arrived in Canada, the routes of the railways that took them to their new homes, and the location of settlements.
   b) a *poster* advertising free land in Canada
   c) a *description* of Canadian immigration policy under Clifford Sifton and its results
   d) a *drawing* of a settler's home
2. At the turn of the century, electricity greatly changed the way of life for many Canadians. Write a newspaper article describing how your life today would be changed without electricity. Your opening might be "Our community has been without electricity for almost a week, and life is so different."
3. Find out more about life in the cities in the early 1900s. Present your findings in the form of a diary entry that might have been written by a teenager in a poor working class family or by a wealthy factory owner. Do you think that anything should have been done about the differences between the rich and the poor? If so, what and by whom?
4. Do further research about the Boer War. Should Canada have been involved? Assume you were living at the time and write a letter to your member of parliament explaining your views.

You Are There

It is 1911. A vigorous election campaign is being fought on the issue of reciprocity, or lower tariffs with the United States. You attend meetings held by both the Liberal party and the Conservative party in your riding. The candidates make the speeches below.

How will you vote? Why? Try to persuade other voters to agree with you. Write a letter to relatives living in another part of Canada explaining the attitude of people in your region.

Borden in Ontario.

Laurier in Alberta.

The Conservative Candidate

My fellow Canadians:

In 1879, John A. Macdonald introduced a protective tariff. This was a customs duty which was added to the cost of manufactured goods imported from the United States. We all know that because American manufacturers are producing goods for a larger market, these goods are often cheaper than Canadian goods. Without the tariff, American goods would flood into Canada. The entire farm implement industry, stove, shoes and clothing manufacturers, would go out of business. The cities of Hamilton, Winnipeg, Halifax, Montreal and Toronto would lose their main industries. Workers all across eastern Canada would lose their jobs. Without these industries, we would be a nation of farmers, fishermen, and lumberjacks — a land of "hewers of wood and drawers of water" providing raw materials for others to process.

No, my friends, low tariffs, or "Reciprocity" would not only cause mass unemployment; it would be the first step towards Canada losing its existence. If you follow the Liberal policy, we will all soon not only buy our manufactured goods from the U.S., we will soon be part of the United States. We would lose our ties to Britain and the Empire.

If you want a prosperous, independent country, vote for the Conservative party. Vote to maintain the protective tariff.

The Liberal Candidate

People of Canada:

For many years we have had a protective tariff. This policy has helped the factory owners in the big cities like Toronto and Montreal. They have become wealthy selling their goods in a protected market. But at whose expense?

I say it is the farmers of the Prairie provinces who have paid the price. I say it is the farmers and people of the small valleys of eastern Canada who are losing out. It is the fishermen of British Columbia and the Maritimes. It is the lumber workers of Ontario, Quebec, New Brunswick, and Nova Scotia. These people have had to pay higher prices for Canadian goods. They could have bought less expensive goods from the United States. And the farmers of the West would not have had to pay those high freight costs to bring goods from Ontario and Quebec.

But this is only the beginning. Our tariffs have caused the Americans to place tariffs of their own against our grain, fish, and lumber.

I say reduce the tariffs. If elected, the Liberal party will arrange a treaty with the Americans. If we agree to reduce tariffs on manufactured goods from the U.S., they will reciprocate by reducing tariffs to let in our raw materials.

Fellow Canadians, We have a great future if we increase our trade. Join with the Liberal Party. Let us reduce the tariffs. Let us have a policy that benefits all Canadians, not just the wealthy factory owners in eastern Canada.

Canada Goes to War
ADVANCE ORGANIZER

1 By the 1900s, Europe was divided into two armed camps. One consisted of Germany, Austria and Italy — the Triple Alliance. The other was made up of the British Empire, France and Russia — the Triple Entente. Only a spark was needed to set off an explosion of war. It came on 28 June 1914, when the crown prince of Austria was assassinated. Within one month the two alliances were at war.

2 Canadians volunteered to fight for the British Empire in 1914. Few knew what war would be like. Soldiers had little or no protection except for the trenches that they dug on the battlefield. They lived in these night and day. For months on end they fended off the enemy while trying to gain a little territory. This went on for four years. Often a long and bloody battle meant winning or losing only a few metres of ground. In battles like those at Ypres and Vimy Ridge, Canadians gained a new pride in their country.

3 At the beginning of the war, planes were used mainly to observe the movements of enemy troops. Then pilots began carrying rifles and firing upon enemy aircraft. Soon machine guns were mounted on the planes, bringing the war in the air to full force. Many Canadians were among the best fighter pilots of the war. The airplane changed the face of modern warfare forever.

Word List

armaments	fortify	regulation
armistice	income tax	suffrage
artillery	mobilize	tradition
conscription	regiment	trench

4

Disasters at sea were not limited to the war front. One thousand passengers drowned when the British liner *Lusitania* was sunk by a German submarine. In the Halifax harbour, two supply ships collided. One was laden with high explosives. The resulting explosion killed and maimed thousands.

5

With war came the need to produce wartime machinery and equipment. New factories were opened. 500 000 soldiers were overseas, and workers were in short supply. Women served as munitions workers in the new war factories. They also replaced men in other important jobs in Canadian society. To pay for the war, the government issued Victory Bonds and introduced new taxes.

6

The Canadian army was made up of volunteers. By 1917 so many soldiers were being killed and wounded, volunteers could not replace them. The Conservative government introduced conscription, forcing young men to join the army. This policy caused one of Canada's major crises. Most English Canadians felt loyal to the British Empire, and were in favour of conscription. But almost all French Canadians were opposed to forcing people to fight in a foreign country. Conscription caused bitter hostility between French and English Canadians, and seriously threatened the unity of Canada.

7

On 11 November 1918 the armistice was declared, ending the war. The Allies had won. Canadian troops could finally return to their country. But the cost to all sides was enormous: 50 000 Canadian soldiers lay buried in the cemeteries of France and Belgium. All told, more than 13 million soldiers lost their lives in the war.

The Road to War

At the beginning of the twentieth century some of the nations of Europe were more powerful than they had ever been before. Germany had always been divided into many small states. During the 1800s it had become a united country. Much the same happened in Italy. Germans and Italians were very proud of their new united countries.

The Slavs of southeastern Europe also wanted a united country. Even though Serbia was an independent Slavic country, many Slavs lived in parts of the Austrian and Turkish Empires. Russia wanted to help its "Slavic brothers" gain independence from their foreign rulers.

Austria feared this would break up its empire. Turkey feared Russia's real aim was to take over Turkish ports on the Mediterranean Sea. Their fear of Russia led Austria and Turkey to seek friends. They turned to Germany.

The big powers of Europe were jockeying for position. Ambition was leading them to make enemies. Fear and suspicion were forcing them to seek allies.

The Struggle for Power

Britain controlled the British Empire. This included Canada, Australia, New Zealand, India, and much of Africa. France had colonies in Africa and Asia.

Because Germany had become a united country so late, its empire was very small — only a few colonies in Africa. Some Germans wanted more. They felt Germany was a great country. It should have a great empire. The German army and navy should be built up. The ruler of Germany, Kaiser Wilhelm II, agreed with these ideas. Germany had an agreement, called the Triple Alliance, with Austria and Italy. With the help of these allies, Germany planned to catch up to Britain and France.

Wilfrid Laurier, prime minister 1896-1911

Robert Borden, prime minister 1911-1919

Conservative and Liberal Policies in Canada

Canada had close ties with Britain — in fact as a member of the British Empire, Canada was officially bound by British foreign policy. Therefore, when Britain declared war, Canada was at war too. Both Conservatives and Liberals accepted this as natural and right.

The parties had disagreed on policy before the war, especially on the naval question. Once the war started, the Liberal opposition under Laurier supported most of Prime Minister Borden's war policies. There was only one issue on which Laurier could not support Borden. This was the conscription issue of 1917.

Borden and his defence minister insisted that Canadian soldiers serve in their own units, not just as part of the British army. Borden told the British that Canadians would not support the war effort blindly. As prime minister of Canada he had to be informed of war policy. He also obtained British war contracts for Canadian industry.

Borden's policies continued Laurier's efforts to establish Canada as an independent country. By 1919 Canada and the other dominions were recognized as nations, not colonies.

The Triple Alliance alarmed France and Russia. They agreed to co-operate if either country was attacked by Austria or Germany.

By the 1900s Germany was expanding its navy. The British grew worried. The German navy might become stronger than their own! A "naval race" started — each country tried to stay ahead by building more ships. Britain had thought the British Empire was strong enough without allies. Now it began to fear Germany and to seek friends in Europe.

First Britain joined with France in an agreement called the Entente Cordiale (the Cordial Understanding). In 1907 France brought Russia and Britain together in the Triple Entente.

List the members of *a)* the Triple Alliance, *b)* the Triple Entente.
Why did each country join the alliance or entente?
How did Britain's declaration of war affect Canada? Was Canada a
completely independent country at that time (1914)?

The Alliance System

In 1914 Europe was divided into two armed camps, the
Triple Alliance and the Triple Entente. All that was
needed was a spark to cause the explosion. It came on
28 June 1914 in Sarajevo, Austria-Hungary. Archduke
Ferdinand, heir to the Austrian throne, was making
an official visit. A terrorist from a Slavic patriotic group
based in nearby Serbia shot and killed him. In little
more than a month, the world was at war.

HMS Dreadnought, built in 1906,
gave her name to a new class of
fighting ships.

The Steps to War, Summer 1914

28 June	Archduke Ferdinand is assassinated at Sarajevo.
23 July	Austria sends ultimatum to Serbia.
25 July	Serbia replies, rejecting one term.
28 July	Austria invades Serbia.
29 July	Russia mobilizes army along borders with Austria and Germany. Germany declares war on Russia. Canada sends telegram to Britain promising support.
3 August	Germany declares war on France.
4 August	Germany invades Belgium. Britain declares war on Germany.
5 August	Canada and the rest of the British Empire are at war.

Italy left the Triple Alliance with
Germany and Austria and came into the
war on the side of France and Britain.
Japan also fought against Germany in
World War I, taking over German bases
in China.

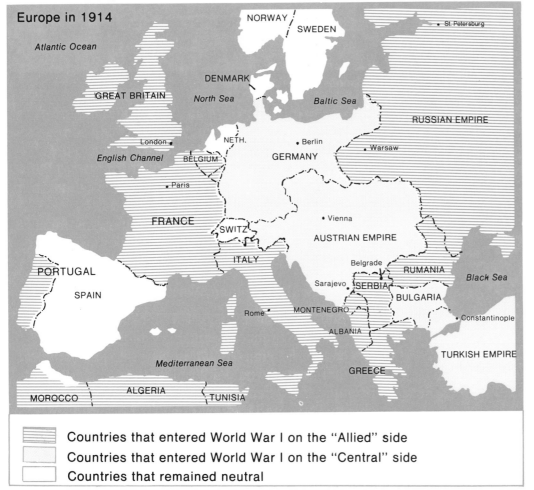

Europe in 1914

Countries that entered World War I on the "Allied" side

Countries that entered World War I on the "Central" side

Countries that remained neutral

The War Begins

In the late 1800s Germany had tried to keep on friendly terms with Russia. If war came, Germany expected it to be with France. This would mean battles to the west — a western front. If Russia joined in on the side of France, it would mean battles to the east — an eastern front.

When Germany allied with Austria, Russia's friendship was lost. Russia became France's ally. How could Germany avoid a war on two fronts at once?

The Schlieffen Plan

General von Schlieffen developed a plan. He figured that the Russians would take a long time to mobilize their army. Therefore he planned to move rapidly against the French. He would mislead the French as to where the main attack would come from. The French army would concentrate along the German border.

In a two-front war, the whole of Germany must throw itself upon one enemy: the strongest, the most powerful, the most dangerous enemy. That can only be France.

General von Schlieffen

Wearing kilts and pith helmets quite unsuitable for modern war, the 48th Highlanders leave Toronto for overseas on a rainy September day in 1914. The photographer used a glass negative which has broken. Prints made since then have a crack down the centre of the picture.

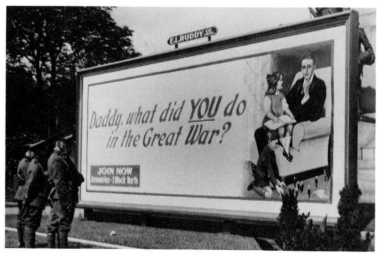

A famous recruiting poster.

Meanwhile, the German army would invade France from the north. They would sweep across the flat lands of Belgium and northern France to the English Channel. Then they would turn toward Paris like a curved claw. They would fall on the capital from the west. All this would take about six weeks.

The French would be knocked out of the war. The Germans could then turn all their armies against the Russians.

How the Schlieffen Plan Worked

The Schlieffen plan was based on a gamble. Over 70 years before, France, Germany, and Britain had agreed that Belgium should be neutral. The gamble was that Britain would not object to the invasion of Belgium. But when the war started, the British did object. They used the invasion as a reason to enter the war.

You will be home before the leaves have fallen from the trees.

The German Kaiser speaking to his troops, August 1914

What was the main aim of the Schlieffen Plan?
Why did it fail?
How did its failure affect the war on the western front?

1900 1910 1920 1930 1940 1950 1960 1970 1980 1990 2000

▲

General von Schlieffen had died in 1913. The new German generals decided to use his plan. But they made a few changes. Instead of approaching Paris from the west, they turned south too soon. This meant the French army from the French-German border could reach them. And they were also attacked by French and British troops moving out from Paris.

The German advance was halted on the Marne River. The Schlieffen plan had failed. Instead of knocking France out of the war, the Germans found themselves bogged down. On the western front they faced the combined armies of France, Britain, and their empires, including Canada.

Instead of a short, swift campaign, it became a long, dreary, and horrible war. Four years of trench warfare had begun.

The lamps are going out all over Europe. We shall not see them lit again in our lifetime.

Edward Grey, British foreign secretary, August 1914

The western front, 1914-1918
General von Schlieffen's planned route
Actual route of the German army

Canada, a daughter of Old England, intends to stand by her in this great conflict. When the call to duty comes, our answer goes at once: "Ready, aye, ready."

Wilfrid Laurier, leader of the opposition, August 1914

Sam Hughes

1853 — born in Darlington, Ontario. After attending teachers' college and the University of Toronto, taught until 1885. Was member of volunteer militia.

1885-97 — owner and editor of newspaper in Lindsay, Ontario.

1892 — elected as Conservative MP.

1899 — served as volunteer in Boer War.

1911 — appointed Minister of Militia and Defence in new Conservative government.

1914-16 — organized Canadian Corps. Refused to allow Canadian troops to be divided among British regiments. As an Irish Protestant, hated Roman Catholics and seemed to antagonize French Canadians. His vanity, and violent temper also created problems for officers working under him.

1916 — was asked to resign as minister because of his unpopularity. Though he was a forceful **administrator**, he lacked judgement.

1921 — died at Lindsay, Ontario.

War in the Trenches

Mud. Barbed wire. Lice. Hardtack and bully beef. Rain, sleet, and snow. Mud. Rats. Shell holes full of stagnant water. Bodies. Machine-gun bullets. Sandbags. More mud.

Digging In

The Schlieffen plan had failed. The Germans could not advance. The French and the British could not drive them back. Both sides set about fortifying their positions.

They dug trenches to protect their troops. Each trench was a ditch about 2 m deep topped with sandbags. Soldiers could stand in the trench without being seen by the enemy. Between the front-line trenches was a narrow strip called no man's land. Rifle and machine-gun fire spattered across no man's land whenever a soldier detected a movement in enemy territory. Shells flew from the artillery behind the front lines, spraying shrapnel everywhere.

Over the Top

Sometimes the officers would order an advance. This meant "going over the top" of the trench and across no man's land fully exposed to the enemy's fire. Sometimes the troops managed to capture the enemy's front line. The enemy retired to their reserve trenches. Barbed wire was stretched across the new patch of no man's land. A few metres of land had been lost or won. Hundreds of soldiers might have been killed in the process. Then the whole dreary business started all over again.

Soldiers fought, ate, and slept in the trenches. Eventually they would be relieved for a few days by fresh troops. In winter they froze in the snow and sleet. Spring rains sometimes filled the trenches waist-deep with icy water. In summer the rich farmlands of Belgium and northern France turned to mud. For 4 years the war went on.

Fix bayonets . . .

. . . and over the top.

OCUS

Why is there such a difference between the two letters from the front? Imagine you are a soldier in the trenches and write a letter about fighting conditions. Your letter could begin, "We have had a horrible week in the trenches. . ."

1900 1910 1920 1930 1940 1950 1960 1970 1980 1990 2000

Two Letters Home

Before heavy action: 24 March 1915

We have been put in the trenches for a week with British troops. Then we'll be taken back for further training. Then we will be in the trenches for 5 weeks, and then we get a rest.

Our German friends opposite have a sense of humour. One day they stuck a toy horse up above their trench. Our chaps shot it down. They put it up again with a bandage round its neck.

They call out things like "We no shoot, you no shoot."

"If you come halfway, we'll give you cigarettes."

"Hello, B.C., how'd you like to be walking down Hastings Street?"

Our men are so light-hearted—full of life and ginger. Somebody is going to be badly hurt when these boys let loose.

A soldier with a close haircut was less likely to suffer from head lice.

Machine guns, shellfire, and newer, more efficient bombs caused injuries never seen before.

After heavy action: 15 May 1915

We were called out from Ypres about 5 o'clock. The sky was a hell of bursting shrapnel. We lay in reserve until nearly midnight. Then they told us to take the wood. We charged across 500 m of open country. We lost many men during that charge.

I saw poor Charlie go down and stopped to help him, but he urged us on. Then Andy fell, shot right through the head. When we got to the edge of the wood we found a trench just dug by the Germans. This is when the hell began. They had 2 machine guns, and the fire was like hailstones on a tin roof. Somehow they missed a few of us, but other fellows were cut in half by the stream of lead.

I have often wanted to see a fight. Never again. I remember the next morning, all the dead and dying lying about in twisted shapes. War is hell.

We are going back to the base to be reorganized. We had 26 officers before, and 2 after, so you can see it was pretty bad. I shall try to transfer, as most of my nerve has gone.

On 1 July the Royal Newfoundland Regiment went over the top at Beaumont Hamel on the Somme River. The regiment was mown down by enemy machine-gun fire. Of the 840 officers and men who took part in the action, 293 were killed and 468 injured. Only 79 were present at a roll call following the battle.

Taking a wounded soldier out on a stretcher, the battle of the Somme, 1916.

Canadian and German wounded help each other through the mud to the field hospital.

THE COURSE OF WAR   67

A Tale of Two Battles

In October 1914 the first Canadian troops arrived in England. The British officers sneered. These "colonials" were sloppy. They didn't even salute properly! The only way to lick them into shape would be to divide them up among British units. They would be no use in their own regiment.

The Canadian minister of militia, Sam Hughes, was furious. He refused to let the Canadians be divided up. As a result, Canada had her own army. The Canadian Corps soon proved its worth.

Ypres

After training, the Canadians arrived in Europe in March 1915. They were sent to Ypres, a city near the Belgian coast. The object was to stop the Germans breaking through to the English Channel. Since the failure of the Schlieffen plan the year before, there had been little fighting here.

The Germans wanted a way to break the stalemate. They decided to use a new weapon—poisonous chlorine gas. On 22 April a gentle breeze blew toward the allied lines—perfect for a gas attack.

The Canadians had been assigned a section of the front-line trenches. To the left were troops from the French colony of Algeria. The Algerians saw a green cloud drifting across no man's land. As it reached the trenches, they found themselves choking and gasping for breath. Those who were not suffocated fled.

People had talked about gas warfare. However, the Allied commanders did not think it would be used. So the Canadian soldiers had no gas masks. All they could do was to soak cotton pads in urine and hold them over their faces. The acid in the urine neutralized the chlorine. Then they moved into the gap to prevent a German breakthrough. They held on for two whole days. Finally British relief troops took over.

The Canadians had proved themselves. Nobody sneered at them after the battle of "Wipers."

John McCrae was our brigade surgeon. "In Flanders Fields" was born of fire and blood during the battle of Ypres. Our headquarters were in a trench on the top of the bank of the Ypres Canal. John had his dressing station in a hole dug in the foot of the bank. Wounded men were actually rolled down the bank into his dressing station. Many times during the 16 days of battle, he and I watched the regiment burying their dead whenever there was a lull. "The crosses row on row" grew into a good-sized cemetery. We often heard "the larks still bravely singing" high in the air between the crash of shells and the reports of the the guns in the battery just beside us. He wrote "In Flanders Fields" between the arrival of batches of wounded.

General Morrison, Colonel McCrae's Brigade Commander

Gas masks were issued to everybody, including the horses, after the battle of Ypres.

In Flanders Fields

John McCrae

In Flanders fields the poppies blow
Between the crosses, row on row,
That mark our place; and in the sky
The larks, still bravely singing, fly
Scarce heard amid the guns below.

We are the Dead. Short days ago
We lived, felt dawn, saw sunset glow,
Loved, and were loved, and now we lie
   In Flanders fields.

Take up our quarrel with the foe:
To you from failing hands we throw
The torch; be yours to hold it high.
If ye break faith with us who die
We shall not sleep, though poppies grow
   In Flanders fields.

FOCUS
Canadian soldiers played a brave and important part in the fighting in World War I. Describe the battle of *a)* Ypres, *b)* Vimy Ridge. For each battle explain why the part played by the Canadian army was especially important.

CANADA
THE TWENTIETH CENTURY
Art Gallery page 9

Vimy Ridge

"Zero hour will be 5:30 a.m."

The word spread through the Canadian army on Easter Sunday, 1917. Every soldier was aware that Vimy Ridge was the key to the German lines. If the Allies were to break the stalemate of the war, Vimy Ridge would have to be taken. In two years of tough fighting, Canadians had done well. The doubtful honour of storming Vimy Ridge would fall to them.

The soldiers looked across no man's land. About 100 m across the mud was the front line of German trenches. It would be sheer hell to get across. That night they got a final hot meal, and a shot of rum to heat their stomachs. It might also give them courage.

For the past two weeks the artillery had been firing shells into the enemy lines. Easter Monday dawned cold, with sleet and snow falling. At exactly 5:30 the command was given to go over the top. Covered by more shellfire, 15 000 soldiers moved in the first wave

of attack. They valiantly struggled across the mud and through what was left of the barbed wire. The return fire from German machine guns and artillery was murderous. But the Canadian shellfire had wiped out the German frontline! In the snow, the soldiers had passed it without knowing it. They surprised the second line of defence. Some fled, but others surrendered to the Canadians then and there. Despite massive losses, by midmorning the Canadians had seized the heights. Vimy Ridge was in Allied hands.

Vimy Ridge was the first great Allied victory since the beginning of the war. Canadian pride got a great boost that cold morning in northern France.

But this pride was dampened by the cost. In just a few hours, 3 598 brave Canadian soldiers had died.

Germans captured at Vimy.

The artillery bombardment before the battle of Vimy Ridge.

Triumphant Canadians return from Vimy Ridge.

The War in the Air

The Wright brothers built the first successful airplane. They flew it at Kitty Hawk, North Carolina, in 1903. Six years later John McCurdy flew the *Silver Dart* at Baddeck, Nova Scotia. The *Silver Dart* had been designed by McCurdy and Alexander Graham Bell.

However, airplanes were regarded as "too expensive a luxury for Canada to indulge in." At the outbreak of World War I Canada had no airplanes and no pilots.

This attitude did not appeal to young Canadian flying buffs. Many went to Britain to join the Royal Flying Corps. They were among the best fighter pilots of the war.

Aircraft Design

By 1914 aircraft design had not advanced greatly. Most planes flew at about 150 km/h. They had open, single

A Canadian aircraft factory. The planes were sent to Europe with the wings detached to save space aboard ship.

Billy Bishop in the cockpit of his single-seater fighter, the French-designed Nieuport 17. The machine-gun controls are on the upper wing just above the pilot's head. The gun fired above the propeller. It could be raised or lowered but not swung from side to side. Bishop scored 36 of his confirmed victories in this plane.

seater cockpits. At first planes were used mainly to observe enemy troop movements. The thrill of flying united all pilots—British, German, French. As their planes passed above the lines of battle, they would wave to each other. But then some pilots started to bring rifles into the cockpit. They shot at enemy planes in order to stop information reaching the enemy generals. The friendly game was over. The war in the air had begun.

The next step was to mount a machine gun on the plane. The problem was to avoid hitting the propeller. One British design mounted the gun behind the pilot. The French placed it above the propeller, on the top wing of the biplane. The Germans had a gun timed to fire through the propeller without hitting the blades. When the British tried this system, it did not always work perfectly. These guns had fixed mounts. The only way to aim the gun was to point the entire plane directly at the target.

FOCUS Draw a picture of an airplane at the beginning of the war. Imagine you are Billy Bishop and write a letter describing a dogfight. Your opening could be: "Our 3 planes took off on a sunlit morning. Suddenly we sighted 3 enemy planes . . ."

Some Canadian World War I Air Aces

	Enemy aircraft destroyed
Billy Bishop V.C. (Owen Sound, Ont.)	72
Raymond Collishaw (Nanaimo, B.C.)	60
Donald MacLaren (Vancouver, B.C.)	54
Billy Barker V.C. (Dauphin, Man.)	50
Fred McCall (Vernon, B.C.)	34
William Claxton (Gladstone, Man.)	31
Albert Carter (Pointe de Bute, N.B.)	31

V.C. stands for the Victoria Cross, the highest military honour in the British Empire. King George V awarded the Victoria Cross to 10 airmen—including 3 Canadians. Altogether, 68 Canadians won the Victoria Cross during the war.

Dogfights

Meetings of enemy aircraft became deadly "dogfights." Pilots tried to get on the tail of an enemy plane where the enemy could not return the gunfire. Being shot down usually meant instant death. Pilots did not carry parachutes. If they did, they might bail out. Their officers wanted them to try to save the planes instead. The expected life span of a pilot was three weeks before being shot down.

One of the leading "aces" of the Royal Flying Corps was a Canadian, Billy Bishop. He shot down 72 enemy planes. The greatest flying ace was Manfred von Richthofen, the famous Red Baron. He shot down 80 planes.

The Red Baron's Last Flight

One day in April 1918 Richthofen took his pilots on their usual daily patrol. They were met by a British squadron led by Roy Brown of Carleton Place, Ontario. Soon the two groups were in a fierce dogfight.

Wop May was on his first combat flight. The young Canadian realized his guns were jammed and drifted out of the battle. The Red Baron moved onto his tail. Preparing for the kill, he did not notice that Roy

Wilfred (Wop) May
1896 — born in Carberry, Manitoba.
1902 — family moved to Edmonton where father opened a farm equipment shop.
1916 — joined Canadian army. As soon as possible, transferred to Royal Flying Corps.
1917 — after training, assigned to observation flights. Wanted more excitement so requested transfer.
1918 — in first combat flight was saved from Red Baron by Roy Brown. Did not have the record of "kills" some Canadian aces had, but was convinced he wanted to fly.
1919 — returned to Edmonton. Wop was expected to join family firm, now a car dealership — had changed with times — as a mechanic. But Wop wanted to fly. Rented a JN4 Canuck. Delivered city newspapers to small towns by dropping them over the side of the plane; did stunt flying at town fairs; gave flying lessons.
1924 — Married. Quit flying to take steady job. It didn't last: Wop was soon flying again.
1929 — Flew vaccine north to Fort Vermilion to combat a midwinter diphtheria epidemic. Trip took 3 days in an open plane. Returned to find himself an instant hero; the country had followed the trip through radio reports. In December flew 1st official airmail to Aklavik.
1932 — Helped RCMP find Albert Johnson, "The Mad Trapper of the North" by tracking from the air. In the shootout when mounties on the ground caught up with him, Johnson was killed, a mountie badly injured. May flew the man back to Aklavik for emergency treatment.
1935 — Gave up active flying due to loss of right eye.
1940-45 — taught in Commonwealth Air Training Plan.
1942 — set up northern Parachute Rescue Squad to rescue U.S. pilots lost while ferrying planes to bases in Alaska.
1946 — planned commercial air route to Japan
1951 — manager of a company making jet planes.
1952 — died while hiking in Utah with 17-year-old son.

Brown had moved behind *him*. Brown got the German ace in his gun sights and knocked him out of the sky.

A Canadian had downed the legendary Red Baron.

The War at Sea

Workers at Alexander Graham Bell's laboratory at Baddeck, N.S., turned to building lifeboats.

When the war began, Canada had only the beginnings of a navy. Wilfrid Laurier had decided Canada should have her own navy, not contribute to Britain's. Canada had two mid-sized cruisers. The *Niobe* was based in Halifax and the *Rainbow* in Vancouver. Canada's navy did little fighting at sea. But by the end of the war, the Royal Canadian Navy had grown to about 100 ships, mostly small coastal vessels.

Atlantic Trade

Canada's main part in the war at sea was in shipping Canadian troops and Canadian products to Europe. Through most of the war, the United States was neutral. Americans sold goods to Britain, France, and Germany. But they sold more to Britain and France. Most Americans were sympathetic to the Allies.

Britain tried to block goods being sent to Germany. The British navy mined the North Sea so neutral ships could not get to German ports. Meanwhile the German navy wanted to stop goods reaching Britain. They declared a war zone in the waters around the British Isles.

The Germans used submarines to attack ships bound for Britain. In 1915 a German submarine sank the *Lusitania,* a British passenger liner. Over 1000 people died, including 114 Americans. The tragedy contributed to anti-German feeling in the United States.

The British started to collect ships into large groups called convoys. Convoys would sail together from Quebec, Halifax, or St. John's. They could be protected from submarines by warships. The convoy system greatly reduced the number of ships sunk.

Halifax after the explosion.

1900 1910 1920 1930 1940 1950 1960 1970 1980 1990 2000

The Halifax Explosion

Thursday 6 December 1917 dawned clear and mild in Halifax. At 7:30 the *Mont Blanc*, a French freighter loaded with benzene, picric acid, and TNT, started to move through the Narrows to Bedford Basin, the city's inner harbour. She had come from New York to join the next convoy across the Atlantic. At about 8:00 the *Imo*, a Norwegian tramp steamer carrying relief supplies for Belgium, headed out through the Narrows.

In the city, factory workers were already at their jobs. Children were assembling in school playgrounds. Offices and stores were getting ready for the day's business. Ships must take care as they pass in the Narrows. As the *Mont Blanc* and the *Imo* drew close to each other, they signalled their intentions. But suddenly the *Mont Blanc* was across the *Imo's* bow. At

Two young victims of the explosion.

8:43 the *Imo* rammed her. The two ships drifted apart. People in the city out enjoying the winter sunshine watched as a wisp of smoke rose from the harbour. At 9:06 the *Mont Blanc's* cargo of high explosives blew up.

Schools, factories, stores, and houses in a 5 km² area were completely destroyed. Part of the two-tonne anchor of the *Mont Blanc* was found 4 km away. Over 2000 people died and another 9000 were injured. That night, with 10 000 people homeless, the temperature plunged to -8°C and a blizzard was on the way.

Within days relief supplies began to pour in from Canada and as far away as Jamaica and New Zealand. The state of Massachusetts sent a special relief committee.

The Halifax explosion was the biggest man-made explosion the world had known to that time.

The War at Home

Wars have always been fought by soldiers in the front line. World War I was the first war to involve all sections of society. In Canada, far from the battle lines, people were making their contribution.

Farming

The war disrupted farming in Europe. Canada had been exporting wheat to Europe for many years. But now Europe needed far more. Canadian farmers had to fill a large part of this need.

By the end of the war "sodbusters" in the West had doubled the land used for wheat farming. Cheese exports tripled. Pork and beef exports shot sky high.

Do you know that last year's grain crop in Europe was half its normal size? That 90 million food animals have already been slaughtered? That over 60% of the 50 million soldiers fighting the war came off the farms? In addition, thousands of ships are being sunk by enemy submarines. Most of these ships are carrying food. Our duty is simple: Produce more and waste nothing.

Speaker from the Department of Agriculture to a housewives' group, Victoria, B.C.

Industry

Canadian business also found new markets. Before the war factories produced goods for the Canadian market. Few tried to compete outside the country. Most of our exports were raw materials—to be processed elsewhere.

Now businesses saw new opportunities. Canadian companies started to make armaments for the Allied forces. Steel companies turned to making shell cases. Others made fuses and explosives. By 1917 one-third of the shells used by the British were made in Canada.

A Ukrainian family brings in the harvest.

Red Cross supplies for the battlefields of Europe.

Canadians made guns, airplane parts, and ships. Aluminum, nickel, railway track, and timber were all sent to Europe. Uniforms, equipment, and medical supplies were made for the Canadian army.

What new Canadian industries were created by World War I?
What is "profiteering"? Give 2 examples during the war. What do
you think should happen to wartime profiteers?
List 3 ways the government raised money to pay for the war.

CANADA
THE TWENTIETH CENTURY
Art Gallery page 10

Profiteering

Most Canadians worked hard to help the war effort. City workers gave up their free time to help farmers bring in the crops. Women turned to new kinds of jobs. Businessmen and government officials worked long hours without extra pay. All this activity created great opportunities for profit.

Most businessmen were content to take a fair mark-up. But some tried to "corner the market" on a product. They would not sell until they could get the best price. Others used cheap materials and did sloppy work. The boots the first Canadian troops were given wore out in less than two months! Canned meat for soldiers sometimes came from diseased animals. Some industrialists used bribery to get government contracts.

Ordinary people did the same sort of things. On one hand, some made up parcels for soldiers and planted "war gardens" with vegetables. On the other, some hoarded supplies, wasted food, and tried to get around government regulations.

Back Him Up!
Buy VICTORY BONDS

Victory Bonds

War is expensive. Canadians paid no income or profit taxes. The government could not raise enough money by other means. How was the war to be paid for?

To raise money, Canada issued Victory Bonds. Canadians were urged to buy bonds to help the war effort. After the war they could cash in their bonds and get their money back with interest. Most bonds were bought by banks and large companies. But ordinary citizens did their part as well.

Two new "temporary" taxes were introduced. The first was a business profits tax. The second was an income tax. These taxes are still with us.

An armament factory.

Women at War

Even before World War I women were breaking out of their traditional role. Many wanted to be more than housewives and mothers. Women stayed in school longer. Some went to university. A few even became doctors and lawyers. But these were special cases. It was almost impossible for women to get hired for many jobs. And women could not vote.

The Needs of Industry

The wartime industrial boom created a problem. The young men who would normally work in industry were in the army. Women moved into the war factories. By the end of the war, over 20 000 women were employed making guns, shells, and aircraft. And they held skilled jobs. Before the war, women had only done routine work. Skilled jobs had been for men.

Overhauling a Curtiss OX-5 aircraft in the repair section at Camp Mohawk. Desoronto, Ont.

Women also replaced men in many civilian jobs. They became streetcar drivers, secretaries, and office managers. They moved onto the farms to help bring in the crops.

Women without paying jobs were also doing their part. They knitted socks for soldiers, sent them letters and care packages, visited the families of men who had been killed. Women supported the Canadian Red Cross and other volunteer organizations.

Letters with news of home from a mother or sweetheart helped make life more bearable for soldiers at the front.

The Army Medical Corps

The wounded soldiers on the western front needed medical care. Over 3 000 women became army nurses and ambulance drivers. Most of them served overseas. They willingly shared the dangers of warfare with Canadian men.

The Right to Vote

The efforts and achievements of women could not be ignored forever. Women wanted the right to vote. World War I meant they got that right. But the federal government granted it in a rather grudging way.

1900 1910 1920 1930 1940 1950 1960 1970 1980 1990 2000

An ambulance driver was responsible for keeping her engine in good running order.

In 1917 Prime Minister Borden decided the government needed conscription, the right to force men to join the army. Some people would not like this. It was time for an election. Borden wanted to use the election to prove conscription was "the will of the Canadian people." Before the election, the government passed the Wartime Election Act.

This act took the vote away from citizens who had emigrated from "enemy" countries. (They might vote against conscription.) It gave the vote to women—but not all women. Only army nurses and close relatives of soldiers would be allowed to vote. (They would probably support conscription: if other men had to go to war, their men might have a better chance.)

Obviously this act was unfair to other women. In 1918 all women were given the vote. But they still could not be elected to Parliament. That right did not come till 1920. In 1921 Agnes Macphail was elected to the House of Commons.

The first steps had been taken. The long struggle for real equality had just begun.

About halfway through the war a new form of warfare was begun, warfare that could hit behind the battle lines. Pilots started to drop bombs on military and civilian targets. This funeral was for Canadian nurses killed in an air raid on a hospital in May 1918.

Conscription

For most of the war, the Canadian army relied on volunteers. At first, many young men were excited at the idea of fighting for their country. They rushed to volunteer. They could hardly wait to get overseas.

The horrors of the trenches soon changed this. From 1915 to 1917 Canadian soldiers gained a high reputation for courage. As a result they were often chosen for the toughest battles.

In April 1917 Canadians fought at Vimy Ridge. That month over 10 000 Canadian soldiers died. Less than 5 000 volunteered to join the army. The volunteer system was not recruiting enough soldiers to replace the losses.

Prime Minister Borden had promised that his government would not introduce conscription. They would not force men to join the army. Now he felt he had to break that promise. An election was coming. The campaign was one of the fiercest and angriest in Canadian history.

When the war broke out, the country went mad! People were singing in the streets. Everybody wanted to go to war. We hadn't had a war since the Boer War in 1899. Everybody was going to be a hero, and I wanted to be a hero too!

But I wasn't big enough. I was only 150 cm tall and weighed 40 kg. I was 19 but looked 15. Finally a drill sergeant said, "We need buglers!" So I joined the army as a bugler.

Bert Remington of Montreal, who had emigrated from England in 1910

Me? I was probably as patriotic as most, but mainly I was restless. I joined up because it was a chance to see the world.

Robert Swan, Yarmouth, N.S.

An anti-conscription parade in Montreal, 24 May 1917.

People against Conscription

The biggest group of people against conscription were the French Canadians. When the war started, many had volunteered to enter the army. The Royal 22nd Regiment, the "Vandoos" (from *vingt-deux*) was a French-speaking unit. It had a great fighting record right through the war.

The minister of militia had been Sam Hughes, an Irish Protestant. Hughes did not try to understand the French Canadians. He hated Roman Catholics. He sent Protestant clergymen as recruiting officers to Quebec. He insisted that French soldiers be trained in English. Borden fired Hughes in 1916, but it was too late to save the situation in Quebec.

What was conscription? Why did Borden think it was necessary?
Why did some Canadians object to conscription?
How did the conscription crisis and the election of 1917 appear to
split the country?

1900 1910 1920 1930 1940 1950 1960 1970 1980 1990 2000
▲

Conscription means national division and strife. It will hurt the cause of the Allies more than a few thousand extra soldiers will bring them help and comfort.

Henri Bourassa

French Canadians had felt no duty to support Britain during the Boer War. Some felt the same way now. This was a European war. They were being asked to save Britain, not Canada. Wilfrid Laurier, the leader of the opposition, did not feel this way. He urged French Canadians to join the army. But he did not think they should be forced to do so.

In the West, many settlers objected to conscription. They had come to Canada to get away from European wars. In many countries governments could force men into the army. They thought they had escaped that way of life. Now is seemed to be coming to Canada.

Farmers everywhere objected. Their part of the war effort was to provide much-needed food. Who would work with them if their sons were taken away?

What the Government Did

Prime Minister Borden was convinced that conscription was necessary. Those in favour of conscription had to win.

First he asked Laurier to join him in the government. Laurier could not do this. Although he supported the war effort, he was against conscription.

Borden then approached other Liberals. Some of

vote against the vernment means:

ou are here for life

A vote for the Government means:

Another man is coming to take your place

Soldiers at the front were encouraged to vote for the government and conscription with posters like this.

them were for conscription. Several Liberals joined the Conservatives in a new party. They called it the Unionist Party.

The government took the vote away from immigrants who might be against conscription. It gave the vote to soldiers overseas and to women who would be for it. Borden promised farmers that their sons would not be forced to go. (This promise was broken after the election.)

Voting up the line, December 1917.

The Election of 1917

The results of the election were Unionists 153, Liberals 82. Only 20 of those 82 were from outside Quebec. But the results did not show the true feelings of the people. Many English-speaking Canadians did not want conscription. In fact, if the soldiers' votes were taken out, nearly half the people voted against it.

The conscription issue aroused many bitter feelings. Canadians were divided as they had not been since the execution of Louis Riel.

The War Ends

While the stalemate continued in France and Belgium, Russians and Germans were fighting on the eastern front. But in 1917 the Russian people revolted against their ruler, the czar. The new government wanted peace. A treaty was signed. This meant German troops were freed to fight in the west.

The United States declared war on Germany in 1917. American troops had not yet arrived. Would they reach the western front in time to help against the new threat?

The Blockade

Germany had trouble at home. The Allies had managed to block German trade. There were shortages of raw materials and of food. Even the army did not get enough to eat.

Tank Warfare

Meanwhile Britain had developed a new weapon. Huge tanks started to rumble across no man's land towards the German lines. Machine-gun bullets bounced off

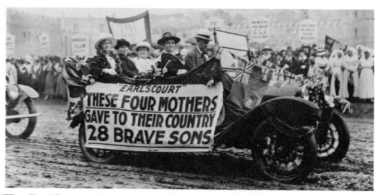

The first Remembrance Day. Each year at 11 a.m. on 11 November Canadians and citizens in many other countries of the world pause to remember those who served in time of war.

these armoured monsters as they crashed through trenches and barbed wire. In August 1918 Canadian troops supported by tanks spearheaded an attack at Amiens. The Germans called this "the black day for the German army." In the following "hundred days" the tanks rolled through the wasteland of northern France. Each victory meant thousands more dead and wounded.

Advancing down a road during the battle of Amiens, August 1918.

Canadian troops enter Cambrai, October 1918.

How did the use of tanks help the Allies to win the war?
What is the origin of Remembrance Day?
List the most important terms of the Treaty of Versailles. Why do some feel that it "sowed the seeds for World War II"?

1900 1910 1920 1930 1940 1950 1960 1970 1980 1990 2000

The blockade and tank warfare combined to defeat Germany. At 11 a.m. on 11 November 1918, the eleventh hour of the eleventh day of the eleventh month, the armistice was declared. The worst war the world had ever known was over.

Over 8 million soldiers had died. More than 20 million more would live out their lives with wounds, shell shock, gassed lungs, lost limbs, sight, or hearing. An equal number of civilians were also victims of war.

The Treaty of Versailles

The arguments were about to begin. The Allies said that Germany had caused the war. They wanted to punish and shame her. They would make Germany too weak ever to start another war.

The Allies met at Versailles to prepare a peace treaty. Many feel that there they sowed the seeds for World War II.

The cemetery at Etaples, France, "where many brave Canadians rest."

Terms of the Treaty

Land Changes

Germany lost control of all overseas colonies.
In Europe, Alsace-Lorraine was transferred from Germany to France; the rich Saar coal region was to be run by France for 15 years; part of east Germany was given to Poland. The Austrian and Turkish Empires were broken up into separate countries.

Military Control

The German army was to be restricted to 100 000 men and to have no tanks or heavy guns. Germany was not to have an air force.
The German navy was to be very small.

Reparations

Germany was to pay money and goods to France and Belgium to repair the damages of the war.

War Guilt

Germany was forced to sign a statement saying that she had caused the war.

Questions and Activities

Test Yourself

Match the people in column A with the descriptions in column B.

A	B
1. Archduke Ferdinand	a) opposed conscription for Canada during World War I.
2. General von Schlieffen	b) was the leading German air ace.
3. Wilfrid Laurier	c) insisted Canadian soldiers fight together in their own unit.
4. John McCrae	d) was assassinated at Sarajevo in an incident that led to the outbreak of World War I.
5. Sam Hughes	e) wrote a poem about soldiers on the western front.
6. Billy Bishop	f) planned the German invasion of France.
7. Manfred von Richthofen	g) was the leading Canadian air ace.

Do Some Research

1. Find out more about the development of one of the following weapons during World War I. Draw a picture and use it to explain the importance of the weapon during the war.
   a) the fighter plane   c) the submarine
   b) the machine gun   d) the tank
2. Do further research on the changing role of women during World War I.
   a) as nurses and workers at the battlefront   b) as workers on the homefront
   c) in getting the right to vote
3. Interview members of the Royal Canadian Legion about Remembrance Day.
4. Find out more about the causes and effects of the Halifax explosion.

Ideas for Discussion

1. Think about the role played by the following groups during the war.
   a) farming families   d) soldiers
   b) city families   e) nurses
   c) armament workers   f) politicians
   Rank these groups in order of importance. Compare your ranking with that of other members of the class.
2. "War brings out the best in people and the worst in people." In small groups, compose two lists: The Best in People and The Worst in People. Compare your lists with those of other groups of students.

3. Here are two different opinions on the Treaty of Versailles. Read them and decide which you agree with most. Discuss the treaty with your classmates, giving reasons for your views.

I think the Treaty of Versailles was fair. Germany had caused the war. She had invaded Belgium, a neutral country, without excuse. Germany had been trying to expand for 75 years. She had to be punished and she had to be weakened. When the new soviet government in Russia wanted to withdraw from the war, Germany imposed much harsher terms in the Treaty of Brest-Litovsk than the western allies did in the Treaty of Versailles.
This kind of treaty was the only way to guarantee that a strong Germany would not cause another war. If the treaty was enforced, it would keep peace in Europe.

I think the Treaty of Versailles was too harsh. The war had not been caused by Germany alone; Austria and Russia were just as guilty. Making Germany pay all that money for the war meant her economy could not recover. Germany should not have had her colonies and so much territory taken from her.
After the war the Allies and the Germans would have to live together. But the treaty was so unfair, the Germans were bound to be resentful. They would look for a chance to get back what they had lost. This might lead to another war.

Hold a class debate on the topic: The Treaty of Versailles was a main cause of World War II.

Be Creative

1. Prepare a newspaper on the Canadian contribution to World War I. Your newspaper could include maps, interviews, letters, statistics, pictures, editorials. Try to cover as many aspects of the war as possible, including recruitment and training, providing supplies and equipment, volunteer work, as well as the actual fighting on land, sea, and air.
2. What does your school do for Remembrance Day each year? Design a Remembrance Day program for your class or school.
3. With another student, choose a person who played a prominent role at the time of World War I. Conduct an interview, with one of you playing the interviewer and the other the historical person. You will need to do further research in order to prepare questions and answers that will highlight the role the person played in World War I.

You Are There

It is 1917. The country is about to vote in an election. The main issue is whether the government should introduce conscription. If you were one of the people described here, what would be your opinion? Why would you feel that way? Write a letter to a newspaper explaining how you feel conscription would affect the war effort, national unity, English Canadians, French Canadians, and recent immigrants.

Albert Jackson was born in London, England. He emigrated to Toronto in 1913. He was brought up to believe strongly in the British Empire and to be completely loyal to King and country. He is convinced Germany caused the war and that she has to be stopped. Canada, as part of the British Empire, is directly involved in the war. Most of his friends in England are already in the army. He believes that all people have a duty to support the war and do whatever the government orders.

Mary Porter was an army nurse in France. She was wounded during an air raid and has been sent home to Vancouver. She has two brothers with the Canadian army. Jack is hoping for a transfer to the Royal Flying Corps. Ed has just been awarded a DSO (Distinguished Service Order) for saving the life of a companion wounded while going over the top during the battle of the Somme. Jack is engaged to Mary's best friend, Susan. Before she left France, Mary was aware that Canadian regiments were not operating at full strength because there were not enough volunteers to replace those killed or wounded.

André Savard's family have farmed on the shores of the St. Lawrence for nearly 300 years. He is one of nine children and has recently married. He and his wife are expecting a baby. When the war broke out, he did not even hear about it for a month or so. He does not see how a war being fought over 5000 km away can possibly affect him. He knows that his cousin Pierre from Quebec City has volunteered and is now a sergeant with the Royal 22nd Regiment. He himself does not want to fight or kill people in a distant land. He is happy to let others fight if they believe in the cause. André sees his life in terms of his village, his farm, and his family.

Stefan Klemens brought his family to Saskatchewan in 1901. They came from Austria to escape the almost constant warfare. Now Stefan farms the 64 ha of land given him by the government when he arrived. He is married with six children. It has been a struggle to provide for his large family, but now they are doing well. Last year they harvested a large grain crop, and got a good price for it. He does not know how he would manage without the help of his sons Kurt (22) and Hans (19). Last week, Greta (7) came home from school in tears because the kids called her a Hunky. It bothers Stefan that Canada is fighting a war against the land where his parents and sisters still live.

Bill McAdam was born and raised in Nova Scotia. His family came here from Scotland over a hundred years ago, and he thinks of himself a loyal son of Nova Scotia. When the war broke out, many of his friends volunteered to join the army. He is still under the age limit of 18 and has not decided whether he will volunteer or not. He sometimes wonders what Canadians are doing fighting in France. His neighbours, Charlie Armstrong and George Macdonald, have already been killed, and nobody knows if Robert Cormier will ever recover from that gas attack. Yet he considers himself a good Canadian and Canada is at war. He has a strong sense of duty. He wonders what would happen if people didn't join up.

Shirley Evans lives in Hamilton and is the mother of three children — Karen (19), Timothy (16), and Daniel (9). Shirley does volunteer work for the Salvation Army. Her group serves refreshments to soldiers on the troop trains that pass through the city. Lately they have helped tend the trainloads of wounded soldiers returning home. Karen's fiancé, Jim Lee from down the street, was killed in action at Vimy Ridge. The Evans family shares the grief of the Lees, who have lost their only son. Timothy had planned to join his father's automobile sales company, but he expects to be in uniform soon. Shirley hopes the war will end before he is old enough to join up.

Boom and Bust
ADVANCE ORGANIZER

1 After the war, returning soldiers expected to find security and well-paying jobs. Instead, factories were closing or cutting back production. Prices had nearly doubled. With the war over, there was no longer a demand for wartime supplies. Workers had to be laid off until new markets were found.

Canadian unions were much stronger than they had been before the war. They were ready to demand higher wages and shorter working hours. The unions joined forces in a general strike in Winnipeg in 1919. Over 30 000 workers left their jobs and the city ground to a halt. The strike lasted over a month. A clash between mounted police and the strikers led to two deaths and many injuries. The strike itself failed, but Canadian unions had demonstrated their strength to industry and government.

2 Women continued their struggle for equal rights. Emily Murphy and Nellie McClung teamed up in a court case to prove women could be appointed to government positions, including the Senate. Women took greater part in business and industry, but still met with prejudice.

3 Business gradually recovered in the 1920s. Jobs became plentiful again, and wages increased. For many it was a decade of plenty. People could afford to enjoy new luxuries of the period, such as movies and phonographs, radios, and automobiles. It seemed that the new prosperity would last forever.

Word List

assembly line	dominion	prohibition
communism	drought	revolution
conspiracy	flapper	socialism
Depression	prejudice	stock market

4

To increase their growth, big businesses sold shares of their companies on the stock exchange. Prices were based on supply and demand. But in the excitement of buying and selling, shares were bought and sold at ever-increasing, unrealistic prices. In 1929 the bottom dropped out of the stock market. The Great Depression had arrived.

With the stock market crash, entire nations could neither buy nor sell. Workers were laid off. Men roamed the country looking for jobs that did not exist. Often they ended up in hobo camps outside the towns. The price of wheat fell to one quarter of what it had been in 1929. To make matters worse, the Prairies suffered a five-year drought. Life was bleak on the farm and in the city during the thirties.

5

During the twenties and thirties Canada relied less on Britain to handle world affairs. The Statute of Westminster was passed by the British parliament in 1931. This confirmed Canada's independence. With the founding of the Canadian Broadcasting Corporation and the National Film Board, Canada was developing her own voice as a nation. By 1939 the country was a respected member of the world community. In that year World War II began. Airplane and armament factories opened up, creating jobs. The Great Depression was over. Amid all this activity, one lingering question remained: Is war the only way to end a depression?

After the War

The war was over! Canada's soldiers were coming home to take up their lives again. What would they find? How would a grateful nation welcome her heroes?

The troop ships tied up at the government docks in Halifax. From there the troop trains steamed westward. Cheers greeted them at every station. On the hometown platform family and friends hugged their brave boys with pride in their eyes. The next day the ex-soldiers headed down Main Street. The first thing they noticed was the prices. Why did everything cost so much?

Rising prices, Ottawa, 1919.

Welcome home!

Wartime Economics

During the war, industry had grown greatly. Canada had supplied shells to the western front. Ships were built and maintained for the Atlantic convoys. The steel industry boomed. Soldiers needed boots, clothes, blankets. Many factory owners became very wealthy. Farmers grew more wheat. Because of the great demand, prices had risen. The soldiers found goods cost nearly twice as much as they had in 1913.

Canadians who had stayed at home were also feeling the pinch. Wages had risen during the war, but only about 18%. They had not kept up with prices. In "real income," what their money would actually buy, workers were much poorer.

To add to people's troubles, many industries were now going through a slump. War supplies were no longer needed. Factories were closing or cutting back. The jobs that remained were already filled. Nobody needed to hire ex-soldiers. They had expected a better deal after their sacrifices in the fields of France.

Who was to blame? Some soldiers blamed the immigrants who had come to Canada before the war. They felt these newcomers, whom they regarded as aliens, had the jobs that were rightfully theirs. Others blamed the economic system and the "profiteers." They wanted a better deal for everybody.

One Big Union

The number of trade union members had doubled during the war. Now the unions were preparing to demand higher wages and better conditions. With their larger membership they would have more power.

Why were many ex-soldiers dissatisfied when they returned to Canada after World War I?
What was the One Big Union? How did the O.B.U. plan to use general strikes?

 Art Gallery page 12

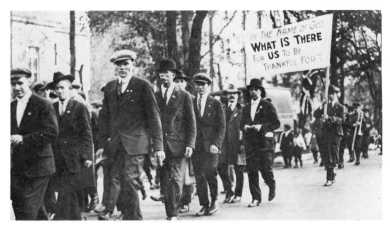

Returning soldiers march to protest the lack of jobs, Thanksgiving Day, 1920.

In March 1919 a convention of western labour leaders was held in Calgary. The purpose was to organize One Big Union. Many workers, particularly unskilled workers, had not been members of unions before. The O.B.U. would represent all workers. There was strength in numbers. Together, workers could press for a better deal. Before the convention broke up, the delegates sent greetings to the new communist government in Russia.

In some ways this was a mistake. Factory owners and businessmen did not like unions. They said this "proved" the O.B.U. was run by communists. Many people in Canada were afraid of communism. They did not want a revolution that might change their whole way of life.

The O.B.U. delegates returned to their homes. They were determined to have a say in the way things were run. First they would organize general strikes in cities across the West. This would demonstrate the power of the workers.

Would general strikes work? The first test came in Winnipeg that May.

Robert Boyd Russell

1888—born in Glasgow, Scotland.
1900—became an apprentice machinist, learning how to build machines and engines from engineers' drawings.
1911—immigrated to Winnipeg. Got job in CPR machine shop. Soon started to organize union.
1914-18—refused to support war. Felt ordinary people were being asked to work harder and go and fight for nothing while bosses sat back and made fat profits. Union leaders in East supported the government and the war. Only leaders from West seemed to agree that the real war was with the bosses.
1919—helped start the One Big Union and organize the Winnipeg General Strike. Was arrested, tried, and sentenced to 2 years in prison.
1920s—travelled and gave speeches to gain support for O.B.U., but the idea was losing ground. Some members returned to regular trade unions, others joined the Communist party.
1930s—backed idea of one industrial union for all workers in one industry. Supported new CCF party.
1956— secretary of Winnipeg branch of CLC.
1964 — died in Winnipeg.
1967 — R.B. Russell Vocational School in Winnipeg named in his honour.

CARD OF MEMBERSHIP

ONE BIG UNION

NATIONAL INDUSTRIAL UNION OF THE DOMINION OF CANADA

"Money is the Root of All Evil," saith the Lord.

I, the undersigned, do hereby declare that, by the help of God, I will STRIKE against the use of money at any time I may be called upon.

Name ....

Address ....

Witness ....

O.B.U. membership card.

The Russian Revolution
In 1917 the Bolsheviks under Lenin led a revolution against the czar of Russia. The new government planned to follow the communist ideas of Karl Marx.

Their slogan was "From each according to his ability; to each according to his need."

Private property was abolished. The state would own all the land, the factories, and the stores. They would be run for the benefit of the workers. Workers would be the most important members of society.

The Winnipeg General Strike

The RNWMP charge the strikers on "Bloody Saturday."

On 1 May 1919, 2000 building and metal workers went on strike in Winnipeg. They wanted higher wages (85¢ an hour) and shorter hours (44 hours a week instead of 60). The Metal Trades Council also wanted to be recognized as a union with the right to bargain for the workers. The employers refused to negotiate.

The workers appealed to the Winnipeg Trades and Labour Council. The council asked all the city's union members if they would strike in sympathy. If all workers went on strike, the city would be paralysed. The employers would have to give in. The members voted 11 000 for a general strike, 600 against. The strike began on 15 May.

By 11 a.m., the city ground to a halt. Firemen, streetcar drivers, telephone operators, storekeepers, garbage collectors, street cleaners, butchers, bakers, dairy workers—all left their jobs. Non-union workers came out too. Within three days over 30 000 people were off the job. The police wanted to strike. The Strike Committee asked them to keep working in case they were needed to keep order. The committee also asked bakers, milkmen, and other essential workers to go back to work.

A Divided City

For six weeks Winnipeg was a city of two rival camps. The strikers were led by the Strike Committee. Businessmen and employers organized the "Citizens' Committee of One Thousand."

The Citizens' Committee said they wanted to maintain essential services, but their main purpose was to break the strike. They feared the workers wanted more than just higher wages. They claimed the strike was a communist plot. This might be the beginning of a revolution in Canada. The union leaders seemed to speak in the same terms as the Russian Bolsheviks. The Citizens' Committee urged the federal government to step in.

After a month the strike was petering out. Many workers could not afford to stay out any longer. They started to drift back to work. All might have ended peacefully. But then the government decided to act. They brought in extra members of the Royal North West Mounted Police. They organized and armed a volunteer police force. The mayor banned all public marches.

The volunteer police march up Main Street.

Why did the Trades and Labour Council call a general strike?
What events led to the violence of Bloody Saturday?
Do you think the strike was a communist plot? Why or why not?
Explain 4 ideas of J.S. Woodsworth. Why were they important?

The Arrests

On 17 June the strike leaders were dragged from their beds at gunpoint. They were taken to Stony Mountain penitentiary. Protests erupted all over the country. Why had these people been arrested? What law had they broken? In Winnipeg a group of ex-soldiers decided to hold a protest march. That Saturday they led the strikers down Main Street. They were met by Mounties swinging clubs and firing pistols.

In the riot which followed, two people died. The volunteer police were called in. They patrolled the streets with machine guns. "Bloody Saturday" would long be remembered by Canadian workers.

A week later the Strike Committee called off the strike.

A Communist Plot?

There is no proof the strikers were planning a revolution. It is most likely they were simply trying to get higher wages and better conditions. But the leaders did not talk that way. Their angry speeches led many to believe there was a plot to overthrow the government. Seven of those arrested were convicted of conspiracy. They received sentences of up to two years in prison. Five were never brought to trial. J.S. Woodsworth, a church minister, social worker, and writer, and two others were acquitted.

The general strike had failed. Workers found other ways to try and solve their problems. However, people had become more aware of these problems. The trade union movement gained support. Some of the strike leaders, such as J.S. Woodsworth, turned to politics. They brought the workers' viewpoint into parliament.

When wilt thou save the people, Lord? O God of mercy, when?
The people, Lord, the people. Not crowns and thrones, but men.
Labour Hymn, 1919

The ONE BIG UNION is Bolshevism Pure and Simple

NOTE THE STRIKING PARALLEL

Bolshevism

Extract from the constitution of "The Federation of Unions of Russian Workers in the U.S. and Canada," the almon pure Bolshevik organization plant which instituted by paid agents of Lenine and Trotzky.

One Big Union

Extract from the official stenographic record of the proceedings at the Western Canada Labor Conference at Calgary last March, where the One Big Union movement was launched by labor delegates from all western cities, including 30 from Winnipeg.

Fundamental Principle of the Federation

The struggle between the classes still continues at the present time and will terminate only when the laboring masses are organized in ONE UNION and USE FORCE to take possession of all wealth through the violence of Social Revolution."

Resolution Creating the One Big Union

"Resolved that this conference place itself on record as favouring the immediate re-organization of the workers along industrial lines, so THAT BY VIRTUE OF THEIR STRENGTH, the workers may be better prepared to ENFORCE ANY DEMAND they consider essential to their maintenance and well-being."

Business interests said the people behind the strike were communists.

J.S. (James Shaver) Woodsworth

1874—born in Etobicoke, Ont. Father a minister.

1900-06—Methodist minister in Ontario and Manitoba. Believer in "social gospel": improving life on earth rather than worrying about heaven.

1906-16—became a social worker. Wrote *Strangers Within Our Gates* about problems faced by immigrants.

1916—lost his government job because he was a pacifist and wrote against conscription.

1917—minister at Gibson's Landing, B.C.

1918—fired because had favoured idea of a co-op store. To support family, went to work on Vancouver docks. Joined the dockers' union.

1919—While on speaking tour, took over Winnipeg strikers' paper when editor was arrested. Was arrested himself for an editorial he wrote. Charge dropped when prosecutor discovered one passage was quote from Bible.

1921—elected in Winnipeg as Independent Labour MP. Communists opposed him because he said socialism should come democratically, not by revolution. In Ottawa spoke on behalf of workers. Uncovered RCMP spies in labour unions. Fought for old age pensions, unemployment insurance, fair treatment for immigrants.

1933—chosen as leader of new CCF party.

1939—stood alone in parliament to oppose Canada's entry into World War II. Even his own party could not support his pacifist beliefs, but all respected his views.

1942—died at Vancouver, B.C.

Women Are Persons

Women first were given the right to vote in the West. In 1918 the federal government gave women the vote on the same basis as men. By 1922 women could vote in provincial elections in all provinces except Quebec.

Women also began to run for office. In the Alberta election of 1917 two women, Louise McKinney and Roberta MacAdams, were elected. In 1921 two more, Nellie McClung and Irene Parlby, entered the Legislature. In British Columbia Mary Ellen Smith became the first woman cabinet minister in the British Commonwealth. At the federal level, Agnes Macphail was the first woman to enter the House of Commons.

Women in provincial legislatures worked for social changes. They pressed for laws on better housing, health, and education. They wanted laws to make marriage fairer to women. They asked for minimum wage laws and safe working conditions. Naturally, these measures were not achieved by women alone. Men supported them too. But it was a sign of changing attitudes that laws like these were being passed.

It seemed that women were finally able to take an equal place with men in public life. Yet very few women were actually running for office. Even fewer were being elected. And there was one branch of government where they were not accepted at all. This was the Canadian Senate.

Agnes Macphail

1890 — born near Owen Sound, Ont.
1900s — attended high school and teachers' college at Stratford, Ont. Taught school in Ontario and Alberta.
1921 — elected as United Farmers of Ontario MP for her knowledge of farmers' problems and her work in farm co-op movement.
1921-40 — As first woman MP, found she had to speak on women's issues even though she'd never been active in the women's rights movement. Said what women needed was absolute equality, not special favours. Her real interest was in helping the powerless — farmers, workers, the old, the handicapped. Worked for old age and disability pensions, better health care, prison reform. With J.S. Woodsworth supported Nova Scotia miners in a bitter dispute with their employer and the government. As a socialist and pacifist, often supported Woodsworth and later the CCF party's policies.
1940 — defeated in federal election because of pacifist views. Worked as newspaper columnist.
1943 — elected to Ontario legislature.
1945 — lost election because of heart attack.
1948 — re-elected to Ontario legislature as CCF member.
1951 — retired from politics.
1954 — died in Toronto of a heart attack.

The lord chancellor of Britain on his way to deliver the Privy Council's judgement in the "persons case." The procession is part of a ceremony hundreds of years old. The British Privy Council was the final court of appeal for Canadians until 1949. In that year Canada asked Britain to amend the British North America Act to make the Supreme Court of Canada the final court.

How did Agnes Macphail work to help "the powerless"?
Who was Emily Murphy? How did she and the "Alberta Five" gain
for women the right to be appointed to the Senate?
Who became the first woman senator?

1900 1910 1920 1930 1940 1950 1960 1970 1980 1990 2000

Emily Murphy

In 1916 Alberta had appointed Emily
Murphy to be a judge. She was the first
woman judge in Canada. In her first
day in court a lawyer challenged her.
He said that only a "qualified person"
could be a judge. According to British
law, only men were "persons."

That word "persons" kept cropping up. The British
North America Act, Canada's constitution, said
senators should be "qualified persons." Did that mean
women could not be senators? In 1921 the Montreal
Women's Club asked Prime Minister Borden to
appoint Murphy to the Senate. He said this was
impossible.

Women's groups thought this was unfair. For
many years Murphy had worked for poor people,
blacks, Chinese immigrants, Indians, children,
women. She would make an excellent senator.

In 1927 Murphy teamed up with McClung, Parlby,
McKinney, and a long-time women's rights worker,
Henrietta Muir Edwards. They fought the "persons
case" in the courts. The Supreme Court said women
were not persons. It based its decision on conditions at

McClung and Murphy

Nellie McClung fought against the abuse of alcohol. She urged
governments to introduce prohibition which forbade the sale of
alcohol. Emily Murphy wanted to change the drug laws. She
thought drug addicts should be treated as sick people, not as
criminals. She felt sentences for drug dealers should be more
severe.

Both women were writers. McClung wrote novels, short stories,
and essays. Most of her writing was about women's issues or
prohibition. Murphy, under the name Janey Canuck, wrote about
western life. Her book *The Black Candle* was different. It was
about the drug trade. It was regarded as a textbook on the subject
all over the world.

the time of Confederation. No one then had expected
women in public office. When the BNA Act
mentioned persons, it did not mean women.

The "Alberta Five" took their case to the final
court of appeal. This was the British Privy Council.
The council ruled that women were persons. "The
exclusion of women from all public offices is a relic of
days more barbarous than ours."

After her long battle, people expected Emily
Murphy would be made the first woman senator. She
was not. In 1930 Liberal Prime Minister Mackenzie
King appointed Cairine Wilson of Montreal to the
Senate. Wilson was a Liberal. Murphy was a
Conservative. Some thought King just wanted to
ignore her because she had caused so much trouble.

In 1938 the Canadian Federation of Business and Professional
Women's Clubs presented this tablet in honour of the "Alberta
Five." The tablet was unveiled by Prime Minister King. Nellie
McClung, the only one of the five to attend the ceremony, is at
the right.

New Fields for Women

During and after World War I women were granted the right to vote. At about the same time reformers achieved another goal. Prohibition, or a ban on the sale of alcohol, was introduced.

Officially the ban was part of the war effort. The grain used to make alcohol could be used for food instead. But people expected there would be social benefits from the ban. They thought family life would improve. There would be fewer broken homes and abused wives and children. For a few years after the war, prohibition was in force in every province of Canada.

Unfortunately, prohibition did not work as people hoped. Those who really wanted to drink found the alcohol somewhere. Criminals turned to bootlegging—making and selling liquor illegally. By 1924 most provinces decided liquor control was better than a liquor ban. If people could buy alcohol legally, the criminals would be forced out of the business. The government could make money from liquor taxes. The licensed beverage room replaced the illegal speakeasy.

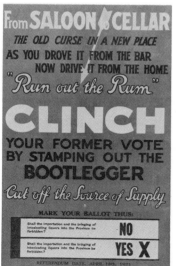

However, the temperance workers had made their point. Society had become aware of the problem. Alcohol abuse is not as widespread as it was in the late 19th century. Drinking still causes many social problems, but help is now available for alcoholics and their families.

Because prohibition was such a sensitive issue, the government asked the people to vote on it in referendums.

The United States kept prohibition after it had been given up in Canada. There were big profits to be made rum-running from the Maritimes to New England, across the Great Lakes, down the Pacific coast, and all along the border. As an American official said, "It's impossible to keep liquor from dripping through a dotted line." The United States gave up prohibition in 1933.

Working

During the war women had turned to jobs they had never done before. When the men came back from the front they took over most of these jobs again. Still, women now had a better foothold in the world of work outside the home.

Yet society had its prejudices. It was not considered respectable for a married woman to work. Many employers automatically fired women when they married. Also, many of the gains of the war and the twenties were lost during the Depression of the thirties. Then people thought it was unfair for a woman to hold a job—especially a well-paying job—instead of a man. They thought the man needed the job more.

What social problems did people hope prohibition would solve?
Why did governments change from prohibition to liquor control?
What gains did women make in the 1920s in employment and
recreation? How were some of these gains lost in the 1930s?

CHIC SILK FROCKS
FOR MISSES
WITH THE
GAY AIR
OF
YOUTH

T. EATON C?

Sports

Women found new freedom in sports. They played
basketball, hockey, and baseball, often for company-
sponsored teams. Women's basketball was broadcast
on radio. Sunnyside Stadium in Toronto drew 6000
spectators for women's baseball. Crowds for men's
games were often not as large.

In 1928 Canadian women went to the summer
Olympic Games for the first time. The track and field
team won medals in nearly every event.

Women's sports had only a brief period of glory. As
professional sport grew, companies stopped
sponsoring women's teams. Women's teams began to
have trouble getting time in public sports arenas. The
"real" athletes (men and boys) were seen as more
important. By the thirties women were discouraged
from active sports. Some doctors claimed it might
harm their ability to have babies. This attitude lasted
well into the fifties. Girls in school continued to play
some games but often with "girls' rules." Instead of
taking part in hockey and football, girls became cheer-
leaders. Team sports for adult women became rare.

Clothing

The new woman needed new styles of clothing. She
wanted the freedom to move easily. The young
"flapper" was not going to climb into the corsets and
long skirts her mother wore before the war.

By 1928 skirts barely covered the knee. Clothes
were loose and comfortable. Women gave up long hair
and hairpins for "bobbed" and "shingled" haircuts.
Other freedoms followed. It was not uncommon to see
flappers smoking—and even drinking—in public.
Needless to say, their parents did not always approve.

Beauty contests like this Miss Toronto contest would have been
considered immoral before the twenties.

Elsie MacGill

1905 — born in Vancouver, B.C., daughter of Helen G.
MacGill, a journalist and women's rights worker.

1917 — mother appointed a juvenile court judge, one
year after Emily Murphy became 1st female judge.

1927 — Elsie was 1st woman to graduate in electrical
engineering from University of Toronto.

1929 — 1st woman to graduate in aeronautical engineering
from University of Michigan. Caught polio. Became lame.

1933 — did further work in aeronautics at Massachusetts
Institute of Technology (MIT).

1934-37 — worked at Fairchild Aircraft, Longueuil, Que.
Helped test-fly first Canadian designed and built all-metal
aircraft.

1939-43 — in charge of engineering on Canadian-built
Hawker Hurricanes and U.S. Navy Helldivers (planes
launched by catapult from aircraft carriers) at Canadian
Car and Foundry, Fort William, Ont.

1943 — married Eric Soulsby, an executive at Canadian
Car. Opened her own consulting business.

1946 — at ICAO (International Civil Aviation
Organization), helped set up airworthiness regulations.

1947 — chaired Stress Analysis Committee for ICAO.

1955 — published *My Mother the Judge.*

1967 — served on Royal Commission on the Status of Women.
(Mark, son of Nellie McClung, worked for Commission.)
Continued consulting business into the 1970s.

1980 — died on visit to sister in Cambridge, Mass.

The Boom Years

Industry took time to change gears from wartime production. An economic slump started in 1919 that lasted into the early 1920s. Then businesses started to make profits. Jobs were available again. The Roaring Twenties had arrived.

People wanted to invest in the future. They bought shares on the stock market, expecting them to double or triple in value. The economic bubble was getting bigger and bigger. Things were going to get better and better. Or so it seemed.

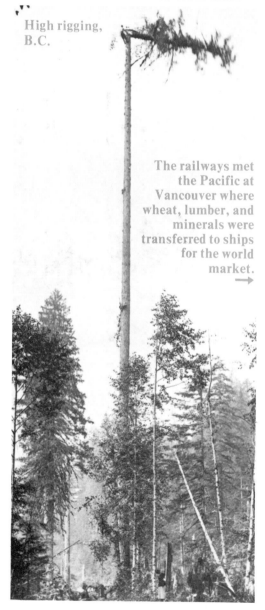

High rigging, B.C.

The railways met the Pacific at Vancouver where wheat, lumber, and minerals were transferred to ships for the world market. →

British Columbia

Timber exports to the world.
A new smelter at Trail.
Vancouver — Canada's third largest city.
Port of Vancouver — Gateway to Pacific.

During the 1920s and 30s the airplane became a vital link in Canada's developing transportation system.

The Prairies

New motor-driven tractors and other farm machinery.
New types of grain needing a shorter growing season lead to opening of northern Prairies to farming.
New mines at Flin Flon, Man.
Construction of railway and new port at Churchill, Man., so wheat exports could be shipped through Hudson Bay.

Hanna, Alberta, a typical prairie town on the CNR.

Ontario

New hydro-electric plants.
Massey-Harris expands farm machinery factories.
American firms like Esso, Ford, GM, GE set up Canadian branch plants.
Hamilton steel mills expanded.
More lead, nickel, zinc, silver, and gold mines open in northern Ontario.

Quebec

Expansion of pulp and paper industry.
New hydro-electric plants.
Electricity used at Arvida to power new aluminum smelter.
Cities like Sorel, Trois Rivières, Chicoutimi attract new industry.
Canada's largest port and greatest city, Montreal, continues growth.

The Maritimes

Fishing, farming, and part-time lumbering still main way of life.
Some growth in coal and steel industry in Cape Breton.
Ports and shipbuilding decline.
Few new industries — Maritimes considered too far from main population centres.

Hydro-electric plants were set up wherever water power was easily available. This new turbine being assembled at Chippewa on the Niagara River was typical.

New facilities at the bustling port of Montreal attracted business from the smaller, less modern ports of Saint John and Halifax in the Maritimes.

A new office building, Toronto.　The assembly line.　Fishing schooners, N.S.　Tourists, P.E.I.

Easy Street

Modern inventions became part of everyday life in the 1920s. People could buy electric stoves, washing machines, irons, vacuum cleaners, toasters. They didn't look like the models we use today. They had few automatic features. But the homemaker of the twenties could rely on many of the same electrical appliances to take the drudgery out of housework.

Home Entertainment

Evenings in many homes were spent round the kitchen table building and adjusting the home-made crystal radio set. The problem with crystal sets was that there was no amplification. The listener had to wear earphones. For family listening big electric radios in fancy wooden cabinets dominated the living room. Of course, there wasn't much on the air during the day. There were few Canadian stations except in the big

Minerva Six-Tube, One-Dial Console Receiver
837-1645. Minerva Console, without tubes, batteries or aerial equipment. Price, delivered:
Cash Price **84.00**   By Monthly Payments **89.30**
Terms: $8.40 down and $8.09 a month for 10 months.
Minerva Console with Complete Equipment
837-1646. Price, delivered:
Cash Price **125.00**   By Monthly Payments **132.90**
Terms: $12.50 down and $12.04 a month for 10 months.

cities. At night, though, the radio could pull in stations from halfway across the continent—Montreal, Calgary, Boston, Toronto, Salt Lake City, Winnipeg. Saturday night was "Hockey Night in Canada." Families from Glace Bay, Nova Scotia to Medicine Hat, Alberta, gathered at the radio to listen for Foster Hewitt's excited cry, "He shoots. He scores!"

Near the radio was the phonograph. Which was better, an electric or a hand-wound model? The new electric ones were far less work and kept the record turning at a constant speed. Hand-wound models could be taken on picnics for outdoor listening.

A range cost more than twice as much if you wanted to cook with the technological wonder, electricity, than if you were prepared to put up with the fuss of wood or coal.

List 5 inventions that used electricity. Explain how each made life easier or pleasanter in the 1920s.
What are the advantages of producing goods on an assembly line?
In what ways has the automobile changed our way of life?

The "EMPIRE" Electric Vacuum Cleaner 37.50

Eatonia "GOOD VALUE AND RELIABILITY"

EATONIA Toaster Stove 4.35

Curling Tongs 1.95

EATONIA Electric Iron 3.50

Electric Coffee Percolator 9.95

Automobiles

Parked in front of the house was the family automobile, probably a Model T Ford. Henry Ford had just about cornered the market on economy cars. He invented the assembly line. By having each worker do a single job on many cars, he was able to produce cars more cheaply. In 1917 the "Tin Lizzy" cost $495. By 1925 so many cars were rolling off Ford's Canadian assembly line at Windsor that the price had dropped to $424.

Of course, the car was not much use in winter. Even if it started, the roads were too bad to travel. Most motorists put the car up on blocks until spring.

Driving at other seasons could be a risky business too. Many farmers make a little extra money by lending their horses to pull motorists out of the mud. Most country roads were earth. Gravel was used on main highways. In the cities, some streets were paved.

An early tent trailer.

Buying on Time

With all these wonderful items in the stores, it seemed a shame to do without. Almost anything could be bought on the "easy monthly payment plan." Next year, or even next week, the investment on the stock market might pay off. Then the family could sell Tin Lizzie and buy a McLaughlin-Buick or a Hudson Super Six.

This gas station attendant had probably been wounded during the war.

Not all homes had ice boxes or refrigerators, so the daily milk delivery was an important convenience right into the 1960s.

On the Town

Now that people worked only 9 or even 8 hours a day, they had time for pleasure. The entertainment industry boomed during the 1920s. Those looking for an evening out had plenty of choice.

Vaudeville and Burlesque

In the early years of the century theatres were built in many Canadian cities and towns. Many were part of a chain controlled by Ambrose Small, a Toronto businessman. Travelling theatre companies used these theatres to perform the latest plays from London or New York. Vaudeville, a type of variety show, was very popular. More daring people went to burlesque shows. At burlesque, between the stand-up comics and the skits you could see the ladies of the chorus line, the exotic dancers, and the strip-tease artists.

The Palace in Montreal sold tickets to "bargain matinees" for 25¢. On Saturday afternoons children's tickets were even cheaper.

The Movies

The biggest entertainment of all was the motion picture show. There were movie houses in every city and town across the country. Many people felt the week was not complete without an evening laughing and crying with Charlie Chaplin, falling in love with Rudolph Valentino, or holding their breath while the dashing hero bravely rescued Mary Pickford from the bad guys. By the end of the decade, people flocked to see — and hear — the new miracle, the talking picture. *The Jazz Singer,* starring Al Jolson, spelled the end of the silent movie era.

"America's sweetheart," Mary Pickford, was born in Toronto.

FOCUS

What were vaudeville and burlesque shows?
How did talking movies affect live theatre?
Describe an evening out you might have enjoyed. Your opening
might be: "How shall we choose where to go tonight?"

Music and Dance

In the evenings young people flocked to the night
clubs to listen to the latest music fad — jazz.
Many adults, of course, thought jazz was horrible.
However, they told each other it was a passing fancy—
it couldn't last long.

For more active amusement people went dancing.
In the dance halls live orchestras played the latest
popular tunes. The tango, the Charleston, and the
black bottom were all the rage.

Many theatres did not switch entirely to movies until the 1930s. The New Orpheum in Vancouver advertised "Vaudeville and Photoplays." Showing the feature film Shanghai Bound provided a break for the singers, comedians, and dancers who were the live entertainment. The Orpheum is now the home of the Vancouver Symphony Orchestra.

The Dumbells

The Dumbells were the idea of Captain Mervyn Plunkett. Before the war, Plunkett had been in the hardware business in Orillia, Ontario. He had also worked for the YMCA. The YMCA sent him to France to entertain Canadian troops at the front. Soldiers needed to laugh, and Plunkett wasn't getting the results he wanted. So he became a talent scout. He brought together a group of soldiers who could sing, act, and play the fool. They called themselves the Dumbells.

The Dumbells were asked to perform before King George V and Queen Mary in London. In 1921 they took their zany show "Biff, Bing, Bang" to the Ambassador Theatre in New York. A critic said, "It took a bunch of Canadian soldiers to show Broadway what speed is." They turned down an offer to make a movie so they could take the show back to Canada. Each year, until the talkies killed vaudeville, the company toured the country. They played all the large city theatres. They performed in small town schoolhouses and church halls. Once they had to climb a fence and cross a field to get to the barn which was their dressing room.

The Dumbells used no women in their shows because there had been no women in the original wartime group. The men acted and sang all women's parts. "Marjorie" played by Corporal Ross Hamilton was always a great hit. Many could not believe Marjorie was really a man.

Marie Dressler was born in Cobourg, Ont., in 1869. At 17, she ran away from home with a touring opera troupe. A comedy star, she appeared in plays in New York and London. Her Hollywood breakthrough came with the talkies, though she first appeared in a movie in 1914. Here she appears with Frankie Darrow and Wallace Beery in one of her most popular films, Tugboat Annie.

The Golden Age of Sports

In the 1920s Canadians from all walks of life took part in sports. Town and village teams all competed for space on hockey rinks, baseball diamonds, and soccer fields.

Canadians were also making a name for their country in international and professional sports. The 1928 Olympic Games were a high point. The Canadian track and field team, particularly the women, who were competing for the first time, won medal after medal.

The daughter of Russian immigrants, Bobbie Rosenfeld shone in almost every sport she tried. She was a star in Toronto in softball, tennis, basketball, and hockey. But her greatest success was in track. In the 1928 Olympics in Amsterdam she won a silver medal in a dead-heat in the 100 m race. She went on to lead the Canadian women's team to a gold medal in the 400 m relay. In the 1930s Rosenfeld was a sports columnist for a Toronto newspaper.

Like Rosenfeld, Lionel Conacher was representative of the time before athletes specialized. He grew up in the slums of downtown Toronto. He was a champion in every sport he played. He played hockey for the Montreal Maroons and football for the Toronto Argonauts. He was an all-star in baseball and lacrosse and a champion boxer and wrestler. Later he became a member of Parliament. He died while playing softball at the age of 57.

Percy Williams of Vancouver trained for two years for the 1928 Olympics in Amsterdam. He came first in both the 100 m and 200 m races. He was described as "the greatest sprinter the world has ever seen." No other Canadian has ever won two Olympic gold medals.

The most successful team in Canadian history was the Edmonton Grads. Members of the team were all graduates of McDougall Commercial High School in Edmonton. Started in 1915 by school coach Percy Page, they dominated basketball for the next 25 years. During this period they won 502 games and lost 20. Once they won 147 games in a row. They represented Canada at 4 Olympics and won each time. In 1940 their practice facilities were taken over by the army, and the team folded.

FOCUS

Who were the Canadian athletes of the half-century? Why do you think they were chosen for this honour?
Why are the 1920s remembered as the golden age of sports in Canada?

Canada
THE TWENTIETH CENTURY

Art Gallery page 13

Howie Morenz, "the Stratford streak," became the star of the Montreal Canadiens. He was the fastest skater in the NHL. Sports writer Jim Coleman described him this way:

"When Howie Morenz picked up the puck, circled behind his own net, and started for the opposing goal, he lifted you right out of your seat. He appeared to fly above the surface of the ice. He could skate faster than Davey Keon. He could shoot as hard as Bobby Hull. He was as strong as Gordie Howe."

Ethel Catherwood, "the Saskatoon lily," contributed to Canada's success at the 1928 Olympics by winning the gold medal in the high jump.

The *Bluenose* was built as a fishing schooner in Lunenburg, Nova Scotia, in 1921. Skippered by Captain Angus Walters, she competed in races against the best schooners in Canada and the United States. She won almost every race. In 1938 the *Bluenose* was sold as a cargo boat. She sank in a storm off the coast of Haiti in 1946. Today the *Bluenose* is remembered on the back of the Canadian dime.

In 1963 an exact replica, *Bluenose II* was built in the same shipyard. She is owned by the Nova Scotia government.

The women's Olympic relay team, 1928. The uniforms of the Canadian athletes were considered quite daring in 1928. By 1932 women from all over the world were wearing "brief" uniforms like these to compete in the Olympics in Los Angeles.

Did the Twenties Really Roar?

During the twenties more people were able to afford the comforts of life than ever before. For example, by 1928 one out of two Canadian families owned a car. Rich factory owners made big profits. Even middle class Canadians could invest in the stock market.

What was happening to the others, the half who could not afford cars? Life was particularly hard on immigrants in the cities. They arrived not knowing the language and with few skills. Employers took advantage of them, paying them as little as possible. Women, too, were paid much less than men doing the same type of work. Wages of factory workers stayed low. The company might be making huge profits, but workers did not share in them. Businessmen priced goods as high as possible. Often the workers could not afford to buy the things they had helped produce. As a result, unsold goods piled up in warehouses and stores.

Most people thought the boom would go on forever, but some economists saw danger signals. They did not like the unequal distribution of wealth. The rich got richer while workers and farmers did not have enough money to buy their share of goods.

Children look for pieces of coal among the cinders dumped outside the coal-gas plant, 1923.

The International Picture

Countries like the United States, Canada, Britain, France, Italy, and Germany were dependent on international trade. If something happened to upset the trade pattern, all countries would suffer. For example, Canada's economy was based on the export of lumber, pulp and paper, wheat, and minerals. What would happen if other countries could no longer afford to buy our exports?

The Stock Market

By the 20th century, many businesses were too big to be owned by one person or one family. Big companies financed themselves by selling shares on the stock market. The price of shares was determined by supply and demand. If a lot of people wanted to buy, the price was high. If more wanted to sell than to buy, the price dropped.

Careful investors made sure they got their money's worth. They checked that the company had good prospects. But as the excitement of buying and selling took over, some people forgot what the whole business was about. Shares were traded at higher and higher prices. Often the price bore no relation to the real value of the earnings and profits of the company.

Daring investors took risks. They bought "on margin." They paid the stock broker 10% or 15% of the price of the shares. Later, when the price had risen, they sold. They could then pay the broker what they owed and still make a profit. Of course, the deal was that the broker could make a "margin call" if the stock fell. Then the investor would have to pay all the money owed. No one worried about margin calls. Stocks might dip a little, but in the long run they always rose. Why should things ever change?

Why did many *a)* immigrants; *b)* women; *c)* factory workers not share in the prosperity of the 1920s?
Explain what happened to cause the stock market crash of October 1929.

The Crash

Nobody knew on 3 September 1929 that the stock market had reached its peak. After that, prices began to slip, but this had happened before. Most investors thought there would be a turnaround soon.

This time there was no turnaround. Brokers started to make margin calls. Investors couldn't pay up. The brokers were forced to "sell them out."

On Thursday 24 October thousands of shares bought on margin were dumped onto the stock market. There were no buyers. Prices took a nose dive.

When the news hit the newspapers, other investors panicked. On 29 October, "Black Tuesday," things were even worse. This time the sellers were small investors rushing to sell out before they lost everything. The bubble had burst.

The New York Stock Exchange three days before the crash. By 1929 economic conditions in Canada were closely tied to those in the U.S.

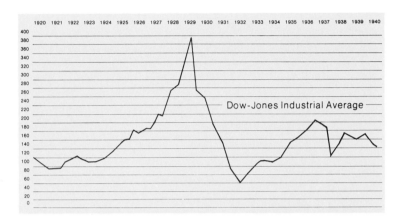

It is likely that more than half of the Canadian people were never anything but poor between the wars, although they were worse off in the thirties than before. For these people the twenties had not roared. The decade has come to seem almost a golden age of prosperity. This is probably because *nostalgia* has a bad memory. Also, for many Canadians, the Depression seemed so terrible that whatever came before it was bound to seem more attractive by comparison.

from The Dirty Thirties *by Michiel Horn*

Here am I, working all day long for $25 a month, while the poorest man in the mines has $4 a day and only works 8 hours. It sure is the limit!

Helmi, an immigrant woman from Finland working as a domestic servant, speaks her mind in Painted Fires, *a novel by Nellie McClung.*

. . . A pupil went to school till he was 14. If you passed high school entrance at 13, you could quit and go to work. The boys were apprenticed to some trade. I think the rate was $4 a week, 10 hours a day, and 5 hours on Saturday.

Q. What would be a typical house of that class?
A. The average home is a shack of three or four rooms.
Q. Do they have running water?
A. Yes, but no baths. At least 80% have no hot water.
Q. What about child mortality?
A. The parts of town where juvenile delinquency is highest are the parts where the greatest number of children die. The two go together.

Two quotes from The Canadian Worker in the Twentieth Century *by Irving Abella.*

The Great Depression

The panic that caused the stock market crash had started in the United States. It quickly spread to all countries involved in trade. The crash triggered the Great Depression.

The Downward Spiral

After the crash small investors thought they would still get by. For many of them investing in the stock market had only been a sort of hobby. True, their savings were gone, they had nothing to fall back on. But most people had never invested in the stock market anyway. They hadn't had enough money in their pay envelope to do more than feed, clothe, and house the family. Like those who couldn't afford to invest, small investors still had their jobs. They thought nothing more could happen to them.

They were wrong. Many Canadian products were made for export. When the crash came, foreign countries bought much less. Prices fell. Canadian farmers still had unsold wheat in storage. Many Canadian companies had been overproducing. They already had goods piled up in warehouses. There was no point in producing more. They closed down or cut back until the backlog was sold. Their workers were laid off. Those lucky enough to keep their jobs had to accept pay cuts. Unemployed people did not have the money to buy luxuries like radios and vacuum cleaners. Workers who make these products were laid off too. Next came the workers who supplied the raw materials. Soon people could not afford to buy shoes, coats, dresses. A sad spiral had set in.

By 1933 one in five Canadian workers had no job. There was no system of unemployment insurance. Two million people were "on relief."

A Depression Dictionary

Bennett buggy vehicle created by people who could no longer afford gas, oil, licences, etc. They removed the motor from the car and hitched horses to it instead. Named after Prime Minister R.B. Bennett.

Food vouchers paper given to people "on relief" to exchange for basic food supplies. Vouchers were used instead of money because it was assumed people would spend money foolishly.

Funny money term used to ridicule Social Credit party's plan to give all citizens a credit to spend of $25 a month.

On relief or **on the dole** receiving public welfare.

Pogey public relief, welfare. **Pogey house** hostel for people with no place to live. Also **pogey pants,** etc.

Riding the rods hitchhiking on a freight train by climbing onto the undercarriage. Actually this was too dangerous to be practical. Most hobos sneaked inside the cars or rode on the roof.

Soup kitchen place giving free meals to poor people, usually run by municipal relief office, a church group, or private charity.

A soup kitchen.

Compare the upward economic spiral of the 1920s with the downward spiral of the 1930s.
How did people survive during the Dirty Thirties when there were few jobs and no unemployment insurance?

1900 1910 1920 1930 1940 1950 1960 1970 1980 1990 2000

Evicted because they cannot pay the rent, Montreal.

The Prosperous Twenties	The Depressed Thirties
Industrial expansion	Industry slowing down
New businesses opening	Bankruptcies and business failures
Stock market values high	Stock market values low
Prices high	Prices low
Wages high	Wages low
Plenty of jobs	Few jobs
Mood of optimism	Mood of pessimism

Freight hopping.

Learning to Survive

Perhaps the worst part of living through the Depression was the shame of being out of work. People had been taught that if they were poor, it must be their fault. Only lazy people failed. Every time they lined up at a soup kitchen or accepted food vouchers, the despair went deeper.

A woman seeking a well paying job was frowned on because "Men needed the jobs more." On the other hand, many women accepted low wages. Therefore they sometimes found jobs when there were none for men. They left their husbands to keep house and went out to work long hours for $3 or $4 a week. Society said that men should be the breadwinners. Every day husbands, brothers, sons, lost a little more self-respect.

People did not give up. They made do. They patched old clothes. When the clothes fell apart, they wore flour sacks. They put wads of newspaper in worn-out shoes. They used tea leaves and soup bones three and four times. When there was nothing left at home, they set out across the country looking for work.

Riding the Rods

They stole into empty freight cars. They hitch-hiked along the highways. Perhaps there would be work on the next farm or in the next town. A knock on the farmhouse door got them a meal but no work. When they lined up at the factory gates, the sign was always out: No Help Wanted.

In summer they slept beside open fires in "hobo jungles" on the edge of town. In winter they might be allowed to sleep on a jailhouse floor.

For many, this way of life went on for ten years. These were the Dirty Thirties.

The Prairie Dustbowl

No work in Edmonton. This family from Saskatoon is on the move again.

The worst place to be during the Depression was on the Prairies. In 1929 wheat had fetched $1.60 a bushel. In 1932 farmers could hardly get rid of it for 38¢. In 1933 world conditions started to improve a little. Some factories in eastern Canada took on a few more workers. Mines were being reopened. On the Prairies, though, the troubles had only just begun.

Drought

The summer of 1931 had been very dry. In 1932 the rains came again. In 1933 the drought returned. There was no real rain for five long years.

Crops depend on the soil on the surface of the land. The subsoil beneath contains no nourishment. Without rain, the fertile prairie topsoil turned to dust. Strong winds whipped it up into a black blizzard. Farmers stood in sorrow as the land that fed them blew away. They watched the few wheat plants that survived the wind storms shrivel and die in the parched subsoil.

With the drought came the grasshoppers. They hatched by the millions in the prairie desert. Farmers looked up to see dark clouds of hoppers blotting out the sun. When they had passed by, nothing would be left alive. One farmer reported they had even stripped the bristles from his broom. Only the metal band that had held the bristles and a chewed handle remained.

In the bumper crop of 1928 Saskatchewan had produced 8 750 000 tonnes of wheat, or 1.6 tonnes per hectare. In the worst year of all, 1937, production fell to 920 000 tonnes, or 0.2 tonnes per hectare.

What did farming families do, hit by the double blows of Depression and dustbowl? They went barefoot. They dressed in flourbags. They burned

> Feb 11, 1935
>
> Dear Sir –
>
> Please don't think I'm crazy for writing you this letter, but I've got three little children, and they are all in need of shoes as well as underwear but shoe's are the most needed as two of them go to school and its cold, my husband has not had a crop for 8 years only enough for seed and some food, and I don't know what to do. I hate to ask for help. I never have before and we are staying off relief if possible. What I wanted was $3.00 if I could possible get it or even some old cloths to make over but if you don't want to do this please don't mention it over radios as every one knows me around here and I'm well liked, so I beg of you not to mention my name. I've never asked anyone around here for help or cloths as I know them to well.
>
> Yours Sincerly
> Mrs. P.E. Bottle

Prime Minister Bennett, who was a millionaire, received many letters like this one from Alberta. He sent Mrs. Bottle $5.00.

Give 3 reasons why the Prairies were the worst place to be during the Depression.
Write a report on conditions on the Prairies for a newspaper in your community during the 1930s.

1900 1910 1920 1930 1940 1950 1960 1970 1980 1990 2000

wheat instead of wood—it was cheaper. They ate gopher stew. They gave up the telephone, the newspaper, the car. They fell behind on their mortgage payments. When the bank foreclosed, they were forced off the land. Others just gave up. They headed for the cities of Ontario or moved farther west to British Columbia. Over one quarter of the wheat farms on the Prairies were abandoned during the thirties.

Most families just hung on. Perhaps next year the rains would come. They might have a good crop. The price they got for it might cover the cost of growing it.

In 1938 the rains came again, but so did hail and grasshoppers. It was not until 1939 that things returned to normal. And it took World War II to bring the price of wheat back to a profitable level.

Dust storm on the Prairies.

The farmers in Saskatchewan are in desperate circumstances. Only about half of them have sown seed this year, and much of that seed has blown out. The soil has drifted completely over fences to a depth of 60 cm on one road.
Quoted in The Dirty Thirties *by Michiel Horn*

The church at Brussels, Ontario, sent us a railway car of mixed fruit and vegetables, apples, potatoes, beets, carrots, onions, cabbage — 26 000 kg in all. We also received clothing, mostly second hand, but all good.
The United Church — particularly from Ontario — surely responded nobly. Over 130 carloads of fruit and vegetables were donated to Saskatchewan, and the railways transported it all free.
Quoted in The Dirty Thirties *by Michiel Horn*

Here's how it was. Let me tell you. The wind blew all the time, from the four corners of the world. From the east one day, the west the next. If you were working outside, you didn't notice it too much, but the women did. Ask my wife — but she's dead now — she said the wind used to make the house vibrate. It was just a small wind, but there, always steady and always hot. A hot sucking wind. It sucked up the moisture. So this wind just blew and blew, and we had dust storms and times when we kept the lanterns lit all day.
Quoted in Ten Lost Years *by Barry Broadfoot*

The On-to-Ottawa Trek

The Depression was probably hardest for young single men. When employers had to cut staff, they let the young and single go first. They assumed older, married employees needed the jobs more. While young women were often unemployed as well, it was considered natural for them to be supported by their families.

The young men set off to look for work in other cities across the country. Usually there were no jobs anywhere. City relief officers worried about these drifters. They did not want to have to support them. They had enough trouble giving food and clothing to their own people. So they tried to make the newcomers move on.

But what if these desperate people turned violent? What if communist agitators organized them? There could be a revolution! The cities demanded action from Ottawa.

A flophouse during the Depression.

Relief Camps

The federal government decided to stop any revolution before it started. Relief camps were set up to get the drifters off the roads, out of the cities, and out of trouble. Men in the camps worked 8 hours a day. They built roads, dug ditches, planted trees. In return each received work clothes, a bed, food, and 20¢ a day. The camps were run by the Department of National Defence.

Men found the camps to be a cross between an army camp and a prison labour camp. After the work was over there was nothing to do. Conditions were terrible. One bunkhouse was 24 m by 7.3 m. It had no windows. The 88 men slept 2 to a bunk.

Men in the camps felt cut off from the world. There was no future for them. They were not even allowed to vote.

Reaction

In June 1935 over 1000 camp workers from the Vancouver area jumped some empty freight cars. They were headed for Ottawa to complain directly to the prime minister. On the way, other discontented workers joined them. People in the cities they passed through welcomed them, fed them, and wished them well. Even the train crews co-operated.

The government was terrified. They had set up the camps to avoid trouble. They had even forbidden the camp workers to form committees. Now a mass movement had begun. The On-to-Ottawa trek had to be stopped.

The trekkers were met in Regina by the RCMP. Eight delegates were allowed to go to Ottawa to meet with Prime Minister Bennett. It was a stormy meeting. Soon each side was calling names. Bennett called the

Why did the government set up relief camps?
Why did camp workers start the On-to-Ottawa trek? What
happened? Think of a recent mass meeting or march to try to
influence government policies. What happened at it?

leader a criminal. The leader called Bennett a liar.
Bennett refused to listen to their demands. The
delegates returned to Regina determined to continue
the trek.

The On-to-Ottawa Trek reaches Regina.

The Regina Riots

On 1 July, Dominion Day, the trekkers held a meeting
to raise money in the Market Square. The police were
afraid the crowd might get out of hand. Soon after the
meeting started, a large furniture van pulled up at each
of the four corners of the square. At the blast of a
whistle the vans opened and out poured Mounties and
city police waving batons. In the words of one trekker,
"We took it for a few minutes, and then we let go
against them."

The riot lasted until late evening. The On-to-
Ottawa trek was over. The government realized that
the relief camps were a failure. Within a year they had
been closed down. Closing the camps, of course, did
not solve the problems of the unemployed.

Depression Across Canada

If one worker in five was out of a job, four were still working. The
hardship was great, but the country survived. How did people in
each region cope? Everybody suffered to some degree, but those
who produced goods for export had the biggest problems.

The factories of southern Ontario and Quebec produced goods
which were mainly sold in Canada. They were protected by high
tariffs. This kept foreign goods out. Some factories were able to
keep going, even though they were producing much less. The tariff
wall meant they could keep prices high. However, this made
things even harder for those who needed the goods.

Farmers in Central Canada and the Maritimes had mixed
farms—a little wheat, some corn, a vegetable garden, some cattle
and poultry. If they could not sell their produce, they could at
least trade, or barter it. The local storekeeper knew his customers
had no cash. He would gladly accept a few dozen eggs and a barrel
of apples in exchange for a pair of shoes. The Maritimes had
missed out on the boom of the twenties anyway. Conditions in the
Depression were worse, but Maritimers were used to hardship.

British Columbia was almost entirely dependent on export.
Lumbering, mining, and salmon fishing were the major
industries. There were no markets and no jobs.

The Prairies were hardest hit: First they could not sell their
wheat. Then the dustbowl meant they could not even grow it.

Bennett and King

"Prosperity is just around the corner." In 1930 the Liberals under Prime Minister Mackenzie King were prepared to sit and wait for prosperity to arrive. When the provinces (which mostly had Conservative governments) asked Ottawa to help look after the unemployed, King refused to give them "a five-cent piece."

R.B. Bennett

The voters were angry. They elected the Conservatives under R.B. Bennett to form a new government. The Conservative approach to the Depression was not very different from the Liberals'. Both believed it was best for business to "find its own level."

Laissez faire is French for "Let it be," or "Leave it alone." This is the name given to the economic theory that business and industry will make the most profits if the government does not try to control them. If they make good profits, there will be more money, and everybody will be better off. In the 1920s it seemed that *laissez faire* worked well. Some economists knew the crash was coming, but governments in North America and western Europe thought it was wrong to interfere with the economy. Even after the crash they did not feel they could (or should) do anything to get things moving again.

Bennett did try to protect jobs in Canadian factories with high tariffs on imports. He suggested lower tariffs on goods from countries which would offer the same deal to Canada. He managed to get Commonwealth countries to agree to this idea at a conference in Ottawa in 1932. However, ordinary people did not feel any effects from this policy. They were still out of work. The lines outside the soup kitchens got longer.

In 1933 U.S. President Roosevelt promised Americans a "New Deal." Instead of leaving business to run itself, the New Deal brought the government into the economy. Slowly things started to improve in the United States.

In hard economic times people lose confidence in their political leaders. Mackenzie King won this election in 1926, but lost to the Conservatives under R.B. Bennett in 1930. In 1935 the voters chose King and the Liberals again.

Letters to Prime Minister Bennett

Chichester, Que.
March 13 1935

Dear Mr. Bennett.
  I am a little boy 11 years old I live in a very back wood place and I am very poor there is a big bunch of us I am going to school My little Sister and I we have three miles to go and break our own path but we dont mind that if we were only able to buy our books, the Quebec books are very expensive so I just thought I would write you maybe you would give us enough to buy our books if you dont I Guess We will have to stop and try and earn a little money to help out our father please excuse paper and pencil as I have no better Hoping to hear from you real soon I am

Yours Loving Friend
Albert Drummond

Please answer soon soon soon

Murray Harbour P.E.I.
March 24 1935

Dear Sir:
  I am writing you to see if their is any help I could get.
  As I have a baby thirteen days old that only weighs One Pound and I have to keep it in Cotton Wool & Olive Oil, and I havent the money to buy it, the people bought it so far and fed me when I was in Bed. if their is any help I could get I would like to get it as soon as possibile.
  their is five of a family, Counting the baby.
  their will be two votes for you next Election
Hoping too hear from you soon

Yours Truly.
Mrs Jack O'Hannon

FOCUS

What is *laissez faire*? Do you think this policy is effective during a depression? What was Bennett's New Deal? Why did the voters elect King in 1935?

Bennett was a rich man, but he could not solve the problems caused by the Depression from his private fortune. However, when he received letters from desperate citizens he often responded with gifts of money or clothing.

Calgary June 18th 1935

Dear Mr. Bennett,
    Do please raise the Old Age Pension to at least thirty dollar per month. So many of your very old friends, myself included, have really not enough to exist on.
    Very best wishes for your good health,

Sincerely,
Alma Ward

May 20/31

Mr Bennette
    Since you have been elected, work has been imposible to get. We have decided that in a month from this date, if thing's are the same, We'll skin you alive, the first chance we get

Sudbury Starving Unemployed

Regina Sask.
May 24/35

Dear Sir:
    You will. no doubt be surpriced to recived this requaist.
    I thought that you would have second hand clothing that would not be suitable for you to wear. as I am straped for clothes fit to wear to Church I disided to write to you
    My best suit is over 8 years old and pretty well frayed
    Judging you by your picture I beleve you are about the same size as myself
    I might say my people and I have allways been stunch Conservatives I wouldn't ask a Liberal party if I had to go naked.
    I was 69 years of age May 22/35
    I voted as a farmer's son when I was 18 years old for Sir John A McDonald's Goverment and Im still on the list

I am yours respectfuly
J.A.Graydon

In 1935, just before an election, Bennett introduced a "Canadian New Deal." It included many of Roosevelt's ideas. It proposed an 8-hour workday, a minimum wage, unemployment insurance, and price control.

"King or Chaos"

The Liberals under Mackenzie King poured scorn on Bennett's plans. They used the slogan "King or Chaos." The voters also were not impressed. Why had Bennett waited for five years while Canadians rotted without jobs? They felt the New Deal was just a way to try to get votes.

The Liberals swept to victory in the election of 1935. They had few real policies. However, by this time everyone realized that governments had to act to help people out of the Depression. The situation was confused by federal and provincial jealousies. The federal government had most power to raise money through taxes. Social policies like unemployment relief, which cost money, were provincial responsibilities. It seemed an impossible situation.

In 1937 King set up a Royal Commission on Dominion-Provincial Relations. The "Rowell-Sirois Commission" recommended sweeping changes in the tax system to remove the stumbling blocks to co-operation. It suggested equalization payments to poorer provinces. It said the federal government should be responsible for unemployment insurance.

However, this report did not come out until 1940. By that time the Depression was over. World War II had started. The unemployed had found jobs — in the army and the arms factories.

The Depression was not ended by R.B. Bennett or Mackenzie King. It was ended by Adolf Hitler.

The New Politics

From the depths of the Depression sprang new political ideas. The Liberals and the Conservatives both believed the problems would solve themselves, that it was not the duty of government to affect the economy. But some people were not prepared to wait. They formed new political parties.

Co-operation, not Competition

Liberals and Conservatives dominated parliament, but there were members from other political groups as well. In 1920 United Farmers groups in Ontario and the Prairie provinces came together as the Progressives. The first woman to be a member of parliament, Agnes Macphail, was a Progressive. Workers supported Labour candidates. J.S. Woodsworth, one of the leaders of the Winnipeg General Strike, was elected as a Labour member of parliament. Other members of parliament were Independents. They didn't belong to any party.

In 1933 some Progressives, some Labour representatives, and other interested people met in Regina. They formed the Co-operative Commonwealth Federation. The CCF believed in *socialism*. They wanted the government to control much of the business and industry in the country. The

The Regina Manifesto

1. The people (the government) should own all banks and financial institutions.
2. The people should own key industries such as railways, mines, lumbering, telephone systems, hydro-electric companies.
3. There should be a large-scale program of public works (housing, roads, and public buildings) to provide jobs for the unemployed.
4. Laws should guarantee minimum living standards for all through programs like unemployment insurance, family allowances, old age pensions.
5. Farmers' land should be protected from mortgage foreclosures.
6. There should be a guaranteed minimum wage.

Newly elected CCF MPs with their leader, J.S. Woodsworth, 1935. The young Tommy Douglas is seated at the left.

economy should be run on a co-operative basis for the benefit of the people. Under the private enterprise system owners ran things to make profits for themselves. The system lacked controls. Because it was uncontrolled, it had led to the Depression.

The CCF elected J.S. Woodsworth as their leader. They published the Regina Manifesto which described their program.

Many people confused the socialist CCF with the Communist party. There were some big differences. The Communists believed that change would only come through violent revolution. The CCF strongly believed that changes in the system should be made democratically. People must vote freely. The Communists said the rights of the individual were not important. The welfare of the state was all that mattered. The CCF upheld the individual's civil rights. Woodsworth was respected by all political parties when he stood up for immigrants, old people, or trade union members.

Summarize the 6 main ideas of the Regina Manifesto. Why did the CCF support each of these ideas?

What did Aberhart believe was the main cause of the Depression? How did his Social Credit party propose to end it?

1900 1910 1920 1930 1940 1950 1960 1970 1980 1990 2000

William Aberhart advocating the idea of Social Credit

Poverty in the Midst of Plenty

The stores of Alberta were stocked with clothes, radios, and tractors. People had no money to buy them. Farmers had wheat and could not sell it. If they managed to sell, the price they got was often less than it cost to sow and harvest.

Far away in Ottawa, Liberals and Conservatives debated and discussed—and did very little.

William Aberhart was a school principal in Calgary. Albertans knew him as Bible Bill, the radio preacher of the Calgary Prophetic Bible Institute. In 1932 he began to talk about a new political idea, Social Credit.

The root of the Depression, he said, was that people did not have enough money to buy the things that were being produced. If people had more money, they could buy more goods. More people would have jobs. They would have more money. The Depression would be over. He proposed to credit each citizen with a monthly "social dividend" of $25.

This idea made great sense to the farmers and workers of Alberta. They trusted Bible Bill Aberhart.

> You can strip down the appeal of Social Credit to the $25 a month. All of us farmers were in desperate straits. Here was William Aberhart promising $25 a month, and he was a Minister of the gospel. I asked him about that $25 after one of his meetings, and he told me I must have faith.
>
> *A farmer in Central Alberta*

In the 1935 provincial election Social Credit won 56 of the 63 seats and Aberhart became premier.

The federal government ruled that issuing money was a federal power. Aberhart's provincial government had no right to give out money. Many Albertans became convinced that Canada was being run by and for eastern interests. The old parties preferred talking about laws and the constitution to helping people in need.

New parties and new politics sprang up in other parts of Canada during the Depression. In British Columbia, Liberal premier Thomas Pattullo tried to bring the provincial government into the economy with a program of "work and wages." In Quebec Maurice Duplessis came to power in 1936 with the party he founded, the Union Nationale. He is shown here with the fiery Liberal premier of Ontario, Mitch Hepburn, on Hepburn's onion farm.

Enjoying Life

Life in the thirties was not dull and drab all the time. People found their fun in many ways. If they could not afford to travel, they could still get together with friends and neighbours for a picnic. They could go swimming at the community beach. Saturdays there were often concerts in the bandstand in the local park.

Radio

Amos and Andy, Eddie Cantor, Bing Crosby, Fanny Brice, Jack Benny—these were the entertainers of the decade. If you had a radio, your pleasure was free. Soap operas ran daily. People could hardly wait to learn more of the loves, fears, disasters, and joys of Helen Trent, Our Gal Sunday, or Ma Perkins. Monday evenings Lux Radio Theatre presented radio versions of the latest movies. Other nights people pushed aside the furniture and danced to the music of the big bands.

The Canadian Radio Broadcasting Corporation (later the CBC) was established in 1932. Canadians from coast to coast could now listen to their own programs. They tuned in to the music of The Happy Gang from Toronto. They laughed at Stag Party from Vancouver. Sunday mornings boys and girls listened to the stories of Just Mary from the Maritimes. At Christmas the whole family gathered round the radio for the King's Message. French Canadian farmers were the first to receive farm news. The programs were so popular that English farm broadcasts were soon started too. J. Frank Willis gave the first on-the-spot news coverage at the rescue operations after the Moose River Mine disaster in Nova Scotia. People learned about the confrontation between Ontario Premier Mitch Hepburn and the strikers at the General Motors plant in Oshawa. Each week on Hockey Night in Canada Foster Hewitt greeted them: "Hello, Canada and hockey fans in the United States and Newfoundland."

Jeannette MacDonald in Rose Marie and Shirley Temple in Susannah of the Mounties. Mountains and Mounties were Hollywood's impression of Canada. Add some snow, birchbark canoes, handsome lumberjacks, and wicked French Canadians, and the picture was complete.

Flash Gordon movies were Saturday afternoon favourites.

Movies

In this era before television, every town had its own movie house. When there was 15¢ to spare, kids went to the Saturday afternoon show almost every week. The cartoons, the latest episode in the adventures of The Shadow or Tom Mix, a full-length movie, sometimes even a free comic book—all could be had for 10¢. The extra nickel bought a chocolate bar or

Which 1930s radio programs might you have enjoyed? Describe an afternoon at the movies during the 1930s. How did sports fans find out about the achievements of their favourite stars and teams?

some jelly beans. A generation grew up on cowboy and Indian movies. These movies painted a distorted picture of the Indians' struggle for survival when European settlers moved in. Native people are still fighting the warped attitudes these movies created.

Few movies dealt with real life as it was in the Depression. People wanted to escape all that. They flocked to laugh at the Marx brothers, Laurel and Hardy, Charlie Chaplin, W.C. Fields. They shivered in their seats as they watched *Frankenstein* or *Dracula*. They thrilled to the adventures of Errol Flynn and Virginia Mayo in pictures like *Captain Blood*.

Canadian movies? Impossible! Everyone knew movies were made in one place only — Hollywood. Of course there were plenty of movies *about* Canada. The fact that these movies painted a pretty strange picture of the country didn't seem to bother anyone.

Sport

Is sport something people watch or something they do? Before television helped create superstars and super salaries there was a lot more "doing."

Winter in the thirties found Canadians of all ages on the ice—skating, curling, playing hockey. Spring and summer brought baseball, swimming, soccer, football. Every town had its own teams. Kids worshipped the local allstar rather than some national figure.

Professional sports were popular too. The Montreal Royals and the Toronto Maple Leafs were the only professional baseball teams. Football was beginning to attract attention. Each year the best western team travelled east to meet the eastern champions. Each year the West was defeated. Then in 1935 Fritz Hanson led the Winnipeg Blue Bombers to victory. National rivalry for the Grey Cup had begun.

The excited public followed the birth and upbringing of the Dionne quintuplets through magazine articles and radio reports. The quints became a great tourist attraction in Callander, near North Bay, Ont. They lived in a hospital built especially for them and were used in movies and advertisements for baby food.

Then, as now, hockey was the Canadian sport. The excitement was carried across the country by the magic of radio. Kids who had never seen the Montreal Canadiens or the Toronto Maple Leafs play knew all the details of the latest game. If they missed the game on the radio, they picked up the story on the sports page of the newspaper the next day.

Young people today either don't care about the Great Depression or have an exaggerated view of it. It was tough, but it wasn't all hunger and sadness. There were picnics, corn roasts, and cheap dances. Young people fell in love and got married. People learned to cope with being poor and out of work. Many rose to heights of bravery and unselfishness they never would have reached in normal times. Babies were born, whether their fathers were employed or not, and their young mothers made do with handmade or hand-me-down layettes. . .

Do you want to know something? I don't think I'd have wanted to miss the Great Depression for the world.
Hugh Garner

Changes Between the Wars

In 1914 Canada did not declare war. Britain's declaration meant the whole British Empire was automatically involved. By 1939 things had changed. Canada issued her own declaration of war.

What is a Dominion?

When Canada became a dominion in 1867, nobody thought that this meant she was an independent country. She handled her own internal affairs, but foreign affairs were still handled by Britain. Canadians soon discovered that Britain was not always interested in what was best for Canada.

During World War I people in Canada were proud of their country and their part in the war effort. They began to feel "Canadian." At the peace treaty discussions in Versailles, Canada and the other dominions of the British Empire sat as separate nations. Canada was an independent member of the new League of Nations.

In 1923 Canadians and Americans worked out a treaty to protect halibut on the Northwest Coast. The British ambassador to Washington expected to sign the treaty on Canada's behalf. Canada announced that her own minister of fisheries would sign the treaty. No British signature was required.

The British Commonwealth of Nations

It was obvious that the new relationship of countries in the British Empire had to be spelled out. Other groups—the Boers of South Africa and the Irish—were also unhappy. They were threatening to leave the empire. The Imperial Conference of 1926 issued the Balfour Report. It stated that the dominions were free and equal. They were united by the Crown and associated as members of the British Commonwealth of Nations.

In 1931 the British parliament passed the Statute of Westminster. This act declared that the British parliament had no power over the laws of the dominions.

Canada's constitution, the British North America Act, was an act of the British parliament. When the Statute of Westminster was passed, Canadians had not worked out how they could make changes to their constitution. So Canada asked Britain to keep the power to amend the BNA Act for the time being.

A Changing Identity

As British traditions faded, the American influence on Canadian life became stronger. If Canada was to be a nation, it was important that Canadians should have a sense of their own country. This was why the Bennett government established the Canadian Radio Broadcasting Corporation. The CBC would give Canadian actors and singers a chance to display their talent. It would provide a news service to tell Canadians about things from their own point of view. In 1939 the King government set up the National Film Board. It was to make films not only for Canadians but also to tell others about Canada.

Transport by Air

Radio could take the human voice to out-of-the-way places. The airplane brought food, supplies, mail, and medical assistance. After their exploits during World War I, Canadian aces had not given up flying. Flyers like Punch Dickens and Wop May became bush pilots. Bush pilots flew under incredible conditions. They performed deeds of great bravery. But airline companies in the twenties and early thirties were small, often with only one or two planes. None could afford to serve the whole country.

How did the Statute of Westminster of 1931 describe Canada's position within the British Commonwealth?
Name 3 organizations in Canada established by the government.
List some Canadian achievements in art, medicine, and writing.

1900 1910 1920 1930 1940 1950 1960 1970 1980 1990 2000

A travelling medical clinic in Alberta. Medical services to the public improved dramatically between the wars.

On TCA's first aircraft, oxygen was required over the Rockies.

The government stepped in. In 1937 Trans Canada Airlines (later Air Canada) was formed. Within two years the company had 15 ten-passenger aircraft. Former bush pilots made up the crew. To ensure the safety of passengers, all the flight attendants had to be registered nurses.

The Government in Business

Laissez faire economics said governments should leave business alone. In Canada provincial governments ran hydro-electric and telephone companies. The federal government ran a railway, and airline, a radio network, and even a film studio! In the United States private companies handled these things. Why was it different in Canada?

Here investors said the distances were too vast, the risks too great. Yet Canadians needed services and transportation. They needed to know about themselves and each other. If private industry could not provide these things, the government had to.

Achievements

Canada was no longer a colony. She was an independent nation, proud of the achievements of her citizens. Diabetics all over the world were being kept alive with insulin, the discovery of Frederick Banting and Charles Best. A Montreal hospital had become a world leader in brain surgery under the guidance of Wilder Penfield. The Group of Seven and Emily Carr had changed Canadian painting forever. Stephen Leacock was regarded as the funniest writer in the English language. Canada was a respected member of the world community.

Frederick Banting

1891 — born on a farm near Alliston, Ont.
1903 — schoolfriend died of sugar diabetes.
1916 — graduated from medical school and joined army as doctor in France.
1921 — with Charles Best began research on diabetes. Knew disease was result of a malfunctioning pancreas. Experimenting with diabetic dogs, they found that an extract of the pancreas (later called insulin) controlled sugar build-up in the blood. Found way to extract insulin from slaughter cattle for human use.
1922 — only known treatment for diabetics was practically to starve them to slow sugar build-up. Insulin tested on a 14-year-old, Leonard Thompson, who had lost so much weight he was near death. In a few weeks he regained normal health. Banting sold patent for insulin to University of Toronto for $1, profits to go to medical research.
1923 — Awarded Nobel Prize for Medicine. Upset that Best was not honoured, shared prize money with him.
1923-39 — directed Banting and Best Dept. of Medical Research, supervised work on cancer, lead poisoning, silicosis. A good amateur painter, became friend of A.Y. Jackson of Group of Seven.
1939 — investigated effects of high altitudes on pilots for RCAF.
1941 — died in plane crash in Newfoundland on way to England on "a mission of high national importance."

Questions and Activities

Match the items in column A with the descriptions in column B.

A	B
1. One Big Union	a) stated the original program of the CCF.
2. Social Credit Party	
3. Regina Manifesto	b) granted Canada full independence within the Commonwealth.
4. Alberta Five	
5. Statute of Westminster	c) fought for the right of women to be made senators.
	d) wanted to give each citizen $25 a month.
	e) sought bargaining power by uniting all workers.

Ideas for Discussion

1. If a general strike like the one in Winnipeg were organized in your community, what industries and services would be closed down? How would you personally be affected?
   Do you think workers should have the right to organize general strikes? Why or why not?
2. Was prohibition a good idea? Discuss this in relation to the ways we deal with alcohol abuse today. Are today's methods more or less successful than prohibition was?
   Compare prohibition of alcohol to today's ways of handling drugs. Do you think the use of marijuana should be legalized?
3. **Summarize some of the main advances in rights and freedoms for women made in the period 1914 to 1930. Compare these to advances for women made in the period since the 1960s.**
4. Discuss the impact of the automobile on:
   a) shopping patterns   d) travel and holidays
   b) city and community planning   e) jobs and industry
   c) convenience   f) morality
5. In the 1930s the government set up work camps for unemployed young men. Some people suggest that a similar system, but with more freedom, should be set up for the unemployed today. There would be a choice of:
   working in local parks, public buildings, etc.
   helping the aged or handicapped
   clearing land in unsettled areas like the North
   joining the armed forces
   Hold a debate on the topic: Resolved that unemployed young people should work for the government rather than being given unemployment insurance.

6. How involved should the government be in running industries and providing services? Here is a list of organizations run by the federal government. What does each one do?
   Why did the government become involved in this area?
   a) CNR   d) TCA (Air Canada)
   b) CBC   e) Petro-Canada
   c) NFB
   List other industries and services run by the federal and provincial governments. Do you think the government should continue to be involved in these areas? Are there other industries or services that you think the government should run? Why?

Do Some Research

1. Do any members of your family belong to a trade union? Compile a list of unions that people in your community belong to. Name some other unions in Canada today. What are their objectives? How have union aims changed since the time of the Winnipeg General Strike? How have they remained the same?
2. Find out more about one of the following:
   a) J.S. Woodsworth, "a saint in Canadian politics"
   b) Agnes Macphail, Canada's first woman MP
   c) Mary Pickford, "America's Sweetheart"
   d) The mystery of Ambrose Small, theatre owner
   e) Bible Bill Aberhart
   f) Banting and Best
   g) The Alberta Five
   h) The Group of Seven
3. Write a report about an outstanding woman in Canada today in one of the following areas:
   a) industry and commerce   c) sports
   b) politics and law   d) entertainment
   Describe her background and accomplishments.
4. Do some research on automobiles of the 1920s. Describe the basic features and options that were available.
   How have automobiles changed since the 1920s? What features have disappeared? What new features have been introduced? What "options" of the 1920s are now standard equipment?
5. Find out more about one of the following:
   a) Movies of the 1920s   c) The early days of radio
   b) Movies of the 1930s   d) Records and record players
   Write a paragraph describing their main features and importance.
6. Find out more about the success of Canadians at the 1928 Olympics. Compare their record to that of Canadian athletes in more recent Olympics. Can you draw any conclusions from this comparison?

7. The Edmonton Grads were one of the most successful sports teams ever. Do further research on the Grads or another Canadian sports team of the 1920s and 30s. Your report might include information under the following headings:
   a) Beginnings   c) Star players
   b) Coaches   d) Win-and-loss records
8. Memories of the Depression. Interview a member of your family or a neighbour who lived through the Depression. Prepare a list of questions you want to ask before you start, but be ready to follow up any interesting points that come up during the interview. Your list of questions might include some of the following:
   a) Where did you live during the 1930s?
   b) What jobs did people in your family do?
   c) What wages did they make?
   d) What kind of home did you live in? Did you move during the Depression? Why?
   e) What kind of food and clothing did you have?
   f) What did you do for entertainment?
   g) What was, for you, the saddest part of the Depression?
   h) What are your happiest memories of the 1930s?
   If you record your interview on a tape, you will be able to refer to it as you write a one-page summary for the class. Some of the best sections might be edited into a class tape of Memories of the Depression.

Be Creative

1. Write a letter from a soldier who has just returned home at the end of World War I. Your opening might be: "I am so pleased to see my family and friends again, but this town sure has changed!"
2. With a group of other students prepare a folder on the changing role of women from 1914 to 1930. Your folder should include:
   a) a *poster* advertising a women's rights rally;
   b) a *speech* by a supporter of women's rights;
   c) a *picture* of women's fashions and hairstyles in the 1920s with an explanation of how these gave women new freedom;
   d) an *editorial* favouring or opposing the right of women to be senators;
   e) a *letter to the editor* disagreeing with the editorial.
3. Design an advertisement for a product or appliance that became available during the 1920s. Let your ad explain how buying the item will make life easier, more convenient, or more entertaining. Compile a class brochure called Advertisements of the Roaring Twenties.
4. Make a mural or picture-map of Canada showing industries across the country in the 1920s.

5. Write a letter to Prime Minister Bennett asking for help for you and your family. Write Bennett's reply.
6. Prepare an edition of a newspaper in your community for a specific date in the 1920s or 30s. Your newspaper might include:
   a) reports on local, provincial, national, and international events
   b) entertainment and sports news
   c) information on new inventions and scientific discoveries
   d) human interest stories
   e) editorials
   f) letters to the editor
   g) political cartoons
   h) business news on local industries and job opportunities
   i) advertisements for new products
   j) fashion news
   k) want ads
   For some of these items you will need to do additional research.

You Are There

Starting a business — a store, a factory, an industry, a mine — takes a lot of money. Most companies get this money by asking people to *invest* in the business by buying *shares* or portions of the company's *stock*. If the company does well and makes a profit, the shares will pay the investor *dividends*. More importantly, the value of the shares themselves will go up. If the company does not make a profit, there will be no dividends and the value of the shares will go down. Shares are bought and sold on the stock market.

You're a big investor!
Your Uncle Fred has died and left you $5000 on condition you invest it on the stock market.
1. Start by consulting the business section of the daily newspaper over several days in order to establish the trends in the value of stock shares.
   a) Find a stock that has gone up in value.
   b) Find a stock that has gone down.
2. Invest Uncle Fred's $5000 in stocks of your choice.
3. Record the value of your stocks each day. Remember that if you think your stock has "peaked," or if you don't like its performance, you can sell it at the going price and re-invest in another stock.
4. At the end of a month, calculate the current value of your shares.
Did you make a profit? Compare results with other members of the class.

The World at War
ADVANCE ORGANIZER

1

After World War I life was not easy in Europe. The war had left many countries heavily in debt. Some people resented the new borders that had been drawn at the end of the war. They distrusted the new democratic forms of government that had been set up. The Depression made these problems even worse. In all this uncertainty, dictators easily gained control. They offered simple solutions and promised glory for their country. They silenced all who spoke against them. In Italy and Spain, Mussolini and Franco came to power. In the Soviet Union, Stalin ruled.

2

Most dangerous of all was Adolf Hitler, who gained power in Germany in 1933. He told Germans they were the "master race." He blamed all Germany's problems on scapegoats — "non-German traitors" within the country — and the unfair terms of the treaty that ended World War I. Hitler's sweeping racism became government policy. Fear of his secret police gripped the country while Hitler urged Germans to dream of ruling the world.

3

Other nations knew Germany had real causes for complaint. They hoped that if they let Hitler take a little, Germany would be satisfied. In 1938 Hitler's armies swept into Austria and Czechoslovakia. When Poland fell to German tanks and dive bombers in 1939, world leaders knew they had to fight back. Their resistance came too late: soon most of Europe was under Nazi rule.

Word List

appeasement	fascism	ration
blitzkrieg	liberation	recruit
demilitarized	partisan	scapegoat
dictator	purge	unity

4

Canadians figured prominently in World War II. The Royal Canadian Navy organized huge supply convoys to Britain. Canadian pilots helped stop Hitler in the Battle of Britain and other air battles. Canadian soldiers fought bravely on the battlefields of Europe and Asia. They suffered a tragic defeat at Dieppe, France. They played a valiant part in the slow advance through Italy and the final invasion of western Europe after D-Day.

5

Canadians at home produced airplanes, ships, and armaments. They bought Victory bonds to help pay for the war. Food and gasoline were rationed so more supplies could go to Europe. Women entered the factories and joined the armed forces. Young people ploughed up their schoolyards to plant "victory gardens."

6

Japanese army officers also dreamed of a vast empire. They attacked China, American bases in the Pacific, and British and French colonies in Asia. Many Canadians feared and hated the Japanese who had moved to Canada. Japanese Canadians were taken from their homes on the Pacific coast and held in camps until the end of the war.

7

The war ended with the dropping of atomic bombs on two Japanese cities. This was the final horror in a war marked by crimes against humanity. Millions of Jews and other minorities had been murdered under Hitler's rule. Too many powers had been willing to prove their might through warfare. The United Nations was founded in the hope of maintaining peace for all in the future.

Dictators in a Changing World

For people in Europe the 1920s were a time of change, insecurity, and frustration. The treaty of Versailles was expected to straighten out the chaos caused by World War I. However, it created as many problems as it solved. The losers of the war felt they had been unfairly treated. The winners could not see that they had gained anything. Both felt cheated.

A New Map of Europe

The diplomats at the conference in Versailles believed every national group should have its own country. So they gave lands that had been part of Germany to Poland and to France. They broke up the Turkish and the Austrian empires into independent countries. But it was impossible to draw neat lines and put all

EUROPE AFTER 1919

Germans or Slavs on one side, all Poles or Italians on the other. Within the new borders there were still minority groups. The minorities resented being part of these new countries. The majority groups feared the smaller nationalities might cause trouble.

New Politics in Europe

Before the war there had been elected assemblies in most countries of Europe. These assemblies had rarely had much power. It was the princes, kings or emperors and their advisors who made the final decisions. Now Europeans had lost faith in their old leaders. The old system had led them into a useless war. The diplomats at Versailles, under the leadership of U.S. President Woodrow Wilson, wanted to set up democratic forms of government. But these new democracies had not grown naturally. As a result, few people knew how to run a country in a democratic way. Voters had no experience to help them judge the new politicians.

Then came the thirties. The Depression caused huge social, economic, and political problems in stable democracies like Canada, the United States, and Britain. In unhappy Europe the effects were disastrous. People felt they had to find a way out of the hopelessness, frustration, and insecurity that surrounded their lives.

They were ready to follow a leader—one who promised better things. They wanted to be told their country was great—and would become greater. They were prepared to believe their problems were somebody else's fault—the foreigners, the communists, the democrats, the Jews.

It was conditions like these that led to the rise of fascism. Mussolini, Hitler, and Franco rode to power on the backs of broken hopes, fears, poverty and hatred.

Why did the new national boundaries created by the Treaty of Versailles fail to bring peace to Europe?
Why did the people fall under the influence of dictators?
Do you think a dictator could come to power in Canada today?

The Fascist symbol, a bundle of rods and an axe, was taken from the ancient Roman Empire. The rods represented the power of corporal punishment and the axe represented the power of capital punishment.

Fascism in Italy

In Italy Benito Mussolini formed the Fascist party to fight communism and socialism. Fascists in black shirts gathered to listen to their great leader. The black shirts were a sort of uniform. They made the wearers feel like a private army. The "blackshirts" broke up trade union meetings and communist rallies with clubs and fist fights. They conducted a campaign of terror against those who protested their actions.

In 1922 Italian unions called for a general strike. Mussolini said that if the government didn't stop the strike, the Fascists would. Fascists from all parts of Italy marched on Rome. In panic, the king asked Mussolini to form a new government.

Mussolini promised great things for Italy. He introduced an economic program that was to make Italy self-sufficient. Meanwhile the blackshirts continued their bullying tactics to silence all criticism. Soon Mussolini was dictator of Italy. There was no opposition. Only Fascists were allowed to run for election.

The hammer and sickle of the Communist party symbolize the power of the workers.

Stalin's Russia

Ten years after the communist revolution, Joseph Stalin came to power in the Soviet Union. He proved to be an able but ruthless dictator. Stalin set up a "five year plan." Under the plan Soviet citizens worked and sacrificed together to expand industry. The plan was exciting because it looked to a better future. It worked, but the cost was high. Stalin conducted "purges" of those the police said were against him. They were sent to prison camps in the Arctic or Siberia. Thousands were executed in secret.

Japan was "the land of the rising sun." On the military ensign, rays spread from the sun to show how the armed forces could spread out to conquer the world.

The Army in Japan

Meanwhile, on the other side of the world, army officers prepared their nation for conquest and empire.

The Japanese emperor was considered divine by his loyal subjects. The Japanese armed forces were responsible to him, not to the elected government. In the late twenties a group of young officers took control of the army. They dreamt of a vast Pacific empire. They were supported by businessmen who wanted raw materials and a guaranteed market for Japanese industry. Government ministers who opposed them were often assassinated.

Franco's symbol was a crossbow and arrows. Adapted from the Spanish coat of arms, it represented military might.

The Spanish Civil War

In 1936 General Francisco Franco led a revolt against the government of Spain. The government was made up of several political groups, including the Communist party. Franco wanted to stamp out communism. He was supported by the army, landowners, factory owners, members of the Roman Catholic church, and the Falange (the Spanish fascists). Mussolini and Hitler sent help from Italy and Germany. Stalin supported the government side.

The world looked the other way as a democratically elected government was crushed by fascist rebels. Some were not content to stand aside. They formed the International Brigades to fight alongside the government forces. Among them were 1200 Canadian volunteers who formed the Mackenzie-Papineau battalion. Other Canadians, especially Roman Catholics, were more worried about communism than about fascism. To avoid offending anyone, the Canadian government did its best not to get involved.

The war lasted 3 years. By 1939 Franco was dictator of Spain. He ruled Spain until his death in 1975.

Adolf Hitler

In Germany the leader of the National Socialist (Nazi for short) party watched Mussolini's rise to power with admiration.

Adolf Hitler was born in Austria in 1889. After an unhappy childhood be became a homeless drifter. The outbreak of World War I found Hitler in Germany. He eagerly joined the German army. He proved an able and courageous soldier.

Germany surrendered in 1918. Soldiers everywhere cheered because the war was over. Hitler cried because Germany had been beaten. He swore revenge on the "socialists and Jewish traitors who," he said, "had stabbed Germany in the back." He joined the Nazi party. Its aim was to rebuild Germany and defeat her enemies. Hitler's passionate speeches soon made him the party leader.

An outdoor rally in Berlin, 1937.

In 1923 Hitler was jailed for plotting to overthrow the government. While in jail, he wrote *Mein Kampf,* a book which explained his political aims. On his release Nazis welcomed him as a hero.

Being a Nazi was made exciting. Hitler organized the party on military lines. The Nazis marched through the streets of German towns. They had their own salute, their own uniforms, their own songs, their own symbol—the swastika. They listened to stirring speeches from their leader. The brown-shirted "storm troopers" broke up Communist party meetings, attacked the homes and businesses of Jews, and struck terror in the hearts of other "traitors."

Many Germans were not won over. Germany had a new democratic system of government—with 27 political parties. By 1933 the Nazis were the largest party in the German parliament, but they never won a majority in a free election. As leader of the largest party, Hitler was asked to be chancellor. He accepted on condition that he be given dictatorial powers. That evening, the Nazis held torchlight parades. Swept along by excitement, the crowds roared "Sieg Heil! SIEG HEIL!" (Hail victory!).

List 5 reasons why many Germans supported Adolf Hitler when he came to power.
What actions did Hitler take when he came to power?
Why might young people be attracted to the Nazi party?

Why Germans Supported Hitler

Even people who had not voted for Hitler were glad to see a strong man in charge. They thought he would solve the country's problems. Few understood his real intentions.

Hitler blamed Germany's troubles on the treaty of Versailles. In many ways he was right. The treaty demanded that Germany pay for the war with money and goods. This had made life difficult for Germans in the 1920s. Hitler, his face red with rage, tore the treaty to shreds before cheering crowds.

The Depression hit Germany hard. Perhaps the Nazis could put Germany back to work.

Few Germans liked or trusted the new democratic system of government. It had never really worked. It

The Hitler Youth was formed to inspire young people with Nazi "ideals."

was easy to blame democracy for Germany's problems. Hitler promised a return to strong government. His private army of storm troopers paraded through the streets. They broke up the meetings of other political parties. Many people supported the Nazis out of fear.

Hitler gave the Germans targets to blame for all their problems. His favorite scapegoats were the communists and the Jews. The Nazis preached "racial purity." They claimed Germans were the "master race." Jews, Slavs, and other minorities were to be regarded as "impure aliens."

Many saw Hitler as an inspiring leader. He had become a brilliant, hypnotizing speaker. Nazi rallies were full of colourful parades and rousing marching songs. People who attended felt they were part of a great movement.

And Hitler delivered on his promises. Germany was put back to work. New roads and bridges were built all over the country. Guns, tanks, warships, planes—all forbidden by the treaty of Versailles—started to pour from German factories. Young men flocked into the army. In 1936 they rode the new tanks down the new highways, across the bridges and into the Rhineland. The Versailles treaty had declared this part of Germany to be demilitarized forever, but Germany was on the way back to glory!

Meanwhile, all traces of democracy in Germany were being destroyed. Socialists, democrats, communists, religious leaders, teachers, scientists—all who spoke out against the Nazis—found themselves in concentration camps. Jews found they couldn't get jobs. Instead of the truth, newspapers printed Nazi propaganda; radios blared it forth. The unions, the schools, the army, even the churches were under Nazi control. The Gestapo, Hitler's secret police, were everywhere.

The Gathering Storm

In 1919 the nations of the world had come together in the League of Nations. The League was to settle international arguments through debate. The nations wanted to prevent another war.

During the 1920s the League managed to settle a number of disputes between nations. By the 1930s things weren't working as well. Some countries had learned they could defy the League and get away with it.

Manchuria

In 1931 a group of Japanese army officers created an excuse to invade the Chinese province of Manchuria. Within weeks Manchuria was torn from China. The League of Nations was not prepared to act. Asia seemed so far away. All the League did was to refuse to recognize the new government of the province. The only result of that was that Japan withdrew from the League.

By 1937 World War II had already begun in Asia. Japan set out to conquer the rest of China and to build an empire in the Pacific.

Ethiopia and the Rhineland

In Italy Mussolini's economic program was not working. Mussolini decided a war would take people's minds off the problems of the Depression. He would rebuild the Roman Empire. He saw himself as *il Duce,* a leader greater than Julius Caesar.

His victim was Ethiopia. All through the summer of 1935 Italian troops gathered in Italy's colonies on the borders of the ancient African kingdom. In October they poured into Ethiopia. The Ethiopians fought bravely, but spears were no match for machine guns, planes, tanks, and poison gas.

Emperor Haile Selassie of Ethiopia appealed to the

While Mussolini invaded Ethiopia, Hitler's armies were welcomed by cheering crowds as they entered the Rhineland.

League of Nations. The League members agreed that Italy was in the wrong. They said they would cut off Italy's oil supplies. "Oil means war!" replied Mussolini. In fear, the League backed down. In any case, it was more worried about the consequences of Hitler's march into the Rhineland. Would France declare war? France, at the urging of Britain, decided not to press the issue.

Hitler and Mussolini soon realized they had served each other well. They had kept the League from acting against either of them. With the military rulers in Japan, they formed the Rome-Berlin-Tokyo Axis. This was an agreement to support each other against communist Russia. Now Hitler had allies. He was ready to gamble that the leaders of Europe would agree to anything to avoid war.

Why did the League of Nations fail to act against Japan, Italy, and Germany?
What countries did Hitler take over before invading Poland?
How would you have dealt with Hitler at Munich in 1938?

1900 1910 1920 1930 1940 1950 1960 1970 1980 1990 2000

The Appeasement of Germany

Hitler declared that his vision of the "master race" required that Germans everywhere belong to one united Germany. In 1938 he announced that Austria was to be part of Germany. The German army marched in. The Austrians had had no way of defending themselves. France and Britain said nothing. Seven million Austrians were now German. And Hitler had his next target almost surrounded.

The rich industrialized Sudetenland area of Czechoslovakia was home to 3 million Germans. Hitler claimed they were being oppressed. He threatened to occupy the area. France, Britain, and Russia promised to stand by the Czechs. At the last moment the leaders of western Europe met at Munich. They gave in to Hitler's demands rather than have another war. British Prime Minister Chamberlain went home to cheering crowds. He claimed he had achieved "Peace with honour, peace in our time." Many people in Canada and elsewhere heaved a sigh of relief. Others warned of greater threats to come.

Within months the German army swallowed up the rest of Czechoslovakia. Hitler now demanded German-speaking areas of Poland. Finally the leaders of France and Britain realized they had to take a stand. They declared they would guarantee Poland's borders.

The government of the Soviet Union decided it could not rely on the western democracies for help against Hitler. Look at what had happened to Austria and Czechoslovakia! So the Soviet Union and Germany signed a treaty not to fight each other. A secret agreement was also made to divide Poland between them. With the Soviet Union out of his way, Hitler was now ready.

On 1 September 1939 German tanks thundered across the Polish border. Bombers flattened the great city of Warsaw. On 3 September France and Britain declared war against Germany. One week later, a hastily assembled Canadian parliament voted to stand by Britain.

Norman Bethune

1890 — born in Gravenhurst, Ont. Strong minded from early childhood, often not popular with others.
1907 — After high school worked as a logger, teacher in one-room school and with Frontier College. Started university, got bored and dropped out for a while, but by 1914 was halfway through medicine.
1914 — dropped out to join Canadian Army Medical Corps.
1915 — wounded. Returned to university.
1916 — graduated in same class as Frederick Banting.
1917-19 — served as surgeon with Canadian navy.
1920s — worked as doctor. Enjoyed easy, 20s lifestyle.
1927 — developed TB. Insisted doctors try an experimental treatment, collapsing the lung. Cured. Decided to dedicate life to helping others.
1928-33 — working in Montreal, invented many surgical instruments for chest operations.
1935 — visited U.S.S.R. Impressed by government-run system of medical care for all. On return, advocated it for Canada.
1936 — shocked at Canadian opposition to socialized medicine, joined Communist party. Volunteered to help government forces against Franco in Spanish Civil War. Set up mobile blood transfusion clinic to take blood right to the wounded in front lines of battle.
1937 — returned to Canada for speaking tour on Spain.
1938 — went to China to help Chinese forces under Mao Tse-tung in war against Japanese. Worked under incredible conditions with almost no medical supplies to help Chinese wounded. Wrote own textbooks to train medical workers.
1939 — a cut on his finger infected during an operation (was not wearing rubber gloves). Died of blood poisoning. A hero in China, not recognized in Canada until 1970s.

Blitzkrieg

The Nazi armies crushed Poland in less than a month. By October 1939 the Polish armed forces had collapsed under the pounding of German tanks and Stuka dive bombers. Hitler had taught the world a new word—blitzkrieg or "lightning war."

After the defeat of Poland came a lull in the fighting. People called this the "phony war" or "sitzkrieg." But most knew it was a time of careful preparation for the bloody struggle to come.

In the spring of 1940 Germany struck in a new wave of blitzkrieg. Denmark fell in one day, Norway in two. The Netherlands were smashed in five days. Belgium took eighteen. Even mighty France was shattered in six weeks. Hitler was master of Europe.

Dunkirk

British and French troops were pinned against the English Channel near the French port of Dunkirk. If British ships could reach Dunkirk in time, they could be rescued. The navy had few ships to spare. The word got round. English fishermen, weekend pleasure sailors, ferry captains, all took their boats across the channel. Canal boats and river tugs towed rowboats and empty coal barges out to sea. The volunteer fleet brought back 350 000 men — ten times the number the government had hoped to save.

Britain stood alone in Europe. The new prime minister, Winston Churchill, promised nothing but "blood, toil, tears, and sweat." It seemed that the war would soon be over. German forces were preparing for the invasion of Britain.

In the distant port of Halifax, Nova Scotia, ships were assembling to steam in convoy across the Atlantic. As well as fighting soldiers they carried the food and weapons needed for one of the most important battles in history — the Battle of Britain.

A convoy of ships sets out on the dangerous voyage across the Atlantic.

The Battle of Britain

On 10 July 1940 the German air force, or Luftwaffe, set out to clear the Royal Air Force (RAF) from the skies. Wave after wave of German Messerschmidts and Heinkels streamed across the channel. They spread out over Britain to their bombing targets—airfields, ports, factories. Slowly but surely the RAF was being wiped out. At one point every British fighter was in the air. Had the Germans launched another attack, no planes were available to respond.

Then suddenly the German tactics changed. The RAF had made a surprise bombing raid on Berlin. The Germans decided to "blitz" the cities in revenge. They would terrorize the civilian population into surrender. The plan backfired. The bombs rained on London

Was Dunkirk a victory for the Germans or the British?
Why did the Germans fail to win the Battle of Britain?
Why do you think Lord Beaverbrook was nicknamed Tornado?
What was his contribution to the war effort?

 Art Gallery page 20

night and day. Londoners moved into air raid shelters and subway stations. Each day they set about repairing homes, reopening stores, carrying on. British resistance grew stronger, not weaker.

However, with this breathing space the few remaining RAF Spitfires and Hurricanes could regroup. Newly trained pilots could join those who had been flying almost constantly since the battle began. New planes were coming off the assembly lines at the rate of 500 a month.

On 15 September German planes almost blackened the skies. The RAF was ready for them. When the day was over the Luftwaffe was decidedly beaten. Two days later, Hitler called off the attack. If he could not wipe out Britain, he would turn against the Soviet Union.

The Battle of Britain was won by a few hundred pilots. They included 80 Canadians as well as Britons, Poles, Americans. The Luftwaffe lost 1733 planes, the RAF 915. Canadian pilots accounted for 60 definite and 50 probable "kills."

> Never in the field of human conflict was so much owed by so many to so few.
>
> *Winston Churchill*

Max Aitken, Lord Beaverbrook (Tornado)

1879 — born in Maple, Ont., son of a minister.
1880 — family moved to Newcastle, N.B.
1895 — left school. Worked first in a drugstore, then as R.B. Bennett's law clerk.
1898 — discovered talent as business promotor. Sold insurance, bonds, re-organized Maritime coal, steel, and lumber industries.
1906 — married. On honeymoon in Caribbean bought a hydro-electric company and a streetcar company.
1907 — at age 28, a millionaire. Moved to Montreal, the financial capital of Canada. Bought Montreal Trust Co.
1910 — organized founding of Canada Cement Co. and Stelco. Moved to England. Elected as British MP.
1914-18 — as Canadian military representative in Britain, arranged that Canadian army would serve as a unit. For Canadians at home, wrote reports, hired war artists, and made 1st films of soldiers in action. Made British minister of information (wartime propaganda).
1916 — Made Lord Beaverbrook.
1918-39 — established huge newspaper empire. Warned Britain of threat of Hitler.
1940 — as minister of aircraft production, broke all rules to boost monthly production from 183 to 471. "Cannibalized" old and damaged aircraft to fix others.
1941 — as minister of supply, set up "lend-lease" program with U.S. Organized supplies for U.S.S.R. after Nazi invasion.
1946-64 — set up scholarships, art galleries, community centres, especially in N.B. Wrote 6 history books.
1963 — remarried at age 83.
1964 — died in England.

These Boulton Paul Mark I fighters were pressed into service for the Battle of Britain, but proved more successful as night fighters.

The Dieppe Raid

As France fell to Hitler's armies, Mussolini decided Italy was ready to join in. By 1941 nearly all Europe was under German or Italian control. British and Australian troops were fighting Germans and Italians in North Africa. In December the Japanese attacked American and British positions in the Pacific. The British colony of Hong Kong fell to Japan on Christmas Day. The main thrust of German might was turned against the Soviet Union.

Hitler's Drive to the East

Germany and the Soviet Union had signed a treaty in 1939. However, both Hitler and Stalin knew that in the end their countries would go to war. It was only a question of time.

Germany needed *Lebensraum*—living space. She needed the grain and oilfields of the Soviet Ukraine. The people of the Soviet Union were communists and Slavs—almost subhuman in Hitler's eyes. For the time being, Hitler had given up on conquering Britain. It was time to attack the Soviet Union.

In June 1941 war erupted along a front 2000 km long. German armies raced for Leningrad and Moscow. Both Germans and Russians adopted a "scorched earth" policy. They set fire to everything so the other side could not use it. Occupied Russia was soon a lifeless desert.

Then the advance bogged down. The harsh Russian winter set in early and caught the Germans unprepared. The more territory they conquered, the harder it was to control.

Stalin and his generals had time to recover. Britain and the United States sent large shipments of arms. The war in the Soviet Union was to be a long and bitter struggle. Before it was over, 20 million Soviet citizens would die.

Why the Dieppe Raid?

The Soviet Union was bearing the full weight of German attack. Stalin pressed his western allies to open a second front. If they would attack in France, the Soviet Union might get a little relief.

The British knew they were not ready to start a second front. But the whole Commonwealth was enraged at the fall of Hong Kong. The Americans,

German soldiers tend their wounded Canadian prisoners.

their new allies, wanted to get moving. Also Canadian soldiers in Britain had been waiting for action since the start of the war three years ago. A raid might satisfy the Soviets, the Americans, and the Canadians. It might be useful, too. It could test German coastal defences. It could help plan a full-scale invasion.

Give 3 reasons for the decision to conduct a raid on Dieppe.
Why were Canadian troops chosen for the raid?
Do you think the lessons learned from the Dieppe raid were worth
the heavy losses? Explain.

1900 1910 1920 1930 1940 1950 1960 1970 1980 1990 2000

▲

The Raid

On the morning of 19 August 1942, 5000 Canadian
soldiers crouched in landing craft off the heavily
fortified French port of Dieppe. They were to seize the
town, destroy the port facilities and airport, and take
prisoners. The key to victory was surprise.

When the first Canadians hit the beach, the
Germans were ready and waiting. The ships had been
spotted during the night. Also some ships had gone off
course and arrived late. As a result the raid did not
start till broad daylight.

The Canadians were facing 15 km of cliffs fortified
with cannon, barbed wire, tank traps, and mines.
Many landing craft were blown right out of the water.
In one boat of 80 men that made it to shore, 40 were
killed and 20 wounded within minutes. One regiment
had 96% casualties. Only a few soldiers ever reached
the town.

Crippled landing craft and abandoned tanks litter the beach
near the bodies of the dead and dying.

Rev. John Foote V.C.

Chaplains are priests or ministers. Their job is to give
spiritual and personal guidance to soldiers. They are not
fighters. They do not carry weapons. They are not sent on
daring raids. When Captain John Foote, chaplain of the
Hamilton Light Infantry, heard his men were going to
France, he insisted on going with them.

When the Canadians hit the Dieppe beaches, Foote was in
the thick of the battle. His mission was to aid wounded and
dying soldiers. When it was clear the battle was lost, he
worked frantically to save lives. "Every man carry a man!"
he urged the retreating troops. He himself moved 30 soldiers
into the boats.

As the Germans moved closer, Foote's soldiers grabbed
him and dragged him into a boat. He fought them off, and
waded back to the beach yelling, "The men ashore need me
far more than you."

Captain Foote was taken prisoner. He was forced to
march for two days without boots. He was sent to a prison
camp for officers where conditions were better than in
camps for ordinary soldiers.

Foote requested and got a transfer. He served his men as
chaplain for two more years. After the war, he was awarded
the Victoria Cross for his courage.

When the smoke cleared 900 men lay dead. Nearly
2000 had been taken prisoner. The boys from
Winnipeg, Hamilton, Montreal, Calgary, Windsor,
Regina and Toronto had been savagely defeated.

The British military leader Field Marshal
Mountbatten claimed "Dieppe gave the Allies the
precious secret of victory." Military leaders now knew
they had to develop greater firepower and new battle
tactics. Only then could a full-scale invasion of Europe
be attempted.

Others have been more critical. They describe the
raid as a disaster — poorly planned and poorly carried
out. Whatever the lessons learned, they were paid for
in Canadian lives.

Canada at War

There is more to war than sending soldiers to the battlefield. How could Canada, Canadians, and Canada's resources best be used to fight World War II?

The War Plan

The Canadian government drew up a war plan. The plan covered the areas that were most important to Canadians. It also dealt with the areas where Canada could make the biggest contribution to the Allied war effort. The plan was carefully co-ordinated with the war plans of other countries.

Weapons of War

One thousand ships, 15 000 aircraft, 700 000 trucks. Countless guns, bombs, and bullets. Under C.D. Howe, the no-nonsense minister of munitions and supply, war products poured from Canadian factories.

Howe wanted to avoid the profiteering that had soured the war effort in World War I. A wartime prices and trade board limited prices to "cost plus 10%." Even with these controls the government was paying up to $65 million a week for war supplies.

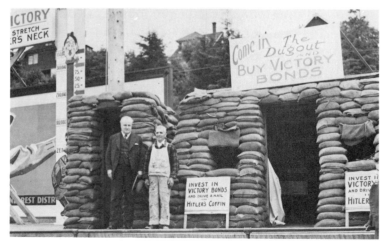

Victory Bond drive, Prince Rupert, B.C., 1941.

Where did the money come from? Income taxes rose to new heights. Canadians lent their money to the war effort by buying Victory Bonds. Victory Bonds paid for two thirds of the cost of the war.

The Canadian War Plan

1. The defence and security of Canada.
2. The production of food supplies for Britain.
3. The production of weapons and ammunition for Allied forces.
4. Training for Allied pilots.
5. Development of the Royal Canadian Air Force (RCAF) for home defence and overseas duty.
6. Development of the Royal Canadian Navy (RCN) for home defence and convoy duty.
7. Development of the Canadian Army for home defence and overseas duty.

Rationing

If people had money left after paying taxes and buying bonds, there was little to spend it on. In 1942 every Canadian received a ration book. When you bought sugar, butter, meat, tea, or coffee you had to hand over some coupons from your book. When your coupons were gone you couldn't buy—except on the "black market." If you were caught, you had to pay a stiff fine.

Gas was rationed. You could fill up once a month. You couldn't buy a new car. The last car was produced in 1942.

Canadians had good jobs. They could afford good food, new cars, clothes, and appliances. Why did they go without?

Anything that Canadians could spare went to the war effort. The butter and cheese Canadians didn't eat went to the tables of Britain where rationing was much more severe. The steel that once had made washing machines went into bombers. Even the common nickel changed—it was made of zinc instead.

Describe 5 ways in which ordinary Canadians contributed to the war effort.
In times of war people often co-operate and sacrifice more than they do at other times. Why?

The Children's War Effort

Kids collected paper, metal, rags, rubber, bones. Contests were held to see who could make the biggest ball of aluminum foil. All these things could be recycled into war materials.

Lunch hour was time for the knitting circle. Socks and scarves were made for soldiers. Letter writing campaigns cheered up lonely prisoners of war. The school baseball diamond was ploughed up to plant a "victory garden" to produce food for the war.

Boys drilled as cadets. Young people were let off school to help bring in the harvest. This kind of war work meant you didn't have to write exams!

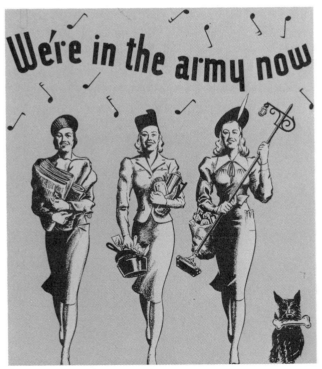

Many Canadians think recycling is an idea of the 1970s and 80s, but in the 1940s patriotic Canadians saved anything that could be re-used in the war effort.

Volunteers

Canadians volunteered to be air raid wardens. They patrolled the coasts to guard against an invasion that never came. They studied aircraft to serve as "spotters" in a bombing raid. They got together to build public air raid shelters. Wealthy Canadians gave their work to the government for a dollar a year. The war drew Canadians together in a spirit of co-operation.

> Thanks to the skill and devotion of our men and women, Canada is a granary, an arsenal, an airdrome, and a shipyard of freedom.
> *William Lyon Mackenzie King*

The Japanese Canadians

The Pacific War

War had been raging in Asia since 1937. China was weak and divided. Japan took advantage of this to expand her empire. When France fell to the Germans, Japan moved into the French colony of Indo-China. Once Hitler attacked the Soviet Union, the Japanese knew they had nothing to fear from the north. They turned their attention south to Hong Kong, Indonesia, and Malaya, and east to the Pacific.

At the American naval base in Pearl Harbour, Hawaii, sailors were turning over in their bunks. Most were looking forward to a lazy day off on that pleasant Sunday morning of 7 December 1941.

Out of the west came the Japanese bombers. In two hours the American Pacific fleet lay at the bottom of the harbour. The United States had been brought into the war.

The next day the Japanese laid siege to the British colony of Hong Kong. Among the defenders were 2000 Canadians. These troops from Manitoba and Quebec had been hurriedly sent to Hong Kong when the British realized attack was certain. They had almost no training. Some had never fired their rifles. They didn't even know you had to pull the pin before you threw a grenade.

The green Canadians fought bravely alongside the British and Australians at Hong Kong. They wouldn't give in. The battle lasted for 17 days.

On Christmas Day 1941 Hong Kong surrendered to the Japanese. The men who had defended it spent the rest of the war in Japanese prison camps. In the battle for Hong Kong 290 Canadians had died. Another 264 would die in the camps.

Today the graves of those who died defending Hong Kong lie on a hillside above the city.

Japan's entry into the war caused near panic for many people in Canada. To Canada's east, Hitler ruled in Europe. Now Japan was sweeping through Asia to the west. The fall of Hong Kong seemed like the end of the world. Canadians wanted revenge and struck out at the handiest target — the Japanese Canadians.

Canadians or Japanese?

Canadians had never been really welcoming to Asian immigrants. After 1913 few Asians were even allowed to enter the country. As a result, by 1942 more than half the 23 000 "Japanese" living in Canada had been born here. They were Canadian citizens. Few had any sympathy for Japan's ambition to take over the Pacific.

A family waits to be "relocated" to a camp in the B.C. interior, 1942.

What led the government to take action against the Japanese Canadians?
What did the government do?
Do you think this action was fair? Why or why not?

1900 1910 1920 1930 1940 1950 1960 1970 1980 1990 2000

Most Canadians paid no attention to these facts. They decided the Japanese Canadians were dangerous. They might be spies. They might help the Japanese attack North America. In 1942 the government ordered that they be moved away from the coastal regions of British Columbia.

Many Japanese Canadians were forced to move to camps in the B.C. interior. Often families were separated. The men were sent to one camp, women and children to another. Others were sent as labourers to farms on the prairies and in Ontario.

The government held auctions to sell these people's personal possessions, their homes, and their businesses. For the buyers there were great bargains. The Japanese Canadians never got a fair price for the things they had lost.

Husbands and fathers say goodbye to their wives and children.

David Suzuki

1936 — born in Vancouver. Parents born in Canada but of Japanese descent. Spoke only English at home. Father encouraged his interest in nature — birds, trees, animals, fish, insects.
1942-45 — with mother and sisters sent to camp near Slocan, B.C. Other kids jeered at him because he spoke no Japanese. White kids jeered because he was an "enemy." Only kids he had fun with were from Doukhobor community near Slocan. Later family moved to Ontario. Father told him: "You have to be ten times better than a white, because if you're just as good as a white, you'll lose out every time."
1954 — an outstanding high school student, he won scholarships to pay for his university education. Studied and taught at universities in the U.S. and Canada. Specialized in *genetics* (how characteristics are inherited through genes). Remembering own experiences with discrimination, worked with civil rights groups to fight racial prejudice.
1968 — became professor of zoology at UBC.
1970s — produced and starred in popular science shows: Suzuki on Science, Science Magazine, and The Nature of Things on TV; Quirks and Quarks on radio. Dedicated to making science serve the world. Warns of dangers of letting science (and scientists) get out of hand: "Science does good things, but science also produced the atomic bomb."
1980s — continues to star on various science shows. Hobbies: scuba diving, skiing, fishing, camping, football.

Why the Japanese?

Since the war, many Canadians have criticized this treatment of the Japanese. They suggest that it was less a matter of military security than of racial prejudice. It was not until 1949 that all wartime restrictions on Japanese Canadians were lifted. Only then could they buy property, travel, and live where they wished.

Behind the Scenes

In a total war not all the action is on the front lines. Many important battles are fought behind the scenes. Some are out in the open. Others are highly secret.

The British Commonwealth Air Training Plan

Military leaders knew that air power would be vital in World War II. Air crew must be trained before they can go into action. Canada provided the bases for the British Commonwealth Air Training Plan.

Trainees came from all over the Commonwealth — Australia, South Africa, Britain, West Indies, and New Zealand. Volunteers who had escaped when Poland, France, and Norway fell to the Germans also trained in Canada.

Courses were short and often inadequate. The rush to get pilots and service crews ready to fight caused many accidents. In one horrible month, 500 aircraft were put out of service by inexperienced fliers. All told, there were 850 deaths during training. On the other hand, 130 000 graduates, over half of them Canadian, went on to fight the battle of the skies.

Bombers on the tarmac, Manitoba, 1943.

The Secret War

On the shores of Lake Ontario somewhere near Oshawa was Camp X. Few knew of its existence. Those who did know said nothing. Camp X was a top secret training post for spies, secret agents and sabotage experts. It was under the direction of Canadian master spy, William Stephenson.

Agents from Camp X were dropped behind enemy lines to spy and report by radio. They connected with underground movements in occupied countries to disrupt enemy activities. One agent who trained at Camp X was Ian Fleming. After the war he wrote the James Bond spy stories.

Station M was a vital part of Camp X. It was staffed by forgers, safecrackers, chemists, movie set designers, and costume experts. Station M provided agents with false passports and money, battered suitcases, and European style toothpaste, eyeglasses, shabby suits, and underwear. Everything an agent carried had to look right to enemy eyes.

The Sheepdog Navy

Far from land, on the chilly north Atlantic, Canadians and Newfoundlanders also showed courage and endurance. Some were sailors in the "merchant navy," the cargo ships that bore food, fuel, and weapons to Britain. Others were part of the Royal Canadian Navy (RCN), which shepherded the convoys. The RCN's job was to find and sink the German U boats before these submarines found and sank the ships of the convoy.

By 1943 the U boats were on the run. They were being destroyed by weapons, sonar equipment, and shore-based aircraft. By the end of the war, the RCN had 400 fighting ships, the third largest navy in the world. It had shepherded 25 000 ships across the ocean. The Atlantic lifeline had been kept open.

FOCUS

How did Canada contribute to the air war?
What part did the Canadian navy play in the war at sea? Why was it important?
Who was Intrepid and what did he do?

1900 1910 1920 1930 1940 1950 1960 1970 1980 1990 2000

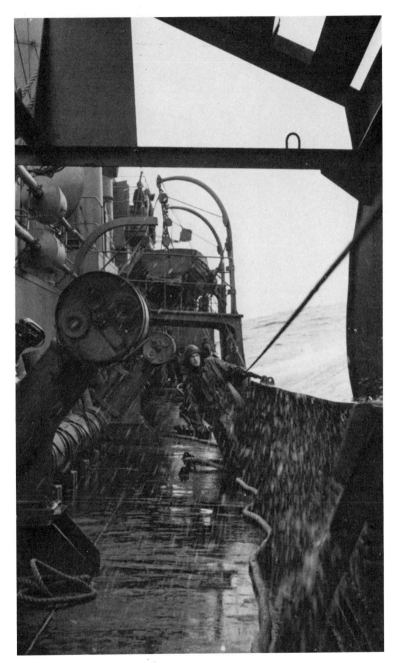

Rough weather in the North Atlantic, March 1942.

Two Canadian Agents

"Set Europe ablaze!" Churchill told the special agents parachuted into enemy-held territory. Among the 28 Canadian agents who went into Europe, 8 died. Even today, little is known of what they did.

Guy Bieler was born in Montreal. His spine was badly injured when he parachuted into France. Even so, he organized a sabotage group. They derailed and blew up trains carrying troops and arms. They sabotaged locomotives. In the end Bieler was captured and shot.

Frank Pickersgill of Winnipeg was captured when he landed in France. Nazi double agents had given him away. He refused to break under questioning. When his captors switched from threats to bribery, he broke a bottle on his interrogator's desk, slashed the throat of an SS guard, and jumped out a 2nd floor window before being stopped by 4 bullets. In prison camp he organized resistance, helping prisoners regain some lost pride. The Nazis finally executed Pickersgill and 15 other agents by hanging them from meat hooks.

William Stephenson (Intrepid)

1896 — born in Winnipeg. As teenager invented his own secret "Morse code."
1914-18 — joined army. Survived 2 gas attacks and declared unfit for service. Falsified medical records and joined Royal Flying Corps. After 5 hours' training, flew as pilot. Shot down 26 planes, including that of Lothar von Richthofen, the Red Baron's brother. Downed himself, captured, and escaped to British lines. Wrote report on German prison camps.
1920s — interested in broadcasting, with Beaverbrook helped set up the BBC. Pushed "wild" ideas like television, splitting the atom, and laser beams. Set up film studio.
1930s — became involved with British intelligence.
1939-45 — as "Intrepid," ran British Security Co-ordination, a secret army of code-breakers, spies, robbers, assassins, and sabotage experts. Many trained at Camp X.
1979 — made Companion of the Order of Canada.
1980s — living in Bermuda, still taking active interest in world affairs.

Women go to War

In 1939 Canadian women were eager to defend their country. Unfortunately, Canadian leaders saw little room for women in the war effort. As more and more men left for the battlefront, the role women could play became more obvious.

Industrial strength was the key to success in the war. Canada had vast resources. Canada's women put their brains and muscles to turning raw materials into tanks, planes, and ships. By 1943 over one million women were working in Canadian industry.

Managers had to change some of their ideas about workers and how to run a factory. Women often proved to be more careful and patient than male workers. Day care centres were set up in many plants. Production rose as workers donated free time to produce another tank or bomber. Men were often outnumbered. They sometimes had to endure female wolf whistles. They learned that in the right circumstances women could swear as well as men could.

Women volunteered to visit wounded soldiers. They sent packages to prisoners of war. They made dressings for the wounded. The family garbage shrank.

Railway workers.

Machine shop mechanics.

Housewives saved paper, scrap, fat, and bones for recycling. They made sure food was eaten, not thrown away.

Women in Uniform

Society had wanted to keep women out of the factory. It was determined to keep them out of the armed forces. When women were refused by the forces they set up their own volunteer units.

By 1941 the armed forces were in desperate need of recruits. Women were finally allowed to join up. One young woman walked 30 km to get to a recruiting station. By the end of the war Canada had 45 000 servicewomen. Many of them had been posted overseas.

These women often found themselves in the heat of battle. They were bombed, shelled, and torpedoed. Some were made prisoners of war. 244 won medals for gallantry.

List 5 ways in which women contributed to the war effort.
Were women treated with full equality? Explain your answer.
Imagine you are one of the Canadian heroines listed on this page.
Write about your wartime experiences.

1900 1910 1920 1930 1940 1950 1960 1970 1980 1990 2000

The Canadian Women's Army Corps conducts a fire-fighting demonstration in London, England, 28 February 1943.

Taking a break, London, February 1943.

Women Prove Themselves

During the war women succeeded in a society dominated by men. Many men had doubted their worth. Now women gained freedom and self-respect. They knew the satisfaction of earning their own money. They also knew the injustice of getting less pay than a man for doing the same work.

After the war many women were happy to return to a more "traditional" role. Many young couples had postponed marriage and babies for the course of the war. Peace meant it was time to start a family. Women became housewives and mothers. It was not until the sixties and seventies that women began to build again on the gains they had made in wartime.

Canada's Servicewomen	Total	Posted Overseas
Canadian Women's Army Corps (CWAC)	21 624	2 900
RCAF Women's Division (WDs)	17 018	1 400
Women's Royal Canadian Naval Service (WRENs)	6 781	1 000
Nursing Sisters		4 172

Canadian Women at War

Molly Lamb Bobak—first female official war artist.

Gudrun Bjening—war propaganda film-maker for the National Film Board.

Fern Blodgett — first female wireless operator on a wartime ship. She crossed the Atlantic 78 times during the war.

Margaret Brooke — nurse. While crossing from Nova Scotia to Newfoundland, the ferry she was aboard was torpedoed by a U boat deep in Canadian waters. Held a fellow nurse, Agnes Wilkie, up in the icy water all night. At dawn a giant breaker forced them apart. Wilkie drowned, but Brooke, now unconscious, was rescued.

Kathleen Christie and **Maye Waters** — nurses stationed at Hong Kong. Aided the troops during the battle for Hong Kong and continued to help them during two years of imprisonment by the Japanese.

Elsie MacGill — chief aeronautical engineer for Canada Car (later Hawker Siddeley). This company produced 1650 Hurricanes for the air war.

Charmion Sansom — radio announcer for a London-based station. Much loved by the troops. Like other radio personnel, her real identity was kept secret until after the war.

Helen-Marie Stevens — army nurse. Heroine of a bombing raid during the London "blitz." Worked for hours aiding customers in a bombed out restaurant. She used champagne as an anaesthetic. "I did what any Canadian nurse would do."

Conscription — Again

Should a person be forced to go and fight? This question had almost split the country during World War I. Prime Minister Mackenzie King was determined to avoid another crisis in World War II. He promised his government would not introduce conscription for overseas service.

In October 1939 Premier Maurice Duplessis of Quebec called for a provincial election. Duplessis was a bitter critic of the war policy. He said the federal government was out to take power away from Quebec. If Canada was to remain united through the war, it was vital that Duplessis's Union Nationale party be defeated.

The federal Liberals threw their support to the provincial Liberal party. Three Quebec federal cabinet ministers campaigned vigorously against Duplessis. They told the Quebec people that conscription for overseas service would never be introduced by their government. They would resign first. They also threatened to resign if Duplessis was re-elected. This would leave Quebec without any influence in the federal cabinet. The provincial Liberals were swept into office.

Meanwhile Premier Mitch Hepburn of Ontario wanted to see more Canadians go to war. He accused his fellow-Liberal, Prime Minister King, of being too weak. In early 1940 King called a federal election. The Liberals won an overwhelming victory in all regions of Canada. Hepburn's political career was over. The country was united behind King.

Home Defence

Volunteers filled Canada's fighting forces overseas. Many people felt this might not be enough. In the dark days of 1940 Parliament set up conscription for home defence only. Men drafted into this army were often jeered at because they hadn't volunteered to go overseas. Later they were called ''zombies'' by those who thought every young man should want to fight.

Conscription if Necessary

King had promised not to introduce conscription. In 1942 he asked the country to release him from his pledge. At that time it still did not look as if the government would need to force men into the armed

You won't get to Berlin in an Armchair!

IF Canada and the United Nations had depended upon "Armchair Soldiers" to fight this war, the Nazis and Japs would have grabbed this country long ago. There is no "Royal Road" to Berlin. It's fighting all the way and Canada's Army needs every man it can get. That's why, today, you should volunteer for overseas service. You'll need months of intensive training to make you fighting-fit.

Don't be a stay-at-home and let the other fellow do it. Get into a man's uniform with the G.S. badge of honour on your sleeve. If we're going to win this war, we'll have to do more than just read about it in the papers.

So, come on you fellows, the good old army has got to finish the job.

OVERSEAS BADGE OF HONOUR
GS
WEAR IT ON YOUR ARM

VOLUNTEER TO-DAY
JOIN THE CANADIAN ARMY
FOR OVERSEAS SERVICE

What is conscription? Why is it a sensitive issue in Canada?
Do you think Prime Minister King handled the conscription issue
well? Explain.
Would you have been for or against conscription? Why?

1900 1910 1920 1930 1940 1950 1960 1970 1980 1990 2000

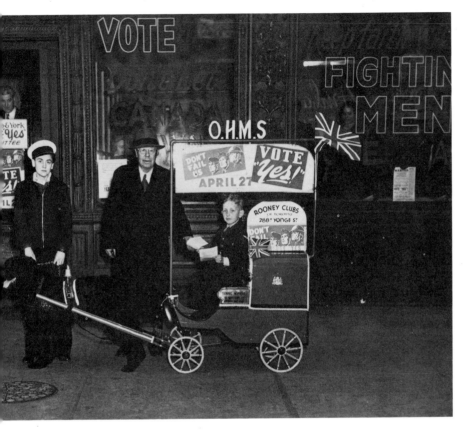

Campaigning in favour of conscription.

services. The Canadian army was sitting in Britain
waiting to go into action. But King knew the situation
might change. If it did, he wanted to be ready for it.

The government organized a vote on the question.
Across the country, 64% voted to let the government
decide. Ontario, Manitoba, and British Columbia were
80% in favour. In Quebec 72% were against. Many
French Canadians felt they had been betrayed. The
unity of 1940 was crumbling. Mackenzie King tried to
cool the issue. He used the slogan "Conscription if
necessary but not necessarily conscription."

The War Heats Up

While the Canadian army stayed in Britain there was
no need for conscription. For two years the issue was
avoided. After the Italian campaign and the invasion
of France, things changed. Now the battle for Europe
had begun and losses were high. The government tried
its best to recruit men voluntarily. Only a trickle joined
up. Reluctantly, in November 1944, King ordered
16 000 "zombies" to be sent overseas.

There was an uproar. One cabinet minister from
Quebec resigned. But other French Canadians stood
by King. Louis St. Laurent, King's "Quebec
lieutenant" told the people of Quebec the decision was
necessary.

Fortunately, the war ended soon after. Only 2 500
"zombies" saw actual fighting. They proved to be good
soldiers.

Unlike the crisis of 1917, all Canadians had been
fairly consulted before conscription was introduced.
The unity of the Canadian people was strained but not
broken.

Prime Minister King casts his ballot in the 1942 referendum.

The Italian Campaign

The Tide Turns

In 1942 the tide of war turned. In North Africa British and American troops drove back Italian and German forces under Field Marshal Rommel, "the desert fox."

In the freezing Russian winter, German troops faced disaster. In the territory they had conquered the people rose up and attacked them from behind the battle lines. The decisive battle was fought at Stalingrad. In February 1943 the once proud German army surrendered. The Russians took 90 000 prisoners. Soviet forces began to roll towards Berlin. They had suffered starvation, torture, and atrocities at the hands of Hitler's troops. They were prepared to take revenge on the German people.

In the Pacific the Americans had recovered quickly after Pearl Harbour. By the end of 1942 the ships sunk there were raised, refitted, and back in action! In June the Americans decisively defeated the Japanese navy at Midway. Island by island, they crept closer to Japan. In China communist and nationalist armies were rallying against their Japanese conquerors. British and Commonwealth forces began to drive the Japanese from Southeast Asia.

Each Allied victory was paid for in blood. Winning the war had become a matter of time and of lives.

Advancing under sniper fire, Campochiaro, Italy, October 1943.

In May 1943 General Montgomery's British army and General Eisenhower's American army surrounded the German and Italian troops in North Africa. It was time to cross the Mediterranean Sea to Europe.

The Invasion of Sicily

Since the disastrous raid on Dieppe, Canadian soldiers had seen no action. Now the 1st Canadian Division was to take part in the invasion of Sicily under General Montgomery.

The battle for Sicily was fought under the blazing July sun. Within 38 days the victorious Allied troops were preparing to invade the Italian mainland. Mussolini's dreams of a new Roman Empire were shattered. His own people rebelled and threw him out of power. Hitler swiftly moved German troops into Italy. The fact that the Italians had surrendered was not going to stop him.

The Liberation of Italy

The Italian campaign was long and difficult. 92 000 Canadians fought in Italy. 30 000 were wounded or killed. A few snipers in the rugged mountains could slow an army to a crawl. And the German forces fought brilliantly. Even with the help of Italian partisans, the Allies paid heavily for each kilometre they won.

FOCUS

Why do you think the Italian people rebelled against Mussolini?
Why was the battle for Italy long and difficult?
What reputation did Canadian troops get from the way they fought
and won the battle for Ortona?

CANADA THE TWENTIETH CENTURY **Art Gallery page 21**

The battle for Ortona was a terrible lesson for Canadian troops. The Germans turned it into a series of house-to-house fights. It took a month to capture the town. The Canadians became known as experts at street fighting.

On 4 June 1944 the Allied armies entered Rome. Canadian soldiers marched with their British, American, New Zealand, Indian, South African, French and Polish comrades to the cheers of the Italian people.

While one Canadian force crept up the boot of Italy, another prepared for the greatest land-sea invasion in history. Two days later came D-Day — the long awaited Allied invasion of France.

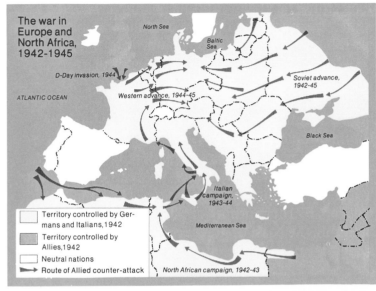

The war in Europe and North Africa, 1942-1945

North Sea
Baltic Sea
D-Day invasion, 1944
ATLANTIC OCEAN
Western advance, 1944-45
Soviet advance, 1942-45
Black Sea
Italian campaign, 1943-44
Mediterranean Sea
North African campaign, 1942-43

☐ Territory controlled by Germans and Italians, 1942
■ Territory controlled by Allies, 1942
☐ Neutral nations
➤ Route of Allied counter-attack

An abandoned German tank near Ortona, April 1944.

D-Day to V-E Day

Everything had been carefully planned. The tide was right. The moon was right. Would the weather be right for D-Day, the big invasion planned for 5 June 1944? Or would it have to be put off for a month?

The south of England was one big army camp. Everybody knew the invasion of France was about to begin. Only a very few knew when and where the landing would be made.

On 4 June the troops were ordered to the ships. Some ships set out. Suddenly, the weather reports got worse. The landing was postponed. The ships were recalled. By the morning of 5 June, violent winds were battering the coast of northern France. The troops stayed crammed aboard the ships, awaiting further orders.

Then the weather forecasters said there would be a lull in the storm. General Eisenhower made the decision. D-Day would be June 6, a day later than planned.

The Normandy Beaches

Across the English Channel the Germans were waiting at Calais. Pilots returning from bombing raids had told them the main build-up of troops and equipment was at Dover. What they had seen were empty tents, dummy ships, plywood gliders, and inflated rubber tanks.

The invaders struck 200 km to the southwest—on the beaches of Normandy. The Dieppe raid had taught them the Germans would destroy any harbours they tried to capture. So they wouldn't use the ports. Two complete harbours were built in Britain, towed across and assembled on the spot. Fuel for trucks and tanks would flow through "Pluto," an underwater pipeline.

All through the night bombers struck at the German defences. Just before dawn, paratroopers dropped behind enemy lines. The main force hit the beaches. The liberation of Europe had begun.

Canadian troops land in Normandy.

Why was the weather an important factor in planning D-Day?
What preparations did the Allies make to be sure the invasion would be a success?
What part did Canadians play in the fighting after D-Day?

The Push to Berlin

It was 11 months before western troops met their Soviet allies near the Elbe River in central Germany. They were 11 months of hard struggle. Hitler was determined to fight to the bitter end. He was prepared to destroy Germany and the German people rather than surrender.

In the long push towards Berlin, Canadians were given the task of clearing the French, Belgian, and Dutch ports. This was slow, dangerous work. Enemy forces fought from behind strong fortifications. Every port taken meant more Allied ships could unload more tanks, weapons, and troops.

The ports fell, one by one. On 8 September 1944 Canadian forces entered Dieppe. This time they came by land and as conquerors. The stain of defeat was erased as they marched into the port.

German children surrender to Canadian troops, April 1945.

A chaplain gives the last rites to a soldier dying at the roadside.

In 1945 Canadian forces liberated the Netherlands. The Germans opened the dykes that held back the water from the low-lying fields. Canadian troops found boats and kept moving. As the Germans retreated, grateful Dutch families poured out of their homes to welcome their liberators. Even today, Canadians are warmly received in the Netherlands.

The End of the Dictators

On 27 April 1945 Mussolini was captured and shot by his own people. His body was displayed hanging upside down on a meat hook in Milan. Three days later in his underground bunker, Hitler listened to Soviet guns bombarding Berlin. He placed a revolver in his mouth and pulled the trigger. His body was burned so it could not be displayed by his enemies. On 8 May 1945, Germany surrendered unconditionally. This was V-E Day — Victory in Europe Day.

The Holocaust

When Hitler came to power in 1933 he began his war on the Jews. He ordered Germans to boycott Jewish stores. He forbade Jewish lawyers and doctors to practise freely. Jews lost the right to vote. In many places, Jews were not allowed to use public parks, swimming pools, or sports fields.

Other nations made feeble protests. They did nothing.

The First Boat People

Early in 1939 the *St. Louis* sailed from Hamburg, Germany. Aboard her were 907 Jews. They were looking for a safe home far from the persecution of Nazi Germany.

They tried to land in Cuba. They were turned away. They headed for the United States. They were forbidden to enter the country. They came north to Canada. Canadians, too, turned their backs.

Most countries tried to keep all immigrants out during the Depression. Many people were particularly prejudiced against the Jews. In Canada over 100 000 people signed a petition to stop Jewish immigration. As a result of attitudes like these, few Jews were able to escape Europe during the 1930s. When Hitler overran the continent, they were caught in a trap.

The *St. Louis* returned to Europe. The Dutch agreed to give its passengers a home. A year later the Germans occupied the Netherlands. The Dutch were powerless. Most of the passengers on the *St. Louis* perished in Nazi death camps.

Extermination

Even before the war German Jews were rounded up and sent into forced labour camps. Once Hitler controlled Europe his terrible plan grew. From 1943 on special death camps were set up to kill people systematically.

At Auschwitz in Poland Jews were stripped of their clothes. Men, women, and children were herded into "showers." When the "showers" were turned on, they rained poison gas.

Once the gas was clear, the piles of bodies were shovelled out. Dentists examined them looking for gold fillings. Sometimes human hair was shaved off to stuff mattresses. Bodies were boiled to make soap.

Before the camps were liberated, six million Jews died in Nazi Europe. Six million other "enemies" of the German state — French, Dutch, Slavs, Poles, Gypsies, communists, homosexuals — also lost their lives. This mass butchery is known as the Holocaust.

Jews on the way to the gas chamber at Auschwitz.

What actions did the Nazis take against the Jews after 1933?
Why do you think Canada and other nations did so little to help the
Jews in Germany at that time?
Do you think there will ever be another Holocaust? Explain.

OCUS

1900 1910 1920 1930 1940 1950 1960 1970 1980 1990 2000

Who Bears the Guilt?

Many war criminals were hunted down and punished. The Allies set up a court at Nuremberg to try the Nazi leaders. Many less prominent people were never brought to trial.

What about clerks who filed identity cards? Chemical workers who made poison gas? Railway engineers who carried millions to their deaths? Ordinary citizens who watched their neighbours disappear? Were they guilty? Did they know what they were doing? Did they try to find out? What could they have done to stop it?

What about the nations who looked the other way before the war? What about Canadians who refused to give a helping hand before it was too late? Who bears the guilt?

The State of Israel

After the war many Jews who had survived the Holocaust wanted never to see Europe again. Some decided to go to Palestine, their ancient homeland. In 1948 they proclaimed the new state of Israel.

Arabs in the region bitterly protested. The resentment and conflict that arose continue to this day.

Jack Kuper, Child of the Holocaust

1932 — born Jankel Kuperman in Pulawy, Poland. Poland was a predominantly Roman Catholic country with a large Jewish minority.

1939-41 — after Nazi invasion of Poland, father escaped to Soviet Union. Sent home money to support family. Mother took 2 boys to her parents in Warsaw. Nazis confined Jews to one section of the city called the ghetto. Family escaped ghetto and lived by begging for food in the country. Grandfather was stopped by German soldiers and shot for being in a prohibited area and not wearing special Jewish badge. Mother and brother captured and taken to concentration camp where they died in the gas chamber. By this time, Jack had lost all contact with his father.

1941 — taken in by a peasant woman but had to leave when it became too dangerous to be caught sheltering Jews. Met an uncle only 4 years older than he. They survived together until uncle gave up hope and turned himself in. Jack, at age 9, was on his own. Using many false names and disguises, wandered through eastern Poland pretending to be a Roman Catholic orphan. Went to church, adopted local accent.

1945 — by end of war had lost all feeling of who he was. Felt praying to Jesus had saved him, so wanted to become a Roman Catholic yet wanted others to know his story. Found people would not accept him. Went to a priest hoping to be baptised. Priest advised him that he'd never be happy unless he found God through his own people. Taken into a Jewish orphanage. Here children would not accept him as

Jewish because he no longer spoke Yiddish or knew Jewish traditions. Joined a Zionist organization working to help Jewish refugees moving to Palestine. Began to have pride in his heritage and to understand that Jews were not second-class citizens. Left communist Poland for Germany. Met another uncle who took him to family in Belgium.

1947 — one of 1000 Jewish war orphans sponsored as immigrants by Canadian Jewish Congress. Delighted by real bed on train (he hadn't slept in one for years), stayed on till Toronto, though supposed to get off in Montreal. Had almost no schooling, so at age 15 was put in grade 1. In 6 months he was in grade 8. Went on to study art at Central Technical School.

1950s — worked for CBC as radio and TV actor and graphic designer. Wrote radio and TV plays.

1952 — located his father in Soviet Union.

1961 — produced Run! an award-winning short film still popular at film festivals, in schools and art galleries. Wrote *Child of the Holocaust,* about his wartime experiences.

1967 — Finally met his father at Expo 67 in Montreal. Father now lives in New York. Runs successful film company in Toronto. Is writing another book about the search for his father.

The Mushroom-Shaped Cloud

On 6 August 1945 a lone American bomber flew high over the Japanese city of Hiroshima. The plane dropped a single bomb, nicknamed "Little Boy." For the first time in history an atomic bomb was unleashed on the world. By the end of the day 173 000 people were dead or dying.

The bomb drifted over the city hanging from a small parachute. It exploded with a burning white flash "brighter than a thousand suns." Shock waves mowed down buildings. Fireballs burned through the streets. Pieces of the city tore through the air. Finally a huge mushroom-shaped cloud billowed over the city.

People who looked up at the sound of the explosion had their eyes melt from the heat of the blast. Skin turned black and dripped from bones. Those who died at once were lucky. Many more suffered slow painful deaths from radiation poisoning. Decades later, deformed babies were born to the survivors of Hiroshima.

The Americans asked the Japanese to surrender. There was no reply. Three days later the same horror was repeated at Nagasaki. 80 000 more people were cremated in a nuclear inferno. Japan surrendered unconditionally on 14 August 1945 — V-J Day.

Hiroshima, ten years later. The city decided to preserve this ruined building as a reminder of the bombing.

Why do you think the Americans decided to use the atomic bomb?
Do you think atomic bombs will ever be used again?
What was the chief aim of the United Nations?
What 2 superpowers emerged at the end of World War II?

The United Nations

Even before V-E Day the leaders of the world were looking for a way to maintain peace in the future. The old League of Nations had failed. They would learn from its mistakes and build a better, stronger, United Nations.

It was not going to be easy. The war had created new borders, and new hatreds. The "old" world powers — Britain, Germany, France, Japan — lay shattered and exhausted. Two new rival superpowers — the United States and the Soviet Union — had gained strength and influence.

World War II left a bitter, confused and divided world. The shadow of the atomic bomb and a new arms race lay across it. Could the United Nations keep the peace?

A model shows what remained of the city after the bomb.

In the Hiroshima museum, visitors read a technical description of the bomb and the explosion.

Halfway around the world, Ottawa celebrated V-J Day.

Questions and Activities

Test Yourself

Match the items in column A with the descriptions in column B.

A	B
1. Blitzkrieg	a) spy training centre near Oshawa
2. Little Boy	b) allied retreat from France
3. The Axis	c) city in Italy
4. The *St. Louis*	d) conscripted soldiers
5. Pearl Harbor	e) an atomic bomb
6. Camp X	f) Jewish refugee ship
7. Ortona	g) alliance led by Germany
8. Dunkirk	h) allied invasion of France
9. Zombies	i) lightning war
10. D-Day	j) American naval base in Hawaii

Who Am I?

Identify the following people from the clues.
1. I served as British prime minister during World War II. I promised the British nothing but "blood, toil, tears, and sweat." Who am I?
2. I am a scientist of Asian ancestry. My people suffered greatly in Canada during World War II. Who am I?
3. I ran a brilliant spy organization during World War II. In 1979 I was honoured by the government of Canada. Who am I?
4. I led Canada during World War II. I engineered a solution to the conscription crisis. Who am I?
5. I grew up in New Brunswick but moved to Britain. I was in charge of British aircraft production during the Battle of Britain. Who am I?

Ideas for Discussion

1. The conscription issue divided Canadians in two world wars. Arrange the classroom to look like the House of Commons. Have each student be the member of parliament for a different constituency in Canada. Be prepared to give a speech in favour of or against conscription in World War II. After the debate, hold a vote on the issue. If your class had been the House of Commons, would conscription have been introduced?
2. The decision to drop the atomic bomb on Japanese cities has often been criticized. Imagine you are an adviser to U.S. President Truman. Write a memo either supporting or attacking the plan to drop the A-bomb on Hiroshima and Nagasaki. Then hold a meeting of the president's "advisers" at which you should be prepared to defend your views.

3. Many Nazi supporters were tried for war crimes at Nuremberg after the war. However, Hitler had committed suicide and could not be brought to trial.
Imagine that Hitler had been captured alive. Organize a trial with judges and defence and prosecution lawyers. Select students to play the parts of witnesses, members of the jury, court reporters, guards, etc.

Do Some Research

1. Find out about one of the following and write a brief report:
   a) a famous Canadian soldier in World War II;
   b) a famous general of World War II;
   c) some new weapons invented during World War II;
   d) a Canadian winner of the Victoria Cross in World War II.
2. People's memories often tell historians a different story from the one recorded in books, papers, and reports. Interview someone who remembers World War II. Find out about his or her experiences at home in Canada and/or at the battlefronts of Europe, Africa, or the Pacific. Assemble a class booklet or tape of Memories of World War II.
3. Make a map of the world showing:
   a) the major Allied powers
   b) the major Axis powers
   c) ten major battle sites
4. With a small group of other students, prepare a folder on life on the Canadian homefront during World War II. Your folder might include:

a) posters	e) brief biographies
b) pictures	f) advertisements
c) songs	g) wartime regulations
d) slogans	h) ration cards

5. Find out what life was like in Hitler's concentration camps. Imagine you have been sent to one of these camps and write a secret diary about your experiences.
6. Find out more about one of the following war heroes. Write a "biocard" like the ones that appear in this book.

Buzz Beurling   Anne Frank   Winston Churchill

7. Design a wall chart comparing Canada's involvement in World War I and in World War II. You may wish to compare some of the following items:

a) length of the war (dates)
b) number of soldiers fighting
c) number of people killed
d) important battles
e) types of weapons
f) activities on the homefront

Add other ideas of your own to complete the chart.

8. Governments often ask artists to paint pictures of wartime scenes. What can be shown in a painting that might not appear in a photograph? Study the pictures on pages 20 and 21 of the Art Gallery. Go to the library and find out more about war artists. Report to the class, explaining which war artists you feel best convey the atmosphere of war and why.

Be Creative

1. Reporting the news as it happens is always an exciting job. During wartime it is also very dangerous. Reporters from all nations risked their lives to bring news of the battlefront to people back home. Imagine you are a Canadian war correspondent. Give an on-the-spot news report about one of the following:

a) the fall of Hong Kong
b) the Battle of Britain
c) the battle for Ortona
d) the Normandy beaches on D-Day
e) the liberation of the Netherlands

Make your report as authentic as possible. You could present it as a newspaper article, a radio report, or a commentary to a news film that will be shown in a movie theatre before the main feature.

A German soldier offers a light to a Canadian prisoner of war.

A wrecked and abandoned landing craft.

2. In a group of four or five students, prepare a brief play showing a scene from the life of some Japanese Canadians during the war. Present your play to the class and watch the plays of other groups. Discuss your reactions to the plays.

3. Make a model or draw a diagram of a ship or plane used in World War II. Write a brief paragraph on its role in the war.

4. Design posters to point out the horror of war and to promote world peace.

You Are There

The Dieppe raid was a stunning disaster for the Canadian troops that took part. Today the debate still rages over the real military worth of the operation. Your class has been appointed to conduct an investigation into the Dieppe raid.

Some of you are *investigators,* whose job is to prepare questions, analyze documents, interview witnesses, and report your conclusions. Others among you are *witnesses.* You may be called upon to testify on the raid in your role as:

a) citizens of Dieppe who saw the raid
b) German officers and soldiers
c) Canadian officers and soldiers who were captured
d) Canadian officers and soldiers who escaped
e) Canadian and British officers who planned the raid

Still others are *reporters.* Your job is to report on the proceedings on a day-by-day basis.

The pictures below, taken by German photographers, may be introduced as evidence.

Canadian prisoners of war are marched through the streets of Dieppe as citizens watch from the sidewalk.

Midcentury
ADVANCE ORGANIZER

1

In 1949, Newfoundland entered Confederation as the tenth province. Joey Smallwood spearheaded the movement for union with Canada. He became Newfoundland's first premier. The province has since progressed rapidly in many areas. Once solely dependent upon the fishing industry for its economy, Newfoundland developed the industries of mining and forestry. The province now faces the prospect of new wealth in the form of oil and deposits of natural gas.

2

A wave of prosperity swept Canada in the fifties. Western oil and natural gas reserves yielded new sources of power for Canadian industry. Pipelines for oil and gas were built. Large bodies of water were harnessed to generate electricity. Uranium deposits were found, promising future benefits from nuclear power. As new resources were discovered, new industries developed. The St. Lawrence Seaway was constructed to aid in the transport of materials.

This economic growth was largely due to foreign investment, much of it American. Such investment brought Canada a much-desired prosperity during the fifties and sixties. It unfortunately also led to future conflicts over the ownership and financial control of Canada's resources.

3

With the end of World War II, the future looked bright for Canada. Returning soldiers and their brides were ready to raise families in these peaceful and prosperous times. Over four million babies were born in Canada during the fifties. The educational system had to accommodate the unexpected youth explosion.

For the first time, teenagers became a driving force in Canadian society. Business began looking to the new teenage market. There arose a new "pop culture," one that often rebelled against society's traditional values. It found its greatest voice in a new form of popular music: rock 'n' roll.

4

The era of the post-war boom saw Mackenzie King's resignation as prime minister. His successor, Louis St. Laurent, was defeated by John Diefenbaker's Conservatives. Diefenbaker in turn was defeated by Lester Pearson's Liberals. Labour union leaders and members of the CCF party saw the need for a strong third voice, one that would uphold workers' rights. The two groups banded together and in 1961 formed the New Democratic Party. NDP ideas have found their way into important policies such as Medicare.

5

The rebellious streak of the fifties came into full bloom in the sixties. The youth culture was now accompanied by more concrete ideas. Social and political protest was typical of the times. The new patterns of lifestyle, music, and dress reflected a desire for tolerance and peace in the world. Much of the rebellion was focused on the hopelessness of the Vietnam War.

6

Canada celebrated its 100th year of Confederation on July 1, 1967. This was a year that Canadians gloried in their country. People from all over the world attended Expo '67, held in Montreal. The election the next year of the new prime minister, Pierre Trudeau, gave people hope for a bright future.

Adjusting to Peace

Once again Canadian soldiers, sailors, pilots, mechanics, nurses were returning home from war. Over a million men and women were coming out of uniform. Another million had worked in war-related industries. How would the Canadian economy cope with these people? Those who remembered the slump after World War I and the Depression shuddered at what might happen.

However, economic planners had learned from experience. The American government set out to help countries like the Soviet Union, Germany, and Japan that had suffered most from the war. If the factories in these countries could be reopened, if people could afford to buy clothes to wear and food to eat, international trade would increase. The whole world would benefit.

The experts were right. Economic recovery after World War II was spectacular. Canadians shared in the good fortune.

Wheat sales boomed. New resources of iron ore, oil, and uranium were developed. People went on a buying spree. Now they could get all the things that they had done without during the war. Washing machines, nylon stockings, automobiles were sold as fast as they poured out of the factories. At last there was enough meat and butter on the table to please everybody.

William Lyon Mackenzie King

Canada's prime minister, William Lyon Mackenzie King, must have been glad to see how his nation adjusted to peace.

King had been Laurier's minister of labour before World War I. He became leader of the Liberal Party after Laurier's death in 1919. He was prime minister through most of the boom period of the 1920s. When the people got tired of Bennett's Depression policies, they returned King to power in 1935. He remained in office through the war years until he retired in 1948. All told, he had been prime minister for nearly 22 years, the longest of any prime minister in the British Commonwealth.

King was a curious mixture of opposites. He never married and had few close friends. Outsiders regarded him as a practical, down-to-earth, and ruthless politician. Yet his diary reveals that this tough political

Future, past, and present prime ministers. Louis St. Laurent and Mackenzie King sit before a portrait of Laurier at the 1948 Liberal leadership convention.

Give 3 examples of the way Canada boomed after the war.
How did King's policies change during the period he was in power?
In what way did American influence in Canada grow after the war?
Do you think this influence was good or bad?

1900 1910 1920 1930 1940 1950 1960 1970 1980 1990 2000

realist wept for hours at the death of his pet dog. He also believed he received messages from the spirit of his dead mother.

King's policies changed with the times. In the 1920s he had believed that government should stay out of business and out of people's lives. The Depression taught him that government could not be that simple. In 1940 he introduced a system of unemployment

Mackenzie King with Pat.

insurance. During the war his government brought in rationing and measures to control business profits and to strengthen trade unions. At the end of the war he established family allowances. Canada was slowly changing from a "laissez-faire state" to a "welfare state."

American Influence

Some people claim King was far too willing to allow American influence into Canada. During World War II he made military and economic agreements with the United States. By combining their operations the two nations could contribute more to the war effort. After the war this association expanded further. American companies moved in to develop Canadian resources and invest in Canadian industry. The prosperity of the 1950s was largely based on American investment. When Mackenzie King handed the reins of power to Louis St. Laurent on 15 November 1948, he saw a rich country looking confidently to the future.

Clarence Decatur (C.D.) Howe
"American by birth, Canadian by choice"
"Minister of everything"

1886 — born in Waltham, Mass., U.S.A.
1907 — on graduating from Boston Tech, went to Dalhousie in Halifax to teach in new dept. of civil engineering.
1913 — moved to Fort William (Thunder Bay), Ont. to build grain elevators. "I've never seen one of these things in my life, but I'll take the job."
1913-1929 — built elevators from Prince Rupert, B.C. to Prescott, Que.
1930s — business collapsed with Depression and dustbowl. Decided to enter politics.
1935 — elected as Liberal. Made minister of transport.
1936 — re-organized harbour system, CNR, and set up CBC.
1937 — set up TCA, Canada's first national airline.
1940 — as minister of munitions and supply, harnessed government, industry, and entire work force to support war effort, allocating materials and workers where most needed to produce tanks, planes, ships. Encouraged experts to serve country for "a dollar a year." On trip to Britain, torpedoed by German U boat. Rescued from lifeboat after 8 hours on open sea in December.
1945 — Minister of reconstruction and supply and minister of trade and commerce.
1951 — also appointed minister of defence production during Korean War.
1954 — organized all-Canadian route for Trans-Canada Pipeline for natural gas from Alberta to central Canada.
1956 — in order to get pipeline construction started that season, arranged huge loan from government. Forced the legislation through parliament by using "closure."
1957 — defeated in election mostly over closure issue. Retired from politics, but stayed active in business.
1960 — died New Year's morning at home in Montreal.

Newfoundland Joins Canada, 1949

Canada cannot be considered complete without Newfoundland. It has the key to our front door.

John A. Macdonald

The island of Newfoundland thrusts out from the coast of Canada far into the Atlantic. For centuries islanders have felt closer to Britain than to any part of North America. In 1867 they refused to join Canada. They felt they had little in common with the mainlanders. They would remain a self-governing colony of Britain.

Newfoundlanders continued to fish for cod, to jig for squid, and to hunt seal. They developed the lumbering industry in the island's interior. They mined iron ore on Belle Isle and found other deposits of copper, lead, and zinc. The merchants of St. John's sold these goods mainly in Britain and the West Indies. In return they bought the manufactured items and the farm products the islanders could not make or grow.

Depression and Newfoundland

Independence meant isolation. When the Depression hit, Newfoundlanders had nothing to fall back on. The market for lumber and minerals disappeared. Other countries could not even afford to buy fish.

By 1934 one third of the workers were unemployed. The average family income was $150 a year. There was little health care and few schools. The government was in debt. It couldn't raise enough money even to pay interest. The dominion of Newfoundland was bankrupt.

The islanders turned to Britain for help. Britain decided the island should be governed by a "commission." The commission was made up of three Newfoundlanders and three non-Newfoundlanders. All the commissioners were appointed to their jobs. None were elected by the people.

A Strategic Position

During World War II, Newfoundland's isolation came to an end. British, American, and Canadian money and technology poured into the island. Its location between North America and Europe was vital to both the sea war

RCN corvettes at St. John's.

Flatrock, an "outport" village during the Depression.

Railway workers in St. John's study their new country, 1951.

What jobs did the people of Newfoundland depend on?
What happened in Newfoundland during the Depression?
Who led the campaign for Newfoundland to join Canada?
Why did Newfoundlanders decide to enter Confederation?

1900 1910 1920 1930 1940 1950 1960 1970 1980 1990 2000

and the air war. St. John's became a headquarters for ships on convoy duty. New modern airports sprang up at Goose Bay in Labrador and Gander on the island. Aircraft from the factories of North America refuelled there on the way to the battles of Europe. Newfoundlanders became used to seeing American and Canadian uniforms everywhere.

Referendum

After the war Britain felt it was time to return Newfoundland to a more democratic form of government. A national convention was elected to discuss the future. Should the island go back to "responsible government" and run its own affairs? Should it stay with the appointed commission? Some delegates brought up a third idea— confederation with Canada. A few urged union with the United States, but this option was not officially considered.

The people voted on the three main options in a referendum. The result was unclear. No one option received more than half the votes. Another referendum was held on the two more popular options — responsible government or confederation.

The campaigning was fierce. People who worked for the government thought they would lose some of their power if Newfoundland joined Canada. The merchants were afraid Canadians would move in on their markets. Fishery workers, loggers, and miners wanted more security. Joining Canada would give them benefits like unemployment insurance and old age pensions. A popular broadcaster named Joey Smallwood led the campaign for union with Canada.

This time the vote was for union with Canada. Newfoundland and Labrador entered Confederation as the tenth province on 31 March 1949. "The Last Great Step of Confederation" had been taken.

The Way the Vote Went:

	1st Referendum	2nd Referendum
Commission Government	14%	dropped from ballot
Responsible Government	45%	48%
Union with Canada	41%	52%

Joseph R. Smallwood (Joey)
"The only living Father of Confederation"

1900—born in Gambo, Bonavista Bay, Nfld., the oldest of 13 children. Did not speak until age 3, "but made up for it later."
1915—organized student strikes. Quit school. Worked as apprentice printer. Continued studies while working as reporter in St. John's, Halifax, Boston, New York.
1920s—organized unions and co-ops all over Newfoundland. Once walked 1100 km to urge workers to fight a pay cut.
1930s—starred on radio as Joe the Barrelman, talking about island people, events, stories.
1939-45—made fortune raising livestock to feed troops stationed in Newfoundland.
1948—campaigned vigorously in referendums for union with Canada, saying it would lead to more jobs and security.
1949—became province's 1st premier. "I love this job. I love it to death. I love every minute of it." Stayed close to people. Always answered own phone. With financial aid from federal government, built hospitals, schools, roads. In order to provide better services, moved people from "outports" to larger centres.
1967—after Expo 67 bought several national pavilions and moved them to Newfoundland to serve as community centres and theatres.
1971 — his Liberals defeated by Frank Moores' Conservatives. Some of his schemes had been costly failures. He was said to be out of touch with younger people.
1973 — published his autobiography *I Chose Canada*. Now spends time writing and travelling in his beloved province.

The Boom in Resources

On 13 February 1947, the Alberta sky was seared by a soaring column of orange flame. After drilling 133 dry wells and spending $23 million, Imperial Oil had struck black gold! Leduc Number 1 was the first major strike in a vast new oil field.

Soon other oil companies joined the search. More fields were discovered — Redwater, Pembina, and Joffre in Alberta, Steelman and Weyburn in Saskatchewan. Along with oil, the searchers found natural gas. Canada now had her own supplies of power for industry, fuel for transportation, heat for homes, schools, and business. By the early 1960s Canada had drilled over 20 000 oil and gas wells.

Energy and Minerals

Besides oil and gas, Canada was developing other energy sources. The waters of the St. Lawrence River, Labrador, Northern Quebec, Manitoba, and British Columbia were harnessed to provide electricity.

Canada also proved to be rich in another energy source. The atom bomb that exploded over Hiroshima brought great tragedy. It also focused attention on the possibilities of nuclear power. In northern Ontario and northern Saskatchewan were deposits of uranium, the new nuclear fuel.

Factories in the United States were producing more goods than ever before. War-torn Europe and Japan were rebuilding their industries. Everyone wanted Canadian minerals. They were prepared to spend money to find them.

Soon the vast mineral wealth of Canada was being tapped. Companies sent out prospectors to pinpoint mine sites. The forest was cleared almost overnight. Mines, plants, airstrips, roads, railways, homes, stores sprang up in the wilderness. The fifties was the era of the boomtown.

The day that Leduc No. 1 blew in, 13 February 1947.

The riches from natural resources spurred industry. Steel production doubled. Factories produced heavy equipment for use in mines, on farms, and in other factories. Goods were also made for the consumer. The country went crazy for automobiles. During the fifties Canadians bought nearly three and a half million new cars.

Boomtowns of the Fifties

Schefferville, Que. — iron ore.
Sept Iles, Que. — new port and railway bringing ore from Schefferville and Labrador.
Elliot Lake, Ont. — uranium.
Thompson, Man. — nickel.
Uranium City, Sask. — uranium.
Kitimat, B.C. — smelter for imported aluminum ore (bauxite) using nearby hydroelectric resources.

Prospectors at work. Will this be the site of a new boomtown?

Name 3 sources of energy that helped create the economic boom.
What regions of Canada did best from the boom? Why?
What regions gained little from the boom? Why? What problems
grew from the resource development of the 1950s?

1900 1910 1920 1930 1940 1950 1960 1970 1980 1990 2000

Below the Surface

Few considered the longterm results of this ride to riches. There were grave problems in the making.

The boom was not shared by all Canadians. Much of the Atlantic region was barely touched by the new wealth. The Prairies still relied on wheat farming. They were rich one year and poor the next because of rapidly changing world markets. Poverty was still a reality across Canada.

Central Canada did best from the growth in activity. The main industries and cities were located here. Many of the resource developments in other provinces were owned by corporations with headquarters in Toronto and Montreal. They rarely worked in the best interests of the local area. Profit was the motive, not people.

Even the boomtowns rarely maintained their

The final weld on the Trans-Canada Pipeline, Kapuskasing, Ont., 10 October 1958.

frenzied growth. Within ten years markets dried up; towns died. Ghost towns were often all that remained of the dreams of limitless prosperity.

The landscape was often treated with little respect. Developers simply tore the wealth from the earth. They left permanent scars behind them. They poured pollution into the rivers and blew it into the air.

Canadians did not pay for the exploration and development of their resources. The money came from outside the country, mainly from the United States. This seemed fine at the time. Foreign investment meant jobs. It also meant loss of ownership and control. In 1956 American firms controlled over half the manufacturing in Canada. Of the sixty largest firms in Canada, less than half were Canadian owned. It was a trend that was increasing rapidly.

The fabulous fifties brought prosperity to Canada. They also sowed the seeds for major problems in the future.

Pipelines

How were oil and gas to reach those who wanted to use them? Trucks and railway cars could carry them, but they would have to return empty. The answer was a "one-way" transport system — a pipeline. Soon pipelines were creeping across Canada.

The first pipeline east was for oil and went partly through the United States. When the Trans-Canada natural gas pipeline was built, the Liberal government wanted an all-Canadian route. This would cost more. The minister of trade and commerce, C. D. Howe, agreed to lend the pipeline company money to cover the extra cost. The Conservatives wanted to debate the loan in Parliament. Howe cut short the debate by using a parliamentary procedure called *closure*. Parliament, led by the Liberals, approved the loan.

The Conservatives said the company would never be able to pay back the money. The voters were worried too. They thought the Liberals had been too high handed. In the next election they chose the Conservatives under John Diefenbaker. As a matter of fact, the pipeline was such good business the government loan was paid back ahead of schedule.

To the Heart of a Continent

In 1535 Jacques Cartier sailed up the great St. Lawrence River. When he came to Hochelaga (Montreal) he found he could go no further. Upstream lay a turbulent stretch of white water that is now called the Lachine Rapids.

Four hundred years later North Americans still could not travel by ship up the St. Lawrence River through the Great Lakes to Fort William, Ontario and Duluth, Michigan, on Lake Superior. In 1941 Canada and the United States signed an agreement to build a canal deep enough to allow ocean ships to reach the Great Lakes. Ten years later, the Americans were still studying the project. Canada needed the new transportation route badly. The new mining towns of Quebec and Labrador needed to get their ore to the factories of Toronto, Hamilton, Detroit, and Chicago. The West needed to move its wheat to market. The growth of industry meant Ontario needed new power sources. Hydro-electric plants could be built at the same time as the canal or "seaway."

Canada decided to build the seaway alone. This spurred the United States to action. Talks started up again. In 1954 a final agreement was reached. Each country would pay to build the part of the seaway that was in its territory.

Building the Seaway

Canadian technology got to work. Five of the seven new locks were designed and built completely by

"Moving house" to make room for the seaway.

Give 3 reasons why Canada needed the St. Lawrence Seaway.
How did Canadians and Americans divide the work of building the seaway?
How did the seaway affect people in towns that were in its path?

Art Gallery page 28

Canadians. Giant rapids were blown to smithereens. Whole islands were demolished or created from scratch. Cross-river tunnels were carved out. Bridges were raised. When their towns and villages had to be flooded 6500 people were "relocated." Teams of historians and archeologists worked feverishly to remove relics and buildings before historic sites were submerged forever.

On 26 June 1959 Queen Elizabeth II and U.S. President Eisenhower officially opened the St. Lawrence Seaway. Merchant ships could now travel 3700 km into the industrial heart of North America. Grain ships could sail to Fort William and Port Arthur (now joined as the city of Thunder Bay) and meet the freight trains bringing wheat for world markets from the Prairies.

Work on the seaway continues to this day. The original 8.2 m depth is not enough for many modern ships. The seaway continues to adapt and modernize.

Louis St. Laurent (Uncle Louis)
"I know nothing of politics and never had anything to do with politicians."

1882—born in Compton, Que., son of a French father and Irish mother. Until he was 6, thought all children spoke French to one parent and English to the other.
1905—graduated from Laval University as lawyer. Unlike many lawyers was not interested in politics.
1914—by now married with family, saw World War I as European war, not important for Canada.
1919-39—represented both Quebec and federal governments in many cases before Supreme Court of Canada and British Privy Council.
1930—president of Canadian Bar Association.
1941—asked to join federal cabinet as leading Quebec figure to help persuade Quebeckers that conscription might be necessary. Agreed "as a patriotic duty and for the duration of the war."
1945—on Canadian delegation at San Francisco conference founding the United Nations.
1946—planned to retire but persuaded not to.
1948—chosen as new leader of Liberal party to succeed Mackenzie King as prime minister.
1949, 1953—won huge election victories. Led country in period of tremendous growth and change. Made Supreme Court final court of appeal instead of British Privy Council. Tried to bring power to change constitution to Canada but could not get provinces to agree. Started seaway and Trans-Canada Highway.
1957—narrowly defeated by Diefenbaker's Conservatives. Aged 74, retired from politics and returned to law.
1973—died in Quebec City. For many Canadians a symbol of co-operation and national unity.

The St. Lawrence Seaway

La voie maritime du Saint-Laurent

LOCKS	ÉCLUSES
① St. Lambert	① St-Lambert
② Côte Ste. Catherine	② Côte Ste-Catherine
③ Lower Beauharnois	③ Beauharnois (aval)
④ Upper Beauharnois	④ Beauharnois (amont)
⑤ Snell	⑤ Snell
⑥ Eisenhower	⑥ Eisenhower
⑦ Iroquois	⑦ Iroquois
⑧ Welland Section :8 locks and Canal	⑧ Section Welland: 8 écluses et canal
⑨ Sault Ste. Marie	⑨ Sault Ste-Marie

locking procedures

All locks on the St. Lawrence Seaway are filled or emptied by gravity. To raise a vessel, for example, the upstream valves are opened and the water simply flows into the chamber through openings at the bottom of the walls. The following diagram illustrates the procedure:

The diagram portrays the following steps:

1: From the lower level the ship sails through the open gates into the lock and is secured to bollards near the side of the walls. The gates are closed.
2: The valves are opened and water is allowed to flow in, lifting the ship.
3: When the vessel reaches the higher level the upper gates are opened and the ship sails out.

To lower a vessel the above steps are reversed. It takes less than ten minutes to raise or lower the water level.

The Baby Boom

Canada's population grew more quickly in the 15 years after World War II than at any other time. By 1961 there were 50% more Canadians than there had been at the end of the war.

Four Million Babies

After the uncertainty of war, young Canadians were settling down. Many young men had married overseas. They brought their "war brides" home to Canada.

Other men and women found sweethearts at home. All were ready to raise families. The future looked good. They expected to have at least three or four children.

Canada became a youth-centred society. Companies making toys, child-care products, and bicycles did well. Provincial governments struggled to keep up with the mushrooming school population. They built new schools and tried frantically to find the teachers to work in them. Boards of education recruited teachers in Britain and even Australia. They never seemed to catch up. The next year still more children were ready to meet the new teachers in the overcrowded classrooms.

The face of Canada's cities changed. People wanted to live near their work, but they wanted their children to grow up in a healthy environment. They moved to the suburbs. Builders couldn't keep up with the demand for houses. Shopping malls, cars, and expressways became part of the Canadian way of life.

Building, equipping, and maintaining schools were all big business in the fifties. Above, a new cafeteria offers school lunches at reasonable prices. Below, an early "portable" classroom.

Shopping malls were designed to serve the new suburban lifestyle. Instead of going downtown to shop at a number of stores along the main street, the homemaker with several small children could use the mall for one-stop shopping convenience.

What was the baby boom? How did it affect Canada?
What new groups of immigrants came to Canada during the 1950s?
Imagine you are a refugee and write an article on the reasons you
left your homeland and your first impression of Canada.

1900 1910 1920 1930 1940 1950 1960 1970 1980 1990 2000

Hungarian refugees in Vienna, Austria, wait to register for
camps that will provide food and shelter until they are accepted
as immigrants to a new country.

Immigration

In this post-war period more immigrants came to
Canada than at any time since the turn of the century.
Many were refugees from Eastern European countries
like Poland, Yugoslavia, and Latvia. Now that their
homelands were ruled by communists they felt they
could no longer live there. They brought to Canada a
strong belief in democracy and a love of their own
traditions.

People from all over Europe felt there was more
opportunity in Canada. The new mines and factories
needed workers. Immigrants came by the thousands.
Canada began to lose its British accent. By 1951, only
47% of Canadians had their roots in Britain. The
multicultural society had arrived.

The Hungarian Revolution

In 1956 Hungarians revolted against their communist
government. Within days help for the government came from
the Soviet Union. Soon Soviet tanks were rolling through the
streets of Budapest. Before the government regained control,
thousands of people had poured across the border into Austria.

Canada offered to help. Immigration requirements were
relaxed. 36 000 Hungarians were airlifted to Canada. They
arrived with little more than the clothes on their backs and
Canadians took them into their homes. They found them jobs.
They gave them clothes and furniture. They taught them
English or French. The refugees repaid their hosts well. They
became hard-working and loyal citizens of their new country.

Czechoslovakia, Uganda, Vietnam

Canada has taken in large groups of refugees on three more
occasions since World War II.

In 1968 the Soviet Union stepped in to prevent liberal
government policies in Czechoslovakia. Many people fled the
country and 10 000 of them came to Canada.

In 1973 President Idi Amin of Uganda stripped the Asians in
his country of their property and told them to leave. Canada
took in 5000.

In 1975 Vietnam was united under a communist government.
Many people in the south, especially business people and former
government workers, were persecuted. They started to leave the
country in small boats. There is evidence that the government
organized their departure in return for huge sums of money. By
the end of 1980 Canada had taken in 60 000 "boat people."

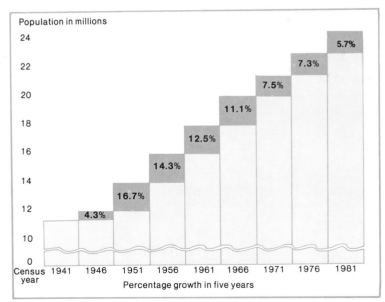

Population growth in Canada, 1941-1981

The Fabulous Fifties

Confidence and fear. Life in the fifties revolved between these two poles. The confidence was based on the new prosperity. The fear came from the shadow of the Cold War.

Even though World War II was long past, the fifties were still years of fear. The fear of nazism had been replaced by the fear of communism. The development of the hydrogen bomb made nuclear war an ever-present possibility. International politics were tense. Yet inside Canada things seemed better than they had ever been.

The Confident Years

In economic terms things looked secure. People couldn't live as if an H-bomb was going to fall tomorrow. They enjoyed life and the new technological wonders of prosperity.

Around 1952 a new article of furniture began to appear in Canadian living rooms. The baby boom generation grew up glued to the television screen. Youngsters rushed home from school for Howdy Doody. Their older brothers and sisters watched I Love Lucy. The entire family gathered round the set to see the latest entertainers on the Ed Sullivan Show. And at last sports fans could *see* the game described by Foster Hewitt on Hockey Night in Canada.

17-inch Table Model
060-G-660. Price, delivered 189.50

21-inch Table Model
060-G-662. Price, delivered 289.50

21-inch Console Model
060-G-664. Price, delivered ... 309.50

THE EATON TELEVISION WARRANTY

Every VIKING Television Set carries a full year warranty on the picture tube; 90-day warranty on all other tubes and parts. While we are convinced that VIKING Television Receivers will perform as well or better than other nationally advertised makes, we suggest you recognize the distance limitations on TV reception. Only if you live well within a 100-mile radius of a powerful TV station, or if an immediate neighbour is receiving satisfactory programs, should you order a television set. If in doubt, please write more specific details regarding your area to EATON'S Mail Order, Dept.

CBC camera operators prepare for the first football game on TV, fall 1952.

Advertisers used special lenses to make cars look longer than they really were, because longer, lower, and wider cars were what people were expected to want. With gas at less than 10¢ a litre, who cared about fuel economy?

What new item or change in the 1950s do you think has most affected Canadian life?

Describe a day in the life of a teenager in the fifties. Try to include as many aspects of "fifties lifestyle" as possible.

NEW

Shopping malls
Sunday sports
Expressways
Sputnik
Stereophonic sound
Queen Elizabeth II
Television
The Stratford Festival
Polio vaccine
Computers
Transistor radios
Jet travel

Teenagers at a rock 'n roll concert.

The Teenager

A new species of person, commonly known as a teenager, appeared in the fifties. In earlier times a child had gone straight from school to the responsibilities of adulthood. The new prosperity meant parents could afford to let their kids finish high school and even go on to college or university. This new group of students were certainly not children. They were not part of the adult world. This did not worry them. With 1 300 000 other teenagers in the country by the end of the decade, they created their own culture.

This cohesive and energetic group soon made its presence felt. Teenage fads in boys' hairstyles ranged from crew-cuts (short and bristly) to duck-tails (long and greasy). Girls wore bobby sox, sweater sets, and ruby red lipstick. Fitting in with the crowd was all important. A teenager's greatest fear was to be thought "an oddball."

Teenagers danced to a new form of music. Despite the agonized complaints of parents and church ministers, rock 'n roll was here to stay. Songs with meaningful lyrics like Shoop de doo and Da doo ron ron blared from the new transistor radios. Each week teenagers waited eagerly to hear which of their idols had tunes in the top ten — Elvis Presley, Connie Francis, or Buddy Holly? Perhaps a Canadian star like Paul Anka or Juliette, or a Canadian group like the Crewcuts made the list.

The youthful eruption of energy that is the teenager remains with us today. Being a teenager is a stage of life all Canadians pass through. However adults, then as now, did not always understand the phenomenon. The "generation gap" became a matter of concern.

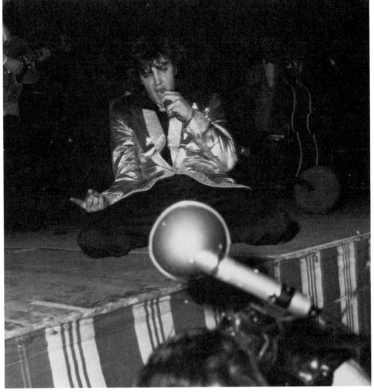

Elvis Presley, Ottawa, 1957.

Side Effects

The fifties brought prosperity and excitement. But rapid change is difficult for society. Some families could not adjust. The divorce rate began to creep up. Juvenile delinquency became a problem in the large cities. The move to the suburbs increased reliance on the automobile. Traffic jams, expressways, and gasoline pollution became part of daily life.

The fifties were years of growth and change. Cities, fashions, lifestyles, and values were transformed. Canadians were sure they were living in the best society in the world. After the long years of depression and world war, the fifties were indeed fabulous.

The Man from Prince Albert

John Diefenbaker scores a point off the Liberal government, 1948.

The Liberals had been in power so long they seemed to regard it as their right to govern the country. Many people felt they were becoming arrogant. They acted as if they knew best and didn't have to listen to anyone. When they wanted to make a loan for the Trans-Canada Pipeline, they used closure to cut off debate in parliament. In 1956 some Canadians felt the government betrayed Britain and France in the way foreign affairs minister Lester Pearson handled the crisis over control of the Suez Canal.

John Diefenbaker

In 1956 the Conservatives chose a new leader. The fiery, colourful John Diefenbaker from the prairies brought new life to the party. His skillful attacks on Liberal policies bore fruit. The voters saw him as a man who cared about the country and the "little people."

In the election campaign of 1957, Diefenbaker hit hard at "Liberal arrogance." He said they weren't achieving anything for the country. He had a "northern vision" for Canada. "Roads to resources" would open up the northland to development and settlement.

Minority Government

Diefenbaker and the Conservatives won more seats than any other party in the election of 1957. However, together the opposition parties — Liberals, CCF, Social Credit — had more seats than the Conservatives. This meant they could block any measure the Conservatives wanted passed. Diefenbaker declared he could not work this way. Early in 1958 he called another election.

Majority Government

Diefenbaker seemed to have hypnotized the nation. The result was a Tory landslide. The Conservatives won 208 seats, leaving only 57 for the other parties.

Diefenbaker worked hard to help all Canadians feel at home in their country. He invited Ellen Fairclough to be the first woman in the Federal Cabinet. He appointed James Gladstone as the first native Indian in the Senate. He chose Georges Vanier to be the first French Canadian Governor General.

Perhaps Diefenbaker's greatest joy was the passage of his Bill of Rights. This law guarantees all Canadians certain basic rights such as freedom of religion, freedom of speech, equality before the law, regardless of race, colour, religion, or sex.

Give 3 reasons why voters chose the Conservatives over the
Liberals in the election of 1957.
How did Diefenbaker try to protect the rights of all Canadians?
Why was this a difficult time to be in power?

The Arrow on a test flight over Niagara Falls, 1958.

Diefenbaker was proud of his German and British background. He wanted to promote the multicultural nature of Canada without weakening her British heritage. He worried about the growing Americanization of Canadian economic and cultural life. His policies certainly helped many Canadians appreciate themselves and their country. But despite his good intentions, the politician from the prairies never fully understood Quebeckers and their view of Canada.

Disappointments

Diefenbaker is remembered for his efforts in the field of human rights. At the time, the disappointments in other areas seemed more important. He had been a brilliant opposition leader, but he and the Conservatives had little experience at governing. They made mistakes.

This was a difficult time to be in power. The great economic boom of the fifties was slowing down. At one point the government had

to devalue the Canadian dollar. "The Diefendollar" people called it, a blow to Canadian pride.

Perhaps the turning point in Diefenbaker's political career came in 1959. He decided to cancel the Arrow, a Canadian-built supersonic jet fighter. Many people never forgave him.

Minority Government Again

In the election of 1962 the Conservatives lost 92 seats. The voters' confidence in Diefenbaker's stirring speeches had been shaken. He was still prime minister, but once again he headed a minority government.

The Fall of the Arrow

Canadian aircraft manufacturers had become world experts during the war. In the 1950s the A.V. Roe Company was developing a new jet fighter, the Arrow. Engineers and air force officials said it was at least 20 years ahead of its time. Just as the first prototypes rolled out of the Malton factory and took to the air, Diefenbaker cancelled the project. He said Canada should buy American Bomarc missiles instead.

Diefenbaker was surprised at the reaction to this decision. People were furious. They said he had dealt a crippling blow to the Canadian aircraft industry. Overnight 15 000 people lost their jobs. Canadian aircraft experts became part of the "brain drain," leaving the country to find work. Worse, the American missiles needed nuclear warheads. Canadians weren't sure they wanted to be a nuclear power.

Perhaps as a result of the public outcry, Diefenbaker was never able to make up his mind to accept nuclear warheads for the Bomarcs. No Arrow. No nuclear warheads. Diefenbaker had great trouble explaining Canadian defence policy. Even his cabinet ministers lost confidence in him. This lack of decision helped lead to his defeat in parliament in 1963.

In 1967 the Conservatives chose a new leader, Robert Stanfield. Though he was bitter about the way his party had treated him, Diefenbaker continued to represent Prince Albert in his beloved House of Commons His wit and energy kept him in the public eye. Reporters knew that if they wanted a pithy comment on Liberal government policy, they could always get one from John Diefenbaker.

He lived to see his party regain power under Joe Clark in 1979. Later that year, shortly before his 85th birthday, "Dief the Chief" died as he had wanted — "a politician with his boots on."

The Quiet Diplomat

In 1957 the Liberals lost their first federal election in 22 years. Their leader, Louis St. Laurent, decided it was time he resigned.

Lester Pearson had been St. Laurent's minister of foreign affairs. He had just been awarded the Nobel Peace Prize for his role in the Suez crisis of 1956. He had suggested the United Nations send a peace-keeping force to the area. By hard work, he got all the countries involved to agree. Not surprisingly, at the leadership convention soon after, the Liberals chose Pearson.

However, the Nobel Peace Prize was not enough to win the next federal election for Pearson and the Liberals. In 1958 the Conservatives racked up the biggest parliamentary majority in Canadian history. The voters were impressed by Diefenbaker. They thought of Pearson as a diplomat, not as a politician. Pearson did not seem really comfortable in parliament. He lacked Diefenbaker's dramatic flair. He seemed more at home watching a baseball game or playing tennis than making angry speeches in the House of Commons.

In 1962 another international crisis, this time over Soviet missile bases in Cuba, gave Pearson and the Liberals the chance they needed. Diefenbaker had refused to arm Bomarc missiles in Canada and at Canadian NATO bases in Europe with nuclear warheads. Without them, the Bomarcs were almost useless. In the light of the crisis, Canada's allies and members of Diefenbaker's own cabinet pressed the prime minister to accept the warheads. When he still would not move, three cabinet ministers resigned. Pearson made a speech in parliament. He said. "We must honour our commitments." We had taken the missiles, so we had to take the warheads. This made sense to many Canadians.

Parliament had lost confidence in Diefenbaker. Early in 1963 his government was defeated in the House of Commons. He was forced to hold another election. The result was another minority government. But this time the Liberals under Pearson would try to run the country.

Walking a Tightrope

Pearson never had a clear majority in the House of Commons. This meant he had to exercise all his diplomatic skills to stay in power. In order to keep the support of the New Democratic Party (the new name for the CCF) he brought in policies they would approve. All the time the Conservatives kept sniping at Liberal policies and unearthing scandals to embarrass the government.

Foreign Affairs Minister Lester Pearson is interviewed by CBC reporter René Lévesque outside the Canadian Embassy in Moscow, 1955.

Why was Lester Pearson awarded the Nobel Peace Prize in 1957?
What 2 problems continued to grow during this period?
Do you like the Canadian flag? Design an alternate national flag for
Canada.

Diefenbaker had urged Canadians to appreciate their country's unique heritage. The Pearson government took this a step further. On 15 February 1965, Canada's official flag was raised over the Peace Tower for the first time. The Canadian army, navy and air force were unified as the Canadian Armed Forces. A system of federal-provincial conferences was set up. Pearson hoped these conferences would help the federal and provincial governments co-operate to provide the best programs and services for Canadians.

Shadows for the Future

The relationship of French and English Canadians became a matter of concern in this period. Pearson set up a Royal Commission on Bilingualism and Biculturalism. The "Bi and Bi Commission" warned Canadians that the French had good reasons to complain about their position in Canada and the way other Canadians treated them. Unfortunately, Canadians largely ignored the findings of the Commission. The government did agree that the civil service should be bilingual. Then it could serve all Canadians equally, and give all a chance at the top jobs.

Under Pearson, American control of the economy grew even greater. Finance Minister Walter Gordon tried hard to reverse this trend. However, he warned too loudly of the dangers of American domination, and became very unpopular. Canadians did not want to be told that their comfortable way of life was based on American interests.

Pearson's last full year as Prime Minister was 1967. Beneath the excitement and joy of Centennial celebrations lay problems his government had not been able to beat. The next year Pearson handed over the reins of power to a very different leader of the Liberal party. His name was Pierre Elliott Trudeau.

For 98 years Canadians discussed the idea of a national flag. Not until 1965, two years before the Centennial celebrations, did Canada acquire a flag of her own. Before then Canada had "borrowed" two British flags. The Union Jack was used at home. The Red Ensign was used to represent Canada at international conferences, to identify Canadian embassies, for Canadian athletes to carry at the Olympic Games.

Many Canadians, especially those of British origin, were quite happy with this compromise. They liked the emphasis it placed on ties with Britain and the Commonwealth. Those who had come from other parts of the world did not feel the same way. And many French Canadians resented it because it was a reminder of the British conquest of New France in 1759.

The flags Canada was using divided Canadians more than uniting them. Pearson wanted a symbol all Canadians could identify with. In 1964 he announced Parliament would choose an official flag.

In the election of 1891, John A. Macdonald's Conservatives used this poster to appeal to loyalties to Britain.

A committee studied over 2000 designs submitted from across the country. Slowly the choice was narrowed down and modified to the single red maple leaf we know today. However, the debate in parliament was long and furious. It took 33 days and 252 speeches before the flag was approved.

The bitterness of the flag debate led people to expect that the new flag would be rejected by many. On the contrary, it met almost universal acceptance. It became more than a flag. It appeared on T-shirts, knapsacks, coffee mugs, and bumper stickers. Canadians today have trouble remembering what all the fuss was about in 1964.

The New Party

Canada has two major political parties, the Liberals and the Conservatives. Third parties have found it hard to survive in this country, especially in federal politics.

After World War II the CCF had trouble attracting voters. The Liberals under Mackenzie King had "stolen" many CCF ideas such as old age pensions and unemployment insurance. Many Canadians thought of the CCF as a party of the past. It had sprung from the bleak despair of the Depression that few wanted to remember. CCF slogans warning of the evils of capitalism seemed out of place in the booming fifties. In fact, against the background of the Cold War, they seemed dangerously radical. Some business people and journalists attacked the CCF as being "commie."

The party was almost wiped out of federal politics in the great Diefenbaker landslide election of 1958. CCF supporters felt it was time for a new vehicle for their hopes.

The Labour Movement

At the same time, Canadian labour unions were becoming more involved in politics. Traditionally, since the disastrous Winnipeg General Strike, unions had kept out of political affairs. This attitude was changing.

Business was booming. Giant corporations donated money to the Liberal and Conservative parties. They expected these parties to reflect the interests of big business.

As business grew, so did labour. The two clashed in long and bitter strikes. Government leaders tended to be on the side of business. Labour unions often found themselves with few allies in government. More and more labour leaders were feeling the need for political power. In 1956 the unions formed the Canadian Labour Congress. The CLC was an "umbrella" organization that would help them work together.

Union leaders were still looking for a political party to represent their views and interests. Two years later representatives of the CCF and the CLC agreed to start a "New Party," which would revive the CCF and provide workers with a political voice.

The idea of a New Party caught fire. New Party clubs held conferences across the country. In 1960 a New Party candidate was elected to parliament — even though the party did not yet officially exist.

The Birth of the NDP

In 1961 the largest political convention in Canadian history met in Ottawa. The delegates gave the New Party its official name, the New Democratic Party. The NDP was an alliance of labour leaders, farmers, intellectuals, and former CCFers. They elected as their leader a tough

Mayor Charlotte Whitton welcomes the delegates.

Why did the CCF lose support after World War II?
What two groups came together to form a "New Party"?
What is medicare? Do you think it has been successful in fulfilling
its aims?

1900 1910 1920 1930 1940 1950 1960 1970 1980 1990 2000
▲

witty orator, Tommy Douglas, the premier of Saskatchewan. The country now had a clear choice from the increasingly similar Liberals and Conservatives. When the delegates left for their homes across the country, they were sure that Canadian politics had been changed forever.

In a sense, they were right. The NDP found greater acceptance than the CCF. Since 1961 the NDP has won provincial elections in Saskatchewan, Manitoba, and British Columbia. The party has shown increasing strength in Ontario.

However, in federal politics the NDP has remained a distant third. In western Canada the NDP is the major alternative to the Progressive Conservatives at the federal level. It has found it difficult to win seats in the Atlantic provinces and to maintain its level of support in Ontario. In Quebec the party is almost non-existent.

Journalists and other politicians no longer dismiss the NDP as commies and pinkos. The Liberals have often taken NDP policies and made them their own. This has been especially true in the areas of social welfare and control of the economy, particularly of natural resources.

In the 1980 federal election the party gained the support of over 2 million voters and won 32 seats. Under dedicated principled leaders like Tommy Douglas, David Lewis, and Ed Broadbent, the NDP has won the respect of voters, politicians, and the press. The "New Party" has come a long way.

Medicare

Perhaps the greatest contribution the NDP has made to Canadian society is universal free medical care. "Medicare" was first introduced by the CCF-NDP to Saskatchewan in 1962.

Doctors in the province were violently opposed to the plan. It restricted the amount doctors could charge for their services. Medical fees would be paid by the government not the patient. The doctors claimed this would destroy the "doctor-patient relationship." The government, under Premier Tommy Douglas maintained that good medical care was a right that belonged to everyone, not just those who could afford to pay.

The doctors fought by going on strike. The government issued an international appeal. Doctors who believed in the idea of medicare came from other countries, especially Britain. They gave free medical care to the people of Saskatchewan until the issue was settled.

Eventually the striking doctors accepted the program. It soon became clear that medicare did not destroy the doctor-patient relationship. Nor did it greatly affect doctors' incomes.

The Liberals in Ottawa watched the Saskatchewan experiment with interest. The government of Lester Pearson soon offered all the provinces medicare on a "shared cost" basis. Today all provinces have some sort of medicare program. Medicare does not always work smoothly, but residents in Canada have access to medical care regardless of the size of their pay cheque.

T.C. (Tommy) Douglas
"Tommy doesn't have to kiss babies. Babies kiss him."
1904 — born in Falkirk, Scotland, father an ironworker.
1910 — family migrated to Winnipeg. Almost had leg amputated because family could not afford proper medical care. As an experiment a doctor decided to try to save it. The fact that only blind luck had saved leg later led him to support medicare.
1919 — during Winnipeg Strike sided with workers.
1922 — lightweight boxing champion of Manitoba.
1930 — became Baptist minister at Weyburn, Sask.
1933 — helped start CCF.
1935 — elected to House of Commons for CCF.
1944-61 — led CCF government of Saskatchewan, first socialist government in North America. Introduced government hospital plan, air ambulance system, and medicare.
1961 — chosen as 1st leader of federal NDP.
1962 — defeated in federal election by opponents of medicare. Ran again in B.C. by-election and elected.
1970 — refused to approve War Measures Act during Quebec October Crisis.
1971 — resigned as leader but continued as MP to 1979.

The Swinging Sixties

Changing the world was almost a way of life during the sixties. The decade was one of rebellion, excitement, and creativity. People, especially young people, seemed to question everything. They "organized." Groups were ready to do battle for the causes they believed in.

Social change was never more obvious than in the world of fashion. A fashion fever swept the world. Extremes were the order of the day. The miniskirt invaded the school, the factory, and the office. Only the most daring women, however, sported the topless bathing suit. Men replaced white shirts with bright colours and patterns. Narrow ties gave way to flamboyant wide ones. At the same time appearances lost their importance. What one looked like mattered less than what one was.

Miniskirts attract no attention in this Winnipeg lunchtime crowd.

Human relationships were altered dramatically when the birth control pill was introduced in 1960. Canadian attitudes to personal morality and sexuality changed. The idea of trial marriages became less shocking than it had been in the conservative past.

Canadian family life showed signs of cracking under the pressure of unrelenting change. Divorce became more common. The "generation gap" that had appeared in the fifties widened to reveal the divisions that existed in many families.

The sixties heralded a search for identity. People looked to religious cults, psychology and even drugs in order to discover "reality." Young people in particular turned to "grass" and "acid" in their search for understanding in a confusing and changing world. The problem of drug abuse is a terrible legacy of the "swinging sixties."

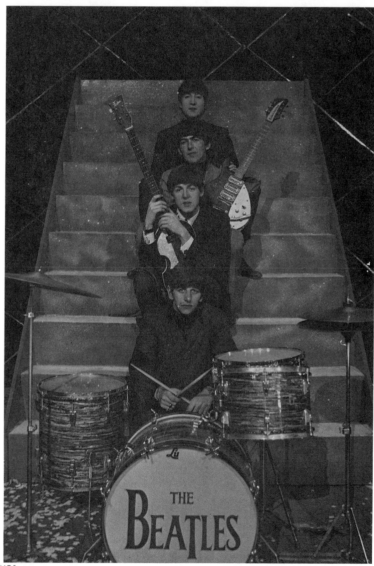
"You say you want a revolution," but "All you need is love!"

Name some changes that took place in Canadian society during the 1960s. In your opinion what was the most important event or change of the decade?
Why do you suppose the 1960s were termed "the swinging sixties"?

Peace and Love?

Peace and love were the watchwords of the decade. Yet violence was evident everywhere. For many people it came to a head in the brutal Vietnam War. This revealed that the United States could be ruthless in pursuing its goals. Young Americans were drafted into the armed forces. As the sixties became the seventies thousands of "draft dodgers" burned their draft cards and fled to Canada to avoid fighting in a war they could not believe in.

The fifties had been a time where everyone had known what was right and what was wrong. The turmoil of the sixties changed all that. The world would never be as self-satisfied and sure of itself again. Yet the decade ended on an optimistic note. As Canadians watched in amazement, an American astronaut set foot on the surface of the moon. His words matched the decade: "One small step for man; one giant step for mankind."

Movements of the Sixties

Canada's native people fought back in the face of racism and neglect. Indian and Métis leaders like Harold Cardinal, Howard Adams, and Kahn Tinehta Horn called attention to the plight of their people. They demanded justice and equality from Canadian society.

Women became aware of their inferior role in Canadian society. The women's liberation movement burst out into the open. Conservative Canadian men had been quite comfortable with the idea that women were there to make their beds, cook their meals, and look after their children. Now they reeled from shock as women questioned this concept.

Women protested and marched for changes in abortion laws, divorce laws, and employment practices. More and more women entered the work force. Some needed the pay cheque. Some were eager for a career and identity of their own.

The province of Quebec emerged from long isolation. Quebeckers protested the place their province held in Confederation. A group of extremists, the Front de Libération du Québec (FLQ), rocked Canada with repeated bombings and robberies. More peaceful Quebeckers who wanted Quebec to separate from Canada formed the Parti Québécois.

Canadian students were no longer willing to accept the ideas of their parents and teachers without question. They organized strikes and sit-ins and refused to write exams. Sometimes these activities led to riots and violence. Students campaigned for everything from an end to war and poverty, to an end to marks and fees.

Demonstrators protest the war in Vietnam and Canada's role in selling arms for U.S. troops fighting there.

Canada's 100th Birthday

1867 | 1967

 There had been no plan to select a popular Centennial song. But Bobby Gimby's CA-NA-DA was so bright and sparkly it was quickly adopted.
Judy LaMarsh, secretary of State

On 1 July 1867 four provinces had come together to form the Dominion of Canada. The new nation's motto was "From sea to sea." Six other provinces joined the confederation until the motto became a reality. Territories to the north were added, and the nation was bounded by a third sea, the Arctic Ocean. In area, Canada was the second largest country in the world. In 1967 Canadians set out to celebrate their country's 100th birthday. All across the land, in every village, town, and city, they planned how they would mark Centennial year. They held parades, dances, banquets, and carnivals. They built libraries, schools, concert halls, and stadiums. That year Canadians gloried in being Canadian.

Expo 67

Canada invited the entire world to help celebrate! The city of Montreal was host to a world fair, or exposition. Man and His World was the theme of the show. It soon became known to Canadians as "Expo 67."

 For one beautiful and unforgettable summer, Expo took us into the future that can be ours.
Robert Fulford

Montreal was chosen for its charm, vibrancy, and international flavour. It was the largest city in Canada and the largest French-speaking city in the world after Paris. Montrealers, led by Mayor Jean Drapeau, set out to make Expo the biggest and best party ever.

Bowsman, Manitoba, held a privy parade, with balloons.

What sort of things did Canadians do to celebrate the first hundred years of Confederation?
Do you think Man and His World was a good theme for Expo 67?
Will Canada still be here to celebrate its 200th birthday?

Expo was held on three islands in the St. Lawrence River. One of the islands was totally man made! Early in 1967 futuristic domes, and towers began to rise. They were carefully planned to blend with each other, the newly landscaped parkland, and the waters of the river. And these were only the shells that held sights, sounds, and ideas the world had never seen before.

A world fair is an advertising display. Each country wants to show itself at its best. The last world fair had been held in 1956 in Brussels, Belgium. Since then there had been great progress in such fields as film, architecture, and science. These developments had grown behind the walls of studios and laboratories. Many were on show at Expo 67 for the first time.

People walked through the glorious array of national pavilions. They saw technology put to work in exciting ways they had not dreamed possible. They listened to the babble of strange languages and felt that Man was truly enjoying the beauty and riches of his World. Canadians and their guests learned new ways of seeing, thinking, and living.

After we have all seen Expo, how can we ever again be content with the cities in which we live?
Ron Haggart

A Good Year

Centennial year came at a happy time for Canada. Most Canadians could not remember the hopelessness of the Depression. Many could not remember the shock of World War II, which had ended 22 years before. Even the Cold War, when people lived in fear that some American or Soviet general would "push the button" and start a nuclear war, was fading from people's minds. Canadians lived in peaceful and prosperous times. They forgot their own differences within the country. They did not worry about gloomy economic forecasts. They simply enjoyed their pride in Canada and her place in the world.

Bells pealed from coast to coast. People danced in the streets. Ships in our harbours blew their horns. Aircraft showered our towns with thousands of tiny flags, and the flares the air force dropped over Trenton, Ontario, were so brilliant you could see them 50 miles away. Soldiers marched, 100 gun salutes boomed. Alberta's birthday cake for Canada weighed 1600 pounds. People on foot, on horses, in canoes, and even in wheelchairs set out on zany journeys to prove their love of country. In Vancouver 100 girls dressed as candles to form a living birthday cake. In a Halifax park Bluenosers downed 20 000 cups of clam chowder. In Saskatchewan every July 1 baby got a silver spoon.
Harry Bruce

Questions and Activities

Who am I?

1. I led Newfoundland into Confederation with Canada. I became known as "the only living Father of Confederation." Who am I?
2. As prime minister, I gave Canadians their first Bill of Rights. My political supporters knew me as "the Chief." Who am I?
3. I was called "the king of rock 'n roll." Teenagers greeted me with screams of delight whenever I appeared. Who am I?
4. I set up the CBC and TCA (now Air Canada). I had so many jobs in government I was nicknamed "Minister of Everything." Who am I?
5. I won the Nobel Peace Prize in 1957. I was prime minister when Canadians got their own national flag. Who am I?
6. I was premier of Saskatchewan from 1944 to 1961. I became the first national leader of the NDP. Who am I?
7. We were the most popular musical group of the sixties. We came from England, but our music conquered the world. Who are we?

Ideas for Discussion

1. What would have happened in Newfoundland if Newfoundlanders had voted *not* to enter Confederation in 1949? Write your thoughts down in a brief paragraph. Be prepared to read your paragraph aloud during a class discussion.
2. List the good and bad results of the boom of the early fifties. Hold a class debate on the topic: Resolved that the economic boom of the fifties created more problems than it solved.
3. With a group of other students discuss the statement, "Parents rarely understand teenagers — and teenagers rarely understand parents."
4. Canada underwent a "baby boom" in the 1950s. Today Canadians are having fewer children or none at all.
   a) Suggest reasons for this drop in the birth rate.
   b) What does the drop mean for the future of our country? Some possible areas for discussion are schools, the labour force, immigration, and supporting the elderly.
5. What are the characteristics of a good prime minister? Working in small groups try to decide which of the following best fulfills the role of prime minister:
   a) Louis St. Laurent
   b) John Diefenbaker
   c) Lester Pearson
6. How has rock 'n roll changed the world? Have these changes been good or bad? In your opinion what song, singer, or group has had the greatest influence? Why?
7. If you had a choice, would you have preferred to live during the fifties or the sixties? Why?

Do Some Research

1. Visit the library to find out more about the province of Newfoundland since it joined Canada in 1949. You might use the following headings:
   a) Geography
   b) Culture and Traditions
   c) Transportation
   d) Towns, Villages, and Outports
   e) Political Leaders
   f) Economic Development
2. Research the recent history of a "boomtown" in your region. Why was the town established? Has the town continued to develop? What do you think will be the future of your boom town?
3. Find out more about the cancellation of the Avro Arrow project by the Diefenbaker government. Make a list of the reasons for this decision and the arguments against it. State your personal conclusions clearly and firmly.
4. Write a brief biocard of an important Canadian of the fifties or sixties. Here are a few suggestions:
   a) Judy LaMarsh
   b) Marilyn Bell
   c) Paul Anka
   d) Kahn Tinehta Horn
   e) Normie Kwong
   f) K.C. Irving
   g) Maurice Richard
   h) W.O. Mitchell
   Make a class folder or wall display for your biocards.
5. Summarize the achievements or changes won by one of the protest movements of the 1960s.
6. Find out what projects your community undertook to celebrate Canada's 100th birthday. Were these projects a good idea?

Be Creative

1. Make a working model to demonstrate how a lock operates on the St. Lawrence Seaway.
2. Divide into teams and prepare time capsules for the fabulous fifties or the swinging sixties. Include photo records, magazines, records, souvenirs, fashions, news items. You might celebrate the end of your project with a theme party.
3. Write a newspaper article on one event in the celebration of Canada's 200th birthday. Use exciting headlines and pictures to present your story. Place your articles together in a class bicentennial newspaper. (Do you think we will still have newspapers in 2067?)
4. Prepare a department store catalogue for the 1950s. Compare this catalogue with a modern version. What differences do you find in the products available, design, prices?
5. Compare the hit songs of the fifties and sixties with each other and with the songs of today. What differences do the songs reveal about attitudes to
   a) values   b) technology   c) teenagers   d) love

In periods like the fifties Canadians regarded almost all economic development as "progress." In the sixties people began to look at some of the side effects of development. They wondered if it was all worth it. Certainly development in some form is necessary for the economic health of a nation. When we examine the question of development today, how do we count the cost?

A Pulp and Paper Mill at River Rock

River Rock is in northern Canada. In the early years of the century copper was discovered nearby. Miners and their families soon created a small town on the banks of the Rocky River. Merchants moved in to open stores. Teachers, lawyers, restaurant owners, and doctors came to offer their services to the community.

River Rock is a pleasant place, surrounded by rich forests. Rushing streams tumble into still lakes that teem with fish. The town is friendly. People enjoy living here.

Three years ago the mine closed because the ore had run out. Now young people are leaving town in order to find work in the big cities to the south. Stores have closed because business is

poor. The town council cannot raise the money to provide the services a modern community needs. Many residents rely on unemployment insurance and provincial welfare benefits. It seems that for the last three years the town has been limping along from one government grant to the next.

Recently U.S. Conglomerate Inc. has shown interest in River Rock. The company plans to develop a giant pulp and paper

A major issue is confronting you, the people who care about the town of River Rock. You are going to a public meeting to discuss it. On a piece of paper jot down the concerns you want raised at the meeting. Be prepared to make a statement, ask questions, or add comments to make sure these concerns are discussed. Keep an open mind. Others may have points you have not thought of.

What is the future for River Rock?

mill. The forests in the valley can be harvested. The Rocky River can be dammed to provide power. All that is needed is the go-ahead from the town council. Then the company will build the mill, provide jobs for local residents, and make profits for its share-holders. River Rock could boom once again.

For weeks all of you — citizens of River Rock, representatives of U.S. Conglomerate, town councillors, and others — have been discussing the proposal. Tonight a public meeting is being held in the school auditorium. A number of groups with special concerns have asked to speak at the meeting:

a) *The town council,* led by Mayor Irene Nadeau: You know the town desperately needs jobs. The taxes paid by the company will help provide new roads, schools, recreation centres, libraries.

b) *Young people* in town: You are eager to get jobs in a highly skilled industry. You also love your valley and fear that its beauty may be destroyed.

c) *Senior citizens:* You want the valley to remain as it was when you were young. Yet you also want your children and grandchildren to be able to live and work in River Rock.

d) *Native people* on the reserve nearby: You are afraid the company will ruin your traditional hunting and fishing grounds.

e) *Jonathan Goldstein's* and *Alice Chan's* families: You have recently moved to River Rock because of its beauty and isolation. You mistrust big business, especially American corporations. You fear the company will be out for profit at any cost.

f) *U.S. Conglomerate's* managers: You feel there is a great future for an operation in River Rock. But millions of dollars will have to be spent in start-up costs. There will be no profits for several years. You are prepared to comply with "reasonable requests" on the way you set up the mill. But you do not want expensive interference from local government. If you feel the citizens are not behind the idea, you are prepared to invest elsewhere.

Creative Tensions
ADVANCE ORGANIZER

1

In the late 1960s, Pierre Trudeau offered a youthful and vigorous approach to government affairs. His fresh ideas and moral strength appealed to the young, and gave new hope to the older generation of voters. World leaders were impressed with his ideas on foreign policy. Trudeau's main objective was a unified Canada. He sometimes achieved his aims by tightening federal controls, which often angered the provinces.

2

In 1973 the oil-producing countries of the Middle East raised their prices. Canadian companies were forced to spend more money for the energy used to make their products. The prices of manufactured goods increased. The workers demanded higher wages to keep pace with the rising prices. Some businesses couldn't afford to keep all their employees. Largely because of this, unemployment rose.

3

In the 1960s, immigration policies meant to be fair to all attracted people of many nationalities to Canada. These people brought with them their own traditions and values, and their own approaches to day-to-day living. Unfortunately many were met with prejudice and hostility in their new country. Although multiculturalism is heartily encouraged by the federal government, racism is still a problem in some Canadian cities.

Word List

budget	energy crisis	multiculturalism
common market	environment	negotiate
conservation	equality	racism
consumer	inflation	standard of living

4 The original natives of Canada are the Inuit and Indian peoples of the North. But industry's desire for northern oil and gas may displace them from their homeland. They are fighting a continuing battle to maintain their way of life in the face of modern technology.

5 Many trends in society and culture developed in the seventies. There was greater activity in modern music, theatre, dance and film. More people participated in hockey, soccer, and other spectator sports. Women were more vocal than ever before in asserting their social and working rights. The general public and the business world began to accept the need for women's equality.

6 High unemployment, inflation, and the energy crisis caused much unrest in the late seventies. People were dissatisfied and blamed the Trudeau government for their problems. They sought a new leader in Joe Clark and his Conservative Party. But the new prime minister was unable to hold to most of his campaign promises, and remained in office for less than a year. The people accepted Pierre Trudeau as their government leader again.

Trudeaumania

The sixties had been a time for youth, colour, and liveliness. Canadians were tired of the same old faces that had dominated the political scene for so long. In the high spiritedness that surrounded Centennial year they wanted fresh blood. Pierre Elliott Trudeau seemed the ideal man. The new minister of justice was much younger than most politicians. He enjoyed sports, dancing, parties, sexy clothes. He had done exciting things like standing up to big business and the Quebec government during the Asbestos strike and visiting communist China in a period when it was cut off from the western world. He had new ideas, a strong sense of justice and a deep love for Canada. Surely this was the man to lead Canada into the seventies. When Pearson resigned in 1968, Trudeau was chosen as leader of the Liberal Party. As soon as he was sworn in as Prime Minister he decided to hold an election. He would take advantage of the mood of the country.

The Campaign

Wherever Trudeau appeared to give a speech, it was a little like a rock concert. Teenagers cheered and screamed themselves hoarse. The crowds swarmed to get close to their hero. Women tried to kiss him (which he clearly enjoyed). People were thrilled by his clear vision of a just society where all Canadians' rights were respected; where all could enjoy the good things of life.

Candidates from other parties had little chance against the Liberals. Voters had been swept off their feet by the new Liberal leader. They were also tired of the compromises minority governments had to make. Canada had not had a majority government since 1962. Voters felt that this was what the country needed in order to get things done. When Canadians went to the ballot box in 1968, they gave Trudeau the majority he had requested.

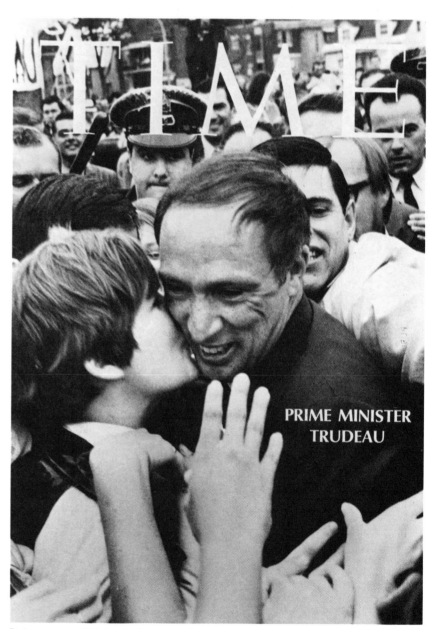

It is every politician's dream to be on the cover of *Time* magazine. Pierre Elliott Trudeau made it because of the excitement and enthusiasm that surrounded his stunning election victory in 1968.

Why were voters attracted to Pierre Trudeau in 1968?
Name 2 areas in which he made changes in Canadian politics.
Why were other nations impressed by Trudeau and Canada?
Was Trudeau a good prime minister? Why or why not?

1900 1910 1920 1930 1940 1950 1960 1970 1980 1990 2000

By the late 1970s cartoonists often portrayed Trudeau as a rich, uncaring person who did not understand the everyday problems of ordinary Canadians.

The Challenge of the Seventies

The 1970s were difficult years. The economy slowed down. It was a time of high unemployment and inflation. Tensions grew between Canadians of different cultural backgrounds — between English and French, between "old" Canadians and recent immigrants. Native people began to demand fairer treatment. Women wanted true equality with men. Many of these matters were beyond the control of the government. But people still expected the prime minister to solve them. When he couldn't, many Canadians felt disappointed and angry.

Trudeau did take steps to deal with many of Canada's problems. People questioned whether they were the right steps to take, whether they went too far or not far enough. Many thought the prime minister didn't listen to advice. He always seemed sure his way was best. People started to say he was detached and arrogant.

The Just Society

Trudeau tried to make Canada a fairer place for all Canadians. He appointed the first Jewish chief justice of the Supreme Court, Bora Laskin. Pauline McGibbon of Ontario and Ralph Steinhauer of Alberta became the first woman and the first native Indian lieutenant governors of their provinces. Another native Indian, Len Marchand, became a member of the federal cabinet.

The Official Languages Act was passed in 1969 to ensure Canadians could be served by the federal government in either French or English. This meant many civil servants had to learn a second language. Companies doing business in Canada were also required to mark their products in both languages. The act only applied to matters under federal control. Trudeau was unhappy that he could not persuade the provinces to follow the federal lead.

Canadian unity was the matter which concerned Trudeau most. In many ways he seemed to be fighting a losing battle. In the early years, the main threat seemed to come from Quebec. By 1980 provincial leaders in many regions of the country were disagreeing with the prime minister. They thought he was trying to take away some of their powers. Many citizens were confused. Which was more important, the province or the country?

Canada in the World

In other countries Trudeau was perhaps more highly respected than in his own. The whole world had been fascinated by the Trudeaumania of 1968. His foreign policy continued to impress other nations. In 1970 he established diplomatic relations with China. He developed new ties with Latin America, an area Canada had often ignored. He tried to increase communications and trade with the European Common Market. By building on the reputation of Lester Pearson, he helped Canada retain a position of respect and influence in the world.

POLITICS **181**

The Economic Crunch

The 1960s had been good years for Canadians. They had good jobs. They were able to afford large cars, stereo sets, and colour televisions. While growth was not as spectacular as in the 1950s, most Canadians still got a little richer each year.

In the 1970s some people found it harder to get work. The rate of unemployment was rising. Those who had jobs got raises every year or so, but they found their pay cheques bought less and less. The rate of inflation was also rising. What had happened? Why were things so different?

The Cost of Fuel

Canadians depend on energy. They use more oil, coal, and electricity than people in any other nation in the world. Part of this is just wastefulness. But part of it is because of the nature of the country.

Canada has long, cold winters. It takes a lot of energy to heat homes, schools, and businesses. A small population lives scattered across a vast area. Canadians use more energy to visit their relatives or to transport raw materials to factories than people in more crowded countries.

The biggest user of energy is industry. Canada's economy is based on raw materials and refining them. Mining, smelting, and building automobiles require more power than growing fruit or making radios and clothing.

Much of the world's supply of oil comes from the Middle East. In 1973 these countries decided to raise their prices: the rest of the world had been taking advantage of them for long enough.

When the price of oil went up, other sources of energy became more valuable. Their prices rose too. Both consumers and business people had to spend more on energy.

A tugboat helps a supertanker make its way to its mooring place in Halifax harbour. There the crude oil it carries will be pumped to the refinery in Dartmouth. Most Canadians receive their oil from western Canada, but the oil pipeline stops at Montreal. Industry and consumers in eastern Canada have depended on imported oil. This situation will change dramatically as oil reserves in the seabed off Canada's east coast are tapped and brought into production.

Why were the 1970s difficult for many Canadians with regard
to *a)* jobs, *b)* pay raises, *c)* prices?
Why does energy cost so much in Canada?
How did Canadians react to wage and price controls? Why?

The Wage-Price Spiral

When companies were forced to spend more to make
their products, they had to raise their prices. When
workers saw prices going up, they demanded higher
wages from their employers. They felt they should be
able to keep buying products the way they always had.
When employers paid higher wages, they had to raise
their prices again. A "wage-price spiral" set in.

This was not the only effect of the rise in oil prices.
It also led to increased unemployment. Business
leaders did not know how high oil prices were going to
go. They were afraid to invest in new ventures in such
an uncertain climate. There were few new companies
looking for workers. Many older companies found that
they could not sell as much at the higher prices they
now had to charge. Many people who had jobs in these
companies were laid off.

Expectations

Canadians had come to expect that the prosperity of
the 1950s and 1960s would last forever. When the oil
price rise made this impossible, they still behaved the
same way. If cash were not available, some people

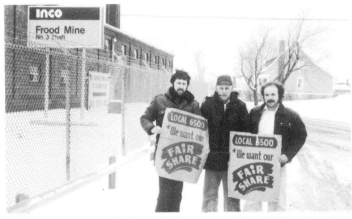

Workers were determined that industry should not take advantage
of higher prices without passing some of the increase on to them.

bought on credit. Then they blamed the government
when they found themselves in trouble.

Prime Minister Trudeau said Canadians would
have to lower their expectations. By this he meant that
they could no longer expect to live the way they had in
the 1960s. Businesses would have to accept lower
profits and workers lower wages. Canadians refused to
listen. Business went on raising prices and workers
went on demanding raises. As a result, in 1975
Trudeau brought in a program of "wage and price
controls." For three years price and wage increases
beyond a certain level were controlled by a
government committee. Many Canadians were angry
at Trudeau for limiting their freedom. They pointed
out that Trudeau had spent the 1974 election campaign
ridiculing the Conservatives for suggesting wage and
price controls. Now he was using them himself. Unions
said that wages were controlled but prices were not. To
a large extent, this was true.

The program may have helped a little. But the twin
problems of unemployment and inflation are still
plaguing the Canadian economy.

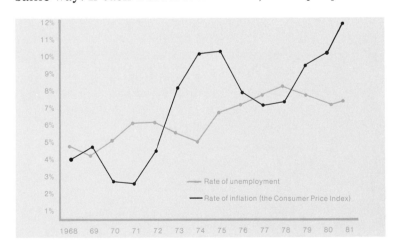

Workers Face the Crunch

In the 1970s workers could no longer expect that things would get better and better each year. A bigger pay cheque would not necessarily buy more goods. There might be no pay cheque at all: workers were being laid off in increasing numbers. In many ways young people suffered most. In a shrinking job market employers demanded "experience." The first job was almost impossible to find.

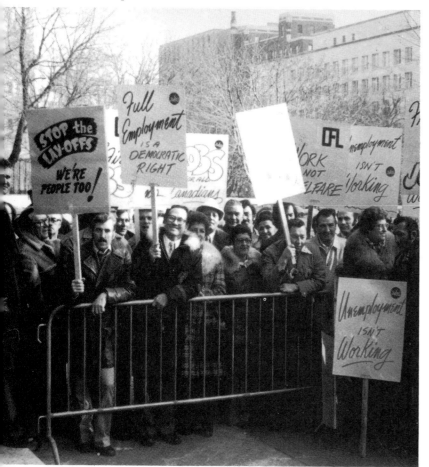

In the late 1970s unemployment reached crisis proportions. People did not want to live on government handouts. They wanted the government to make sure they could find jobs.

The Power of Numbers

Workers who belonged to unions were in a better position to fight the situation. Unions had gained considerably in strength since the early years of the century. Their right to bargain with employers for better wages and working conditions was fully recognized by law. The right to strike if bargaining failed to produce an agreement was being extended to more and more groups of workers.

Workers do not like to go on strike. They need the regular pay cheque to pay the rent and buy the groceries. However, during the 1970s many Canadian union members decided a strike was the only way to protect themselves against inflation. They felt the wages offered them were not high enough. Rather than accept a lower standard of living, they went on strike.

Wages were not the only issue. Unions worked for improved working conditions. They wanted shorter working hours, better ventilation and safer work places. They wanted recreational facilities and better pensions. They fought to protect their members from unemployment. For example, the Union of Postal Workers tried to make sure automatic machinery would not replace members' jobs. The United Auto Workers got companies to agree to pay workers part of their wages when they were laid off. Unemployment insurance and these payments raised their income to 90% of their regular wage.

Unions and Society

Unions affected more than the relations between their members and their employers. When union members got higher wages, employers of non-union workers often found they had to pay more too. When unions

Why was getting a job hardest for young people in the 1970s?
Name 3 issues unions worked for in this period. Which issue do you
think is the most important?
Should more Canadians belong to unions? Why or why not?

1900 1910 1920 1930 1940 1950 1960 1970 1980 1990 2000

A worker receives dental care under a union-sponsored plan.

demanded safer working conditions, provincial governments began to see the need to apply the same rules to everyone.

One issue that unions have been concerned about is health. For example, in the late 1970s unions and medical experts finally convinced people that asbestos was a health risk. Asbestos had been used for fire protection in many large buildings. The asbestos had often remained uncoated. Tiny fibres could escape into the air and be breathed into people's lungs. Exposure to asbestos fibres could cause future cancer. As a result of the publicity unions gave to the problem, action was taken. Offices, factories, schools, and subway systems were inspected for crumbling asbestos.

Most Canadian unions belong to the Canadian Labour Congress. The CLC represents the interests of union members across the country. Provincial federations of labour represent workers within each province. These groups urge governments to pass laws that benefit all workers. For example, unemployment insurance payments were increased to help workers who were laid off. Provincial minimum wage laws are supported by unions. However, as most union members make more than the minimum, these laws mainly help non-union workers.

Safety clothing in a textile factory that uses dangerous chemicals.

New Unions

Workers in many fields do not belong to unions. In fact in 1980 only about 38% of workers in Canada were union members. The union movement has tried to convince other workers of the advantage of union membership.

In the late 1970s unions were started by several groups of workers who had not been unionized before. The Union of Bank Employees signed up members in some bank branches. The Canadian Association of Burlesque Entertainers was set up by performers in bars and night clubs to ensure adequate pay and working conditions. In 1980 there was a union local in one fast food outlet in Windsor, Ontario, and the idea was expected to spread across the country.

New People for a New Society

Who should be allowed to come to Canada? At the turn of the century Clifford Sifton wanted "sturdy peasants in sheepskin coats." The need for farm workers decreased once the West was settled. In 1905 Frank Oliver, the new minister of immigration wanted only "the right class of British immigrant." Until World War II the government made it difficult for people like Asians, Jews, and eastern Europeans to immigrate. It did not think they would "fit in" to Canadian society. This policy was enforced when several hundred Sikhs from India aboard the *Komagata Maru* were turned away from Vancouver in 1914. In 1939, 907 Jews aboard the *St. Louis* were not allowed to enter Canada.

After World War II Canada accepted many refugees from Europe as a humanitarian gesture. However, the basic rules remained the same: white people from the British Commonwealth, the United States, and France were preferred, then other Europeans. Numbers of non-white immigrants were severely limited.

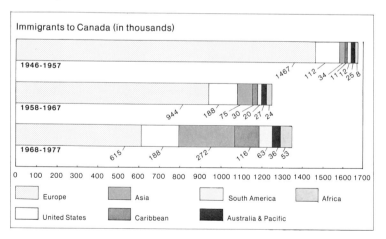

Immigrants to Canada (in thousands)

1946-1957	1467 / 112 / 34 / 1112 / 25 8
1958-1967	944 / 188 / 75 / 30 / 20 / 27 / 24
1968-1977	615 / 188 / 272 / 116 / 63 / 36 / 53

0 100 200 300 400 500 600 700 800 900 1000 1100 1200 1300 1400 1500 1600 1700

- Europe
- Asia
- South America
- Africa
- United States
- Caribbean
- Australia & Pacific

Even before 1976 immigration policy was changing, and more immigrants from "non-white" countries were entering Canada.

Changing Attitudes

By the 1970s many Canadians felt this immigration policy was a scandal. People should not be judged on the colour of their skin, where they came from, or the language they spoke at home. The choice of immigrants should be based on Canada's need for workers in certain fields and the ability of the immigrants to fill that need.

IMMIGRATION SELECTION CRITERIA*
A Summary of the Point System

Factors	Criteria	Max. Points
1. Education	One point for each year of primary and secondary education successfully completed.	12
2. Specific Vocational Preparation	To be measured by the amount of formal professional, vocational, apprenticeship, in-plant or on-the-job training necessary for average performance in the occupation under which the applicant is assessed in item 4.	15
3. Experience	Points awarded for experience in the occupation under which the applicant is assessed in item 4 or, in the case of an entrepreneur, for experience in the occupation that the entrepreneur is qualified for and is prepared to follow in Canada.	8
4. Occupational Demand	Points awarded on the basis of employment opportunities available in Canada in the occupation that the applicant is qualified for and is prepared to follow in Canada.	15
5. Arranged Employment or Designated Occupation	Ten points awarded if the person has arranged employment in Canada that offers reasonable prospects of continuity and meets local conditions of work and wages, *providing* that employment of that person would not interfere with the job opportunities of Canadian citizens or permanent residents, and the person will likely be able to meet all licensing and regulatory requirements; *or* the person is qualified for, and is prepared to work in, a designated occupation and meets all the conditions mentioned for arranged employment except that concerning Canadian citizens and permanent residents.	10
6. Location	Five points awarded to a person who intends to proceed to an area designated as one having a sustained and general need for people at various levels in the employment strata and the necessary services to accommodate population growth. Five points subtracted from a person who intends to proceed to an area designated as not having such a need or such services.	5
7. Age	Ten points awarded to a person 18 to 35 years old. For those over 35, one point shall be subtracted from the maximum of ten for every year over 35.	10
8. Knowledge of English and French	Ten points awarded to a person who reads, writes and speaks both English and French fluently. Five points awarded to a person who reads, writes and speaks English *or* French fluently. Fewer points awarded to persons with less language knowledge and ability in English or French.	10
9. Personal Suitability	Points awarded on the basis of an interview held to determine the suitability of the person and his/her dependants to become successfully established in Canada, based on the person's adaptability, motivation, initiative, resourcefulness and other similar qualities.	10
10. Relative	Where a person *would* be an assisted relative, *if* a relative in Canada had undertaken to assist him/her, and an immigration officer is satisfied that the relative in Canada is willing to help him/her become established but is not prepared, or is unable, to complete the necessary formal documentation to bring the person to Canada, the person shall be awarded five points.	5

*Members of the family class and retirees are not selected according to these criteria; Convention refugees are assessed against the factors listed in the first column but do not receive a point rating.

In the past, what groups of people found it difficult to enter Canada?
How did Canada's immigration policies change during the 1970s?
What does the expression "visible minority" mean?

1900 1910 1920 1930 1940 1950 1960 1970 1980 1990 2000

Vietnamese refugees wait to talk to immigration officers on their arrival at a Canadian airport.

In 1976 the Canadian government announced a new immigration policy. Immigrants would be judged on a system which awarded points for education, job skills, and a knowledge of English or French. No weight would be given to race or country of origin.

The change was immediate. As living conditions improved, fewer people from Europe wanted to leave their homeland. On the other hand, many countries in Asia, Africa, and the Caribbean were poor. Opportunities for good jobs were few. It was hard to get an education. Many people in these countries decided they would have a better chance in Canada.

A Changing Population

As the new policy took effect, the face of Canada changed. White Canadians sat next to blacks and Asians on city buses. Children born in Canada found their new classmates were from Uganda, India, or Trinidad. The line-up in the supermarket included people from all over the world.

When immigrants arrived from Europe they looked the same as Canadians. As a result they were accepted because few even knew they were immigrants. The new immigrants were a "visible minority" — easily recognized as being different. Many Canadians found this interesting and exciting. Others found it frightening. People often fear what they do not understand. Their fear can turn to prejudice and hate.

Prejudice made life difficult for many immigrants. Some found themselves the target of racial attacks. They found they could not get good jobs, not only because of the problem of unemployment but also because employers demanded "Canadian experience." They found landlords would not rent to them even though in most cases discrimination in housing is illegal.

Fairer rules for immigration are only the beginning of the answer. A just society must ensure fair treatment for all once they have arrived in Canada.

Multiculturalism

During the 1970s one million people immigrated to Canada. They were eager to become a part of their new society. They also wanted to preserve the customs and traditions of their native country.

Melting Pot or Mosaic?

Should immigrants become like everyone else as soon as possible? Some people believe they should give up their old ways of life. They should wear Canadian-style clothes, eat Canadian-style food, enjoy Canadian-style radio and TV. In this way, they say, the country will be strong and united. Canadians will understand each other and not argue among themselves. They claim this "melting pot" philosophy worked in the United States. Immigrants were expected to fit into the American way of life.

Others say Canada should not be a melting pot but a "mosaic." While immigrants need to take part in Canadian life, they should keep their traditions as well. Having a variety of cultures adds colour and interest for all Canadians. Why should everyone be the same?

In 1971 Prime Minister Trudeau announced that his government supported the idea of the mosaic, or multiculturalism. They would encourage Canadians to take pride in their customs and traditions. Money was set aside for cultural programs.

The upsurge in cultural festivals and celebrations that followed affected more than recent immigrants. The Gaelic Society Folk Arts and Crafts Festival is run by people whose ancestors came to the Maritimes one and two hundred years ago. Participants in the Dauphin Ukrainian Festival are often the great-grandchildren of immigrants who came to the newly opened Canadian West in the early 1900s. The families of many performers in the Romanian Music Spectacle in Quebec and the Latvian Song Festival in British Columbia left their homelands when they were taken over by the communists after World War II. The Hungarian Dance Bouquet in Alberta is organized by descendants of two groups of immigrants: those who came to farm wheat at the turn of the century and those who left Hungary after the revolution of 1956.

Dragon dance.   Shumka dancers.   Indian girls.   Grey Cup Parade.   Sword dance.   Canoe race.

Compare the American "melting pot" with the Canadian "mosaic."
List 4 cultural festivals in Canada.
Have you ever been guilty of racism or prejudice? Explain.
What steps can be taken to end racism in Canada?

1900 1910 1920 1930 1940 1950 1960 1970 1980 1990 2000

Probably the largest cultural festival is Toronto's Caravan. Caravan is truly international. Each June churches and community centres across the city come alive with music, food, crafts, and celebrations. During the ten days of Caravan people can sample the delights that over 40 different cultures have brought to Canada.

Everyone enjoys a party. These festivals have helped Canadians understand each other. But the pieces that make up the Canadian cultural mosaic often rub each other the wrong way.

Racism

A person's culture is more than songs, meals, and holidays. It is an everyday affair. It is what one wears, how late the kids can stay out at night, how long they stay in school, attitudes to work, ways of relaxing.

Different cultures have different attitudes to family life. In some cultures children are indulged. In some they are expected to obey their parents without question. Rules for girls may not be the same as rules for boys.

Some people ask questions if they don't understand something. Others think asking questions is pushy and rude. Some accept whatever treatment they are given. Others stand up for their rights. What seems a chance remark to one may be an unbearable insult to another.

Differences like these lead to misunderstanding, fear, and hate. Colour of skin, shape of eyes, religious practices, eating habits, and style of clothing can all be the focus of hatred. This type of prejudice is known as racism.

The problem of racism is most severe in the big cities. School boards, police forces, social workers, city governments have all tried to deal with the issue. Often in doing so they are accused of racism themselves. Like other Canadians they may not recognize how their words and actions may be seen as racist by others.

Canadians face a serious challenge. The multicultural mosaic is threatened when people cannot tolerate differences. The alternative is a forced melting pot in which everyone would lose a little.

At the market.　　　　Clog dance.　　　　Loyalist Days.　　　　Old-time fiddler.

Canada's Native Peoples

The native peoples were the first Canadians. Before European settlers came, they lived a life in tune with nature. This special relationship with the environment was highlighted in their religions. The spirit of the land was an important symbol. Conservation was the principle behind the way they hunted and fished.

European traders taught the native people to value the fur more than the animal that bore it. Then settlers moved in and took over the land. Sometimes a treaty was made between the native people and the new government. The native people were usually allowed small areas of "reserved" land and an annual pension that was little more than welfare. For this, they had given up the vast land they regarded as their heritage.

By the 1970s many native people felt the government treated them as permanent welfare cases. Their traditional way of life had vanished. Settlers had destroyed the natural forests and grazing lands where they had hunted. They had lost the customs and values they cherished. They owned only their restricted reserves. If they left the reserves to seek work, they found they did not possess the skills required in the modern cities. They were trapped in a lifestyle that robbed them of their self respect.

Canada's native people suffered from an unemployment rate of over 50%. Some were victims of alcoholism. They were twice as likely as other Canadians to commit suicide. Native people lived in the poorest parts of Canadian cities. On the reserves housing, sewage systems, schools, and recreation facilities were all far below standard.

> If I could just get the people from Treasury Board to come out and visit the reserves it would be easy to get more money. If they could just see the schools, the housing, the roads and the lack of running water.
>
> *Warren Allmand, minister of Indian Affairs, 1976*

A government "white paper" is a statement of proposed policy. In a formal ceremony, native Canadians present a "red paper" containing their views on native affairs in response to a government white paper.

The Search for Solutions

Native people faced a basic problem. They wanted an adequate standard of living like other Canadians. They also wanted to retain the old relationship with the land. There were vast expanses of land they claimed were theirs but the government said the land no longer belonged to them.

Instead of letting the government have its way, the native people took their case to court. Native lawyers argued that their ancestors had never meant to give away their lands. The government had merely acted as if they had. They also argued that the government had not lived up to its side of the terms of the treaties.

The first native land claim case to reach the courts was the Nishga claim to 10 000 km² near the Nass River in northern British Columbia. The Nishga fought the case all the way to the Supreme Court of Canada. The ruling went against the Nishga, but 3 out

Why did the native people's traditional way of life disappear?
What problems did they face a) in the city, b) on the reserve?
What arguments did they use to defend their land claims?
Name other steps they are taking to improve their status.

Art Gallery pages 26-27

of 7 judges disagreed with the verdict. Even though the native people lost the case, this was encouraging. The government had at least been forced to listen to them and reply to their arguments.

Later the same year the Supreme Court of the Northwest Territories ruled that the Northwest Territories Indian Brotherhood "might have a claim" to one million km^2 of land. Partly because of this ruling the Canadian government set up the Mackenzie Valley Pipeline Inquiry.

The James Bay hydro-electric project in northern Quebec was built on land native people had lived on for 5000 years. The Cree and Inuit were able to negotiate a treaty that should have given them adequate land, money, health services, and local self-government. However, they claim that already the Quebec government has not lived up to its part of the bargain. They are not being allowed the language rights specified by the treaty. In 1980 a number of Cree babies died because of inadequate health care.

By the end of the 1970s Canadians were listening to the concerns of native people. Native organizations had been stronger and more outspoken. They had established their right to negotiate for their traditional lands. They were dealing with the social problems of native people both on and off the reserves. They were regaining pride and a sense of purpose. Perhaps native people could play an active part in Canadian society without giving up their customs and values.

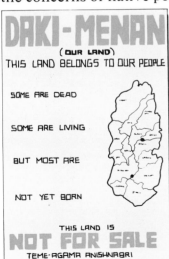

DAKI-MENAN
(OUR LAND)
THIS LAND BELONGS TO OUR PEOPLE

SOME ARE DEAD

SOME ARE LIVING

BUT MOST ARE

NOT YET BORN

THIS LAND IS
NOT FOR SALE
TEME-AGAMA ANISHNABAI

Chief Dan George

"Let no one forget this: we are a people with special rights guaranteed to us by promises and treaties. We do not beg for these rights, nor do we thank you because we paid for them. We paid with our culture, pride, and self-respect. We paid we paid and we paid until we became a beaten race, poverty-stricken and conquered."
from "Lament for Confederation"

1899 — born on a Coastal Salish reserve on Burrard Inlet, B.C. Attended a mission boarding school in North Vancouver.
1916 — started work as a logger.
1920 — became a longshoreman on Vancouver docks.
1947 — badly injured in dockyard accident. Became an entertainer. Soon known all over Burrard Inlet.
1951 — elected chief of his tribe. Lost election in 1963. Later made honorary chief of Shuswap and Squamish tribes.
1960 — cast as Antoine in CBC TV series *Cariboo Country*.
1965 — appeared in Walt Disney film *How to Break a Quarter Horse*.
1967 — as a leading spokesman for native peoples, delivered his "Lament for Confederation" at centennial celebrations in Vancouver. Explained how Indian people had been poorly treated and their interests ignored in 100 years of Confederation.
1970 — starred as Ol' Lodgeskins in *Little Big Man*. Nominated for an Oscar.
1972 — chosen as national chairman for Brotherhood Week. Continued work in film and TV while living on his reserve.
1981 — died in a Vancouver hospital

We want to carry on our own economic and community development so that Indian people can share in the things all Canadians want, and can do so within the framework of an Indian value system. That is what our struggle is all about.
George Manuel, president, National Indian Brotherhood, 1969

Northern Frontier, Northern Homeland

In Canada's North native people can still live close to the land and sea. They now hunt and fish with the aid of modern tools like guns, snowmobiles, and motorboats. Yet their attitudes to nature and conservation remain.

Beneath the Arctic Ocean lie vast resources of oil and gas. The energy crisis of the 1970s meant southern Canadians wanted access to these resources. When a large gas field was discovered in the Beaufort Sea, the easiest way to transport the gas seemed to be by pipeline. A pipeline was planned along the Mackenzie River Valley.

There were problems to overcome. The route stretched for 2000 km before it even reached the Alberta border. Most of the land it would pass through was *permafrost* — frozen all year round. This meant the pipeline would have to be built above ground.

Otherwise the heat from the pipeline would melt the permafrost and cause the line to sink.

Many Canadians in the South thought these engineering problems were all that had to be worried about. The gas was needed in southern Canada. The project would create many jobs. In the South, factories would produce steel pipe and equipment. People would move north to work on the actual construction. Native people could work on the pipeline. Northern businesses would have more customers and hire more workers. The pipeline seemed to be a good idea.

Others thought differently. They feared the pipeline would damage the northern environment. The government decided the project had to be studied before it was started. Justice Thomas Berger was appointed to conduct the Mackenzie Valley Pipeline Inquiry.

The changing northern environment. An oil rig on an artificial island in the Beaufort Sea. In the 1970s oil companies started to build entire islands like this one. The dredge ship *Beaver Mackenzie* at the right pumps a mixture of water and sand from the ocean floor and slowly a new island is formed.

Give 3 arguments in favour of a northern pipeline.
Give 3 arguments against a northern pipeline.
Do you think the pipeline should be built? Explain.
Should native people have their own government in the North?

Canada Art Gallery pages 30-31

The Inquiry

Berger listened to the pipeline experts in Yellowknife. He also took his inquiry to 35 native communities in the Mackenzie Valley and the Western Arctic. He wanted the Inuit and Dene (Den-nay) peoples of the area to be able to speak to the inquiry "in their own villages, in their own languages, in their own way."

He found nearly all the Inuit and Dene were against the pipeline. They were afraid drilling in the Arctic Ocean would disturb the fish and sea mammals and pollute the water. They said the pipeline would cut across the migration routes of the caribou. They did not want southern-style industry in the North. They wanted to hunt and fish in the old ways. The pipeline would destroy their way of life.

Berger's final report suggested that the pipeline be delayed 10 years. This would allow time to solve the native people's problems. He agreed that the Inuit and Dene should have "special status" within Canada. They wanted a new political area in the North controlled by a government of native people. This would allow them to preserve their way of life.

The Canadian government agreed with only part of the report. They felt the pipeline was too important to wait 10 years. They did not accept the idea of "special status." They did agree that native claims had to be dealt with before the pipeline was started.

There are many more people in southern Canada than in the North. They need northern oil and gas. Native people in southern Canada have lost their old way of life. In the North, many aspects of the traditional culture still survive. Should the needs of the majority of Canadians come before the desire of the Inuit and Dene to preserve their way of life?

Pitseolak

"My name is Pitseolak, the Inuit word for the sea pigeon. When I see pitseolaks over the sea, I say, 'There go those lovely birds — that's me, flying!' "

About 1900 — born on Nottingham Island, Hudson Strait, N.W.T. Had a happy, healthy childhood near Cape Dorset, Baffin Island. Father taught her Inuit legends and beliefs in the spirit world. Learned skills expected of Inuit women: food preparation, treating animal skins, sewing clothes, repairing tents and kayaks.
Married childhood friend, Ashoona. They had 17 children, 5 are still living. Became well known for beautiful embroidery on caribou and seal skins brought to her by Ashoona.
Ashoona died on a family hunting trip. Life was hard for Pitseolak and the family.
1950s — James Houston, government administrator and himself an artist, encouraged Inuit to sell soapstone carvings and other crafts to make the money they needed in the new cash-based North American society. When a friend, Oshweetok, recognized possibility of printing Inuit drawings, Houston helped people of Cape Dorset develop their own techniques to make prints. Suggested to Pitseolak that she draw "the old ways." Her drawings and prints based on the legends learned from her father have sold well all over the world.
She has been drawing "the old ways and the monsters" ever since. "I'll keep on doing them. I'll make them as long as I am well. If I can, I'll make them even after I am dead."

Womanpower

In the early years of the century women struggled to get equal rights with men. They achieved the right to vote and to be appointed to government offices. Some went to university to study law, medicine, and engineering. They took part in sports. Many women thought that equality had been won.

A working woman legally had to hand all her salary to her husband. I was prepared to fight. I've been fighting ever since.
Thérèse Casgrain, Quebec women's rights worker, 1930s; protester against conscription and government treatment of Japanese Canadians, 1940s; leader of the Quebec wing of the CCF, 1950s; president of Voice of Women, 1960s; senator, 1970s.

Really, the battle was only just beginning. The women who succeeded in politics, law, or medicine were the exceptions. Very few even tried to enter these "male" fields. Those who did rarely made it to the top.

Women were entering "non-traditional" occupations more frequently in the 1970s. Below, an assembly line worker. Right, Rosella Bjornson, Canada's first female commercial airline pilot. However, it was not until the 1980s that women were accepted as pilots in the armed forces.

Whatever women do, they must do twice as well as men to be thought half so good — luckily it's not difficult.
Charlotte Whitton, mayor of Ottawa, 1950s.

If women were accepted as equal, why did they not succeed at the same rate as men? The answer is simple: They were *not* accepted as equal. Those who might have encouraged women did not do so. And women were not brought up to expect very much of themselves.

Expectations

In theory, women could do anything they wanted. In practice, only certain jobs were regarded as suitable. Women could be office workers, waitresses, nurses, and teachers. They were not accepted as truckers, scientists, plumbers, or administrators.

Even when a woman showed ability she was often passed over for promotion. "What's the use of promoting a woman?" managers said, "She'll only marry and leave. Besides, you can't have a woman supervising men. They won't respect her."

It was not until the 1960s that women really became conscious of these attitudes. Many were not concerned. It took long hard work by those who recognized the problems to convince others that the situation was unfair.

In 1967 the government appointed a royal commission on the status of women. The commission gave convincing evidence that women were not treated equally with men in Canada.

Changes in the 1970s

During the seventies women began to assert their rights. They took more active part in politics. They went into jobs that had been held only by men. They demanded attention be paid to the problems of women.

Why were women often less likely to succeed than men?
How did attitudes to women change during the 1970s?
What advances were made by women in this period?
Are women today treated as full equals to men?

Discrimination starts at birth. Girl babies are dressed in pink, boys in blue. Girls are given dolls to play with, boys get trucks. Girls who climb trees are called tomboys. Girls should be neat and clean. Boys should be tough.

In school girls are expected to be good at literature and art. Boys are expected to be good at math and science. Girls are encouraged to take shorthand and typing. Then they can get an office job for a couple of years until they get married. Boys are encouraged to take courses that will lead to a career.

These general statements do not apply in every case. But it is attitudes like these that have helped to keep women "unequal" to men.

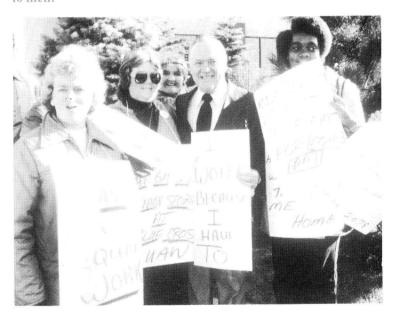

Changes in the 1970s

Most women can now get maternity leave when they have a child. They no longer have to quit their jobs completely.
Most provinces now have "equal pay for equal work" laws. Employers must pay men and women the same for doing the same job.
The idea of equal pay is being extended to "work of equal value." Some employers were using different job descriptions for men and women in order to pay different rates.
Family laws were changed so that a husband could not claim all property if the marriage broke up.

Attitudes changed. Businesses realized they could promote women successfully. New family laws were passed to make sure that women received a share of family property if a marriage broke up. Day care centres were set up so mothers of young children could go out to a paying job.

You can't fight, fight, fight all the time without becoming less feminine. In politics you have to.
Judy LaMarsh, lawyer, 1950s; Liberal cabinet minister, 1960s; author and broadcaster, 1970s.

This certainly did not mean the seventies was an easy time for women. Many women were confused by their changing relationship with men — and so were many men! Women who chose to stay home as full-time housewives felt they were being "put down" by the women who went out to work. Many mothers who wanted paying jobs found there wasn't room for their children in the new day care centres. Working wives often found their husbands still expected them to do most of the housework as well. The idea of equal pay for equal work was established in most provinces. Yet some employers looked for ways to get around it.

Many people working for real equality for women say that little progress has been made. They point to statistics like these: Women working full time in Canada make only 60% of the money that men do. This percentage remained unchanged through the 1970s. Yet there is one very basic change. In the early sixties few people were aware that women had problems. Twenty years later women's issues are a matter of concern in government, business and family life.

The true liberation of women cannot take place without the liberation of men.
Thérèse Casgrain.

Is There a Canadian Culture?

What is culture? In its broadest sense it is an entire way of life. Many use the word to mean the books, magazines, and papers people read, the music they listen to, the films, TV, and live theatre they watch.

During most of the twentieth century popular "culture" in Canada came largely from outside the country. People enjoyed American movies. They read books published in the U.S., Britain, and Europe. When television started in the fifties nearly all the popular shows were American. If Canadian artists were known in Canada, it was usually because they had become famous in another country.

Many Canadians were concerned about this. They argued that the problem was largely a matter of *access*. Canadian talent could not become known if it wasn't given a chance to perform. Movie houses should show some Canadian films. Rock concerts should feature some Canadian groups. Theatres should use Canadian actors in Canadian plays. Schools should teach children with Canadian textbooks, stories, and poems. Art galleries should display Canadian paintings and sculptures. When people saw how good Canadian culture was, they would become interested in it.

During the thirties the CBC had given Canadians their own coast-to-coast radio network. In 1939 the National Film Board was established. The NFB kept busy during World War II making propaganda films about the Canadian war effort. Since the war several NFB documentaries and cartoons have won Oscars and other international awards.

In the fifties the federal government had set up the Canada Council. The council gave money to artists and arts groups to help them put their work before the public. As Centennial year approached in 1967, interest in Canadian culture blossomed. Through the sixties dance companies, theatres, and rock groups

Alice Munro, novelist.

Canadian artists in a variety of fields

The rock group Triumph.

Norval Morrisseau, painter.

Alden Nowlan, poet.

The Royal Winnipeg Ballet, Canada's oldest ballet company.

How "Canadian" is your culture in the following areas: a) books; b) films; c) records; d) TV; e) live concerts and theatre?
Name 5 organizations that support and develop Canadian culture.
Is there a Canadian culture?

Art Gallery page 33

sprang up all across the country. The growth was amazing. By the seventies Canadian artists were more popular than they had ever been. Some of this popularity was a direct result of government policy.

Gaining Access

In 1968 the Canadian Radio and Television Commission (CRTC) took over the job of granting licences to radio and television stations. In 1970 the CRTC announced that in order to keep their licences, radio and TV stations had to broadcast a certain percentage of Canadian material. This would give Canadian artists an opportunity to perform and become known.

In order to supply this "Canadian content," recording companies started to look for Canadian talent. Singers like Anne Murray and Gordon Lightfoot and groups like Rush, Trooper, and Bachmann Turner Overdrive were signed up. Once Canadians heard their music on the radio, they wanted to see them in person. Booking concert tours became

Yvan Deschamps, Gilles Vigneault, and Claude Léveillée consult with director Jacques Bissonette during a rehearsal for a St. Jean Baptiste Day concert on Montreal's Mount Royal.

easier for Canadian musicians. On television, Canadian actors were hired to perform in series like the Beachcombers and King of Kensington.

The Canadian Film Development Corporation (CFDC) was established to encourage Canadians to make feature length films. With the CFDC's help, successful films such as The Apprenticeship of Duddy Kravitz and Why Shoot the Teacher? were made. On the other hand, the CFDC also gave money to films like Meatballs, which some people thought were really low grade. Some Canadians protested that many of the films weren't "Canadian" at all. They had American stories and American stars. They were shot in Canada only so they could get Canadian government money.

During the 1970s Canadians continued to enjoy books, films, and music from other parts of the world. They were also interested in the work of Canadian artists and performers.

Stratford, Ont., probably Canada's best-known theatre.

Fitness and Sport

Sports are fun. Canadians at all times in history would agree with that statement. Yet they might not agree on what it meant. In 1900 Canadians assumed it meant sports were fun to play. By 1970 most Canadians thought it meant sports were fun to watch. During the seventies professional sports became big business. Several times a week Canadians could buy tickets or turn on their TV sets to watch "the big game."

Professional Football

Unlike most other professional sports associations, the Canadian Football League is an "all-Canadian" league. Nine teams form the CFL. Each year the champions of the East meet the champions of the West in one final test of skill — the Grey Cup game. The Grey Cup is one of Canada's greatest sports festivals. Even Canadians who have little interest in football get caught up with the colourful Grey Cup parade and all the hoopla the surrounds the game.

Yet during the 1970s Canadian football was a matter for heated discussion. Which made a better game, Canadian rules or American? Many fans preferred the excitement of the American game, which they could see regularly on the television. Others claimed that Canadian rules demanded greater skill and made a faster game. In 1976 the government felt it had to protect the CFL. It refused to allow a new World Football League team, the Toronto Northmen, to be formed in Canada.

At the same time, most CFL teams included a number of American players. These "imports" were expected to be the stars of the team, but some fans felt they were not worth the huge salaries they were paid. The CFL entered the eighties in poor financial shape. Fewer spectators were coming to games. Only the Grey Cup game itself was guaranteed to draw a crowd.

Hockey

Many Canadians regard hockey as their national sport. Yet for years Canada had only two professional teams — the Montreal Canadiens and the Toronto Maple Leafs — in the National Hockey League. In the seventies investors decided that more money could be made out of the interest in hockey. They began to start new teams like the Vancouver Canucks — and a new league.

In 1972 the World Hockey Association was formed. It had twelve teams, four of them in Canada. The two leagues competed for fans and players. Hockey salaries soared as star players were lured from one league to the other.

The WHA survived until 1978 on a shaky footing. Then it became clear that it was not making enough money to continue as a league. A deal led to some WHA teams joining the NHL. They included the Edmonton Oilers, the Winnipeg Jets, and the Quebec Nordiques. In 1980 the Calgary Flames also joined. The NHL, which had six teams in 1967, now had twenty-one, seven of them in Canada.

Canadians dominated international hockey from the 1920s to the 1950s. Then, teams from the Soviet Union began to defeat the best Canadian amateur teams. Canadians consoled themselves with the theory that their professional teams were still superior.

In 1972 the first great test of the best Canadian and best Soviet players took place. Team Canada was expected to win easily. In fact, only a dramatic last-minute goal by Paul Henderson in the final game in Moscow let Canada squeak through to victory.

In 1976 the Canadian team won the Canada Cup series against the best players from five other countries, including the Soviet Union and Czecho-slovakia. But in 1978 and 1981 the Canadians lost again to the Soviets. By the 1980s it was clear that Canada could no longer expect automatic victory against the best players of other nations. European-style hockey began to influence the game in Canada, NHL scouts brought in outstanding European players. Fans began to expect more skill in skating and passing rather than the "hockey violence" popular in the 1970s.

Paul Henderson's winning goal.

What is your favourite sport? Do you play it, watch it, or both?
Give 2 examples to show that professional team sports are not only big business but also risky business.
What is Participaction?

Art Gallery page 23

Soccer

Professional soccer, long popular in the rest of the world, was not played in North America until the 1970s. By 1981 the North American Soccer League included four Canadian teams — the Vancouver Whitecaps, the Edmonton Drillers, the Toronto Blizzard, and the Montreal Manic. Amateur soccer began to rival baseball and football in popularity as people found the game was fun for all players, male and female, age 6 to 60.

Amateur Sport and Participaction

For years Canada had paid little attention to amateur sport. This began to change during the 1970s. In 1976 the summer Olympic Games were held in Montreal. Canadians naturally wanted to put on a good showing. Government and private industry gave grants to help amateur athletes with their training.

Two years later the Commonwealth Games were held in Edmonton. Graham Smith won six gold medals for Canada in swimming. Diane Jones Konihowski amazed spectators with her skill in the pentathlon.

As interest in amateur sports events rose, Canadians became aware that in general they were in poor physical shape. The example often used was that a 30-year-old Canadian was less fit than a 60-year-old Swede. To change the situation the federal government started "Participaction." Participaction was an advertising program. It pointed out the joys of jogging, swimming, tennis, or cycling.

By the 1980s many Canadians were once more thinking of sports as fun to do as well as fun to watch.

Baseball

Big-league baseball came to Canada when the Montreal Expos joined the National League in 1967. The Toronto Blue Jays entered the American League in 1976. In 1981 the Expos almost — but not quite — made the World Series. Interestingly enough, in 1981 there were no Canadians on either "Canadian" team. However, there were Canadian players, such as Ferguson Jenkins, on other teams in both leagues.

Diane Jones Konihowski

1951 — born in Saskatoon. As child, kept busy with gymnastics, ballet, figure skating, drama.
1963 — started training with Bob Adams who had competed in decathlon in 1952 Helsinki Olympics.
1969 — entered University of Saskatchewan. In sports concentrated on pentathlon (hurdles, shot put, high jump, long jump, 800-metre run).
1970 — lost confidence in herself and performed poorly. Quit track and ballooned up to 82 kg.
1971 — moved back home to "Mom's cooking" and a correct diet. Started a ten-year training program aimed at winning an Olympic gold medal in the penthathlon.
1975 — won pentathlon at Pan-American games in Mexico.
1976 — came sixth, ahead of all other Canadians, in pentathlon at Montreal Olympics.
1977 — married John Konihowski, a fellow track star and member of the Edmonton Eskimos football team.
1978 — won pentathlon before her home fans at Commonwealth Games in Edmonton.
1979 — voted Canadian Woman of the Year. Trained for Moscow Olympics.
1980 — forced to miss her chance for an Olympic gold medal when Canada joined boycott of Moscow Olympics because of Soviet invasion of Afghanistan.

The Conservative Interlude

Joe Clark.

The 1970s were a challenging and confusing period. Groups like native people, new immigrants, women, and working people spoke up about their special interests and concerns. Canadians recognized that these social issues were real, but did not always agree on what should be done.

Canadians argued about economic problems too. Unemployment remained high. Inflation affected everyone. The energy crisis created more confusions.

Political issues also caused disagreement. Many people in Quebec thought they would be better off in a separate country. In the West and in the Atlantic region, some felt the federal government had too much power and the provinces too little. They also felt the country was being run for the benefit of the central region, Ontario and Quebec.

It is easy to blame the person at the top. Many Canadians blamed Pierre Trudeau and his government's policies for their problems. In 1968 they admired his clear mind, his vision for Canada, and his sense of purpose. By 1979 they saw these characteristics as "arrogance."

Trudeau seemed to believe he had all the answers. He no longer asked people for new ideas. Sometimes he lost his temper. He often seemed cold and uncaring.

In the spring of 1979 Prime Minister Trudeau called an election. This was the opportunity the Conservatives had been waiting for. Under their new young leader, Joe Clark, they made Pierre Trudeau the main issue of the campaign. In the election on 22 May, the Conservatives won more seats than any other party. However, they were a minority government. They won less than half the seats in the House of Commons. This would cause them trouble.

Election Promises

The government of Joe Clark got off to a poor start. During the election campaign Clark had made some promises that had not been properly thought out. As a result he had to go back on them, or at least not act on them immediately.

However, every politician makes promises during an election. Often these promises cannot be kept. People usually forget about them before the next election. Unfortunately for the Conservatives, the next election came too soon. The broken promises were still fresh in people's minds.

Probably the biggest mistake the Conservatives made was in strategy. They did not handle the House of Commons well. A minority government usually tries to make policies that please at least one other party in the house. Then they will get enough votes so their measures will pass. The Conservatives decided they would govern in the way they felt was best whether other parties agreed or not.

In December the minister of finance, John Crosbie, introduced the Conservatives' budget. The budget called for higher taxes. It also included a price rise of 4 cents on a litre of gasoline.

John A. Macdonald and Flora MacDonald may spell their names differently, but both have been Conservative MPs for Kingston, Ont.

Why was Trudeau defeated in the election of 1979?
Explain the problems that led to Clark's fall from power in a) foreign policy, b) the economy, c) managing parliament.
What challenges faced Trudeau at the start of the 1980s?

Problems with Promises

In order to appeal to Jewish voters, Clark promised to move the Canadian Embassy in Israel to Jerusalem. Jerusalem had been fully taken over by Israel 12 years before. Many Arabs had never accepted this. Moving the embassy would have been a slap in the face for the Arabs. After the election, Clark began to see the dangers of the move. He appointed Robert Stanfield to study the proposal. Stanfield reported that the move would cause trouble and the idea was dropped.

Clark promised that home owners would not be taxed on the interest they paid on their mortgages. This program would have cost the government a lot of money. In the end, only a partial tax break was offered.

Clark promised to sell Petro-Can, the government-owned oil company. Many Canadians did not like this idea as they felt Petro-Can was one way Canada could control her energy supply. The Clark government did not act on this promise while they were in power.

Clark promised to lower interest rates. Soon after he was elected interest rates rose in the United States and he allowed them to rise in Canada as well.

Clark promised to lower taxes. After the election he announced the Liberals had left the country in a worse mess than he had expected. To correct the situation, the Conservative budget in December called for higher taxes.

Number of MPs elected by province, 1979 and 1980
The percentage of the vote for each party is shown in parentheses

	Conservative		Liberal		NDP	
	1979	1980	1979	1980	1979	1980
Nfld.	2 (29%)	2 (36%)	4 (40%)	5 (47%)	1 (30%)	0 (17%)
N.S.	8 (45%)	6 (39%)	2 (35%)	5 (40%)	1 (19%)	0 (21%)
P.E.I.	4 (52%)	2 (46%)	0 (40%)	2 (47%)	0 (6%)	0 (7%)
N.B.	4 (40%)	3 (32%)	6 (44%)	7 (50%)	0 (15%)	0 (16%)
Que.	2 (13%)	1 (12%)	67 (61%)	74 (67%)	0 (5%)	0 (9%)
Ont.	57 (42%)	38 (36%)	32 (36%)	52 (42%)	6 (21%)	5 (22%)
Man.	7 (43%)	5 (38%)	2 (23%)	2 (28%)	5 (36%)	7 (33%)
Sask.	10 (41%)	7 (39%)	0 (22%)	0 (24%)	4 (36%)	7 (36%)
Alta.	21 (65%)	21 (65%)	0 (22%)	0 (22%)	0 (10%)	0 (10%)
B.C.	19 (44%)	16 (41%)	1 (23%)	0 (22%)	8 (32%)	12 (35%)
N.W.T.	0 (32%)	1 (24%)	1 (34%)	0 (36%)	0 (32%)	1 (38%)
Yukon	1 (44%)	1 (40%)	0 (30%)	0 (39%)	0 (25%)	0 (20%)
CANADA	136 (36%)	103 (32%)	114 (40%)	147 (44%)	26 (18%)	32 (20%)

In 1979, 6 Créditiste (Social Credit) MPs were elected from the province of Quebec. In 1980 the Quebec Créditiste vote dropped from 16% to 6%, and no members were elected.

The Liberals and the New Democrats were opposed to the rise in taxes. Clark had to rely on the 5 Créditiste members from Quebec to support the budget. But their leader, Fabien Roy, felt the budget did not offer enough safeguards for Quebec.

On 13 December the Liberals joined the NDP in a motion to defeat the government. The Conservatives were caught by surprise. They had not expected the opposition parties to come together like this against the budget. After less than 7 months in power, the Clark government was defeated. Another election was called for 18 February 1980.

The Return of Pierre Trudeau

Shortly before the election was called, Trudeau had announced his resignation. Now he decided to run again. With the election so soon, the Liberal party felt it was safer not to bring in a new leader.

The Liberals made Joe Clark the main issue. They said he was weak and kept changing his mind. They also attacked the proposed rise in taxes and the gasoline prices. They said the Conservatives did not know how to run the country.

On election day the Liberals got enough seats to form a majority government. Pierre Trudeau was back in power. However, he faced some major problems. Quebec was about to hold a referendum on the issue of a new relationship with Canada. Not one Liberal had been elected west of Manitoba. Many westerners felt that no one in the government would care about what was best for them. Inflation, the energy crisis, and unemployment were as serious as ever.

Once again Canadians had turned to the man they had cheered in the exciting far-off days of 1968. It was Pierre Trudeau who led Canada into the eighties. This time expectations were more down to earth.

Questions and Activities

Match the persons or groups in column A with the sport or field of entertainment in column B.

A	B
1. Pitseolak	a) international sport (e.g. hockey)
2. Anne Murray	b) creative writing
3. Edmonton Oilers	c) soccer
4. Dan George	d) baseball
5. Rush	e) art
6. Montreal Expos	f) WHA and NHL hockey
7. Alice Munro	g) singing
8. Team Canada	h) rock music
9. Vancouver Whitecaps	i) acting

Ideas for Discussion

1. Brainstorm to draw up a list of arguments for and against wage and price controls as a way to fight inflation.
2. Invite a union representative and a management representative to visit your class. Prepare a list of questions to ask them.
3. "There is no Canadian identity." Brainstorm arguments for and against this idea.
4. Petro-Canada, established in 1975, is a "crown corporation," meaning it is owned by all Canadians.
   a) Do you think it is a good idea for Canadians to "own" an oil company?
   b) If you saw two service stations offering gas at the same price and one of them was a Petro-Canada station, would you take your car there or to the other station?

5. Canadian sports heroes include Nancy Green, Cindy Nicholas, Abby Hoffman, and Tracey Wainman. Yet the professional sports teams that attract the most attention and regular TV coverage are almost entirely male. Why do you think this is? Do you think anything could be done to change the situation? Do you think anything *should* be done?
6. Name jobs that before the 1970s might have been considered "for men" or "for women" in the following areas:
   a) offices
   b) factories
   c) farms
   d) hospitals
   e) schools
   f) homes
7. Are boys and girls treated equally in your school? Provide specific examples to support your ideas. Write a letter to the school board outlining any changes you feel should be made in your school. Be sure to send a copy of the letter to your principal.

Do Some Research

1. Find out what the prices of ten everyday items were in 1970 and compare them with the prices today. Some areas to consider are food, clothing, housing, busfares, newspapers, records, tickets to movies and sports events. Compare average salaries as well. What conclusions can you draw?
2. Analyse a recent strike in your community.
   a) What was the position of the workers?
   b) What was the position of management?
   c) What was the final settlement? Were workers and management both satisfied?
   d) How did the strike affect your community?
   e) What are your personal reactions to this strike?
3. On pages 23 and 198 are two artists' very different impressions of Canada's national sport. Go to the library and find a reproduction of a famous hockey picture by artist Ken Danby. Which do you think is the most imaginative? the most realistic? How well do you think each painting captures the true spirit of hockey? Find other works of art inspired by some aspect of sport.
4. Do some research about one of your favourite Canadian sports or entertainment personalities. Write a biocard. Pass the cards around the class and then assemble them in a class folder.
5. Organize a survey of your school to determine the cultural and language background of the school population. Make a wall display of your findings. You might use a world map and graphs to highlight the statistics.
6. Does your school have any special programs to help new Canadians adjust to life in this country?

7. Do you think the "point system" of selecting immigrants is really fair? How would you change it or improve it?
8. There is prejudice in Canada not only against immigrants from other countries but also against other groups that people perceive as "different." Find out more about one such group. What can you do to help them become fully accepted as part of Canadian society?

Be Creative

1. Write a letter to a local newspaper outlining your ideas on an aspect of one of the following:
   a) sexual equality   c) Canadian culture
   b) native rights   d) immigration policy
2. Organize a radio or television program to re-enact a famous sporting event of the 1960s or 1970s. Present your program to the rest of the class.
3. Present a visual or sound collage on one of Canada's most famous musicians, singers, artists, actors, dancers, or writers.
4. Organize a multicultural "caravan" or pageant in your class or school.
5. Design a Participaction exercise program your family might enjoy.

You Are There

You and the other members of your class work for Alpha Corporation. Your jobs involve assembling high technology radio and radar equipment. The work force is about 75% female and 25% male. Four weeks ago, you and the other members of your union voted to go on strike. You have been walking the picket lines ever since. The union's strike fund has given you some money, but not nearly enough to cover your living expenses.

Now your union negotiators and the company have agreed on issues affecting wages, fringe benefits, and safety. However, issues of special importance to the women working in the plant have been rejected by the company.

Union leaders have called a meeting today to decide whether to accept the company's offer or to continue the strike. As you enter the hall in a nearby community centre, you are handed a sheet summarizing the state of negotiations. You read the list of accepted and rejected demands, and make up your mind on how you will vote. When the meeting is called to order, you should be prepared to speak up for your point of view.

Would your position be any different if you were male or female? Why or why not?

Electronic Workers' Union Local 198

Report of the Strike Committee

Fellow workers, as you know, our negotiating team has been meeting with Alpha Corporation representatives. Last night we began to feel we were getting somewhere. The company has finally agreed to some of our demands, but not all. However, we felt we should put the offer to a vote, even though it is not entirely satisfactory.

UNION DEMANDS	COMPANY POSITION
1. Wage increases as requested over a two-year contract period.	Accepted.
2. Better fringe benefits including a dental plan.	Accepted.
3. Improved pensions.	Accepted.
4. New, tougher safety regulations.	Accepted.
5. Six months' paid maternity leave.	Rejected.
6. Day-care facilities in the plant.	Rejected.
7. Improvement of washroom facilities. (As we all know, the plant was built for an all-male work force.)	Rejected.
8. Equal pay for work of equal value.	The company says it has the right to decide the pay levels of jobs.
9. More equal opportunities for promotion.	The company claims opportunities are already equal and that it does not discriminate against women.

Canada and the World
ADVANCE ORGANIZER

1

Out of the ashes of World War II rose the United Nations. The UN was created to prevent future wars and to promote world co-operation. Most countries, including Canada, are members of the United Nations. Canada has solidly supported the UN with money, people and materials. Canadian soldiers have served in several UN peace-keeping operations.

2

Since the introduction of atomic warfare in World War II, an all-out war can now mean the destruction of our entire world. For this reason there has come about a new form of war, called the Cold War. The Cold War is a war of nerves. The major powers threaten each other with displays of military strength rather than outright warfare. Canada lies between the two main rivals — the United States and the Soviet Union.

To help keep peace and to protect Canadian interests, Canada has joined two major alliances. These are NATO and NORAD. Canada supports NATO to protect Europe against aggression by the Soviet Union or its allies. Canada and the U.S. form NORAD, whose goal is to protect North America from enemy attack. Membership in these alliances could at some time involve Canada in a major war.

3

Not all of Canada's foreign ties are of a military nature. Canada is a member of two non-military organizations — the Commonwealth and la Francophonie. The Commonwealth is a free association of peoples once ruled by the British Empire. La Francophonie is a free association of French-speaking nations of the world. Both of these bodies provide Canada with friendships all over the globe.

4

Canada is concerned about a number of trouble spots in the world. Of increasing importance are the Third World countries. These are the poor, often starving nations of Africa, Asia, and South America. Their people account for well over half of the world's population. Canada has given money and supplies, and has sent people as advisers to help improve conditions within these countries.

At the opposite end of the economic scale are the Arab countries of the Middle East. These countries have vast quantities of oil and therefore hold power over other countries. Canada needs oil from the Middle East, and values the Middle East as a trading partner. To help ease tensions, Canadian soldiers have served as peace-keepers for the United Nations in the Middle East as well as other parts of the world.

Word List

acid rain	Francophonie	Third World
boycott	ideology	United Nations
Cold War	NATO	veto
Commonwealth	satellite	Warsaw Pact

5

Although Canada and the United States share the same continent, it is surprising how little the people of each country know each other. Stereotypes have been created by the movies, television, and other media. Although many of the stereotypes are old ones, for the most part they are still with us. A clear, unbiased image of each other would make for easier social and economic relations. With the increasing tensions in the world today, such mutual understanding would greatly benefit both countries.

6

At the turn of the century Canada considered its ties to the British Empire the most important. Between the wars Canada began to stand independently in foreign affairs but seldom looked beyond its borders. Since World War II Canada has taken full part in both continental and world affairs. Now the most important aspect of Canadian foreign policy is our relationship with the Americans. The United States is our most important trading partner and military ally. Canada and the U.S. share many political, cultural, and economic interests. However, they sometimes disagree over the handling of different problems. In the end, each country tries to protect its own interests. Americans have invested in Canada and promoted Canadian economic growth. At the same time Canadians are anxious to maintain control of their own companies. Still, each country is likely to become more dependent on the other in years to come. It is important that Canada and the U.S. keep their alliance an open and friendly one.

The United Nations

As World War II entered its final days in Europe, representatives of 50 nations met in San Francisco. Their dream was to build an organization to maintain peace and promote friendly relations among all countries of the world. They called this organization the United Nations.

After World War I a similar organization, the League of Nations, had been formed. The League of Nations had not been able to control the actions of nations like Japan, Italy, and Germany because other member nations had refused to act against them. The delegates at San Francisco were determined to learn from the mistakes of the League of Nations.

The United Nations was to be much stronger than the old League. It would help solve all important problems facing the world — political, economic, social, and cultural. In short, the United Nations was to be a centre of international co-operation.

Six Languages

The United Nations is a fascinating but gigantic and confusing organization. An army of interpreters are required to translate debates. Delegates may speak in any of six official languages — Arabic, Chinese, English, French, Russian, and Spanish. About 150 countries are members of the UN. The headquarters are on the banks of the Hudson River in New York City, but the UN has offices in many countries all over the world.

When the United Nations building was opened, Canada's gift was the nickel-bronze doors that lead to the General Assembly. The panels of the doors represent four themes — peace, justice, truth, and brotherhood. Surely these themes are central to the work of the United Nations.

It took the Nations of the world many meetings to decide how the United Nations should be organized. Its structure is the result of compromise.

The General Assembly is the central body of the UN. All other agencies report to it. Each member nation is represented here. Each has one vote. The General Assembly meets once a year to debate important issues.

The Security Council is responsible for maintaining peace and security. Britain, China, France, the Soviet Union, and the United States — the world's big powers — are permanent members. The General Assembly elects 10 non-permanent members for two-year terms. The 5 permanent members each have a *veto*, or the right to forbid action by the council. Many people think this veto power is a serious weakness in times of crisis.

The Secretariat is the permanent staff of the United Nations. It is headed by the Secretary General. The Secretary General is responsible for the day-to-day running of the UN. Another duty is to bring matters that threaten international peace to the attention of the UN. The job requires great diplomatic skill.

Agencies of the UN include many international councils and organizations to deal with specific international concerns. Here is a list of some of these agencies:

ILO (International Labour Organization)
IMF (International Monetary Fund) and World Bank
FAO (Food and Agriculture Organization)
UNESCO (United Nations Educational, Scientific, and Cultural Organization)
UNICEF (United Nations Children's Fund)
WHO (World Health Organization)

FOCUS

What is the main purpose of the UN?
Note 5 ways in which the UN has made the world a better place.
Do you think the United Nations will be able to prevent the outbreak
of another world war?

Girls in Mersa, Ethiopia, collect water for their families from a UNICEF sponsored water system.

1981-1990

City children in Lusaka, Zambia.

The UN asks the world to focus on certain issues by proclaiming "Years" like International Women's Year, World Refugee Year, the Year of the Child, and the Year of Disabled Persons. In addition the UN undertakes longterm projects like wiping out the killer disease smallpox. This was accomplished in the 1970s. The 1980s was declared the Water Decade. The goal: "safe drinking water and adequate sanitation for all by 1990."

The UN's Work

Has the UN succeeded in promoting peace and security? The UN has helped to end wars in Asia, Africa, and the Middle East. UN agencies have fed millions of starving people. They have helped to wipe out bitter diseases like smallpox. UN conferences have established laws for the oceans and the peaceful uses of outer space. The UN has sponsored special programs like International Women's Year, the Year of the Child, and the Year of Disabled Persons.

Yet wars still break out. The threat of nuclear destruction continues to grow. Leaders arm their people instead of feeding them. The big powers often promote their own interests rather than the good of the entire world. They have used military force against others, and avoided working through the United Nations.

Canada has been one of the United Nations' strongest supporters. Along with other nations she has contributed money for general upkeep as well as many special projects. When the UN has organized peace-keeping missions Canadian troops have served with patience and courage. Lester Pearson was once elected as president of the General Assembly. General Burns led the UN peace-keeping force in Suez and worked with the UN Disarmament Commission. Maurice Strong helped provide technical assistance for developing countries.

The United Nations cannot solve all the world's problems. However, it has certainly helped to prevent small wars from becoming big wars. It has helped nations restore peace and ensure that treaties are kept. Its agencies help the world's people in many ways. Without the United Nations, the world would be a poorer and more dangerous place.

The Cold War

Everything of importance that happens in the world is of interest to Canada — often of direct and immediate interest. For us there is no escape in isolation or indifference. Recent events have brought home to all of us the increasing threat to our democracy of the rising tide of communism.

Louis St. Laurent, 1948

What is a "Cold War"? It is not guns, bombs, tanks, and soldiers. It is a war of words, threats, spies, secrets, and fear. It is an arms race, in which each side strives to have more and better weapons than the other. The big powers now possess enough nuclear weapons to kill everyone in the world several times over. The world spends more on arms than it does on food, housing, or medicine.

When World War II came to an end, the Soviet Union met her western allies along a line through central Europe. That line was to become an "Iron Curtain" dividing the world into two rival camps. The Soviets did not withdraw from the lands they had occupied. They helped people in these countries to set up communist governments. The United States and other western nations protested. But the nations on the other side of the Iron Curtain became the Soviet Union's allies or "satellites."

The Cold War is based on the clash of ideas. The "communist world" believes that economic equality for all citizens is more important than free elections and free speech. The "free world" believes the opposite.

Fear and Suspicion

The Cold War overshadowed the peace and prosperity of the fifties. The climate of fear in the West was intensified when the Soviet Union exploded its first hydrogen bomb in 1953 just 7 months after the United

The Hooded Spy

In September 1945 Igor Gouzenko left the Soviet Embassy in Ottawa with 109 top secret documents hidden under his shirt. They revealed the existence of a spy ring that had passed vital atomic secrets to the Soviet Union.

Canadian authorities believed Gouzenko had made the whole thing up until he was nearly kidnapped by Soviet agents. Then the RCMP put Gouzenko under their protection and began to hunt the spies down.

Thirteen spies were on the staff of the Soviet Embassy, but others were Canadian military officers, scientists, and one member of parliament. Canadians became nervous about anyone who had ever expressed admiration for communism or for the U.S.S.R. One result of the Gouzenko affair was a "witch hunt" for possible communists in the CBC and the National Film Board.

When Gouzenko appeared in public he always wore a hood to protect his new identity. In 1948 he wrote a book about the affair called *This Was My Choice*. He died in 1982.

States. It reached a peak in 1957 when the Soviets launched a space satellite, Sputnik, long before the American space program was ready to do so. Americans began to build nuclear fall-out shelters. Some expected nuclear war was very near.

In the decades that followed, the world learned to live with the Cold War. At times the Soviet Union and the United States seemed to come closer together. They have signed treaties limiting the size and type of weapons they will develop. At others it seemed a single spark might turn the Cold War into a "hot war." Certainly there have been numerous "brush-fire wars" over local issues in many parts of the world. The two super powers have often tried to increase their influence by supplying "military assistance" to one side or the other in local wars.

What is the Cold War?
Why is the Cold War a matter of concern for Canadians?
Should Canada be the United States' ally in the Cold War?
Explain your answer.

1900 1910 1920 1930 1940 1950 1960 1970 1980 1990 2000

Canada and the Cold War

Canada lies directly between two giant war machines, the United States and the Soviet Union. Therefore, Canada has a special stake in maintaining world peace.

Canada is firmly on the side of the United States. She is a member of the American-led NATO alliance. She is a partner in NORAD, the North American defence system. At the same time Canada has tried to serve as a peace-maker. She has maintained friendly relations with communist countries like the Soviet Union, China, and Cuba at times when the United States would not do so. This has been useful in times of crisis, because both sides have been ready to respect Canadian diplomats.

Until World War II Canada had stayed out of international affairs as much as possible. After the war Canadian politicians realized that in the modern world such "isolationism" was no longer practical. The first test of the new attitude came when the Cold War turned hot in Korea in 1950. The U.S.A., along with Canada and 30 other countries, contributed to a UN army to fight in Korea. Though the Korean War ended in 1953, UN troops still patrol the border between North and South Korea.

CBC reporter René Lévesque carries his portable tape recorder on his head as he crosses a stream on the way to do an on-the-spot report on the Royal Canadian Regiment in the heart of enemy territory. Korea, 14 August 1951.

Will the world survive the twentieth century without a nuclear war? There are good signs and bad signs. Certainly, governments understand that no one wins such a war. Yet people fear that international tensions may become so great that one side or the other may "push the button." Canada and Canadians will do what they can to act as peacemakers in the future as they have in the past.

Canada's Alliances

Several times a year, a Canadian Forces officer is found in charge of the largest, most sophisticated defence system in the world. This officer has the power to start a massive nuclear strike almost anywhere on the planet. Yet Canada has no nuclear weapons and limited armed forces. It is Canada's alliances that have gigantic military strength.

An alliance is formed when two or more nations agree to help each other. Most are military alliances for defence. Canada belongs to two major alliances — NATO and NORAD. Canada joined these alliances because of the threat of the Cold War, and the lessons learned from two world wars. It is a strange thought that in order to prevent another war, Canada is part of two massive military machines.

Canada and Europe

Canada was an active founding partner of the North Atlantic Treaty Organization (NATO) in 1949. This alliance includes the United States, Britain, and other European nations. The main purpose of this alliance is to protect western Europe. In response, the Soviet Union brought the Communist countries together in an alliance called the Warsaw Pact. Both alliances are ready to fight an all-out war.

All countries in NATO are pledged to support each other if attacked. They contribute to the defence of western Europe and the North Atlantic. Today Canadian ships patrol the ocean for NATO watching for submarines. Five thousand Canadian troops are stationed in Europe.

Canadian forces on NATO exercises in West Germany.

What is the purpose of NATO and NORAD?
Why do some Canadians question our participation in these alliances?
Should Canada continue to be a member of NATO and NORAD?

1900 1910 1920 1930 1940 1950 1960 1970 1980 1990 2000

Canada in North America

In 1958 Canada and the United States entered an alliance for North American Air Defence (NORAD). NORAD is designed to protect North America from attack by the Soviet Union by detecting and intercepting manned bomber or missile attacks.

North America is defended by lines of radar stations and air bases in the North. Hundreds of missiles are aimed at targets in the Soviet Union. Bombers and fighters are in the air at all times ready for combat. It would take only few pushed buttons for destruction to be unleashed on the Soviet Union.

HMCS *Iroquois* tests a Sea Sparrow missile near Puerto Rico.

NORAD headquarters are located deep inside a granite mountain in Colorado. The commander of NORAD is always an American. The second-in-command is always a Canadian. When the American is absent, the Canadian officer is in charge of this huge military machine.

Recently, however, Canadians have raised serious questions about our alliances. Some of these questions concern costs. Others are about the basic nature of the alliances.

The F-18 A Hornet, Canada's new fighter aircraft.

The Alliances Today

Maintaining NATO and NORAD is extremely costly. Perhaps Canada should spend more on foreign aid or social programs at home. In a cost-cutting move, Canada reduced the size of her armed forces during the 1970s. This angered other members of the alliances.

Many Canadians feel it is dangerous that these alliances are so heavily dominated by the United States. They fear war may break out before Canada is properly consulted. They feel the alliances would be more useful if they were cultural and economic as well as military.

The world is once again in a period of tension and uncertainty. In times like these, there is little desire to pull out of NATO and NORAD. Rather than pull out, Canada is starting to re-equip her armed forces. Up-to-date weapons like the CF18 Hornet fighter have been ordered so Canada can better fulfil her commitments to these alliances.

Alliances would be no protection from the tragedy of a nuclear war. The only hope is that they may help to prevent it happening.

Commonwealth and Francophonie

Canada is a member of two multiracial and multicultural associations: the Commonwealth and La Francophonie. These two world-wide "clubs" have helped Canadians establish friendly ties with many nations.

The Commonwealth

Britain once ruled countries located all over the world. As these countries gained their independence it was decided a new form of association should take the

Queen Elizabeth II, head of the Commonwealth, at her coronation in 1953.

place of the British Empire. In 1926 it was given the name of the Commonwealth of Nations. The king or queen of Britain was recognized as the head of the Commonwealth.

The Commonwealth is a loose economic and cultural association. Members often give each other easier terms in trade agreements. The Colombo Plan was organized in 1950. This scheme gave aid and technology to the poorer nations of the Commonwealth. Canada's contribution through the Colombo Plan has been over $2 billion. In sports athletes find the Commonwealth Games a stirring challenge. Commonwealth scholarships are available for students from all member nations.

Commonwealth leaders meet regularly. Even though it is such a loose association, it can take some tough policy decisions. In 1961 South Africa left the Commonwealth because of criticism over the treatment of non-white South Africans. In 1980 the Commonwealth was involved in solving a 15-year-old racial and political crisis in Zimbabwe (at that time called Rhodesia). The Commonwealth will probably take similar stands in the future, especially on the issue of human rights.

> **The Commonwealth is people meeting together, consulting, learning from each other, trying to persuade each other, and sometimes co-operating with each other regardless of economy, geography, ideology, religion, or race.**
> *Julius Nyerere, President of Tanzania*

La Francophonie

After Paris, Montreal is the largest French-speaking city in the world. It is natural that Canada should be a member of La Francophonie, a voluntary association of French-speaking nations.

La Francophonie is a little like the Commonwealth. Most of the participating nations were once part of the French Empire. Canada has had no political links with France for over 200 years, but the ties of language and culture remain deep. La Francophonie is less organized than the Commonwealth. The economic connection is less well developed. For example, a lot of Canadian aid goes to poorer countries in La Francophonie. However, it is given directly rather than through the association. On the other hand, cultural ties are probably stronger than they are in the Commonwealth. In 1974 La Francophonie took part in a huge festival in Quebec to celebrate the culture of 25 French-speaking nations.

Membership in La Francophonie is a delicate question in Canada. The federal government maintains the right to control international affairs. This includes sending delegates to La Francophonie meetings. The government of Quebec wishes to be represented independently in La Francophonie. Usually both governments appoint members of the

What types of activity are promoted by the Commonwealth?
What issue has created political problems for Canada in
La Francophonie?
How does membership in these associations benefit Canada?

Canadian delegation. A meeting was scheduled to be
held in Senegal in 1980. The federal government
refused to accept a Quebec cabinet minister as a
delegate. Quebec refused to appoint a less important
official. The president of France said the meeting was
pointless if Quebec was not represented. His country
would not attend. Therefore the meeting was
cancelled.

Windows on the World

The Commonwealth and La Francophonie provide
Canada with friendly contacts all over the world.
Canada, with her two official languages, is a leading
member of both associations. In the long run, such
economic and cultural ties may prove more rewarding
than military alliances.

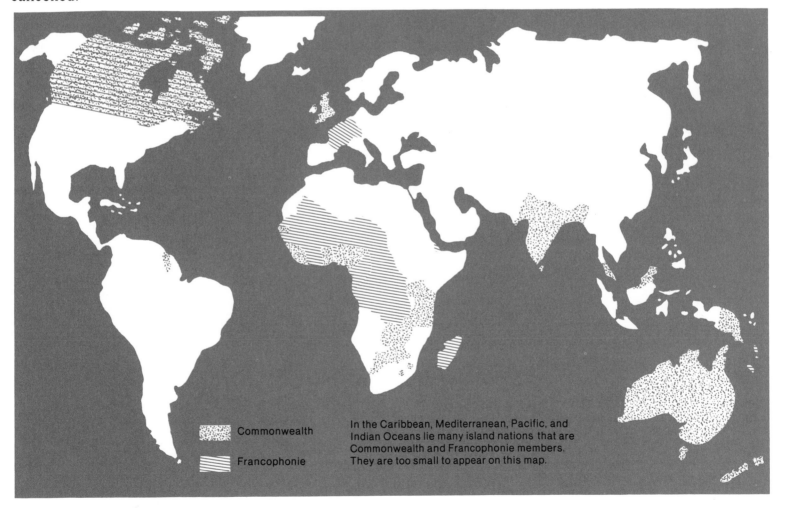

Commonwealth

Francophonie

In the Caribbean, Mediterranean, Pacific, and
Indian Oceans lie many island nations that are
Commonwealth and Francophonie members.
They are too small to appear on this map.

The Third World

Over half the world's population never has enough to eat. Home is often a shack, crowded with children and adults. Many people never have a chance to learn to read and write. If they get sick, medical aid is often non-existent. In times of war, floods, or earthquakes, there are no disaster funds for emergency relief. On top of this many nations are governed by ruthless power cliques. Citizens may have no civil rights.

Why should Canada help the countries of the Third World? Besides humanitarian reasons, Canada has 3 major concerns.
Political: It is in our interest to help Third World countries. Great poverty can push them to try a communist system of government. They might become unfriendly towards us.
Economic: We can help ourselves by helping Third World countries. If countries become richer through Canadian aid programs, they may be able to buy Canadian products and Canadian technology.
Military: Poverty and hardship can lead to violence and war. If poor countries are not given help, they may use war as a tool to better themselves. First and Second World countries could also come to blows over their different hopes for Third World countries.

Yet these concerns are not uppermost in the hearts and minds of Canadians when they reach into their pockets or leave their homes to teach, nurse, or help feed the people of the Third World. Canadians care because fellow human beings suffer.

Observers have divided the modern world into three communities:

The First World is made up of wealthy "democratic" countries with highly developed technological societies. Canada is part of this world.

The Second World is made up of the "communist" nations. The Soviet Union leads this world.

The Third World consists of most of the nations in Africa, Asia, and South America. These nations are generally poor. The bulk of their people are usually non-white. Many are former colonies of First World countries. Some of these countries have found oil and other valuable resources. They are using these resources to improve their position. Most Third World nations, however, are poor and getting poorer. Two-thirds of the world's people live in the Third World.

Left, in the west African country of Benin, learning farming methods is as important as math or shorthand. Below, in Colombia, South America, city children attend a "school of benches" in a neighbourhood backyard. UNICEF helps parents act as "teachers" and provides materials.

FOCUS

What is the Third World?
Give 4 reasons why Canadians should be concerned about conditions in the Third World.
Does aid to the Third World really help? Discuss.

Aid for the Third World

A great deal of assistance from the First and Second World is channelled through the United Nations and UN agencies. Canada contributes to many UN aid programs.

Canada also has her own program of foreign aid, run by the Canadian International Development Agency. Canadian money and expert advice are used in many Third World countries to find wells, build dams, teach good nutrition, or develop farms, fisheries, or factories.

Volunteer groups like the Red Cross, the Save the Children Fund, and the Foster Parents Plan also do their part. Money comes from Canadians in all walks of life. Young people collect money on Hallowe'en for UNICEF or undertake special projects to aid the Third World.

Yet the problems remain severe. The money spent on foreign aid is a small fraction of what the world spends on weapons. Often aid never reaches the people it is intended for because of inefficiency or dishonesty.

Cardinal Léger enjoys a game played by some patients at his Rehabilitation Centre in Cameroon.

Some projects have been poorly thought out and are massive failures. Others have been wiped out by floods or wars.

Is it worth it? International aid seems to be a losing battle. But Canadians must remain hopeful and have faith in humanity's future. They must be prepared to be even more generous. The pinch of inflation does not change the fact that Canada is a rich country. It can afford to help. The alternative is to give up on half the world's people. The future is with the children. Can Canadians turn their backs on them?

Paul-Emile Cardinal Léger
"The bishop who serves"

1904 — born in Valleyfield, Que.
1923 — felt called to priesthood.
1929 — made a priest. Went to France to study and teach.
1933 — sent to Japan to open seminary for priests.
1939 — recalled to teach in Montreal.
1940 — returned to work in Valleyfield.
1947 — rector of Canadian Pontifical College in Rome. Raised money in Canada for poor in the war-torn city.
1950 — made Archbishop of Montreal. "The little ones, the humble, the poor, the sick, and the workers will be the chosen portion of our fold."
1953 — made a cardinal, a prince of the R.C. church.
1962-65 — at 2nd Vatican Council argued for reform of church to make it more relevant to modern world.
1963 — visited Africa. Set up *Fame Pereo* (I am dying of hunger). Organization has aided 82 leprosy colonies in 20 African countries.
1967 — "retired" from high post in Montreal to serve as missionary in Africa. Set up Centre for the Rehabilitation of the Handicapped in Cameroon.
1970 — set up organization to administer and raise money for his many projects.
1979 — appointed with Roland Michener to head special fund to help Vietnamese boat people. Officiated at funeral of brother, Jules (governor general, 1973-79).

Hotspot: The Middle East

World War I started in Europe. World War II had its roots in Europe and East Asia. If there is to be a third world war, many observers expect it will flare up in the Middle East.

The Middle East has huge oil reserves. For that reason alone, the super powers each want to dominate the region. They try to influence the internal politics of Middle Eastern countries and their relationships with the rest of the world.

Canada, like other countries, has a strong interest in the Middle East. Some Canadian homes are heated by Middle Eastern fuel oil. Canadian businesses want contracts to develop industry and technology in the region. Some Canadian families migrated from the Middle East. Others have relatives who have chosen to live in the state of Israel, which was established after World War II. Because Canada wants world peace, Canadian troops have served on United Nations peace-keeping missions in the Middle East.

The Suez Crisis

1956 was probably the first time many Canadians were aware that the Middle East was an unstable trouble spot. Four years before, the Egyptians had overthrown their ruler, King Farouk. The new leader, Colonel Nasser, was determined Egypt should be strong. Britain and France had controlled the country when the hated Farouk was king. Therefore, Nasser turned to the Soviet Union for military and economic aid. This made Israel nervous of the power of her Arab neighbour.

In 1956, Nasser nationalized the Suez Canal, taking it from its French and British owners. Israel invaded Egyptian territory. France and Britain bombed Egypt and captured the canal. The Soviet Union threatened to send troops to help Egypt. The United States announced she was against the use of force. Yet she did little to discourage France and Britain.

This bridge was destroyed by the Jordanian army in 1967 to stop a possible Israeli invasion. Arab refugees from the West Bank of the Jordan River continued to use the crippled structure to cross into Arab-held territory.

The Israeli army moves through the Sinai desert, 1967.

Give 3 reasons why the Middle East is important to Canada.
How did Canada help end the Suez crisis?
Why should Canadians try to be aware of Middle Eastern politics and customs?

1900 1910 1920 1930 1940 1950 1960 1970 1980 1990 2000

The United Nations feared this would mean another world war. Canada worked hard through the UN to end the crisis. Lester Pearson developed a plan to end the fighting. All forces withdrew from the combat zone. They were replaced by a UN peace-keeping force. The force contained 1000 Canadian troops as well as soldiers from other nations. It was led by Canada's General Burns. Although trouble

A Canadian member of a UN peace keeping force on guard duty.

remained, the crisis was over. Pearson received the Nobel Peace Prize for his efforts.

Unfortunately the UN troops left in 1967 at Egypt's request. Later that year war between Israel and Egypt closed the canal. That meant ships, including oil tankers, had to go all the way around Africa to get from the Middle East to Europe and North America. The canal did not reopen until 1978. At that time Egypt and Israel were trying to establish better relations.

Tensions in the Middle East

The Suez Crisis is only one example of trouble in the Middle East. Severe tension exists between Israel and her Arab neighbours. This tension has turned to open war several times. In 1973 it helped lead to the Arab nations' decision to increase the price of oil.

Arab nations cannot be regarded as a united group. They also have differences among themselves. In 1980 war broke out between Iran and Iraq. Some Arab

Arab refugees.

nations supported one side and some the other.

For a country like Canada, maintaining good relations with the Middle East is like walking a tightrope. Canada needs Middle East oil. Canadian businesses want to take advantage of the wealth of the area. They see the Middle East as a market for their agricultural goods and manufactured products. They see opportunities for Canadians technology to help in developing the region. In order to keep these doors open, Canadians must try to understand middle eastern politics and customs. For example, Joe Clark's proposal to move the Canadian embassy in Israel to Jerusalem in 1979 offended most Arabs. The Arab nations consider that Israel's occupation of Jerusalem is illegal. They threatened to cut trade with Canada. The idea of moving the embassy was quickly abandoned. However, some Canadian companies had already lost valuable contracts.

Modern trade and communications make us more dependent on each other. Canadians cannot afford to ignore problems in the Middle East or in any other part of the world.

The American Connection

In the past Canadians and Americans have shot and killed each other. They have also fought and died side by side against a common enemy. Canadians and Americans have invaded each other's territory. Yet today they share the world's longest undefended border.

Canadian governments have made laws designed to keep American money and influence out of Canada. However, they have also co-operated with Americans and jointly spent billions on vast projects that benefit both countries.

Relations with the U.S. are the most important Canada has with any foreign country. These relations will continue to play a central part in the lives of both peoples. Both hope that in the future they will be partners rather than rivals.

Yet how well do Americans know Canadians? How well do Canadians know Americans? Might their views of each other stand in the way of understanding?

Canadians Talk of Americans

Everyone in the U.S. owns a gun, or would like to.

Americans all live in cities in big apartment buildings. They have to breathe their air through filters so they won't die of smog and pollution.

Americans just think about money and big business. They either have big houses or fast cars.

Americans show their feelings more than we do. They might be the first to get angry, but they're the first to help you out of a tight spot, too.

Americans get their foreign policy from those John Wayne movies — "Shoot first and ask questions later."

The major threat to Canadian survival today is American control of the Canadian economy.
The Waffle Manifesto

American Woman — stay away from me!
The Guess Who

Americans Talk of Canadians

Mountains. I think of mountains, and people singing.

Canadians are healthier than we are because they have to fight the elements to survive. Also probably because they're mostly descended from Eskimos, Indians, and Mounties.

The one thing I remember about Toronto is that you can read the map on the subway. In New York I never know where I'll end up, but Toronto's such a neat, itty-bitty place you can't get lost.

Canadians are nice and polite, not rude and noisy like some Americans you see. 'Course, I've only met but two Canadians I know of.

You're the ones who gave India the bomb, aren't you?

Canada will always be remembered by my generation as the nation that stood for peace, whether in the Middle East or Vietnam or Cyprus. If I were a Canadian, I'd rather have that said about me than anything else.

Short and fat and dark mostly and some of them speak French.

OCUS

Why is Canada's "American connection" important?
How well do you think Canadians and Americans know each other?
In your opinion, what has been the most important event
in Canadian-American relations? Why?

Partners or **Rivals?**

1775 — Americans invade Canada during the American Revolution.

1783 — British loyalists leave the U.S. to settle in Canada under the British flag.

1812-14 — War of 1812. Americans and Canadians invade each other's territory from the Atlantic to the Great Lakes.

1866 — Irish-American Fenians invade Canada.

1867 — Nova Scotia, New Brunswick, Quebec, and Ontario unite to form Canada partly in defence against the U.S.

1871 — Treaty of Washington — Canada, Britain, and U.S. settle long-standing differences peacefully.

1878 — John A. Macdonald's National Policy tries to defend Canadian economy from American economy.

1903 — Alaska boundary dispute. Americans gain territory at expense of Canada.

1911 — Election on reciprocity. Canadians reject idea of free trade with U.S.

1939-45 — In 1940 Canada and U.S. create a permanent Joint Board of Defence. From 1941 they fight side by side in the battles of World War II.

1949 — NATO is formed. Canada and U.S. are among founding members.

1951 — Massey Report warns of American cultural influence in Canada.

1954 — St. Lawrence Seaway project started. In 1959 Seaway is opened by Queen Elizabeth II and President Eisenhower.

1958 — NORAD is formed for defence of North America.

1961 — Columbia River Treaty. Gigantic joint power project on West Coast.

1962 — Cuban missile crisis. Canadian and American leaders disagree over action to be taken.

1963 — Canadians divided over issue of nuclear warheads for Bomarc missiles from U.S.

1965 — Auto Pact brings free trade and better job security for large segments of the auto industry.

1965 — Pearson criticizes U.S. role in Vietnam War.

1968 — Watkins Report warns of American domination of Canadian economy.

1969 — U.S. oil tanker _Manhattan_ voyages through Arctic waters against wishes of Canadian government.

1972 — Canada and U.S. agree to clean up pollution in Great Lakes.

1974 — FIRA (Foreign Investment Review Agency) created to screen foreign take-overs of Canadian businesses.

1976 — the American _Time_ magazine loses special tax exemption and ceases to publish Canadian edition. _Maclean's_ magazine grows to fill the gap in the market.

1977 — Canada and U.S. agree to recognize 200 mile fishery limits.

1980 — Canada and U.S. protest Soviet invasion of Afghanistan and join in boycott of Soviet products and Moscow Olympic Games.

1980 — Canadian government aids escape of American diplomats from Iran after U.S. embassy take-over.

1981 — Canadians and Americans debate who is to blame for acid rain pollution killing northeastern lakes.

The Political Connection

Canada and the United States share a vast continent. Relations between the two countries are usually warm and friendly. Sometimes there are moments of tension and concern. The prime minister of Canada and the president of the United States share the job of guiding the course of Canadian-American relations. The management of this intricate process is a true test of political leadership.

Prime Minister Trudeau and President Ford at the White House.

Foreign Affairs

Most of the time Canada and the United States agree about relations with other countries. They share many interests, have the same "friends," and belong to the same military alliances (NATO and NORAD). Occasionally the two countries disagree about how a situation should be handled.

One area where Canada and the United States have common interests is in the Middle East. Both want political stability in the Middle East. For example, they worked together to end the Suez crisis in 1956. Both want to ensure a secure supply of oil from the region.

On the other hand Canada did not approve of American involvement in the war in Vietnam. When

Pearson and Johnson.

Prime Minister Lester Pearson criticized the war to President Johnson, the president reacted in rage. A Canadian aide said he almost hit Pearson. In international affairs an "incident" like that might have been serious.

The United States has not approved when Canada established "diplomatic relations" with communist governments in Cuba and China. On the other hand, American leaders have later used Canada's stand as a stepping stone to creating better relations with these countries themselves.

American laws forbid American companies to sell goods to "enemy" countries. The United States government claims these laws extend to Canadian branches of American companies. Canadians have protested the loss of jobs when a Canadian branch is forced to cancel a sale by its parent company.

The Canadian Caper

Canada showed her friendship for the United States when the staff of the United States embassy were taken hostage in Iran in 1979. Six American diplomats who escaped found refuge in the homes of Canadian embassy officials. Over two months later in January 1980, they left Iran using fake Canadian passports. The Royal Canadian Mounted Police and the American Central Intelligence Agency had co-operated in preparing the passports and smuggling them into Iran. Overnight the Canadian ambassador, Ken Taylor, became an American hero. Perhaps, though, the greatest courage was shown by the wives of the Canadian officials. Night and day they lived in fear that the Iranians would discover the presence of their "house guests." It was up to these women to act at all times as if everything was completely natural in their homes.

Ken Taylor.

Note 3 areas of agreement and 3 areas of disagreement between Canada and the United States.
Did Canada do the right thing in helping the American diplomats in Iran? Why or why not?

The Mica Dam was completed in 1972 as part of the Columbia River Treaty Project. It is the highest earth-filled dam in the world outside the U.S.S.R.

Continental Affairs

Just as important as foreign affairs are direct relations between the two countries. Over the years Canada and the United States have co-operated on a wide range of projects. For example the St. Lawrence Seaway was started as a joint project in 1954. In 1961 a treaty was signed to dam the Columbia River to provide electricity for British Columbia and the State of Washington. The nations also have agreements to build several pipelines in the West. For various reasons these projects have not always run smoothly.

In the 1970s the environment became a matter of increasing concern. For example, the Canada-United States border runs through the Great Lakes. However, the water and the pollution in it flows freely from one side to the other. In 1972 a joint project was undertaken to clean up the Great Lakes.

Canadians are now worried about the effects of acid rain. The industry of central Canada and the northern United States creates air pollution. This is absorbed into the rain that falls on eastern North America. The most noticeable effect is that the rain kills plant and animal life in lakes. Canadians are trying to work out a treaty like the one that started the Great Lakes clean-up. As yet, American leaders have shown little interest in the idea.

Canada and the United States have both extended control over coastal waters to a "200 mile limit." Generally they have supported each other in this move. However, it has created new disputes over fishing rights within these waters. One treaty on fishing rights was signed by both governments, but the United States Senate refused to approve it. Another area for disagreement is the Arctic Ocean. Canada claims Arctic waters to the North Pole, but the United States maintains these are international waters.

Canadian-American relations will remain important in the years to come. Canadians and Americans are likely to rely on each other even more. Diplomats and political leaders will test their skills in keeping the association fair, open, and friendly.

Geography has made us neighbours. History has made us friends. Economics made us partners and necessity has made us allies. Those whom nature hath so joined together, let no man put asunder.

President John F. Kennedy to the Canadian Parliament, 1961

Our relationship has not been easy, but imagine for a moment, just how much worse it could have been. Then realize that with continued hard work and good faith it will last.

Prime Minister Pierre Elliott Trudeau to the U.S. Congress, 1977

The Cultural Connection

Many people claim that Canadians and Americans share much of the same culture. Culture means lifestyle. This includes beliefs, customs, attitudes, language, ways of working and relaxing. Is there any difference between Americans and Canadians?

The United States is a dynamic world power. The effects of Americanization are all over the world. You can sit down to a Big Mac in Europe or sip a Coke in China. Canada, for reasons of geography, numbers, and language, is the country most open to American influence.

Canada and the United States share a border 9000 km long. They have a similar history of settlement, immigration patterns, attitudes and approaches to the rest of the world. Canada's population is only one tenth the size of the United States'. Most people in the two countries speak the same language.

American radio, TV, movies pour across the border. Canadian artists, writers, actors, and musicians have found it hard to earn a living in their own country. Many talented Canadians have had to "make it in the U.S." before their work was accepted in Canada. They claim Canadians suffer from an inferiority complex when it comes to enjoying their own culture. They assume that "If it's Canadian, it can't be any good."

> A Canadian is someone who drinks Brazilian coffee from an English teacup and munches a French pastry while sitting on his Danish furniture having just come home from an Italian movie in his German car. He picks up his Japanese pen and writes to his Member of Parliament to complain about the American take-over of the Canadian publishing business.
>
> *Campbell Hughes, publishing executive, 1953.*

Some Canadians automatically read *Time* magazine rather than *Maclean's*. Their TVs are always on American channels. They listen to American pop songs and go to American movies. Their attitude seems to indicate they would really prefer to be American all the way.

In the 1970s changes in the tax laws made it more expensive for foreign magazines to publish in Canada. Today Canada has a booming "homegrown" magazine industry.

Why is Canadian culture so open to American influence?
Why do Canadian stars often find they must "make it in the U.S."
before they are recognized in their own country?
Does being Canadian mean something special to you?

1900 1910 1920 1930 1940 1950 1960 1970 1980 1990 2000

"International" Canadian stars: Burton Cummings, Anne Murray, Toller Cranston, Donald Sutherland, Karen Kain.

A Canadian Identity?

Yet when these same people go to Europe or Asia, a strange thing happens! If they are taken for Americans they become very indignant. "No, we are Canadians," they say. They paste maple leaves on their bags, so people will not make the same mistake again. Suddenly they are proud of their country and their heritage.

Which is the real Canada? Is is just the United States moved north? Or is there something about Canadian culture that is special and different?

The federal and provincial governments believe most Canadians want to retain an identity that is different from their neighbours to the south. Therefore they have looked for a number of ways to support the arts. The CBC, the National Film Board, the Canada Council, the Canadian Radio and Television Commission, and the Canadian Film Development Corporation have all sprung from the federal government's concern. Many provinces have provincial arts councils which try to support local and regional cultural activities as well as the arts in general. Business, too, realizes the benefits of a strong cultural life. Many companies give generously to sponsor concerts, theatre and dance companies, or art shows.

All this helps to give Canadian artists the opportunity to be appreciated in their own country.

However, the real decision about the future of Canadian culture lies with average Canadians. Only Canadians can decide if they want to be different from Americans. Only Canadians can develop their own dancers, novelists, sculptors, jazz musicians, and architects. If it means something special to be Canadian, Canadians must work to discover their national identity.

A language barrier can sometimes be useful. French Canadian artists like this pop group, Harmonium, can easily find a ready audience.

The Economic Connection

Canada lives next door to a giant. The American economy produces over a trillion dollars worth of wealth a year. Canadians both share and contribute to this wealth.

> **No matter where they locate in relation to where we reside, we're always delighted to hear of branch factories being established in Canada because of the employment they create for Canadian labour, the market they provide for Canadian farmers and merchants, and the business activity they stimulate in countless ways and in countless quarters.**
> *H.H. Stevens, Minister of Trade and Commerce, 1930*

Canadians and Americans are the closest trading and business partners in the world. Each year, billions of dollars worth of goods and services flow across the border. Americans invest and vacation in Canada. Canadians invest and vacation in the U.S. Many foreigners see Canada and the United States as a single economic unit.

> **Our problem is not to divorce the United States but how to live with it**
> *John Holmes, former Canadian diplomat*

However, Canada and the U.S. are not *equal* economic partners. The Canadian economy is much smaller than the American economy. The interests of Canadians and Americans are not always the same. The close relationship does present some problems.

> **The multinational corporation is like the man who came to dinner. You welcome him as a guest and then find that he's making the rules and giving the orders for the household.**
> *from* Gordon to Watkins to You: The Battle for Control of our Economy, *published in 1970*

Dependence

Many Canadians feel that Canada is too closely tied to the American economy. Since Canada is so much smaller, this makes Canadians dependent on Americans for our prosperity. This makes it difficult for Canada to act independently of the U.S. Often the economic well-being of Canadians rises and falls with decisions made "south of the border."

> **The United States is a good neighbour that never forgets self interest.**
> *Harry J. Boyle, author and former head of the CRTC*

The Question of Ownership

Foreigners own 275 of the 500 largest corporations in Canada. It has been said that Canadians are tenants rather than landlords in their own country. Millions of dollars worth of profits and resources leave Canada for the United States each year.

On the other hand, economists point out that American money has helped Canada grow strong and wealthy. Canadians have benefited from American technology and know-how. American investment has created millions of jobs in Canada. The close economic link has helped create friendly political and military relations.

What are some of the positive results of Canada's close economic relationship with the U.S.?
What are some of the negative results of this relationship?
Do you think the CDC and FIRA are worthwhile organizations?

1900 1910 1920 1930 1940 1950 1960 1970 1980 1990 2000

> It is because of American capital investment and the technology that comes with it, that we enjoy one of the highest standards of living in the world.
> *Pierre Elliott Trudeau*

Canada must always make sure that economic ties with the U.S. are in the best interest of Canadians. The Canadian government has taken steps to exercise some control over the relationship.

The Foreign Investment Review Agency (FIRA) investigates the purchase of Canadian companies by foreigners. If the agency feels these "take-overs" will not benefit Canadians, it can forbid them.

> The day is going to come when people are going to say, "Why were you so stupid? Why did you give it all away?"
> *Eric Kierans, Canadian economist and former Quebec cabinet minister and head of the Montreal Stock Exchange*

The Canada Development Corporation (CDC) is designed to help Canadians maintain ownership of their economy. The CDC invests in Canadian companies and projects. It is owned by the government and people of Canada.

In 1975 the Liberal government at the urging of the NDP created Petro-Can, a government-owned oil company. Petro-Can is designed to protect Canada's interest in the vital oil industry.

In recent years the government has encouraged Canadians to invest in Canadian companies through its tax policies. Taxes on profits from Canadian companies are much lower than those from foreign companies.

> If we continue the same way it will not be possible by the end of the 1980s for Canada to retain control over its economy.
> *Mel Hurtig, Alberta publisher*

Most Canadians feel the Canadian economy should be in the hands of Canadians. Canadians have benefited in the past from American investment. Yet in hard economic times like the late seventies and early eighties Canadians can be hurt by foreign control. American companies may decide to supply Canadian demands for their products from U.S. factories rather than keep Canadian branch plants open. This means lost jobs in Canada. The question of economic ties to the U.S. will become increasingly important.

> I say the hell with foreign investors and their investments. Let's make the 1980s the decade in which Canada does for itself what has to be done to bring our country to maturity.
> *James H. Gray, Canadian author and historian*

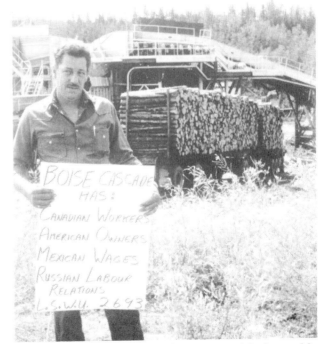

Labour unions often blame American ownership for problems in contract negotiations.

Questions and Activities

Word Scramble

Unscramble the letters to form terms introduced in this chapter.
1. INTUDE STONIAN
2. DHIRT RODWL
3. LCMTENOMAHWM
4. ZSEU RSCISI
5. LDCO RWA
6. 002 LEMI TLIMI

Test Yourself

Match the words in column A with the descriptions in column B.

A	B
1. Lester Pearson	a) person responsible for day-to-day activities of UN
2. NATO	b) Canadian-American alliance
3. Security Council	c) informer who helped break Soviet spy ring
4. NORAD	d) winner of Nobel Peace Prize
5. FIRA	e) leader in aid for Third World, especially to the handicapped
6. Secretary General	f) agency to screen foreign take-overs
7. La Francophonie	g) alliance to defend western Europe
8. CDC	h) body of UN responsible for maintaining peace
9. UNICEF	i) UN agency for children's welfare
10. Cardinal Léger	j) agency to promote Canadian ownership
11. Igor Gouzenko	k) association of French-speaking nations

Ideas for Discussion

1. Assume you have been elected Secretary General of the United Nations. Prepare a speech to be delivered to the representatives of the world in the General Assembly. Your working title might be "What We Must Do to Survive."
2. Between 1947 and 1982 Canada participated in every UN peace-keeping mission. Do you think Canada should continue to volunteer for these activities? Why or why not?
3. There are now over 100 000 nuclear weapons in the world. This is enough to kill everyone on the planet several times over. With a small group of other students, discuss the chances of nuclear disarmament.
4. Working in teams, draw up lists outlining the good points and the bad points of Canada's membership in NATO and NORAD. Using ideas from all teams, draw up a master list on the board. Take a vote on whether Canada should continue as a member of these two alliances.

5.

> You can never really come to terms with the idea of nuclear war. You just put it out of your mind, get on with your work, and hope it never happens. But if it does, you do your duty. I don't think it would worry me, because by the time we're fighting back, I know my family and most everyone else on the outside would no longer exist.
> *Canadian Forces Officer with NORAD*

6. Write down three or four words to describe your reaction to this statement. Compare *your* reaction to the reactions of others in your class.
7. Hold a debate on the topic: "Canadians are Americans in everything but name."
   Draw up two lists showing the positive and negative results of Canada's close relationship with the United States. Which list is longer? Is the longer list necessarily the more important?

Do Some Research

1. Find out more about the Nobel Peace Prize. Your report might answer the following questions:
   a) What are the origins of the prize?
   b) Besides Lester Pearson, who are some of the other winners of the prize?
   c) Why were they awarded it?
   d) Is there anyone you think should be awarded the prize? Why do you think so?
   e) There are Nobel prizes for other achievements as well as peace. What other Canadians have won a Nobel prize? In what field?
2. Since 1945 there have been over one hundred wars involving over eighty countries, and 25 million people have been injured or killed. Examine the causes, events, and results of one of these wars.
3. Find out about an agency that tries to help people in the Third World. By telephone and letter, gather as much information as you can about the projects this agency is concerned with. Some agencies you might study are:
   a) Canadian Save the Children Fund
   b) Red Cross
   c) Oxfam
   d) UNICEF
   Report your findings to the rest of the class.
4. Of the 500 largest corporations in Canada, 275 are owned by foreign interests. Find out the names of ten of these corporations.

5. Keep a record of the TV programs you watch for a week. How many hours did you spend watching:
   a) American programs?
   b) Canadian programs?
   c) programs from other countries?
6. In 1976, Canada hosted the summer Olympic Games at Montreal. Four years later, along with the U.S. and many other countries, Canada boycotted the 1980 games held in Moscow. Find out why. Was a boycott the right thing to do? What would have been your reaction if you were:
   a) a person with relatives in Afghanistan
   b) a member of parliament
   c) a Canadian athlete
   d) "the average Canadian"

Be Creative

1. **The last century made the world a neighbourhood; this century must make it a brotherhood.**
   J.S. Woodsworth

   Write your own short punchy sentence with the same general message.
2. Organize a fund-raising activity to support an aid project in the Third World.
3. Exchange letters and a "school capsule" with a school in another part of the Commonwealth or La Francophonie.

4. Write a poem about a pump that delivers clean water to a village that has had only polluted water for many years.
5. Brainstorm to find as many endings as possible to a sentence beginning "Peace is . . ." Use your sentences as captions for posters.
6. Listen to the song "Imagine" by John Lennon. Write additional lyrics of your own. Collect a peace songbook. Can songs affect peace and/or war?

You Are There

You are the members of parliament for constituencies across Canada. You also make up the new cabinet, led by a young, energetic prime minister. Your party has won the recent election, and you are eager to begin the task of leading Canada into the future.

Canada's relationship with the United States has become an important issue. Your party promised that it would begin a thorough review of Canadian-American relations, and that this review would lead to a new Canadian policy towards the United States.

The prime minister has called you together today to discuss three reports from experts on the subject. Which do you most agree with? What will be the cabinet's decision? Remember that all cabinet ministers must be able to support the final policy in public. This is known as "cabinet solidarity." Good luck, prime minister! Good luck, cabinet!

Dear Prime Minister:

After much research, I suggest that the following actions be taken by your government:
- increasing economic co-operation with the United States
- pooling of all North American energy resources
- dropping laws that discriminate against American magazines
- beginning discussions on the political union of Canada and the U.S.

I have suggested this closer relationship with the U.S. because it is in our best interests. Our peoples are basically the same. Together, Canada and the U.S. will be the world's greatest power. Our living standards will rise only if we co-operate rather than compete. Remember, united we stand, divided we fall.

Sam Union
Continental Consultants

Dear Prime Minister:

Time is very short. The greatest crisis in Canadian history now faces us. Canada has almost become a colony of the United States.

The U.S. now dominates nearly every aspect of Canadian life. The U.S. develops our resources, owns our economy, swamps our culture. Sometimes it seems we look to Washington for every foreign-policy decision we make. To save our country, I recommend the following:
- placing tough restrictions on American money and companies moving into Canada
- take-overs of major American companies by the Canadian government
- firm action to promote Canadian culture and restrict American influences

Act now, or Canada is lost. This is our last chance.

Jane Canuck
Can-Home Enterprises

Dear Prime Minister:

I have made a thorough analysis of all aspects of Canadian-American relations. Quite frankly, I fail to see what all the fuss is about. I can't see any problems.

Some Canadians love Americans; some Canadians hate Americans. Yet in spite of some tension and disagreement, we always seem to survive. I would suggest your government do the following:
- make as few changes as possible
- play down the issue and avoid letting people get too excited about our relations with the U.S.
- act only when and if a real problem arises

This makes sense because our two nations have always solved our mutual problems in the past. We live a good life in Canada. Why rock the boat?

Stan Pat
Status Quo Enterprises

One Nation or Two?
ADVANCE ORGANIZER

1 French Canadians can trace their roots on this continent back over 400 years. Their culture stems from the period when New France was a French colony. They lost most contacts with France after Quebec fell to Britain in 1759. Today 5 million French Canadians call Quebec home.

2 After the conquest the *Canadiens'* goal was survival. They were granted the right to use their own language, laws, and religion. Yet they felt threatened by the growing numbers of English-speaking people in the colony. Confederation in 1867 created special guarantees for the French culture in Quebec. However, in the years that followed there were clashes between French and English over a number of issues. Quebeckers reacted by turning inward to their own society.

3 By 1960 a new generation of Quebeckers wanted more than just survival. They demanded equality. The "Quiet Revolution," a period of modernization, was underway. Vast natural resource projects led to economic expansion. The province took a fresh look at education and social policies. In the new political atmosphere, some Quebeckers claimed that independence was the only way to gain real equality with other Canadians.

In October 1970 headlines all over the world announced that James Cross, a British diplomat, had been kidnapped by the FLQ, a Quebec terrorist group. Pierre Laporte, a Quebec cabinet minister, was also kidnapped and later murdered. In response to the crisis, the federal government proclaimed the War Measures Act. This act gave police special powers. Hundreds of suspected separatists were arrested without charge. Many Canadians objected furiously to the loss of civil rights. However, the crisis convinced Quebeckers that change should only come through peaceful means.

Réne Lévesque had been elected leader of the new Parti Québécois in 1968. The PQ's goal was political independence for Quebec but with strong economic ties to Canada. On 15 November 1976 Lévesque and the PQ won a major election victory. One of the first moves of the new government was to protect the use of the French language in Quebec.

On 20 May 1980 the people of Quebec voted in a referendum. They were asked to choose whether or not their government should negotiate "sovereignty-association," a new relationship with the rest of Canada. Nearly 60% voted against the plan. In other provinces people heaved a sigh of relief. Prime Minister Trudeau vowed to work for changes in the constitution for all Canadians.

Despite many disagreements, French and English Canadians have a long record of mutual respect and co-operation. In the referendum vote, Quebeckers clearly indicated their desire for a united Canada. The task for all Canadians in the future is to build an even stronger partnership.

The French in New France

A modern replica of Jacques Cartier's ship in a park in Quebec City.

Most Canadians recognize names like Guy LaFleur, Pierre Trudeau, Genevieve Bujold, and Gilles Villeneuve. These famous Canadians are the descendants of a French-speaking society that settled in North America nearly 400 years ago.

In the 1530s Jacques Cartier sailed deep into North America up the mighty St. Lawrence River. His stories of rich furs, teeming fish, and gold lured other explorers to North America. In 1604 Samuel de Champlain brought a group of French settlers to the Bay of Fundy. In 1608 he brought another group to Quebec.

The government of France wanted to make money out of New France. They thought of the colony in terms of the furs, timber, and fish it could send back to France. However they soon realized that New France could not survive if it could not grow its own food. Soon farms dotted the shores of the St. Lawrence River. The colony began to have an independent existence. Champlain and other early leaders of the colony had another burning ambition. They wanted to convert the native people to Christianity. They encouraged missionary priests to come to New France. Nuns came as well, bringing with them nursing and teaching skills.

The harsh climate, isolation, and constant warfare with the Iroquois and the English colonies to the south kept the population of New France small. Men and women who prospered created a self-reliant, religious, hard-working society. Yet slowly the villages grew larger and stronger. By 1759 the population was 60 000.

New France continued to look beyond the settled area of farms and towns. The coureurs-de-bois, eager for riches, got their name from "roaming the woods" in search of furs. Champlain himself mapped much of what is now eastern Canada and the northeastern United States. French explorers reached the Gulf of Mexico, the shores of Hudson Bay, and the foothills of the Rockies. Traders established posts at points that later became the cities of Kingston, Toronto, and Winnipeg. By the 1750s the French had made their mark in every future province of Canada east of the Rockies.

By this time many people in New France thought of themselves as "Canadiens" rather than "Français."

Give 2 reasons why France set up a colony in North America.
Why did the population of New France grow only slowly?
How would average Canadiens have felt after the British conquest?
Why do Acadians today feel different from Quebeckers?

They would have felt like foreigners in France. Most had been born in North America and had developed a unique lifestyle suited to their environment. Some had intermarried with the native people, bringing the best of two ways of life together. They had built schools, a university, churches, hospitals, missions, factories, forges, even breweries. They had their own set of heroes like Madeleine de Verchères and Dollard des Ormeaux, coureurs-de-bois like Jean Nicolet and Pierre Radisson, soldiers like Frontenac and Le Moyne d'Iberville, missionaries like Jean de Brébeuf and Jeanne Mance.

The times had not been peaceful. The relentless search for furs brought New France into constant conflict with the English and their Indian allies. In 1756 a war began which was to change New France forever.

The Conquest of New France

The empires of Britain and France were spread all over the globe. In 1756 war broke out between the two rival nations. The colonies were the pawns in this struggle.

France decided it was too difficult to defend the vast and distant colony of New France properly. Outnumbered and outgunned, French forces surrendered their outposts one by one. In 1759 the city of Quebec fell to the British at the battle of the Plains of Abraham. A year later Montreal fell. The Canadiens were under British military rule. In 1763 the British took formal control of the entire colony.

Much of New France lay in ruins. Farms and villages had been burned to the ground. Many of those who had ruled New France returned to their homes and families in France. The Canadiens, born and raised in the new world, remained in the land they knew and loved. They were isolated and under the rule of strangers.

Traditional crafts are demonstrated at the Acadian Historical Village in New Brunswick.

Acadia

France's other colony in North America was Acadia (modern-day Nova Scotia). Acadia was the result of Champlain's first settlement in the Bay of Fundy. Often ignored by France, the Acadians became an agricultural community. They dyked and improved the rich farmlands around the bay. They traded with the English colonies to the south for the things they could not grow.

Acadia was soon caught up in the strife between Britain and France. After 1713, much of Acadia was under British rule. The Acadians tried to remain neutral, but the British never trusted them. In 1755 as tensions grew, the British decided to get rid of the Acadians. They rounded them up, herded them onto British ships, and sent them to the English colonies further south.

Some Acadians escaped this deportation. Others slowly made their way back to their homeland. Eventually many settled in what is now northern New Brunswick.

The French Canadians of the Maritimes have a proud heritage. They feel they are a different people from their neighbours in Quebec. They have a different history, different memories, a different culture. At the same time they look to the larger French-speaking population of Quebec as their allies in the struggle to maintain their identity in the often alien English-speaking culture of North America.

The French in British North America

Many French Canadians probably found their daily lives changed little after the British conquest. The new rulers wanted to win the respect and perhaps even the loyalty of the people. The way to do this was offer respect in return — respect for a language, system of laws, religion, and way of life. In 1774 the British parliament passed the Quebec Act. The Quebec Act was based on these principles.

Yet the colony could never be the same again. English-speaking settlers, some from Britain, some from the south after the American Revolution, were pouring in. These people did not like the French laws and customs they found in Quebec. The relationship between French and English became strained.

The history of the next hundred years shows various attempts to deal with the strain. In 1791 the colony was divided into "Upper Canada" (later Ontario and mostly English) and "Lower Canada" (later Quebec and mostly French).

Rebellions in 1837 in both colonies showed people were unhappy with the system of government. Lord Durham in a report to the British parliament recommended more self-government. However he also suggested that the colonies should be united again. This way the French Canadians would be outnumbered by the English. He hoped they would soon give up their language and way of life.

In 1841 the colonies were united according to Lord Durham's plan. But the arrangement did not work. By the 1860s the government was in a stalemate. English and French were too evenly balanced for either to take a firm lead. Both began to feel they would be better off handling local affairs on their own. A central government could run services both needed.

George Etienne Cartier joined with John A. Macdonald in proposing this "federal" form of

Quebec had to be rebuilt after the British siege in 1759, but today it still retains its character as a French city.

government. By 1867 their efforts had led to a confederation of four provinces — Nova Scotia, New Brunswick, Quebec, and Ontario. All expected other provinces would eventually become part of this new country called Canada.

French Canada after Confederation

Many French Canadians saw Confederation as a bargain with English Canada. In return for French participation in the new nation, Quebec was guaranteed control over religion and education. This ensured the survival of French and English in the new nation.

The partnership was not an easy one. In 1870 Manitoba joined Confederation as a bilingual province. The protection of the French language was largely the result of the armed resistance and negotiations of a fiery young Manitoban called Louis Riel. Fifteen years later

OCUS

What did the Quebec Act guarantee to French Canadians?
Give 3 examples that show that Confederation was an uneasy partnership between French and English.
How did the Union Nationale influence life in Quebec?

1900 1910 1920 1930 1940 1950 1960 1970 1980 1990 2000

Riel led another rebellion in the West against the new Canadian government. He was captured, tried, and executed. The execution pleased English Canadians, who thought Riel was a tiresome rabble-rouser. French Canadians were enraged because Riel had been trying to protect the French-speaking people who had first settled western Canada.

In 1890 the English-speaking majority in Manitoba abolished French language rights. In 1912 Ontario did the same. The conscription crises in the two world wars divided English and French Canadians even more deeply. Canada was in danger of becoming "two solitudes." French Canadians felt their culture was only safe in Quebec.

Church and Homeland

The Depression emphasized the fears and insecurities of the French in Canada. It was easy to believe that Quebec's economic problems were caused by "foreign" control. The Union Nationale, a new political party, swept to power in 1936. Their leader, Maurice Duplessis, promised that decisions about Quebec's industry and resources would be made in Quebec.

The Union Nationale wanted to preserve the French language, religion, and culture. To do this, they worked closely with the Roman Catholic Church. The church controlled the schools and colleges. Young people were taught to respect traditional values. Modern influences were discouraged. As a result, a generation of French Canadians grew up with very little background in business, science, and technology.

Outside investment actually increased under Duplessis. Large companies liked the Union Nationale government. They gave the party money. In return the church, the government, and the companies worked together to keep trade unions weak in Quebec. They

---

Maurice Duplessis (Le Chef)

"I have no family. My only responsibility is the welfare of the province. I belong to Quebec."

1890 — born in Yamachiche, Que., near Trois Rivières.
1900 — at age 10 spoke at political meetings.
1913 — graduated as lawyer from Laval University.
1923 — narrowly defeated in provincial election.
1927 — elected. Announced: "Before you stands the future premier of Quebec."
1933 — elected leader of Quebec Conservatives.
1935 — with his supporters, joined with rebel Liberals to form Union Nationale.
1936 — Duplessis swept to power (UN 76, Liberals 14).
1937 — "Padlock Law" passed, giving police power to close offices of "subversive" groups.
1939 — UN defeated in election called over Canada's role in World War II.
1944 — re-elected, partly because of conscription issue.
1948 — Fleur-de-lis made Quebec's official flag.
1949 — used force to try to break a strike at Asbestos, Que. Many Quebec figures (Léger, Trudeau) supported the strikers.
1953 — appointed Tremblay commission to investigate Quebec society and its place in Canada. Report "woke" Quebec to desire for change.
1959 — died of heart attack at Schefferville, Que.
1960 — UN defeated in provincial election, though returned to power in 1966.

---

thought unions were communist inspired. With weak unions, the companies did not have to improve wages or working conditions.

Except for a four-year period during World War II, Duplessis remained in power in Quebec until his death in 1959. By that time the people of Quebec were becoming restless.

The Quiet Revolution

On 7 September 1959, "le Chef," Maurice Duplessis, died of heart failure. With him died the old Quebec.

Under Duplessis' rule, politics in Quebec had become very corrupt. The rural regions had far more power than the bustling cities. Areas that voted Union Nationale got new roads. Those that voted Liberal did not. The Roman Catholic Church had tremendous influence. English-Canadian, British, and American corporations soon discovered the way to do business in Quebec was to support Duplessis.

The effects were felt in all aspects of life. Labour unions were ruthlessly restricted. The church did not want French Canadians to mix with the English. The church-controlled education system did not prepare students for the modern business world. Furthermore, English was the language of big business. Corporations promoted English speakers rather than French speakers. Quebec was ripe for change.

The death of Duplessis left the Union Nationale in a state of collapse. In 1960 the Liberals under Jean Lesage won their first Quebec election since World War II. The people of Quebec were ready to look at their province and its place in their country and the world in a new way. The Quiet Revolution, a period of wholesale, dramatic change in Quebec society, had begun.

Quebec Seeks a New Identity

The goals of the Quiet Revolution were several. Quebec was to be speedily modernized. The survival of the French language and culture was to be guaranteed. The economy of Quebec was to be in the hands of the citizens of Quebec. French Canadians wanted to feel fully equal in Canada.

The government of Quebec made great changes during the 1960s and 70s. Education and medical services were brought under government rather than church

Quebec has vast energy resources. These lie not in oil or coal or uranium but in water power. Many fast-flowing rivers run into James Bay at the southern tip of Hudson Bay. The James Bay power project has flown thousands of workers and millions of tonnes of supplies and equipment to this isolated part of northern Quebec. There one of the world's largest hydro-electric complexes is being built.

control. Modern schools and hospitals were built for the Quebec people. Laws were passed to protect the use of the French language and to ensure the survival of French-Canadian culture. Other laws guaranteed the rights of labour unions and provided social benefits. In some cases,

List 3 goals of the Quiet Revolution.
What do you think were the most important achievements of this period in Quebec's history?
List 3 groups that developed different approaches to the future.

1900 1910 1920 1930 1940 1950 1960 1970 1980 1990 2000

such as in consumer rights, these laws were stronger than those in other parts of Canada. The government took more active part in developing provincial resources. In 1963 Quebec bought out all hydro-electric companies in the province. In the seventies the province undertook to build the world's biggest hydro power project in the James Bay region.

Quebec was becoming an active society with increasing self-confidence. This could be clearly seen in the arts. Hundreds of new musicians, writers, painters, and film-makers began to use their talents to portray the new Quebec. In politics, provincial leaders were ready to defend Quebec's interests capably and intelligently. People were gaining a new pride in their province. They began to call themselves Québécois (Quebeckers) rather than French Canadians.

Nearly all Quebeckers agreed with the goals of the Quiet Revolution. They had different ideas on the best way to achieve these goals. One group wanted Quebec to have more influence on the federal government in Ottawa. This group was led by people like Jean Marchand, Pierre Trudeau, and Jean Chrétien. Another group felt Quebec would be better off with far fewer ties to the rest of Canada. They saw Quebec's culture and interests as apart from those of other Canadians. They thought Quebec should be politically independent. René Lévesque, a former Liberal, united many people who felt this way in a new political party called the Parti Québécois.

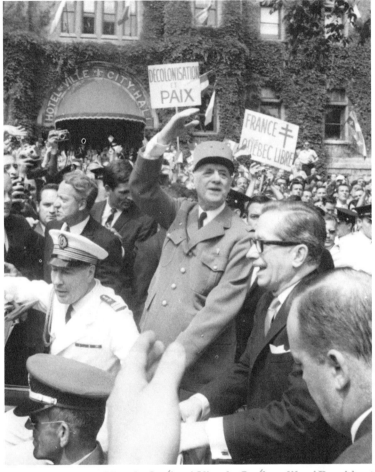

Vive la France! Vive le Québec! Vive le Québec *libre!* President de Gaulle's words from the balcony of Montreal city hall were greeted with a roar of cheers. He had appealed to the deepest feelings of many Quebeckers. In Ottawa, the reaction was very different. By encouraging the Quebec independence movement in this way, the French president had "interfered" in Canada's internal affairs.

A far smaller group believed Quebec could only be free through violent revolution. They called themselves the Front de Libération du Québec (FLQ). They pledged themselves to a war of liberation. The first stage in this war was terrorism.

The October Crisis

On the morning of 5 October 1970 James Cross, a British diplomat, was kidnapped at gunpoint from his Montreal home. The kidnappers soon identified themselves as members of the FLQ terrorist organization. They demanded a ransom of half a million dollars. They also wanted free TV and radio time to broadcast their views to the Quebec people. FLQ members in prison for terrorist activities were to be released and given free passage out of Canada along with the kidnappers. They warned that Cross would be executed if their demands were not met. The FLQ hoped the kidnapping would spark a wave of violence that would result in the separation of Quebec from Canada.

Canadians were numb with shock. Terrorism could be expected on the other side of the world, not in nice, safe Canada. Police seemed to be able to find no clues to the Cross kidnapping. Then, five days later, the terrorists struck again.

On Saturday 10 October Pierre Laporte, the Quebec minister of labour was playing football with his son outside his suburban home. Armed men seized him and dragged him into a car. This second kidnapping drove many people in Quebec into a state of near panic.

For two months James Cross sat facing the wall in a room in the terrorists' hideout. He never saw his kidnappers except with masks over their heads. When he was taken to the bathroom he was always blindfolded so he would not be able to recognize his surroundings. He passed the time by playing solitaire. Sometimes he was allowed to watch TV. This picture, as it appeared in newspapers around the world, was taken by the FLQ to prove he was still alive.

The War Measures Act

The federal and provincial governments acted together in the face of crisis. The police seemed to be getting nowhere. They did not know where the next move might come from. They feared the FLQ might go even further. Finally Premier Bourassa of Quebec asked the federal government to proclaim the War Measures Act. This gave the police special powers to search, question, and arrest suspects.

Soldiers cordon off the street while police negotiate with the kidnappers of James Cross.

What demands were made by the kidnappers of James Cross?
Why did the government proclaim the War Measures Act? How did it use the powers the act gave it?
What were the results of the October Crisis?

An armed soldier mounts guard over the funeral of Pierre Laporte.

Under the War Measures Act 497 people were arrested and held for up to three weeks. Most of them were later released without charge. They had been imprisoned merely "on suspicion." The army was called in to assist the police. Soldiers in full battle dress bearing machine guns patrolled the streets of Montreal, Quebec, and Ottawa.

On 17 October, police were tipped off about an abandoned car. When the bomb squad unlocked the trunk they found the lifeless body of Pierre Laporte. He had been strangled with the chain of his own religious medal.

It was ordinary police work, not the War Measures Act, that finally found James Cross. On 3 December, police and soldiers surrounded the house where Cross had been held for nearly 9 weeks. All Canada watched as the deal for his release was negotiated. Television crews in helicopters followed the kidnappers' car as it raced at 80 km/h through downtown streets to Man and His World, the site of Expo 67. There Cross was released into the custody of the Cuban consul while the kidnappers were flown to Cuba.

On 6 November one of the kidnappers of Pierre Laporte had been found in a closet during a search of a Montreal apartment. Police did not realize till later the others were hiding behind a partition in the closet. It was not until 28 December that they were found in a secret underground tunnel in an abandoned farmhouse 30 km southeast of Montreal.

After the Crisis

The results of the October Crisis were far-reaching. The FLQ was in ruins. Any sympathy Quebeckers had for the organization was wiped out. Those who believed in separatism for Quebec were now firmly convinced it would have to come by peaceful means. Other Canadians, both English and French, became truly aware of the feelings dividing the country for the first time. They resolved to work even harder at co-operation and understanding.

Canadians had learned a bitter lesson. Their country was not immune to violence and terror. How could they prevent similar occurrences in the future?

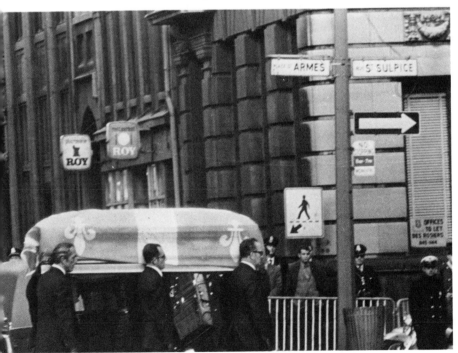

The funeral of Pierre Laporte.

René Lévesque and the Parti Québécois

For many English Canadians, separatism means René Lévesque. He, more than anyone else, represents the separatist movement. Lévesque led the first government in the history of Quebec that avowed the intention of taking the province out of Confederation. In 1980 his government asked the people of Quebec to vote on the question of the political independence of Quebec.

René Lévesque was born in 1922 in New Carlisle, Quebec. He grew up in a town where both English and French were spoken. As a boy, Lévesque often fought and traded insults with English kids.

Lévesque was a bright but restless student. He intended to become a lawyer, but dropped out of law school. He turned to journalism instead. Lévesque's skilled reports on the news soon made him one of the most popular radio and television personalities in Quebec.

After the death of Duplessis, the Liberals were looking for good political candidates in order to win the 1960 provincial election. They recruited the popular Lévesque. The Liberals won the election and Lévesque became a member of Jean Lesage's cabinet. He was one of the leading figures of the Quiet Revolution.

A Liberal Cabinet Minister

"Maîtres chez nous," or "Masters in our own house," became the Liberal slogan. Lévesque believed strongly that Quebec should control its own economy. The provincial government bought out the last privately owned hydro-electric companies in Quebec to make them part of the vast corporation of Hydro-Québec.

During this period of the Quiet Revolution, it seemed that the aims of Quebec often conflicted with the aims of the federal government and of the other provinces. Some Quebeckers became more and more

René Lévesque in the Quebec National Assembly.

frustrated with Quebec's role in Canada. Extremists and terrorists were beginning to fight for the "liberation" of Quebec. The rise of the FLQ was marked by riots and bombings. Other French Canadians were divided and confused as to the future of their province and their country.

Lévesque was frustrated too, but violence was not his answer. He was looking for a political solution to Quebec's problems. In 1967, while the majority of Canadians were celebrating the Centennial of Confederation, René Lévesque came to the conclusion that only an independent Quebec could protect the language, culture, and economy of Quebec. The Liberal party was firmly committed to the federal system. As Lévesque could no longer support this, he left the party.

Lévesque's views on the FLQ kidnappers of October 1970:

If they really thought they had a cause, they killed it along with Pierre Laporte. By shaming themselves, they have given a bad name to the entire separatist movement.

Their act was not only criminal but senseless. One can only hope that they live long enough to see that they stand for nothing and represent no one who matters. That would be the worst punishment they could have.

What was Lévesque's career before he entered politics?
Why did Lévesque leave the Liberal party?
Other than political independence for Quebec, what are some of
the policies of the Parti Québécois?

The Democratic Approach

The next year he was elected as leader of a new political party, the Parti Québécois. This new separatist party attracted a wide range of Quebeckers. Among its strongest supporters were many of the young and well educated. They looked forward to an exciting future in a new, independent country. However, party members believed in democracy. A free and democratic vote was the only road to the political independence of Quebec.

The PQ pledged to end corruption in Quebec politics, protect the French language and aid the weaker groups in society. To ease fears that independence might bring a loss of money and jobs, Lévesque stressed that an independent Quebec would have close economic ties with Canada.

The PQ had many supporters. Yet in the provincial election of 1970 and 1973 they were unable to turn votes into seats in the legislature. In 1976 there came a dramatic turnaround. Quebec voters were tired of what they saw as mismanagement by the Liberals under Bourassa. Lévesque led the PQ to a huge victory over the Liberals.

Many Canadians in other provinces thought that the election of a PQ government meant the end of Confederation.

The Parti Québécois and the Popular Vote

Election year	Number of seats won by PQ	Percentage of total seats won by PQ	Percentage of total votes cast for PQ
1970	7	6.5%	23.0%
1973	6	5.5%	30.3%
1976	71	65.5%	41.1%
1981	80	65.5%	49.2%

In this period, the number of seats in the Quebec National Assembly rose from 108 to 122.

In elections in Canada people vote for candidates in individual ridings. Therefore, the distribution of votes across the country or province is very important. The number of seats a party wins is not always a reflection of the total number of votes it gets. In 1970 and 1973 this worked against the Parti Québécois. In 1976 and 1981 it worked in its favour.

Many Canadians were stunned. It took several months before English Canadians recovered from the shock of having a separatist government in power in Quebec.

Lévesque knew much of his support had come from people who were not really in favour of separatism. Quebeckers had just wanted to get rid of the Liberals. The Parti Québécois had promised that a vote for their party did not automatically mean separatism. That question was to be voted on at a later date. The PQ set to work to persuade the people that independence was the best answer to Quebec's problems. Across the country, Canadians waited anxiously as Quebeckers prepared to vote for or against Canada.

The Referendum

The Parti Québécois had promised to give Quebeckers a chance to vote on their future. Late in 1979 they announced that chance would come on 20 May 1980. For the first time in the history of Canada an entire province would vote on the idea of leaving Confederation.

PQ leaders laboured for years over the exact wording of the question they would put to the voters. They knew many people were afraid of separatism. They wanted to persuade them the idea was not really dangerous. They finally asked the Quebeckers to vote *oui* (yes) or *non* (no) to giving the Quebec government "a mandate to negotiate sovereignty-association with Canada."

What the Referendum Question Meant

By *sovereignty* the question meant that Quebec would be politically independent. Only the Quebec government could collect taxes. Quebec would run its own foreign affairs. No law passed in Ottawa would have any effect in Quebec. By *association* the question meant that Quebec would still be tied to Canada economically. The two "countries" would use the same money. They would have the same tariffs on imports. By *mandate to negotiate* the question meant that a *oui* vote would not necessarily mean Quebec would leave Canada. It only meant the government would try to work out a deal with the rest of the country. The government also promised Quebeckers they would get another chance to vote on any agreement reached.

Oui or *Non*

People for and against the political independence of Quebec feverishly prepared to win over the hearts and minds of the voters. They bombarded the province with rallies, speeches, pamphlets, and radio and TV ads.

Lévesque and his followers launched a passionate campaign. They claimed a *oui* vote was needed to protect the French language and culture of Quebec. Even if a *oui* vote did not lead to sovereignty-association, it would give Quebec the power to negotiate a better deal from the federal government. Lévesque urged his fellow citizens to remember their history and their pride in their homeland when they went to vote.

Leading the *non* side against the idea of sovereignty-association was Claude Ryan. Ryan had been the editor of *Le Devoir,* the influential Quebec newspaper started by Henri Bourassa in 1910. Even though he had no experience in politics Ryan had been chosen as the new leader of the Liberal party. This was his first real political campaign. Many people regarded this as a test of his leadership ability.

Ryan started the campaign by attacking the wording of the question. He stressed that the PQ was trying to disguise separatism by calling it sovereignty-association. Many thought Ryan's approach was too dry. They said he should appeal to people's feelings, not just to their minds. However, as the campaign progressed, Ryan's speeches became more passionate. He began to impress the voters as a sincere and dedicated man.

Members of all three federal parties threw their support to the *non* side. Pierre Trudeau used his personal popularity in Quebec to persuade people of the advantages of staying in Canada. Conservative leader Joe Clark and NDP leader Ed Broadbent put aside party differences to work for the unity of their country. One million Canadians signed a petition to tell the people of Quebec they wanted them in Canada. A group of Ontario high school students made their statement by travelling to Quebec to work for the *non* side on the day of the vote. One man flew a plane over Quebec towing a banner saying "Canada loves you!"

What does the term "sovereignty-association" mean?
How did some non-Quebeckers get involved in the campaign?
How did the "Yvettes" affect the referendum results?
Do you think the idea of separatism is finished in Quebec?

20 May 1980

On referendum day Quebeckers streamed to the polls. People waited in long lines as 85% of the 4 362 588 eligible voters cast their ballots. When the polls closed people across the nation waited in hushed suspense as the first results trickled in. Within an hour the outcome was clear. Lévesque and the PQ had been dealt a considerable defeat. Only 40% had voted *oui*. Almost 60% of Quebeckers had voted *non*. They did not want even to negotiate an independent Quebec. They wanted to stay in Canada.

Prime Minister Trudeau urged Canadians to use this moment of unity. He promised to "renew" Confederation and start a process of peaceful change. He said that this was the time for Canadians to "bring home" their constitution. He would ask the British Parliament to give Canada the sole right to change the British North America Act.

Unfortunately the provinces and the federal government could not agree on how this was to be done. The focus of attention was no longer on the problems of Quebec. The grievances of all the regions of Canada were about to be brought before the nation.

The Yvette Movement

The turning point in the referendum debate came with the Yvette campaign.

Lise Payette, a PQ cabinet minister, made a speech in which she called Claude Ryan's wife an "Yvette." She even went on to accuse all women who voted against the PQ of being "Yvettes." Yvette was the name of a girl in a grade two reader used in Quebec. The reader showed Yvette staying home to cook and sew while her brother had exciting adventures. Payette was implying that women who were against sovereignty-association were submissive to men and unable to think for themselves. Payette soon regretted her careless remark.

Enraged women in Quebec started an Yvette movement. Within a week of Payette's comment, the "Yvettes" held a mass rally of 15 000 women. They showed their love of Canada and their anger at being insulted. One of the speakers proudly said, "We are mothers who have inherited this great country of Canada from our ancestors. We want to hand it on to our children intact."

The Yvette rally was the first serious setback for the PQ. Payette's apology came too late to make any difference. From this point on, the federalist campaign gathered momentum. A large majority of Quebec women voted *non* in the referendum. One PQ organizer commented, "The Yvettes killed us."

Canadians and Canadiens

It is easy to assume that French and English Canadians are always at each other's throats. Nothing could be further from the truth. Much of Canadian history sparkles with the warmth and affection felt between the two founding peoples. Our history records countless examples of co-operation. Even a convinced separatist like René Lévesque has always stressed the need for mutual respect and understanding.

Quebec's demands for greater powers and concern for its identity are not really unusual. Most provincial leaders defend their province's rights very firmly. Other regions in Canada, especially the West and the Maritimes, have felt that Confederation was sometimes against their best interests.

Canadians in all regions of Canada have elected strong provincial leaders. Peter Lougheed of Alberta

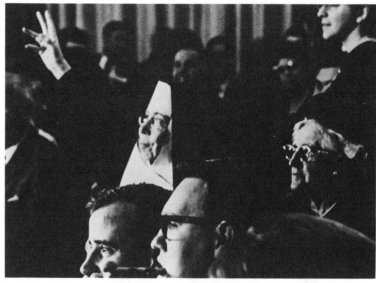

Raising a point of concern at Bi and Bi hearings in Sudbury, Ont.

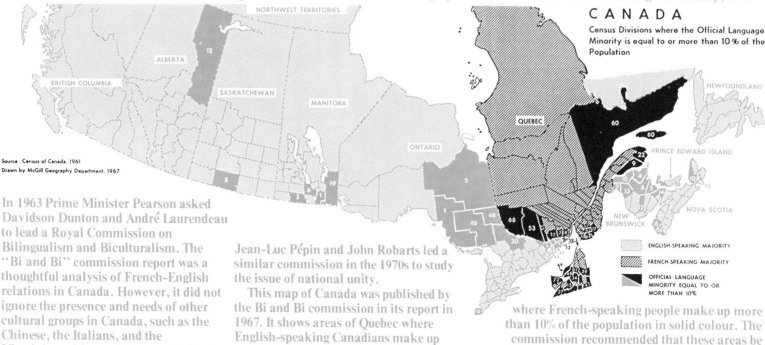

CANADA

Census Divisions where the Official Language Minority is equal to or more than 10% of the Population

Source : Census of Canada, 1961
Drawn by McGill Geography Department, 1967

ENGLISH-SPEAKING MAJORITY

FRENCH-SPEAKING MAJORITY

OFFICIAL LANGUAGE MINORITY EQUAL TO OR MORE THAN 10%

In 1963 Prime Minister Pearson asked Davidson Dunton and André Laurendeau to lead a Royal Commission on Bilingualism and Biculturalism. The "Bi and Bi" commission report was a thoughtful analysis of French-English relations in Canada. However, it did not ignore the presence and needs of other cultural groups in Canada, such as the Chinese, the Italians, and the Ukrainians. Many of the commission's ideas have become government policy.

Jean-Luc Pépin and John Robarts led a similar commission in the 1970s to study the issue of national unity.

This map of Canada was published by the Bi and Bi commission in its report in 1967. It shows areas of Quebec where English-speaking Canadians make up more than 10% of the population in solid black. It shows areas of the rest of Canada where French-speaking people make up more than 10% of the population in solid colour. The commission recommended that these areas be made "bilingual districts." The federal government provides services to these districts in both languages.

How many provinces have districts with a significant proportion (over 10%) of French-speaking people in the population?
Who wrote the music for Canada's national anthem?
What happened in the 1981 Quebec election?

has been a tireless defender of his province. W.A.C. Bennett always defended the interests of British Columbia. Joey Smallwood of Newfoundland was both a patriotic Canadian and a strong spokesman for the concerns of his island voters.

Although Canadian history reveals many bitter battles between various provinces and the federal government, no province has actually left Confederation. Even in Quebec, few people support the idea of a totally independent Quebec nation.

Politics aside, most Canadians treat each other with generosity and respect. Canada will need that spirit of co-operation in order to survive the tough challenges of the future.

In 1880 the song that would become Canada's national anthem was written by Adolphe-Basile Routhier and Calixa Lavallée to help celebrate French Canada's national day, St. Jean Baptiste Day. It was an instant hit.

In 1908, to celebrate the 300th anniversary of the founding of Quebec, Stanley Weir wrote English words to Lavallée's famous tune. His version became popular in English Canada.

However, it was not until 1980 that parliament gave full recognition to *O Canada* as the national anthem. Minor changes were made in the English words, but the French version is as Routhier wrote it.

The National Anthem

Ô Canada! terre de nos aïeux,
Ton front est ceint de fleurons glorieux!
Car ton bras sait porter l'épée,
Il sait porter la croix!
Ton histoire est une épopée
Des plus brillants exploits.
Et ta valeur, de foi trempée,
Protégera nos foyers et nos droits.
Protégera nos foyers et nos droits.

O Canada! Our home and native land!
True patriot love in all thy sons command.
With glowing hearts we see thee rise,
The True North strong and free!
From far and wide, O Canada,
We stand on guard for thee.
God keep our land glorious and free!
O Canada, we stand on guard for thee!
O Canada, we stand on guard for thee.

The things I love most — the arts, sports, music — know no language barriers. Neither do my children. And so for us, a separation of the two cultures would be a kind of amputation.
Roger Doucet who sang O Canada *at Montreal Canadiens hockey games.*

René Lévesque

In 1981, a provincial election was fought in Québec. After nearly five years in power, the Parti Québécois had changed the face of the province. Québec now had Bill 101 to protect the use of the French language. The minimum wage was the highest in Canada. A new auto insurance law had reduced insurance costs for drivers. In general, Quebeckers felt a new sense of drive and confidence. René Lévesque was a very popular premier.

Quebeckers had also shown they had little desire to separate from Canada. The PQ leaders decided to hold no new referendum if re-elected. Premier Lévesque promised to help make the Canadian federal system work. The PQ campaigned for re-election on the basis of good government *not* of separation from Canada.

Liberal leader Claude Ryan fought tirelessly to defeat Lévesque and the PQ. He claimed the economy was collapsing and that Lévesque would still try to pull Quebec out of Canada.

However, few voters liked Ryan's dry, intellectual image. Ryan also seemed to be too close to Prime Minister Trudeau. Trudeau's government had proposed constitutional changes that many Quebeckers felt were against the interests of the province. Voters wanted a leader who would defend Quebec's rights against the federal government. Ryan was accused of being the mouthpiece of his "boss," Trudeau.

Claude Ryan

Finally Ryan failed to convince voters that a vote for the PQ in 1981 was still a vote for separatism. Separatism seemed to be a dead issue. Many people simply felt the PQ had been a good, honest government and deserved to be re-elected. The final vote was close. The PQ received just over 3% more votes than Ryan's Liberals. But they won a smashing victory in terms of seats (PQ 80, Liberals 42).

As this book went to press, the federal government and the 9 other provinces agreed on a new constitution. Lévesque was very bitter. He swore Quebec would never accept it. It seemed that the issue of separatism was not dead yet.

Questions and Activities

Test Yourself

Match the people in Column A with the descriptions in Column B.

A	B
1. Samuel de Champlain	a) leader of the Union Nationale
2. Maurice Duplessis	b) a Father of Confederation
3. James Cross	c) founder of Quebec in 1608
4. Claude Ryan	d) first leader of Parti Québécois
5. George Etienne Cartier	e) leader of the *non* forces in the 1980 referendum
6. René Lévesque	f) kidnap victim of the FLQ

Quick Recall

Identify the following in a few sentences:
1. FLQ
2. Yvette Campaign
3. Quiet Revolution
4. Quebec Referendum
5. Acadia
6. War Measures Act

Instant Analysis

Some statements can be labelled true or false. Others may depend on a variety of facts, opinions, and special situations. Place these statements in three categories: True, False, or It Depends.
1. Quebec wants to separate from Canada.
2. English and French Canadians rarely co-operate.
3. Like other provincial governments, governments of Quebec are usually prepared to defend their provincial rights and responsibilities.
4. The Quiet Revolution was a period of tremendous change for Quebec.
5. Confederation has generally been a bad deal for French Canadians
6. Most French Canadians see Confederation as a bargain or pact between the two major language groups in Canada.
7. All French Canadians live in Quebec.

Do Some Research

1. Find out more about the expulsion of the Acadians. Why did the British government decide the Acadians had to go? How many were forcibly removed from their homes and lands? Where were they sent? How many ever returned to their homeland? Where are there pockets of their descendants in North America today?
2. Do some research into the reasons for the failure of the Conservative and New Democratic parties to win acceptance and parliamentary seats in Quebec. How might this be changed?
3. Most Canadians do not realize that O Canada was originally a French Canadian song. The lyrics in French are quite different from the lyrics in English. Find or make an accurate translation of the French lyrics and compare the two. What conclusions can you draw about the ways the two versions reflect the country?
4. The War Measures Act has been used at two other periods in Canadian history. Investigate these periods and compare and contrast the actions taken under this law.

Ideas for Discussion

1. Assume that you are a Canadian living in New France during the British Conquest. Write a letter to the new British governor outlining both your fears and your hopes for the future.
2. What do you think would have happened if René Lévesque and the *Oui* forces had won the Quebec Referendum in 1980? Write a brief summary of the possible events. Present your ideas to the rest of the class.
3. Organize a class debate on the use of the War Measures Act during the October Crisis. The motion you debate might be: Resolved that the War Measures Act was an unnecessary threat to civil liberties and should not have been used.
4. What does the term "official bilingualism" mean? Do you support the policy? Take a vote to find out the opinion of your class on official bilingualism.
5. Do you think English Canadians have always been fair to their French-Canadian fellow citizens? How can English Canadians help French Canadians feel more at home outside Quebec?
6. What do these pictures tell you about the Quebec people and the Quebec culture? Do you think they give a true picture of life in the province?

Be Creative

1. Exchange letters, tapes, photos, and information packages with a francophone school in Quebec or elsewhere in Canada. Perhaps you can even organize visits between your two schools.
2. Listen to some of the music of French Canada. Perhaps your French teacher could help you translate some of the lyrics.
3. Make a bilingual poster advertising the benefits of living in a nation with two official languages.

You Are There

It is May 1980. In a few days, you, the people of Quebec, will be voting in the referendum on sovereignty-association. A Quebec television network has brought people together from across the province for a live debate. Some are prominent people in the news. Others are ordinary Quebeckers. You are among them, and tonight your opinion will be heard.

Those present include:

René Lévesque
Claude Ryan
Pierre Trudeau
A young student
A single mother
An English-speaking Montrealer
A dairy farmer from the Eastern Townships
A fishing boat captain from Gaspé
A member of the Yvette movement
A former member of the FLQ
A hotel owner from a Laurentian resort
Reporters from small-town French and English newspapers
Reporters from three Montreal daily newspapers

As special guests, the network has also invited:

An Acadian teacher from Moncton, New Brunswick
A worker for Newfoundland Light and Power at Churchill Falls, Labrador
A French-Canadian miner from Sudbury, Ontario
A member of the Alberta cabinet
The mayor of a mainly French-speaking town in Manitoba
A Chinese-speaking political scientist from British Columbia

The debate is chaired by a diplomat from Belgium, a country that also has two official languages.

Are you planning to vote *oui* or *non*? Might this debate change your mind? It's time to find out. The lights are on. The cameras are rolling. The meeting is open.

Regional Report
ADVANCE ORGANIZER

1 **Yukon**
Capital: Whitehorse
Area: 483 000 km²
Population: 22 000
Origins: 46% British, 5% French, 15% native people, 8% German, 26% other
Industries: Mining (lead, zinc, oil and gas production and exploration), fishing, trapping, hunting
Energy sources: thermal and hydro-electricity, oil, gas
Per capita income: $10 853

Northwest Territories
Capital: Yellowknife
Area: 3 380 000 km²
Population: 43 000
Origins: 25% British, 6% French, 33% Inuit, 21% Indian, 15 % other
Industries: mining (gold, lead, zinc, copper, oil and gas productions and exploration), fishing, trapping, hunting
Energy sources: thermal electricity, oil, gas
Per capita income: $10 853

2 **British Columbia**
Capital: Victoria
Area: 949 000 km²
Population: 2 570 000
Origins: (58% British, 4% French, 2% native peoples, 9% German, 6% Scandinavian, 3% Italian, 3% Dutch, 3% Oriental, 12% other

Industries: lumbering, pulp and paper, wood products, mining (coal, copper, lead, zinc, gas), tourism, farming, fishing
Energy sources: Hydro-electricity, coal, gas
Per capita income: $11 024

3 **Alberta**
Capital: Edmonton
Area: 661 000 km²
Population: 2 014 000
Origins: 47% British, 6% French, 2% native peoples, 12% German, 8% Ukrainian, 4% Scandinavian, 21% other
Industries: mining (oil, gas, coal), farming, petro-chemical industries, meat packing, food processing
Energy sources: oil, gas, coal
Per capita income: $14 410

Saskatchewan
Capital: Regina
Area: 652 000 km²
Population: 957 000
Origins: 42% British, 6% French, 4% native peoples, 20% German, 9% Ukrainian, 5% Scandinavian, 14% other
Industries: farming, mining (potash, oil, gas), meat packing, petroleum products
Energy sources: oil, gas, hydro-electricity
Per capita income: $10 191

Manitoba
Capital: Winnipeg
Area: 640 000 km²
Population: 1 030 000
Origins: 42% British, 9% French, 4% native peoples, 12% German, 11% Ukrainian, 22% other
Industries: machinery and metal products, agricultural implements, meat packing, dairy products, farming, mining (nickel, copper, zinc), lumbering
Energy sources: Hydro-electricity
Per capita income: $9 272

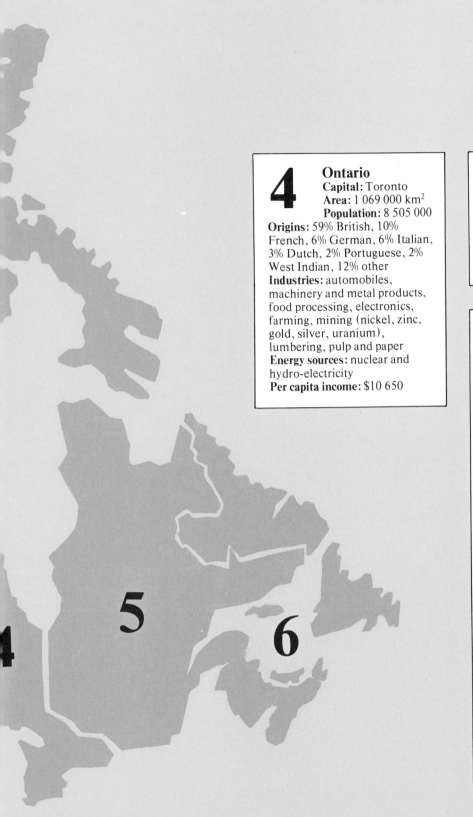

Word List

compromise
decentralized
diversity
freight rates

industrial waste
isolationist
natural resources
regionalism

renewable resources
resource industry
secondary industry
taxation

4
Ontario
Capital: Toronto
Area: 1 069 000 km²
Population: 8 505 000
Origins: 59% British, 10% French, 6% German, 6% Italian, 3% Dutch, 2% Portuguese, 2% West Indian, 12% other
Industries: automobiles, machinery and metal products, food processing, electronics, farming, mining (nickel, zinc, gold, silver, uranium), lumbering, pulp and paper
Energy sources: nuclear and hydro-electricity
Per capita income: $10 650

5
Quebec
Capital: Quebec City
Area: 1 541 000 km²
Population: 6 301 000
Origins: 79% French, 11% British, 10% other
Industries: lumbering, pulp and paper, mining (iron ore, copper, asbestos, aluminum and other metal processing, gold, silver), farming, electrical and transportation equipment, textiles, clothing.
Energy sources: hydro-electricity
Per capita income: $8 941

6
New Brunswick
Capital: Fredericton
Area: 73 000 km²
Population: 701 000
Origins: 58% British, 37% French, 5% other
Industries: Farming, food processing, fishing, mining (zinc, copper, lead), lumbering and pulp and paper
Energy sources: thermal and hydro-electricity, nuclear electricity (potential)
Per capita income: $6 325

Nova Scotia
Capital: Halifax
Area: 55 000 km²
Population: 847 000
Origins: 77% British, 10% French, 5% German, 8% other
Industries: mining (coal), steel, farming, fishing, food processing, tourism
Energy sources: thermal electricity, oil (potential)
Per capita income: $6 701

Prince Edward Island
Capital: Charlottetown
Area: 5 657 km²
Population: 123 000
Origins: 85% British, 12% French, 3% other
Industries: farming, fishing, food processing, tourism
Energy sources: thermal electricity
Per capita income: $5 194

Newfoundland and Labrador
Capital: St. John's
Area: 405 000 km²
Population: 574 000
Origins: 94% British, 3% French, 3% other
Industries: mining (iron ore), fishing, fish processing, lumbering, pulp and paper, oil exploration
Energy sources: hydro-electricity, oil (potential)
Per capita income: $5 250

The Challenge of Regionalism

A typical Prairie landscape with grain fields and grain elevators.

There are three main themes in Canadian history. The first is the drive to build a strong country separate from the United States. The second is the struggle to accommodate the rights of two founding peoples, the French and the English. The third is regionalism — the recognition of the very different histories, geographies, cultures, and economic strengths and weaknesses of the various regions of Canada.

Canada is the second largest country in the world. Its territory covers about 10 million km². Despite this vastness, less than one-tenth of its area is occupied by cities, towns, or farmland. The rest is wilderness, mountains, or the biting cold of the North. The regions of Canada are kept apart by geography. British Columbia is separated from the prairies by the Rockies. Dividing the prairies from central Canada are rocky woodlands of northern Ontario. The mountains of Maine cut the Maritimes off from Quebec, and Newfoundland is kept from the mainland by the sea. The North is isolated by its own geography — the lonely expanse of the Canadian shield and Arctic tundra.

Balancing Powers

Today, many of the provinces want to see a more decentralized system of government. They want to have more say in matters that directly concern them. They seek greater control in many areas of government: cultural affairs, natural resources, taxation, distribution of goods and services, and their general economy. Finding the best balance between federal and provincial powers is an essential task for Canada.

Each region of Canada has been subject to its own forces — history, geography, politics, culture, language, traditions, and economics. Some of these forces help keep the Confederation together; others hold it apart. Are we Canadians, or are we Albertans,

What have been three main themes of Canadian history?
What are the six regions of Canada?
What factors have contributed to the growth of "regionalism" in Canada?
Why does regionalism conflict with centralism? Give examples.

Québécois, Ontarians, and Newfoundlanders? Prime Minister Trudeau once said, "My name is Québécois and my name is Canadian too." What did he mean?

What are the backgrounds of the people of the regions of Canada? What sort of jobs do they have? What are their problems? What are their similarities and their differences?

What do they contribute to Confederation, and what do they expect in return?

In each region, the physical elements helped to shape the attitudes and livelihoods of the people. Natural forces influenced not only regional economics, but social patterns as well. In Newfoundland the sea encouraged tiny, isolated fishing settlements. This in turn bred a relatively slow-paced, "small-town" way of life. Similarly, the harsh living conditions of the Prairies forced the

settlers to adopt a communal, "co-operative" lifestyle. This approach to problem-solving eventually led to many government policies that affected all Canadians.

The isolation of one region from another had a significant effect on Canada's development. Each region had risen from its own cultural roots. It was with some reluctance that they followed one another into Confederation. Local concerns remained more important than national issues. Strong regional loyalty still is a part of the Canadian character.

The idea of Canada was born principally in the areas that are now Ontario and Quebec. They were the largest of the original provinces. They were further strengthened by the policies of the new federal government. As other provinces entered Confederation, they often felt neglected in favour of Quebec and Ontario.

Quebec sculptor
J.J. Bourgault of
St-Jean-Port Joli.

The North

In the past, residents of the North used local materials for buildings. Today, in Tuktuk, N.W.T., most buildings have been prefabricated elsewhere and put together here.

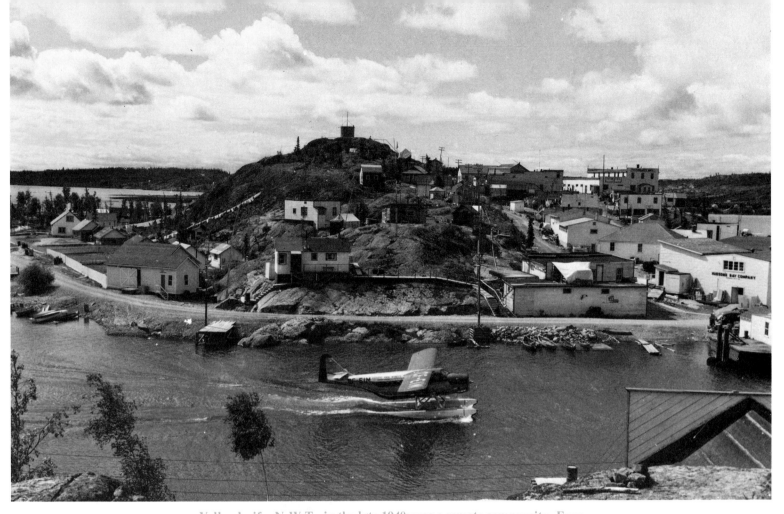

Yellowknife, N.W.T., in the late 1940s was a remote community. Even today the usual way in and out is by airplane.

Musk oxen are hardy enough to survive harsh Northern winters. In summer, their fur helps them ignore the blackflies.

CBC Inuvik announcer/operators who covered the Northern Games at Inuvik in 1979 in English, Loucheux, Slavey, and Eskimo.

Nature and Technology

When Canadians refer to the North they generally mean the Yukon and the Northwest Territories. This immense region occupies 40% of Canada's total land area. Yet less than 1% of the population lives there. Labrador and Northern Quebec should probably also be considered as part of the North. However, Canadians usually reserve the term for the territories.

The population of the North divides roughly into two groups. Immigrants to the North, often from southern Canada or the United States, usually live in the larger communities such as Whitehorse and Yellowknife. Some of these people are permanent residents. Others come to take a job for a few years and then move back south. The other group is the native people of the North. They are over 50% of the population. This is by far the largest proportion of native people in all the Canadian regions.

The native people belong to two main cultures — the Dene (pronounced *Den-nay*) and the Inuit. The Dene live south of the "tree-line," the northernmost point at which trees grow. Traditionally they depended on the vast herds of caribou that once grazed the land. The Inuit live north of the tree-line — mainly where the northern rivers meet the Arctic Ocean. These people lived by fishing and hunting bear, caribou, and seal.

The traditional way of life in the North was first disrupted by Hudson's Bay Company fur traders. They traded modern conveniences for furs, which were greatly valued in Europe and the South. Gradually the people of the North began to depend on the traders. They became used to things like tobacco, tea, and cooking pots, which had previously been unknown. They began to use guns and ammunition to hunt game.

The next major change occurred when mining and oil companies started to explore the North. The mines, transportation routes, and settlements upset the delicate northern balance of nature. In particular, the migration routes of the caribou were disturbed and the herds grew smaller. A fear of pollution of the Arctic Ocean began to develop. Gradually the natural economy of the North was disappearing.

Caught Between Old and New

The federal government wanted to help the native people of the North prepare for a new way of life. In the early years of the twentieth century they felt the best way to achieve this was through education.

Because the native communities were so small, native children were brought to boarding schools. Here, they were completely cut off from their families for periods of several years. They were often punished if they spoke their native language. They were taught by southern teachers from books meant for southern children. The Inuit and Dene students did not understand these books because nothing in them related to their way of life. These children returned to their families as strangers. They had

The old ways.

Describe the characteristics of the three main Northern groups:
a) "southern" immigrants, b) Dene, c) Inuit.
How have the immigrants disrupted traditional Northern ways of
life? Why do so many people of the North want provincial status?

lost important years of training in hunting, fishing and other life skills. Yet they had not really adapted to the "modern" world.

By midcentury the government thought the native people would be better off in permanent settlements. Southern-style housing was erected in a few "central" locations. The people were encouraged to move to these new homes. Here they could be near stores, schools, medical centres, and other government services. However, moving to these permanent settlements meant the people could no longer follow the migrating caribou or choose the best fishing grounds. Their way of life was killed by the combination of the move and the impact of technology.

The government expected new jobs would soon be available for the native people. The South wanted to exploit the North's natural resources — minerals and oil. However, native people don't generally possess the skills needed to work in mines or on oil rigs. The companies

The new ways.

bring in workers from the South. These people come north for a few years. They make a good deal of money, which they take with them when they go home. The native people often get neither jobs nor profit from this invasion of their land.

The change from the traditional, nomadic way of life has given the native people little. Too often it has meant they are no longer dependent on their own wisdom and the skills of their own hands but on a government welfare cheque.

By the 1960s and 70s the native people of the North began to realize that the government's attempts to help them did not meet native people's needs. They decided to take more responsibility for their own future.

Controlling the Future

The people of the North are striving to gain more control over their own land, its resources, and its economy. The North is the only region which is still more or less a colony. The Northwest Territories and the Yukon are administered by the federal government from Ottawa. Before 1905 Saskatchewan and Alberta were part of the Northwest Territories. In that year their population and development had reached the point where they could manage their own affairs as provinces. The newer inhabitants of the North, as well as the natives, feel the northern territories too are now ready for provincial status.

Canada's native people are the true "founding nation" of Canada. They are demanding that this fact be recognized, as they struggle to regain their way of life within the confines of Confederation. To make their voices heard more clearly, the Inuit and Dene are joining forces with the native peoples of southern Canada. Together they hope to achieve direct participation for native people in federal policy making.

British Columbia

Today, water transport is as important to British Columbia as it was in the past. Steamers chugged into Yale during the Cariboo gold rush, and ferries now ply the waters under the Lion's Gate Bridge in Vancouver.

Carving a Kwakiutl totem pole in Thunderbird Park, Victoria B.C.

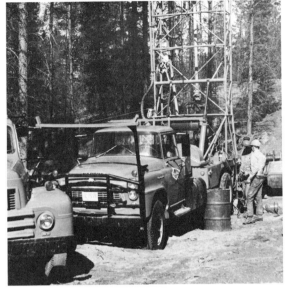

Percussion drilling to prospect for copper and molybdenum.

Skiers on Whistler Mountain.

Butchart Gardens, near Victoria, were created in an old gravel pit.

Mountains and Seacoast

Canada's westernmost province is British Columbia. The area was settled largely by people who arrived by sea rather than overland from eastern Canada. With the Rocky Mountains on one side of them and the sea on the other, the people of British Columbia have always felt somewhat shut off from the rest of the nation. British Columbia is probably the most "isolationist" of Canada's English-speaking provinces.

This trend reached its peak between 1953 and the early 1970s. During this period, Social Credit Premier W.A.C. Bennett tried to keep the province out of national affairs. As much as possible he wanted British Columbia to function independently from the rest of Canada.

After a period of rule by the NDP, W.A.C. Bennett's son, Bill, became premier. Bill Bennett thought his province should have heavier involvement with the rest of the nation. At the same time he demanded certain rights for his province that he felt had been denied by Ottawa since Confederation.

Felling a cedar tree, near Bella Coola.

Bennett said that his province had been a victim in some of the federal government's policies. Ottawa tried to protect Canadian manufacturing industries by placing high tariffs on incoming foreign goods. Most manufacturing in Canada is centred in Ontario and Quebec. Other regions of Canada, like British Columbia, have protested that the tariff policy does nothing for them. Their economies are based on resource industries like lumbering, mining, or farming. These industries depend largely on selling their products abroad. In the past the Ottawa government has done little to help resource industries get good prices. Regions like British Columbia feel it is unfair that Quebec and Ontario are protected by tariffs which all Canadians have to pay. Meanwhile their economies seem to get no protection and little help.

British Columbians would like to insure that their interests are better protected by the federal government. To this end they would like to receive increased representation in Ottawa. B.C. wants to be sure it has a real voice in the making of government policies.

The Vancouver waterfront in the 1980s.

Not for Sale

At the same time British Columbians wish to be firmly in control of their own economy. In 1979, Canadian Pacific Investments, a subsidiary of the CPR, tried to buy British Columbia's largest resource business, the Macmillan Bloedel paper company. The head office of CPI is in Montreal. Premier Bill Bennett saw the take-over bid as an attempt by central Canadian interests to extend their control of British Columbia's economy. He firmly stated that British Columbia was "not for sale" and successfully stopped this take-over. The paper company has since been bought by other "outside" interests, but Bennett was expressing an attitude held by many people in the province.

British Columbians often have different attitudes one from another. The people of the fertile fruit-growing valley of the Okanagan do not have the same outlook on life as the Indian fishermen of the Queen Charlotte Islands. Neither do the people of Victoria and the cowboys of the Cariboo. Yet they are all conscious of their identity as westerners.

British Columbia's demands on the federal government are echoed by many other provinces. But with the isolation already created by geography, British Columbians perhaps feel these issues more keenly.

A ranch in Deadman Valley, west of Kamloops.

The Changing Prairies

Some things change, but cattle herding is the same operation today as it was a hundred years ago.

Chuckwagon races at the Calgary Stampede.

The city of Winnipeg.

Sunset on a northern lake, Saskatchewan.

Oil refinery.

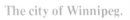

The New West

When Canadians talk of the "New West," they usually mean all the provinces west of Ontario. These provinces are united by the common goal of greater political and economic freedom. These are the Prairie provinces — Manitoba, Saskatchewan, and Alberta — and British Columbia, which lies on the Pacific coast. Because of its geography and individual character, British Columbia is often thought of separately from the other western provinces.

The Prairies were settled more rapidly than any other region. Until the 1880s the area was the territory of Indians and Métis who followed the great herds of buffalo. Then the newly built Canadian Pacific Railway brought in would-be farmers. Until the first World War, immigrants flooded into the Canadian West. The first settlers came from eastern Canada, the United States, and the British Isles. From the 1890s on they were joined by people from Poland, Hungary, the Ukraine, and other countries of eastern Europe. As the railways expanded, wheat farms and cattle ranches gradually filled the land.

A Land of Hardship

Living conditions on the Prairies were harsh. The vast remoteness of the region and its severe weather, created a particularly hostile environment. Farming families had to endure dry, searing heat in summer and intense cold in winter. They lived with the knowledge that a storm could level a year's crop in seconds.

These conditions deeply affected the people's attitudes. In the end they helped shape the society. The Prairies forced people to band together if they were to survive. Families helped one another to gather the harvests and raise barns and homesteads. Their co-operation served them well when bad weather or poor

Today, a troop of harvesters goes through a grain field almost as fast as an army of grasshoppers during the Dustbowl years.

economic conditions brought hard times. This spirit of solidarity led to a number of new ideas in Canadian politics. Women first got the right to vote in Manitoba in 1916. In the 1920s and 30s the first large-scale co-operatives were set up on the Prairies. Saskatchewan started the first government hospital plan in 1944.

The western provinces have long felt that central Canada has treated them as an outpost. They have had to cope with tariff policies that favour the central provinces, Ontario and Quebec. In early years they resented the monopoly the CPR was given on the

How did the settlement of the West differ from that of the east? Why did relatively harsh living conditions of the prairies lead to cooperation and social reform? Give at least three examples. How have natural resources led to feelings of a "New West?"

shipment of grain. They had to deal with banks that were based in Montreal or Toronto and did not understand western farmers' problems. Western Canadians feel they have been ignored by the federal government. They have protested this state of affairs since the days of Louis Riel. Resentment reached its peak with the Depression. Economic hard times lingered over the region for more than thirty years. They ended dramatically with the development of the region's major oil and gas reserves.

Energy Resources

In 1973 the world price of energy, especially oil products, shot up dramatically. Now Ontario and Quebec, as well as other industrial centres, require the West's oil and gas to fuel their factories. As a result, the economy of Alberta, where the largest oil and gas reserves have been found, is now booming. Saskatchewan also has major oil fields.

In comparison with its sister provinces, Manitoba is a low-growth area. But it too has begun to find the way to prosperity. Manitoba has been harnessing its extensive hydro-electric resources to fuel its own industries. The province plans to sell electricity to Saskatchewan and Alberta. In this way Manitoba hopes to profit from the oil boom as well.

The West no longer depends entirely upon agriculture. Though the price of wheat and freight rates are still major issues, the chief concern of the typical prairie dweller today is the demand for western oil. Oil has given the western provinces new economic power. They hope to use this power to get political changes that will benefit themselves as well as the rest of Canada. The New West is rising to take its place as an equal partner in Confederation.

Part of the high cost of searching for oil and gas reserves is the expense of operating a drilling rig.

The Price of Energy

An oil drilling rig on farmland in the Peace River district between Fort St. John and Dawson Creek, B.C.

A study of the regions of Canada is not complete without a close look at how the problem of energy supply is affecting the country now and how it will affect us in the future. In many ways the New West is the product of the energy crisis.

Alberta is the centre of Canada's oil boom. The province has more than half of the country's known oil deposits. In 1980 geologists estimated these reserves at a minimum of one trillion barrels. This is 16 times more oil than Saudi Arabia is believed to have.

The Pricing Debate

Since world oil prices shot up in 1973, the government of Alberta has been involved in a number of disputes with the federal government. Other energy-rich provinces have been watching these disputes with interest and concern. The issues centre on the price of oil and how the revenues should be shared. Prime Minister Trudeau maintained that the rise in oil prices within Canada was a major issue for all Canadians. His government insisted that Alberta sell its oil within Canada at below world price.

At the same time he placed a tax on oil exported to the United States. Eastern Canada could not use the cheap oil from Alberta because the oil pipeline did not reach that far. The eastern provinces had to pay the world price for imported oil. Therefore the federal government gave some of the export tax money to help offset these higher costs.

Trudeau's oil policies angered many Albertans. To them they were yet another example of how the federal government protected central Canadian interests at the expense of the West. Alberta premier Peter Lougheed produced figures in 1979 that showed Alberta had lost almost $20 billion because the province had sold its oil at below the world price. Lougheed believed Albertans were being denied a rightful source of revenue. They felt entitled to their wealth, as central Canadians had been entitled to theirs.

The Heritage Fund

The federal government justified its position by calling attention to the ever-increasing Alberta Heritage Fund. Alberta deposits 30% of the sale value of oil into this fund. At the end of 1980 the fund was near the $8 billion mark. It is expected to reach $50 billion by 1990.

The Heritage Fund is the largest and most powerful government-owned bank account in the western world. Alberta intends to use the fund to finance the future development of the province's economy. Instead of merely extracting oil from the ground, Alberta hopes to develop a petro-chemical industry. This would use the oil to manufacture plastics, textiles, fertilizers and detergents. Alberta has also announced plans for a medical research centre that would serve all Canadians. The Heritage Fund has been used to loan large sums of money to other provinces. Some say this type of investment may give oil-rich Alberta more control over other aspects of Canada's economy. Many Canadians, especially in the eastern and central regions, feel that no one province should have this sort of power. The federal government has been warning of the dangers such decentralization may bring.

Non-renewable Resources

Another concern is shared by all the oil-producing provinces. Fossil fuels like oil and gas are a non-renewable resource. Around 1990 supplies will begin to run low. Then electricity generated from water power and nuclear energy will likely become the new main source of energy. In 1980 electricity accounted for about one third of all energy use. This proportion will grow to about one half before the end of the century. Therefore, the importance of Alberta, Newfoundland, and other oil-rich areas is likely to fade somewhat. In the meantime they naturally wish to sell their resources at the best possible price.

Canada is one of the few western countries that can become self-sufficient in energy. According to government agencies, self-sufficiency may be possible by the 1990s. This will require an immediate upswing in energy research. Alternative energy systems are the key to the future beyond the 1980s. Increased oil drilling is needed now to support these efforts. But cars may one day run on cleaner fuels such as compressed hydrogen or propane gas. Factories may run on the energy of gases distilled from garbage and vegetable waste. Energy from the sun and wind may provide the power needed in our homes.

In 1981 the federal government and Alberta reached an agreement on energy prices. It allows for the price of oil to rise rapidly over the five-year period of the agreement. However, Canadians will still pay less than the world price. Economists and politicians state that in the long term the agreement will be good for all Canada.

Ontario

The frontier communities of early Upper Canada have become the bustling cities of modern day Ontario.

Iron ore open-pit mining at Atikokan, in northwestern Ontario.

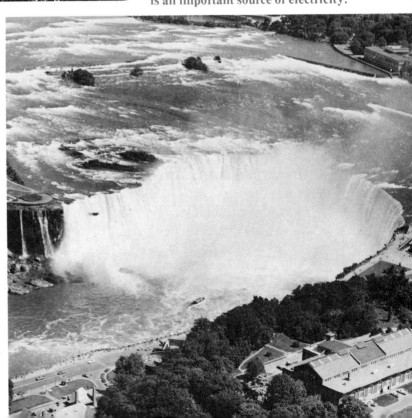

Ontario Place, an entertainment centre on islands specially built in the waters of Lake Ontario. The lighted dome is a movie theatre.

Niagara Falls attracts many tourists and is an important source of electricity.

Moosonee is a favourite tourist centre for "southerners."

The Industrial Heartland

Since the first days of Confederation, Ontario has had the largest population of all the provinces. Today Ontario is home to over a third of all Canadians. Half the nation's manufacturing industries are based in the province.

In recent years most immigrants to Canada have been city dwellers who wish to seek jobs in industry. Therefore they tend to head for the cities of the "golden horseshoe," Canada's industrial centre around the west end of Lake Ontario. As a result, Ontario receives more than half of all immigrants to the country. Ontario has changed from being the most "Anglo-Saxon" province at the turn of the century to being the most "multicultural" one.

Industrial Expansion

Ontario's industries started to grow toward the end of the nineteenth century. The province's forests, farms, and mines supplied the new factories with raw materials. Ontario's natural richness, size, and central situation helped guarantee its success as an industrial region.

Ontario's large population gave the province more seats than any other in the federal House of Commons. This fact, plus its economic importance, helped the province to dominate most national issues.

The development of Canadian industry has been a main concern of this country's economic policies since John A. Macdonald introduced the "national" policy in 1878. The federal government has protected industry by imposing high tariffs on foreign imports. All Canadians had to pay these tariffs. However, a study has shown that over 85% of the jobs protected by tariffs were located in Ontario and its neighbouring province Quebec. Eastern and western Canada have provided, at low prices, the resources that help the industries of Ontario to prosper.

This situation has created much friction over the

The control room in a steel mill in Hamilton.

years between Ontario and the other provinces. By the 1980s the balance of power was shifting. The energy-producing regions of Canada were gaining new economic power. Ontario relied on these regions for much of its fuel. And so Alberta, Saskatchewan, and even Newfoundland were adding a new dimension to the question of economic policy.

This changing balance created new resentments. Many Canadians living in other provinces wanted political power to equal their new economic power. However, Ontario still had the largest population and therefore the most seats in parliament. With support from Quebec, whose economy was also based on industry, Ontario could control political decisions of the federal government.

What natural advantages make Ontario the "industrial heartland?"
How has the tariff, since 1878, encouraged Ontario industries?
Why has northern Ontario not prospered as has southern Ontario?
Why might Ontario lose some of its political and economic power?

People tend to think of Ontario's economy as based entirely on industry. Yet many fertile farms still dot the province. Some of Canada's finest vegetables are grown here. Some parts of the Niagara Peninsula are as far south as northern California. In this mild climate and rich soil, vineyards and orchards yield excellent produce.

Northern Ontario

Ontario's industrial growth has occurred in the south of the province. Northern Ontario is a sparsely settled area rich in mining and timber resources. However, the region has never developed a stable economy of its own. The north has always been dependent on the richer south. The people of northern Ontario are now demanding that the provincial government encourage more industrial growth in the area. This would greatly improve the employment opportunities in the north.

For most of the twentieth century, Ontario has been the richest province. Taxes paid by Ontario citizens and businesses have gone in equalization payments to poorer provinces. The economic slump of the late 1970s and early 1980s has changed this situation. In political affairs, Ontario finds itself in a weakening bargaining position. Political power is bound to shift to some extent to the oil-rich provinces.

Most people in Ontario understand this. This does not mean they are ready to give up their influence without a struggle. For example, Ontario is reluctant to back other provinces in their claims for greater natural resource control. Ontarians would prefer that the federal government continued to control the cost of energy. But Premier Blakeney of Saskatchewan has observed that "Ontario will probably be called upon to make some painful compromises." Even if this is so, Ontario will remain the backbone of Canadian industry.

A Sense of Identity

Most people in Canada have a dual sense of identity. They are both Canadians and Nova Scotians, Canadians and Quebeckers, or Canadians and Manitobans. In Ontario this sense of a provincial identity as distinct from the national one is not as strong.

Since 1867 Ontario has been the province with the largest population. As Canada grew, the province's central location increased its importance. The nation's capital is situated there. Perhaps these facts make it harder for the people of Ontario to distinguish in their hearts between their province and their country. Certainly they are often surprised at other Canadians' strong feelings about their own regions.

A pulp and paper mill in northern Ontario.

Quebec

Montreal, seen from Mount Royal a hundred years ago, and from an island in the St. Lawrence River today.

Bonhomme Carnaval, a familiar figure in Quebec City every February.

The Montréal Canadiens and the Québec Nordiques play hockey.

Alcan's aluminium smelter at Jonquière, Quebec, in the Canadian shield.

A coastal village in the Gaspé Peninsula.

La Belle Province

Quebec has always been different from the other provinces of Canada. Many of the provisions of Confederation were designed to protect these differences.

Quebec was settled by the French before the British took over what is now Canada. All other provinces developed under British influence. Quebec was an established community following its own laws, customs, and language. Quebeckers seldom felt welcome in other parts of Canada. This encouraged a tendency for French Canadians to look to their own province for support.

For nearly 200 years Montreal was the business centre of Canada. It was closest to the bustling cities of Boston and New York. Ocean-going ships dropped and picked up cargo there because they could get no further up the St. Lawrence River. Businesses set up their head offices in Montreal. Industry grew up around the city. It was not until the twentieth century that the focus of business activity moved west to Ontario. It was not until the midcentury that Toronto surpassed Montreal in population.

The Economy of Quebec

The Quiet Revolution of the 1960s and 1970s asserted Quebec's cultural and political differences from the rest of Canada. At the same time it encouraged Quebeckers to learn more about the world about them and to grasp at economic opportunities.

Perhaps the most powerful symbol of the new restless energy of the province is the mammoth James Bay hydro-electric project. Since 1972, 20,000 workers have been carving one of the world's largest energy projects out of the rugged northern wilderness. By 1990 the gigantic dams and generating stations of James Bay will provide Quebec with 40% of its energy needs. Unlike oil and gas, hydro power is a renewable resource. Quebec will be able to prosper because it has a reliable energy supply.

Quebec is also rich in minerals. Asbestos, iron, zinc, and copper are abundant. The rising price of gold in the early 1980s meant a boom for Quebec's gold mines. The

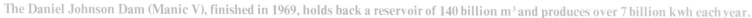

The Daniel Johnson Dam (Manic V), finished in 1969, holds back a reservoir of 140 billion m³ and produces over 7 billion kwh each year.

What is one of Quebec's greatest renewable natural resources?
What is meant by the "Quiet Revolution?"
Why was a referendum held in Quebec in 1980? What was the result?

Olympic stadium, Montreal.

province's vast electricity supplies are harnessed to produce aluminum.

Yet the Quebec economy has its problems. Quebec's manufacturing industries find it hard to compete with cheaper foreign goods. The building of the St. Lawrence Seaway and the growth of air travel meant that Montreal was no longer the nation's natural financial capital. Companies began to move their head offices west — usually to Toronto. This trend speeded up when business people became afraid Quebec might separate from Canada. The same fear meant they were reluctant to set up new factories in the province. Quebeckers hope that the decisive vote to stay in Canada in the 1980 referendum will reverse the trend. Investors should once again look to Quebec as a good place to do business.

The Language of the Workplace

One of the most significant acts of the 1970s was a law that made French the language of the workplace. This meant that the average Quebecker had the right to use French on the job, just as workers in other provinces could use English. Until this law was passed, an employer could insist on running a factory or office in English even if all the workers were French.

The law gave French Canadians access to a whole range of jobs they had been excluded from before. It was hard on some English Quebeckers who had never expected they would need to speak the language of the majority. Most adjusted well. Some, who could not or would not adjust, left the province.

The Future

The 1976 election victory of the Parti Québécois led by René Lévesque, increased separation and confederation tensions. Lévesque proposed a separate nation state connected to Canada only by money and banking systems. In the 1980 referendum results, separatist strength seemed to be dying. When the Parti Québécois didn't support the new constitutional agreement in 1981, separatist feelings revived. Regardless of how this matter is settled, large numbers of Quebeckers will continue to be unhappy with the association with Canada. Yet the majority seems satisfied to continue the development of Quebec within Canada.

Horsepower is still often the most efficient way to gather maple sap.

The Atlantic Region

There are still villages like Grand Pré, Nova Scotia, in Atlantic Canada, but cities like Saint John, New Brunswick, with its port facilities, railways and superhighways, are also part of the present-day scene.

Fish are diverted into a fishing weir where they can be netted easily.

The people of Grand Manan Island in the Bay of Fundy make their living from fishing, lumbering, and tourism.

Prince Edward Island, better known for its potatoes, also grows fine tobacco.

The Maritimes

Sharing the southern shores of the Gulf of St. Lawrence are the Maritime provinces — Nova Scotia, Prince Edward Island, and New Brunswick. French settlers arrived here before the founding of Quebec. They were later joined by English, Scottish, and Irish immigrants. The American Revolution sent north large numbers of Americans loyal to Britain.

Wind and sail power dominated the nineteenth century. This was the golden age of the Maritimes. Situated on the sea, the Maritimes had an ideal vantage point for world trade.

With Confederation a new era arrived. The Maritimes had once profited from their location on the sea. Confederation made them a less significant area on the edge of a much larger territory.

A Canadian Outpost

The main goal of Confederation became developing the country's interior. This involved a new mode of transportation, the railway. To encourage manufacturing industries, a new import tariff was imposed on all the provinces and territories. The Maritimes could no longer trade freely with other ports. The end of free trade and the introduction of the railway meant the age of sail and Maritime prosperity was over. It had been replaced by the new age of steel, coal, and steam.

The Maritimes fell into a period of decline. They were labelled the "weak sisters" of Confederation. They suffered from heavy unemployment and slow economic growth. Unable to find work at home, Maritimers began to move to other parts of Canada.

Many people of the Maritimes blamed their difficulties on the federal government. They had been hurt by the high freight rates and tariff policies that favoured the industrial regions of Quebec and Ontario. Instead of being a centre of commerce and trade, they

were now a Canadian outpost. This, combined with the change from wooden sailing vessels to steel-hulled steamships, had deprived them of their shipping and shipbuilding industries.

The next blow to Maritime fortunes came as homes and industry moved from coal to cleaner oil-based fuels. Even the railways switched — the last coal-burning steam engines in Canada were retired in the midfifties. Production in the coal mines of Cape Breton and mainland Nova Scotia slowed. Miners were laid off. Whole communities almost died.

The New Value of Resources

A turnaround began in the 1970s. The region's natural resources became of increasing value. Industry began to look once again to coal as oil prices shot up. Coal mines expanded or re-opened. Miners went back to work. The price of other minerals rose as well. Lead and zinc mines in northern New Brunswick also prospered. New potash mines have recently been opened.

Hay harvesting in the Saint John River Valley.

Why did the Maritimes enter an economic decline in the years after 1867? Why are there new reasons for optimism in the 1980s? Why do many Maritimers resent the federal government, yet feel the need for federal support?

Farming is also important to the Maritime economy: Prince Edward Island has become world-renowned for its fine potatoes. The orchards of the Annapolis Valley in Nova Scotia produce excellent apples. Dairy farming is good business.

In 1977 the federal government declared a 200-mile fishing limit. This benefited all the Maritime provinces. The new limit gives Canadians first rights at fishing in all waters as far as 200 nautical miles (370 km) from the Canadian shoreline. This gives Canadian fishing boats a new advantage over their competitors from Norway and the Soviet Union. The federal government has recently given financial aid to the Maritime fishing industry. Canada is resuming its role as one of the world's leading fish suppliers.

The city of Halifax is a bustling centre of the Maritime region. Its modern container port allows goods to be shipped in enormous containers without being repacked at any stage. Plans are underway for a new marine industrial park. Here marine equipment such as mini-submarines, fishing gear, and underwater sonar devices will be produced. Projects like these combine the economic benefits of manufacturing with Nova Scotia's location on the sea.

Most Maritimers want a share in the new industrialized society. Yet they want to avoid some of the harsher effects of industry. People in the Maritimes still live differently from people in other parts of Canada. Fewer goods and services are available in this region, and there is less money to buy them with. The pace of life is slower. Maritimers value this. So do the many tourists who visit the region each year. They come not only for the breathtaking scenery but also for the atmosphere. They say visiting the Maritimes is like walking back to a gentler time.

Many Maritimers feel their place in Canada is a frustrating one. They resent the federal government for the policies that made their region so dependent on central Canada. Yet they need federal funding to help them establish independent secondary industries. It is this revitalization of Maritime resources that is giving the region a renewed opportunity for strength and prosperity.

Oyster farming on Prince Edward Island. Malpeque oysters are enjoyed in many areas around the world.

Newfoundland and Labrador

Newfoundland was Britain's oldest colony. In 1949 it became Canada's newest province. For centuries French, English, Irish, and Portuguese fishermen competed for fishing rights in the island's waters. The unique mixture of these founding people has given Newfoundlanders a rich folk culture and a special sense of humour. The province retains its distinct character to this day.

The early settlers lived from fishing out of necessity. Newfoundland's infertile soil yielded only small quantities of potatoes and vegetables. There were few animals to hunt. Most Newfoundlanders lived in isolated fishing villages called "outports." St. John's was the only town to grow to any size.

It is easy to see Newfoundland's economic heritage isn't nearly as great as its cultural one. Historically Newfoundland has been Canada's poorest province. It has always had the highest rate of unemployment.

Despite these bleak statistics, Newfoundland is making great strides in a number of economic areas. The island's fishing and fish-processing industries, are being modernized. Inland, the same is happening to mining and forestry.

Gaining riches from the sea: the fishery . . .

Labrador

Labrador is the rocky eastern coast of the Canadian mainland north of the Gulf of St. Lawrence. At the turn of the century, Wilfred Grenfell became concerned about conditions in the tiny Labrador fishing villages. His Grenfell Mission established hospitals, nursing stations, orphanages, schools and centres for small industry all along the coast. Since that time Newfoundlanders have begun to exploit Labrador's rich resources of lumber, iron ore, and hydro-electric power.

For many years Quebec and Newfoundland both claimed Labrador as part of their territory. This dispute was settled when an international commission established the border in 1927. However, Quebec has never accepted the decision of the commission.

It is partly because of this that the two provinces cannot agree about hydro-electric power from Labrador. Quebec refuses to allow Newfoundland electricity to pass over its borders for sale to other provinces or the United States. It will buy the power for use in Quebec — at a price that was established over 20 years ago when no one expected the tremendous rise in the cost of energy. Newfoundland has been trying to renegotiate the deal but so far without success. Quebec has offered to exchange free flow of Newfoundland's hydro-electric power in trade for Labrador. Newfoundland has refused.

A New Resource from the Sea

Newfoundland may yet become a wealthy province. Offshore oil reserves valued at $15 billion have been discovered. Already a new dispute has arisen. This one is between the federal and the provincial governments. As with Alberta, the dispute centres on taxation and revenue rights to the oil. Newfoundland's Premier Brian Peckford argued that Newfoundland should decide how much oil

What does it mean to say "Newfoundland has a rich cultural heritage yet a weak economic heritage?"
Labrador's sale of electricity to Quebec has caused friction. How?
Why are some Newfoundlanders concerned about offshore oil?

... and the petroleum industry.

revenue it will share with the federal government. Like Alberta's Premier Peter Lougheed and other provincial leaders, Peckford was fighting to gain more financial control over the province's own resources. However, Canada's oceans are a federal responsibility. Prime Minister Trudeau claimed that as the oil resources are off shore they are under the control of the federal government.

No matter how this is resolved, Newfoundland faces a difficult and challenging period of transition. Those in the fishing industry are concerned for the delicate balance of life in the sea. They fear industrial wastes may poison prime fishing grounds. If the fishing resource is looked after properly it will always be there. They argue, "If you kill the fish, what happens when the oil and gas run out?" Employers in the fishing industry fear they may lose many young workers to the oil business where there is big money to be made.

Another concern is the effect that big industry is likely to have on the general way of life. The residents want time to adapt to the influx of new people and technology. Big business isn't likely to make it a gradual process. Many Newfoundlanders feel they are being forced to adapt not only to central Canadian economics, but also to central Canadian values. Says one Newfoundlander, "With oil and all these mainlanders flooding in, who knows? In fifty years we could be just as bland as someone from southern Ontario."

Newfoundlanders are wary of sacrificing their traditions to this new source of income. The new oil revenue, they argue, will be only a temporary one. Their heritage goes back several hundred years! Newfoundlanders have a two-fold challenge. They want to preserve their way of life. At the same time they want to use the oil boom to fuel their economy.

A Pattern of Regions

The falling tide, Nootka Sound, Vancouver Island.

April on the Prairies.

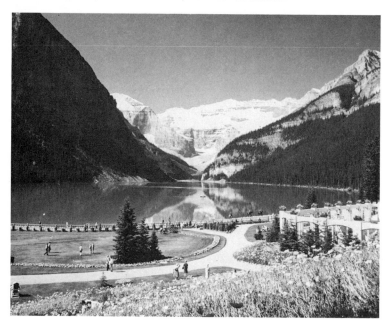

Lake Louise, Banff National Park, Alberta.

Large countries have a problem that small ones don't: their diversity. There are two ways of handling the situation. One way is to force the entire country to share the same cultural and economic structure. The other is to accept this diversity and to make it work for the country. This is the way Canada has chosen. Making it work is one of Canada's main challenges.

The problem of diversity is perhaps greater in Canada than in any other country. Most, if not all, of the larger countries — including the United States, Russia, China, Japan — have chosen the other path. Their people are encouraged to subdue their individual traditions to unite their countries. Canadians are encouraged to remain unified but maintain their own cultural individuality. This makes the task of governing much more difficult. National leaders must try to avoid their own traditions and prejudices. Only in this way can they respond fairly to the needs of each region or group.

Debate: Resolved that only by increasing provincial powers can Canada become a true federal state; **or** Resolved that reducing federal economic, financial, and political powers would lead to disintegration of Canada into separate regions.

Art Gallery pages 22 and 24

Skating on the Rideau Canal at Ottawa.

Notre-Dame-des-Victoires, the oldest church in Quebec City.

Many of the differences between the federal and provincial governments are reactions to unresolved historical problems that have gone unsolved for many years. Others are due to new situations that have arisen out of Canada's development as an industrial power. Such differences are probably unavoidable in any democracy, especially in one that encourages cultural diversity.

The regions of Canada are all seeking greater power and autonomy. The eastern and western provinces in particular want to have a larger say in setting government policies. Each region or province is also prepared to speak up for its own needs. Only in coming to terms with its diversity will Canada become more unified. At that point, the possibilities of a Canada based upon its regional differences may be fully explored.

Cleaning the catch, Peggy's Cove, Nova Scotia.

Questions and Activities

Test Yourself

1. Make a chart for the 6 regions of Canada. For each region list
   a) three main economic features (resources, industries, etc.)
   a) one idea of *agreement* with the federal government
   c) one idea of *disagreement* with the federal government
2. Which region has the highest per capita income? If the region or province is considered poor, what does the federal government do to help?

Ideas for Discussion

1. a) Examine the three themes in Canadian history referred to on page 248 (The Challenge of Regionalism). List the three in order of importance to your region today. Explain your reasons.
   b) How might the order of importance be different in other regions of Canada today?
2. Discuss or debate the topic: "That Canada would be better off with a free trade policy, than with retaining the protective tariff."
3. Hold a debate on the topic: "That separatism will always be an attractive option for many Quebeckers."
4. Discuss the future of the manufacturing industry in Canada. Make all kinds of suggestions — sane or crazy — you can do research later to pick out workable ideas.
   a) Should the federal government continue to support older industries (automobile, farm-equipment, etc.) by tariffs and subsidies?
   b) Should the government shift support to newer high technology industries (computers, electronic equipment, etc.)? Why? How would your suggestions affect the different regions in Canada?
5. Looking at pages 246 - 247, study the "Industries" and "Resources" and discuss the possibility of developing new industries in each region. What might those industries be? Does geography always dictate settlement and industry decisions?

Do Some Research

1. Write a brief research report on the following people from one region.
   a) a premier or political leader
   b) a business person or labour leader
   c) a sports or entertainment personality
2. Find out to what extent the economy of British Columbia is related to the Pacific Rim countries, rather than to the rest of Canada.
3. How much money is currently in the Alberta Heritage Fund? How is the money being used? Find out if any other provinces have similar funds.
4. Do some research on a recent (or upcoming) first Ministers' conference. (The Prime Minister of Canada and the 10 provincial premiers). What are the key issues in the conference? What were the viewpoints of your provincial premier? How were they similar or different from the federal position?
5. Report on the effect that energy resources development has on the economy and on the way of life of the people in Alberta and Saskatchewan.

Be Creative

1. Form a group to prepare a *folder* on *one* region of Canada. In your folder include:
   a) a *map* of your region, showing the key economic resources.
   b) a *poster* for the region, inviting tourists and/or immigrants.
   c) a *written description* of the region, describing the factors that would attract a new wave of immigrants.
   d) a *written statement* of your region's opinions about the current federal government economic policies (i.e., energy prices, manufacturing, unemployment, transportation).
   e) a biography of *one* person from the region.
2. Write a letter to the editor of your local newspaper on one of the following topics:
   a) a statement of *someone from your province,* giving a viewpoint to another province or the federal government.
   b) a criticism of *your* provincial policy from the viewpoint of another region.
   c) a suggestion of the advantages of cooperation by all regions.
3. Prepare a *collage* for one of the regions of Canada from newspaper and magazine materials. Your collage might include industries, tourist attractions, people, sports and entertainment, controversial issues, etc.
4. Prepare a radio or TV program on a recent or future First Ministers' Conference. Focus on the key issues and present regional attitudes likely to be expressed by the different ministers. Include information on such extras as language facilities, dinners featuring regional specialties, and security provided by the conference organizers.

You Are There

The Regional Conference

The prime minister has convened a conference of regional representatives. The objective is to provide recommendations for the federal government to help in deciding on policies to satisfy the different needs of different regions of the country, and to meet the needs of Canada as a whole.

Procedure

1. Elect a prime minister from your class.
2. Each member of the class should become a representative of one region of Canada. A recommended split for representatives:

Atlantic provinces	— 4	Prairies	— 6
Quebec	— 8	British Columbia	— 4
Ontario	— 8	North	— 1

3. The regional conference is to consider several proposals submitted by the federal government.
4. After re-examining the information about each region in this chapter, and other resources, each region is to select the proposals which they would support. It is agreed that all representatives of each region must support their own region's proposals.
5. Representatives from each region should meet with other regions in order to gain support for their proposals.
6. Any region may submit *additional proposals* if the representatives can gain the support of other regions.
7. The prime minister has stated:
   a) The total revenues available to the federal government are $1 500 000 000.
   b) Any proposal to be accepted must have the support of 2/3 of the total number of representatives.
8. The prime minister, in carrying out discussions with regional groups, is concerned about:
   a) the welfare of the whole country.
   b) the need of the government to be re-elected in the next election.
9. Break the conference into five sessions:
   Session 1 — Introduction of topic, explanation of rules, selection of regional representatives
   Session 2 — Development of regional viewpoints, consideration of regional policy on different proposals.
   Session 3 — Negotiations with other regions to try to gain support.
   Session 4 — Formal conference; presentation of viewpoints; final voting on proposals.
   Session 5 — Debriefing — analysis of what happened and why.

List of proposals for discussion

The federal government has submitted the following proposals after consultation with the premiers. Remember, the maximum amount of money available is $1 500 000 000.

A. *Increased industrial subsidy to the Atlantic Provinces*
   Money is required to subsidize a steel mill in Nova Scotia, a pulp mill in New Brunswick, a potato-processing plant in PEI, and a fish-processing plant in Newfoundland. These new industries would provide employment for over 3000 people in the Atlantic Provinces. COST: $400 000 000

B. *Additional grain subsidy to Western farmers*
   Because of a recent drought and the fluctuating prices of grain, a further subsidy is needed to guarantee income to western farmers. COST: $100 000 000

C. *Modernization of Canadian armed forces*
   As part of our NATO responsibilities, we wish to build 3 new military bases in British Columbia, Saskatchewan, and Newfoundland, and to purchase 50 new fighter planes. Parts of these aircraft will be built in Ontario and Quebec. COST: $1 000 000 000

D. *New oil pipeline to Eastern Canada*
   A new oil pipeline is to be built through Quebec to the Maritimes. This will increase the sale of western oil, will reduce energy costs in the Maritimes, and help move Canada towards energy self-sufficiency. COST: $800 000 000

E. *Additional CBC network*
   In order to counteract the influence of American television, and to provide more opportunities for Canadian musicians and entertainers, additional funds are needed to expand the CBC network and Canadian programs. COST: $100 000 000

F. *Unemployment insurance*
   Because of increased unemployment in some areas, and inflation, more funds are required for longer periods of unemployment, and for higher payments. COST: $300 000 000

G. *Increased day-care programs*
   Because of the rising costs due to inflation, more women have to go out to work. Therefore the federal government is proposing greater subsidies to the provinces to support day-care centres for working mothers. COST: $20 000 000.

Government in Canada
ADVANCE ORGANIZER

THE
PEOPLE

BALLOT
BOX

GOVERNMENT
MPs

PRIME
MINISTER

CA

HOUSE OF COMMONS

LEADER OF
OPPOSITION

OPPOSITION
MPs

Word List
ballot
bill/act/law
campaign
candidate

Charter of Rights
constituency
constitution
federalism

municipality
political platform
province
reading

SENATE

GOVERNOR GENERAL

THE COURTS

PUBLIC SERVICE

THE PEOPLE

Why Do We Have Government?

Spaceship *Aurora*

Imagine that your class has been selected to join a spaceship, the *Aurora,* on an exploratory trip to a distant corner of the galaxy.

You and your classmates are assigned a central cabin with individual survival chambers. Travelling swiftly through space, you are soon many light-years from earth.

Suddenly the pilot speaks from the control room. The ship has passed through a mysterious cosmic storm that has damaged it and robbed it of most of its power. There is just enough fuel left to land on a nearby planet. A scan of the surface shows that the atmosphere is breathable and there is enough water and vegetation to support human life. However, the pilot does not know the state of the reverse thrust landing gear. She asks all passengers to return to their cabins and prepare for an emergency landing.

Touchdown is violent. In your padded chamber you are safe, but others may not have been so lucky. Cautiously, you emerge to take stock.

All adults, whose cabins were near the outer walls of the ship, have been killed. Only your classmates, in their individual chambers, have survived. No older people are around to give orders or impose rules. You are "free" to do whatever you want.

But what *should* you do?

At the moment, you have no supplies of food or water. You have no place to sleep and no way to keep warm. It is obvious that you will be on this planet for several weeks, months, or even years.

At first, no one seems to know what to do. People make various suggestions. There is much shouting and arguing, but no useful plan of action emerges. Gradually you realize that you can only solve your problems by working together as a group.

You gather in small groups to discuss and answer the following questions:

1. How will you make your decisions?
2. Who will be your leaders, and how will they be selected?
3. What kinds of people do you want as leaders? What characteristics do you think that they should have?
4. What kind of rules will you make? Who will make these rules?
5. What will you do if some person or group refuses to abide by the rules?

As you examine these questions, you are considering the same problems that are faced by any group of people trying to work together. All societies and nations have faced these problems. Different groups arrive at different solutions, but all must meet the same basic needs. They must establish rules, make decisions, and select people to run the organization. In other words, they must set up a system of government.

Canada has a democratic system of government. Leaders are chosen in elections. Canadian citizens 18 years of age and over vote for the candidate of their choice. The candidate with the most votes wins. This candidate is a representative of the people, who have chosen him or her to make decisions on their behalf.

All groups or societies establish certain basic rules or laws. Imagine a hockey game with no rules, or no referee to enforce them. It would be chaos, just as society would be without laws.

Canada's laws are made either by the federal parliament, or by provincial legislatures, or by town governments. It is the duty of law courts to see that the laws are applied fairly, and to pass judgement on people who break the law.

The basic framework of laws and conventions that a society develops is called the constitution. For example, the NHL rules are hockey's constitution. Canada's constitution is based on the British North America Act of 1867 (now called the Constitution Act, 1867), which sets out Canada's system of government. In 1982, the act was amended to include a Charter of Rights, which adds to the basic framework of rules that Canadians have agreed are important.

Governments in democracies are elected by the passengers to steer the ship of the nation. They are expected to hold it on course, to arrange for a prosperous voyage and to be prepared to be thrown overboard if they fail in either duty.

Senator Eugene Forsey

What Government Does

Government often seems to be something that happens a long way away. Few people think of government as something that affects their daily lives. Yet most Canadians cannot make it through a single day without coming into contact with government.

Consider a typical day in your life. You wake up, turn on the electric light, and take a shower. The chances are that both electricity and water are public utilities, which means that they are run by the government and supported by taxes. The waste from your bathroom is carried away by the public sewage system. The sidewalks you walk on and the bus you take to school are both likely to be provided by the government.

School teachers, fire fighters, street cleaners, and police officers are all paid with money raised through taxes. The food sold in stores is inspected by government officials to make sure it is fresh and clean. Every time you listen to a weather forecast (supplied by government experts) on the radio (all stations must have licences from the government), visit a public library, or go skating at a public arena, you are coming into contact with some form of government.

Testing a lake for the effects of acid rain.

Checking weather data.

Keeping the city clean.

Governments have a lot of power over you. Give an example of how the government can help you in each of the following ways:

1. Provide financial assistance if you are out of work
2. Pay medical bills
3. Help you find a job
4. Support you if you are too old or too sick to work
5. Protect you from robbery or unfair treatment
6. Teach you useful skills
7. Pick up your food waste and other unwanted possessions

Governments can also force you, as a citizen, to do certain things. Give examples of how governments can do each of the following:

1. Send you to jail
2. Require you to risk your life
3. Regulate the movies you watch
4. Control the music you listen to on the radio
5. Demand that you give them some of your money
6. Force you to do things "for your own good," such as wearing safety clothing at work, using seat belts in cars, or avoiding drugs
7. Limit your right to make statements harmful or insulting to others without evidence to support them

Look at the picture of an imaginary Canadian community. Find examples of things that governments do.

In groups of three or four students, make a list of these examples.

Compare your list with other groups' lists. Make a total class list. Save this to refer to later in this chapter.

Choose what you think are the five most important things that governments do. In a class discussion, give reasons for your choice.

All's Well that Amends Well

The "constitution" has been much discussed throughout Canada's history. But can you say what it is? Is it some sort of document, rather like the Official Rule Book of the NHL, that sets out rules and regulations for the government of Canada? Or is it a more vague and abstract thing, a mass of unwritten rules and traditions?

In Canada, the answer is that it is both.

The written part of the constitution consists mainly of the Constitution Act. This used to be called the British North America Act, which was passed by the British parliament in London, England, in 1867. The BNA Act set out most of the rules for the working of the Canadian government. At that time, the newly confederated Dominion of Canada was still part of the British Empire, which is why the British parliament had to pass the law that created Canada.

Canada's parliamentary system of government is very closely modelled on the British system. The Fathers of Confederation took this for granted, so they didn't think it was necessary to include in the BNA Act obvious things like "Canada will have a prime minister" or "The governor general will always act on the advice of the prime minister and cabinet." As a result, many very important parts of Canada's system of government have never been written down. The rules of this "unwritten" constitution are called constitutional customs or conventions. Although they are not laws, conventions are very powerful. If officials disobeyed them, they would probably be removed from office very quickly.

An Obstacle to Independence?

In the years following 1867 the relationship between Canada and Britain changed, and various laws were passed making the changes official. For example, in 1949 the Supreme Court of Canada was made Canada's highest court. Until then, lawyers had been able to appeal to a committee in Britain (the Privy Council) for rulings on Canadian cases.

By the 1980s, Canada was functioning as a completely independent nation. There were still many cultural and trade links between Canada and Britain. But as far as Canada's system of government was concerned, there were only two remaining ties. One was that both countries recognize the queen as head of state. The other lay in the constitution.

For although Canadians had been running their own government for many years according to the rules

It should be borne in mind that there is nothing more difficult to arrange, more doubtful of success, and more dangerous to carry through than trying to change a nation's constitution.
Niccolo Machiavelli, Italian political scientist, 1469-1527

of the BNA Act, the act itself could only be changed, or "amended," by the British Parliament. That is to say, Canadian government could work independently *within* the system; but in order to change the *system* itself, it was necessary to go through the British government. And though a law (the Statute of Westminster) prevented Britain from changing the Canadian constitution except at Canada's request, many Canadians found the situation unacceptable. They felt it prevented Canada from being a truly independent nation.

Patriating the Constitution

What was the problem? The British didn't want to keep the power to change Canada's constitution. For more than fifty years they waited for Canadians to decide on a way to change it themselves. The problem was that the federal government and the provincial governments couldn't work out how to balance their interests. From time to time Canadian politicians came together to look for a suitable "amending formula." Twice they came close, but on each occasion Quebec felt unable to join the agreement, and the idea was dropped.

By 1981 Canadians were beginning to lose patience. The arguments had been going on for years, and nothing ever happened. Some people didn't even think it mattered whether the constitution was "patriated" or not. A great fuss was being made over a technicality, while more important issues, such as the economy, were being overlooked.

At last, on 5 November 1981 the federal and nine provincial governments reached a three-point agreement:

1. The power to amend the constitution would be brought from Britain to Canada.

2. Thereafter, changes could be made to the constitution if the federal government and seven or more provinces, representing 50% of the population, agreed. Provinces that did not agree to the changes would be allowed to "opt out."

3. A "Charter of Rights and Freedoms" would be added to the written constitution to protect human rights in Canada.

Apart from the amending formula and the Charter of Rights, the substance of the constitution remained almost unchanged by the historic agreement of 1981. Canadians would notice few changes in their day-to-day contacts with government.

Earlier, Quebec had agreed with seven other provinces on some points they all wanted to see in the agreement. But the province's premier, René Lévesque, found he could not accept the final form of the constitution. Once again, Canada was divided on cultural lines.

It remains to be seen how well the amended constitution stands up to the needs of a developing Canada.

Discuss the reactions of these provincial premiers to the constitutional agreement of 5 November 1981.

William Davis, premier of Ontario: It represents a feeling around this table that there is something to this nation. That there is something to being a Canadian.

René Lévesque, premier of Quebec: It is an insult done to Quebeckers by English Canada.

Brian Peckford, premier of Newfoundland: I feel more fully a Canadian today than I have ever felt since I have been old enough to think, to know, to understand.

If you had been premier of your province, what would your reaction have been?

The Canada Act

On 2 December 1981 the House of Commons passed a constitutional resolution to be presented to the queen. The resolution requested her to have an act called the Canada Act passed by the British parliament. Members of all parties supported the resolution, and it passed by 246 votes to 24. One MP left a hospital bed where he was recovering from open-heart surgery in order to be on hand for the historic occasion. After the vote was taken, the rafters shook as the members joined in a rousing chorus of O Canada in both English and French.

Within days the Senate also passed the resolution, and the governor general had agreed to have it presented to the queen. The stage was set for the British parliament to pass the Canada Act as contained in the Canadian resolution. This would be the last time Canadians called on the British parliament to approve changes in Canada's constitution. The Canada Act would end all legal authority that Britain held over Canada. It would remove one of the last symbols of Canada's former colonial status.

Now Canadians were faced with understanding the new law. It was long and detailed. Its words and phrases seemed complicated, but this was not to make things difficult for ordinary citizens. It was the only way of making sure it said precisely what it meant. Canadians, including politicians, lawyers, teachers, and students, all worked hard to grasp the full meaning of the new constitution.

Queen Elizabeth signs the proclamation of Canada's constitution

The Canada Act contains the Constitution Act, 1982. On the opposite page is a summary of some of the major provisions. Remember that it is *only* a summary. To understand the act fully, you would have to read the complete version.

What do you think is the most important provision of the act? Be prepared to explain your choice.

Not all Canadians were happy about the passage of the Canada Act. Some groups were upset at what the act left out, such as protection of the rights of the unborn, or recognition of "all" not just "existing" native rights. Civil rights workers felt the provinces should not have been allowed to "opt out" or override the Charter of Rights. The Quebec government felt the act did not agree with its hopes for the people of Quebec.

Still, it was a giant step forward in Canadian nationhood. Canadians from coast to coast knew that their nation was ready to face the future on its own feet and its own responsibility.

Part I
Canadian Charter of Rights and Freedoms

Fundamental Freedoms

Freedom of conscience and religion
Freedom of thought, and expression, including freedom of the press
and other media of communication
Freedom of peaceful assembly
Freedom of association

Democratic Rights

The right to vote
The right to run for election

Mobility Rights

The right to enter, remain in, or leave Canada
The right to move to, live in, and work in any province of Canada

Legal Rights

The right to "life, liberty, and security of the person"
Security from unreasonable search or seizure
Security from arbitrary arrest or detention
When arrested, the right to be told why and to hire a lawyer
When accused of a crime, the right to a fair bail hearing, to a quick
trial, and to be assumed innocent until proven guilty
The right not to be subjected to cruel and unusual punishment

Equality Rights

Equality before the law regardless of race, national or ethnic origin,
colour, religion, sex, age, or mental or physical disability (however,
programs may be introduced to help "disadvantaged" groups)

Official Languages of Canada

Equal status for the use of English and French in the government
and courts of Canada and of New Brunswick

Minority Language Education Rights

The right to education in English or French wherever there are
reasonable numbers of Anglophone or Francophone students (not to
come into effect immediately in Quebec)

These rights and freedoms are to be enforced by the courts.

All provisions apply to men and women equally.

Certain sections of the charter may be "over-ridden" for periods of
up to five years by the provincial legislature (or the federal
parliament in matters under its control, including the Yukon and
the Northwest Territories).

Part II
Rights of the Aboriginal Peoples of Canada

"Existing aboriginal and treaty rights" of the native peoples
(Indians, Inuit, and Métis) are recognized.

Part III
Equalization and Regional Disparities

The federal and provincial governments are committed to promote
equal opportunities for the well-being of Canadians. They also agree
to make equalization payments to poorer provinces.

Part IV
Constitutional Conference

A special first ministers conference is to be called within one year of
the proclamation of the act. It is to define and identify the aboriginal
rights of native peoples. Representatives from the Yukon and
Northwest Territories are to be invited to take part in discussions of
items that affect the territories.

Part V
Procedure for Amending the Constitution of Canada

Amendments to the constitution require the approval of the
parliament of Canada and of the legislatures of at least seven
provinces representing at least 50% of the population. (Proposed
changes will need a great deal of support before they become law. On
the other hand, no one province can permanently stall a change
wanted by the rest.) Provinces that do not approve the amendment
may "opt out" if they wish.

Part VI
Amendment to the Constitution Act, 1867

The Constitution Act, 1867 (the BNA Act) is amended by adding
important new provincial powers to section 92. These powers relate
to the development and management of non-renewable natural
resources, forestry resources, and electrical energy.

Part VII
General

The Constitution of Canada is recognized as the supreme law. No
laws that are inconsistent with it are valid. English and French
versions of the Act have equal force.

Federalism: the Division of Powers

> **Agreements are as necessary between Ottawa and the provinces of Canada as they are between Canada and other countries.**
> *From* Government and You *by Charles Kahn and Richard Howard, McClelland and Stewart, 1979.*

When Canada's system of government was being worked out between 1864 and 1867, two of the most important things to be considered were the size of the country, and the fact that it was made up of several distinct regions. Each of these regions had its own history, its own type of terrain and resources, and its own culture. It would be difficult to govern such a country from a single, central capital.

Instead, a *federal* system of government was established. Power was divided between the central government in Ottawa, often called the federal government, and several provincial governments.

At Confederation, powers were divided up very carefully between the two levels of government. The division of powers was set out in Sections 91, 92, and 93 of the British North America Act (now the Constitution Act, 1867).

The Fathers of Confederation chose to give Canada a strong central and weaker provincial governments. A number of very important powers, such as taxation and defence, were therefore given to the federal government. The federal government was also given any powers which were not specifically assigned to the provinces in Sections 92 and 93.

Canada also has a third level of government: local government. The governments of towns and cities are called municipal governments, and they are responsible for purely local matters. It is up to the provincial governments to see that municipal governments work fairly and legally.

Partners in Government

Canada's provincial governments play a large and increasingly important role in the lives of the people of Canada. As their powers and responsibilities have grown, so has the need to communicate and plan with each other and the federal government. Therefore, they have set up a system of federal-provincial conferences to co-ordinate their activities. At these conferences civil servants and ministers meet regularly to plan policies for all Canada.

First Ministers' Conferences

The conferences that receive the most attention in the news are usually first ministers' conferences. These are often televised. The prime minister and the provincial premiers meet to discuss matters of the greatest concern, such as the economy or amendments to the constitution.

These conferences are often the scene of sharp disagreement and intense political battles — under the full glare of television cameras. They also often result in compromise and co-operation. Whatever the outcome, the cameras give Canadians a chance to view their political leaders at work.

Some commentators have accused first ministers of "showing off" to the cameras to impress people back home. They suggest this makes it harder for the ministers to solve their joint problems.

Some Municipal Powers and Responsibilities

local roads
garbage disposal
public transit
maintenance of schools
police and fire protection
libraries
sewage disposal

matters of purely local concern

Some Provincial Powers and Responsibilities
(Sections 92 and 93):

direct taxation (for example, sales taxes)
setting up and supervising municipal governments
management and sale of public lands, and
   supervision of forests
      development and management of non-renewable
       natural resources, forestry resources, and
       electrical energy (added in 1982)
administration of justice and the courts
public and reformatory prisons in the province
      hospitals and asylums
      shop, saloon, and other licences, in order to
       raise money for local and provincial purposes
        property and civil rights
       provincial highways
       education

         all matters of "a merely local or
         private nature in the province"

Some Federal Powers and Responsibilities (Section 91):

postal services
armed forces and defence
currency and coinage
     banking and the issuing of paper money
     regulation of trade and commerce
     seacoast and inland fisheries
     any form of taxation except provincial sales tax
       matters relating to Indians and land
        reserved for Indians
       the census
       management of penitentiaries
       criminal justice

        all matters not assigned exclusively to the
        provinces

---

1. Do you think it is better for political leaders to meet "in the public eye" or "behind closed doors"? What are the advantages or disadvantages of each method?
2. Make three headings: Federal Responsibility, Provincial Responsibility, and Municipal Responsibility. Put each item in the list below under the appropriate heading.

a) Canadian airforce	g) skating arena
b) new sidewalks	h) automobile licences
c) importing oil from Saudi Arabia	i) post office
d) fire department	j) issuing of gold coins
e) regulations about forests and parks	k) sales tax on gasoline
f) sewers	l) highways

3. Refer to the list of things government does that you made from the picture on page 287. Divide the list into federal, provincial, and municipal responsibilities.
4. The government workers in the photographs on page 286 are all concerned with some aspect of the environment. Can you work out whether they are federal, provincial, or municipal employees?

The Provinces

Examine the coats of arms of Canada, the provinces and territories. Choose one and try to identify the various symbols it contains. What do these symbols reveal about the history, geography, and people of the area? Does the coat of arms include a motto? If so, what does it mean?

The diagram at the top shows boxes labeled: THE PEOPLE — BALLOT BOX — LEGISLATIVE ASSEMBLY — LIEUTENANT GOVERNOR — THE COURTS / PUBLIC SERVICE — THE PEOPLE

1. Who is premier of your province?
2. What political party is in power in your province?
3. What political party forms the opposition in your province?
4. What are the most important political concerns in your province?
5. Perhaps you do not live in a province, but in one of Canada's northern territories. What is the form of your territorial government?

The structure of government in the provinces is very similar to that of the federal government. Elections are fought in much the same way. Elected candidates represent the voters of the province in the Legislative Assembly. In some provinces the legislature goes by a slightly different name. For example, in Newfoundland and Nova Scotia it is called the House of Assembly. In Quebec it is the National Assembly. Bills are debated and passed in the legislature as in the federal House of Commons. (However, they do not have to be debated again in an upper house: the provinces have no Senate.) The premier selects a cabinet and leads the government as the prime minister does.

As the queen's representative, the lieutenant governor of the province signs provincial bills into law. The lieutenant governor is appointed by the governor general on the advice of the prime minister and has similar duties. These are largely ceremonial — opening new hospitals, greeting important visitors, giving the speech from the throne at the beginning of a session of the legislature.

It is in areas of responsibility that provincial governments are different from the federal government. For example, the provinces cannot make laws about the size of Canada's armed forces. The federal government cannot decide how much time grade 3 students should spend on physical education each week, or what rules should control lumbering operations in the province's forests.

Each province is different from every other. Each has its own history, its own heroes, its own strengths, its own weaknesses. The *structure* of government is similar across the land. However, the experience of each province leads to varied political views, attitudes, and leaders. These provide a healthy dynamism to Canadian political life.

The Territories

We tend to speak of the provinces as "Canada." Yet 39% of our land area is not part of any province. The vast regions of the Yukon and the Northwest "Territories" are still largely administered by the federal government.

These territories contain only 0.3% of Canada's population. This is considered too small for them to undertake all the responsibilities of provincial government. However, both territories elect territorial councils that have some limited powers and duties.

In 1982 the people of the Northwest Territories voted in a referendum to divide the vast area in two. This proposal was made because the Inuit in the east live quite differently from the Métis, Dene, and others of the western territories. Some feel that this proposal could lead to the creation of two new provinces in the future.

The call for new provinces in Canada's North will get louder and more forceful in the years to come. The people of the territories point to the rapid development of the oil and gas reserves expected in the near future. This may soon drastically change their way of life. If the territories were provinces, they would have more control over development and the changes it will bring.

The Indian, Inuit, and Métis argue that with full provincial status they could better protect the interests of their people.

Political Parties

It is very difficult for one person alone to bring about change in government. But a large group of people working together can make an impact on the government, change policies, and affect decisions. In your local community, people probably have different opinions about where a new road should be built or whether or not a dump for chemical waste should be set up nearby. On a larger scale, in a country as large and diverse as Canada, people will have very different ideas about how things should be run.

A political party is a group of people who share similar ideas about how the government should work, and who band together to put their ideas into effect.

What Political Parties Do

A political party organizes its opinions on various issues into a statement called a political platform. This summarizes the attitudes shared by members of the party, and sets out the way the party would run the government. The platform tells the public about the party's policies. Voters sometimes discover that they support some "planks" in the platform but do not agree with others. However, most voters find that political platforms make it easier to decide which party they want to support.

The Parties in Canada

Canada has three main political parties: the Liberals, the Progressive Conservatives, and the New Democratic Party.

Political parties know that they need a broad range of support in order to be elected. They therefore try to attract voters from all walks of life — farmers and factory workers, executives and clerks, homemakers and storekeepers, recent immigrants and Canadian-born citizens, students and old-age pensioners, loggers in British Columbia as well as bankers in Newfoundland.

To appeal to so many different groups, political parties must compromise. Often a political platform is a compromise between what members really believe is best and what they think will appeal to most voters.

The Liberals and Conservatives are known as middle-of-the-road parties. They have always attempted to attract support from all groups. NDP leader Tommy Douglas once called them "Tweedledum and Tweedledee," poking fun at the fact that there sometimes seems little to choose between them.

The CCF started out in 1933 as a socialist party. It appealed to workers and farmers, and did not attempt to attract support from other groups. By the forties and fifties, however, the CCF was winning less and less support in federal elections. In 1961 it became the New Democratic Party. The NDP presented a more moderate program in order to attract a wider range of voters.

At the same time both the Liberals and the Conservatives began to adopt some of the CCF's popular social policies such as unemployment insurance and medicare. When these policies were first suggested, they seemed outlandish to the middle-of-the-road parties.

It is difficult to imagine what federal and provincial elections would be like without political parties. Almost all candidates belong to one of the major political parties. When you vote for Mr. X or Ms. Y, you are also voting for a political party. The party with the most supporters elected forms the government.

Each party chooses its leader at a leadership convention. Leadership conventions are among the most colourful and exciting events in Canadian political life. Delegates from local party associations across the country converge on the convention site.

In groups, choose a political party and collect information about it. You can do this by:
a) visiting the local party committee office
b) reading party campaign literature
c) reading newspaper accounts
d) interviewing a member of the party
e) watching television reports
   Summarize your chosen party's viewpoints on the following issues:
a) employment   c) energy
b) inflation   d) one other policy of your choice
   Compile a scrapbook, and prepare your own summary of your party's platform for presentation to the class.

The first days of the convention are spent in speeches, social events, and discussion as candidates try to win support among the delegates. Songs, hats, buttons, banners, and pamphlets describing the candidate and outlining policies, are all part of the campaign. After a succession of votes, the name of the new party leader is announced. This is the person who will become prime minister or premier if the party is elected to power.

Political parties also organize election campaigns. They select and advise candidates, raise funds, prepare advertising campaigns, and provide information to the media and the public. On election day, each party tries to make sure that as many of its supporters as possible get to the polls to cast their votes.

In most countries today, political parties are a vital part of the government. It is important that voters always have a choice between two or more parties, so that no one party can ever put all of its policies into effect without opposition.

Everything a political party does is geared towards the next election. The election is the key. Only if elected, will the party have the power to start putting its ideas into effect.

Liberal Party

Progressive Conservative Party

New Democratic Party

Federal Elections

Politics is a strange game. You *stand* for nomination, so you can *run* for election, to *sit* in parliament.

The scene is set:

The election machinery: The country is divided into electoral districts called *constituencies* or ridings.

The candidates: In each constituency the local branches of political parties are at work. They *nominate* candidates for the next election. Some candidates do not have the support of any political party but run as *independents*.

The voters: During the government's term of office, voters watch the words and actions of both government and opposition parties. They develop opinions about who would be best to govern after the next election.

An election is called:

The election campaign swings into action. The candidates are out to persuade the voters of the constituency to support them. They make speeches, hold meetings, shake hands at bus stops and supermarkets, visit the voters in their homes. Eager campaign workers run the campaign headquarters, canvass from door to door, and give out pamphlets and buttons. A special squad erects posters wherever friendly voters will allow them. Teenagers too young to vote may have strong political opinions. They are often among the most active volunteers.

Many voters feel the real campaign is being waged in their newspapers and on their television screens. They watch the leaders of the major parties as they swing across the country trying to make the headlines. The parties spend millions of dollars on paid political announcements. They make every effort to reach into people's homes to win the voters' support for the party platform, the party leader, and the local party candidate. Many voters find the bombardment of information confusing. But in the end most come to a decision on the way they will vote.

Meanwhile, a list of eligible voters is compiled by *enumerators.* In federal elections all Canadian citizens 18 years of age and over may vote. (The rules vary slightly in provincial and municipal elections.) The *district returning officer* has ballots prepared and hires people to run each *polling station* on election day.

On election day:

Polling or voting stations open up throughout the constituency. Each station is run by a *deputy returning officer* and a *poll clerk.* They work under the watchful eyes of *scrutineers* representing the various candidates. This is only one of many precautions to ensure there is no cheating or sloppiness in the election.

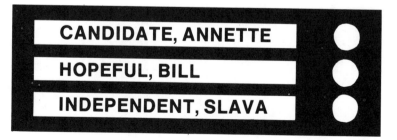

CANDIDATE, ANNETTE	○
HOPEFUL, BILL	○
INDEPENDENT, SLAVA	○

The voters mark their ballots in private. The ballot is secret: no one but you knows how you have voted.

| THE PEOPLE | → | BALLOT BOX | GOVERNMENT MPs | PM | CABINET | | | | THE COURTS | | THE PEOPLE |

Today the candidates' campaign headquarters are scenes of frantic activity. The aim is to "bring out the vote." Workers want to make sure every possible supporter casts a ballot. The phone lines hum as scrutineers call in to report on activity in their polls. Canvassers call to find out who has not yet voted in their area. The office co-ordinates a babysitting service for homemakers with young children and free drives to the polls for the elderly and disabled.

The polls close:

The ballot box is opened. The returning officer counts the ballots while the scrutineers check to make sure the count is accurate. When all polling stations have reported to the district returning officer, the final figures are announced and the candidate with the most votes is named member of parliament.

Tension is mounting at campaign headquarters. During the day workers put up wall charts to list the results from each poll as they come in. Canvassers, drivers, and scrutineers join the office staff to watch the vote totals mount. Has their candidate won? Will they have a victory party tonight?

People want to know more than the result in their own constituency. They want to know the result of the *general election* — the election in every constituency across the country. Most turn on their TVs to find out.

Depending on where a person lives in Canada, the wait for the election results could be long or short. Coverage in the Atlantic provinces starts as soon as the polls close in the Maritimes. By then, the first results are trickling in from Newfoundland, where counting started half an hour earlier. An hour later, the polls close in central Canada, and Quebeckers and Ontarians turn on their sets to see what trends are developing in the Atlantic region. No election results may be broadcast in a region of the country until the polls are closed in that time zone. This means, however, that by the time people in B.C. and the Yukon join the network most of the results from the east are known. This has made some westerners feel that their votes have little influence on the election results, particularly if one party has already gained enough seats to form a government. Actually, of course, their votes are just as important as everyone else's — it is only the timing that causes bad feelings. In the early 1980s a plan was developed to avoid this problem by having the same voting period right across the country, even if the local time is different in each zone. However, it was rejected by Parliament.

Each vote affects the result in one particular constituency. The candidate with the most votes will "sit" in parliament as the member for that constituency. Depending on the number of "seats" won by his or her political party, the elected member will sit on the government or opposition side of the House of Commons.

Hold an election:
- Divide the class into three groups (L, PC, NDP) and let each nominate a member as candidate.
- Make buttons and posters; write pamphlets.
- Select *one* problem as the election issue; decide your party's attitude; and present the candidate to the class. Have each make a short speech giving the party's point of view and its promise to the electors.
- Select a Returning Officer and a Polling Clerk. Have them prepare ballots and a ballot box. After you hold your election, have them count the vote and report the results to the class.

Member of Parliament

Who is your member of parliament? Which political party does your MP belong to? What is the name of the riding or constituency in which you live?

If you are like most Canadians, you probably were unable to answer these questions correctly. That's a pity, because members of parliament make the laws that rule much of our lives. They also represent us in the parliament of Canada.

The MP's Job

Once in parliament, the new MP usually faces a wide range of responsibilities. Members of parliament are expected to perform well in three main areas: in parliament, in the constituency, and as a member of a political party.

The House of Commons has a "seat" for the member of parliament from each constituency in Canada. After the election of 1980, there were 282 seats, for 282 MPs.

Although MPs are paid good salaries and receive free air and rail passes, the workload can be crushing. The MP must spend a great deal of time in Ottawa, often far away from family and friends.

In Parliament

An MP is required to play an important and demanding role in the business of parliament. An MP must:
- attend debates in the House of Commons
- make speeches in the House of Commons, especially on issues that affect his or her constituency
- vote on bills presented to the House of Commons
- work on special committees preparing laws
- maintain a parliamentary office to help constituents (people who live in the MP's constituency) with their problems

In the Constituency

The people back home in the local constituency or riding expect their MP to act on their behalf. A good MP must:
- be available through his or her riding office
- deal personally with constituents' problems, such as old age pensions or local pollution
- attend social and political functions in the riding to meet people and keep abreast of local issues

In the Political Party

Members of parliament are also members of political parties. They must work for the party they represent. These duties can include:
- speech making
- television and radio interviews
- visits to other parts of Canada
- helping make party policy
- attending "caucus" (meetings of all MPs belonging to the same party)
- attending party conventions
- working on election committees, fund-raising, membership drives

Politics involves considerable tension which can affect the health of members of parliament. MPs can never be sure whether they will be "out of a job" after the next election.

One of an MP's most important duties is voting on bills in the House of Commons. A bill is a proposed law. No proposal can become law without the support of a majority of MPs. When MPs vote for or against a bill, they are making decisions that affect the way the country is run. Thus each member's vote is very important.

In making their decisions, MPs must consider their own consciences, the interests of their constituents, and the views of their political parties. It is the duty of the "party whip" to make sure MPs support the party in important votes.

Some MPs

John Crosbie (PC): born 1931, St. John's, Nfld. *Education:* Degrees in political science, economics, and law. *Career:* Lawyer, municipal politician, Liberal MLA and Cabinet member; PC/MLA and Cabinet member 1971-76. *Parliament:* Elected 1976, PC cabinet (Finance) 1979. *Riding:* St. John's West (Nfld.).

Peter Ittinuar (L): born 1950, Rankin Inlet (NWT). *Education:* Political science and sociology. *Career:* CBC announcer, filmmaker, professor of Inuit Culture, editor of *Inuit Today,* hunter, trapper, pilot. *Parliament:* Elected 1979, NDP critic on northern development. 1982, joined Liberal party. *Riding:* Nunatsiaq (NWT).

Jeanne Sauvé (L): born 1922, Prud'homme, Sask. *Education:* Universities of Ottawa, Paris, London. *Career:* Catholic youth organizations, journalist, CBC broadcaster, lecturer on art, director of media firms. *Parliament:* Elected 1972, Liberal cabinet (Science & Technology, Communications & Environment), 1980 Speaker. *Riding:* Laval des Rapides (Que.).

The Decision

Perhaps the most difficult moments for members of parliament occur when their personal views clash with the views of their party or their constituents. Read the following fictional account and decide how you think Albert Martin should vote.

Albert Martin, MP, has only two hours left in which to make the most difficult political decision of his life. The young man has spent a week agonizing over his decision. After talking with friends, reporters, and political opponents, he still isn't sure how he will vote on the government plan to increase the size of the armed forces by 10%.

His party is proposing to expand the armed forces because of increased world tension and the urging of Canada's allies. Albert is being pressured by the party whip to support the prime minister or risk losing the help of the party in the next election.

The voters in his riding seem to be split on the issue. Many feel the expansion is necessary because Canada's armed forces seem too small to defend Canadian interests adequately. Other voters feel the expansion will be too costly, and only add to world tension.

Albert himself is a firm believer in non-violence. He is a deeply religious person who is convinced military might can only lead to more wars.

How should he vote?

He owes the party and prime minister his loyalty. He wants to represent the feelings of the voters in his riding fairly. He also has to listen to his own conscience. Time is running out. . . . He has to decide.

The Prime Minister

Canadians often say they wish they had the chance to run the government, if only for a day. Have you ever wished that you were prime minister of Canada? What would it be like? What does being prime minister involve? What kind of people would seriously want the job? Would you?

The prime minister is usually the leader of the party with the largest number of seats in the House of Commons. The job lasts until the prime minister's party is defeated in a general election, though prime ministers sometimes resign to let new leaders take over between elections. Being prime minister means being the first minister and the most powerful member of the cabinet.

The Prime Minister's Job

The prime minister earns a good salary, lives in a large house with a butler, housekeeper, cook, and other servants, and is treated with great respect. At first glance this seems a very comfortable way of living. Yet the job involves some very serious responsibilities. The prime minister must:
- select and lead members of the cabinet
- appoint senators, justices of the Supreme Court, and many other officials
- lead the government party in the House of Commons
- recommend to the governor general the times for summoning parliament and for calling elections
- keep the party popular with the voters
- work with the provincial premiers
- speak for Canada to other world leaders

Being a leader requires special qualities. Many people are worried that the demands and difficulties of being prime minister scare away some of our brightest potential leaders. Few people want to take on these pressures and responsibilities. The work is difficult, the hours are long. Being prime minister can be very hard on family life. When times are tough, the criticism can be difficult to take. During times of crisis, the prime minister can be a lonely figure.

All things considered, do you have what it takes to be prime minister? Would you really want the job?

Leadership requires special characteristics. Few people have all the qualities necessary to be successful leaders. Here are some descriptive terms that people often associate with leadership. Which do you feel are the most important? Which apply to you?

intelligent	determined	imaginative
bilingual	outgoing	careful
attractive	flexible	financially secure
cool under pressure	well-educated	middle aged
self-confident	power hungry	exciting
decisive	organized	

Write a letter to the present prime minister of Canada. Explain your views or ask for information on an issue that is important to you. Wait for the reply and share it with your classmates.

Remember that when parliament is in session, it is not necessary to place a stamp on the envelope when writing to a member of the House of Commons.

Pierre Trudeau (L): born 1919, Montreal, Que. *Education:* Law, politics, and economics. *Career:* World traveller 1948-49, federal government adviser 1949-52, founded reformist magazine *Cité Libre,* opposed Quebec separatism. *Parliament:* Elected 1965, Minister of Justice 1967, party leader 1968, PM 1968-79, re-elected PM 1980, oversaw patriation of Constitution with Charter of Rights. *Riding:* Mount Royal.

Joe Clark (PC): born 1939, High River, Alta. *Education:* Degrees in history and political science. *Career:* Lecturer in political science, University of Alberta, journalist for CBC, *Calgary Herald* and *Edmonton Journal* 1965-67, special assistant to senior PC's 1967-70. *Parliament:* Elected 1972, PC leader 1976, defeated Liberal government 1979, re-elected 1980. *Riding:* Yellowhead, Alberta.

THE PEOPLE

BALLOT BOX

GOVERNMENT MPs

PM · CABINET

HOUSE OF COMMONS

OPPOSITION MPs · LEADER

SENATE

GOVERNOR GENERAL

THE COURTS

PUBLIC SERVICE

THE PEOPLE

A Typical Day in the Life of the Prime Minister

6.30 a.m. Has breakfast. Listens to the news, reads the newspapers from across the country.

8.00 a.m. Goes to the office. Confers with advisers over the day's schedules, signs letters and telegrams.

9.00 a.m. Series of appointments with leading citizens, politicians, reporters and advisers.

10.30 a.m. Attends weekly meeting of party "caucus" (meeting of all MPs belonging to the same party.)

12.00 noon Working lunch with economic experts.

1.30 p.m. Attends and leads cabinet meeting.

3.00 p.m. Attends Question Period in the House of Commons, when ministers must answer MPs questions.

5.00 p.m. Diplomatic reception at the P.M.'s residence for recently arrived ambassadors.

6.00 p.m. Working supper with Party Pollsters and organizers.

8.00 p.m. Delivers speech to a convention of energy experts, stays to dance and chat with the crowd.

10.00 p.m. Reads various reports and memos in preparation for the following day.

11.30 p.m. Lights out!

The Cabinet

The prime minister chooses about 30 other ministers to help govern the country. Together these people form a group called the cabinet. Most of the ministers are given "portfolios," which means they are put in charge of particular departments, such as external affairs or finance. A minister "without portfolio" has no department to run but may be given special responsibilities. Sometimes the cabinet is divided into an inner and an outer cabinet. The inner cabinet is more powerful, and meets more often with the prime minister.

A Cabinet Minister's Job

Being a cabinet minister usually brings prestige and increased political power. It also means a great deal of work. A cabinet minister has to acquire a detailed knowledge of his or her department. He or she must also:

- oversee the running of the department
- speak for the department in parliament and to the press
- present to parliament new laws that will affect the operations or duties of the department
- advise the prime minister on policy concerning the department
- help the prime minister and the cabinet make other political decisions
- explain the government's policies to the public
- help set up the party's election strategy

Choosing the Cabinet

An outsider might think that choosing a cabinet meant simply picking the best person for each job. It is actually a complicated juggling act. The prime minister has to consider the skills, experience, and personalities of potential ministers. He or she must also guarantee that the various regional, religious, and ethnic groups of Canada will be fairly represented. For instance, cabinets usually contain an equal number of representatives from Ontario and Quebec. The minister of agriculture is often a farmer from the West.

Some Recent Cabinet Ministers

Marc Lalonde (L): born 1919, Ile Perrot, Que. *Education:* Degrees in law, economics, and political science. *Career:* Lawyer, professor, adviser to PM's Pearson and Trudeau. *Parliament:* Cabinet since 1972 — Energy, Health and Welfare, Justice, Federal-Provincial Relations, Status of Women, Constitution reform. *Riding:* Outremont.

Flora MacDonald (PC): born 1926 in North Sydney, N.S. *Education:* Empire Business College and National Defence College. *Career:* Director, Canadian Political Science Assoc., Member of Canadian Institute of Public Affairs, Canadian Institute of International Affairs, and Civil Liberties Assoc. *Parliament:* Elected 1972, re-elected 1974, 1979, 1980. Member of Cabinet and Privy Council, Secretary of State. *Riding:* Kingston and the Islands, Ont.

Hazen Argue (L): born 1921, Moose Jaw, Sask. *Education:* Science and farm management. *Career:* Farmer, CCF member 1945-62, Liberal since 1962. *Parliament:* Elected 1945 as CCF, re-elected 1962 as Liberal, appointed to Senate 1966, Cabinet representation of Western Canada interests.

Iona Campagnolo (L): born 1932 at Vancouver, B.C. *Education:* UBC Extension Dept. Courses. *Career:* Skeena Broadcasters Ltd. 1965-74. Member and Chairman of Board of School Trustees 1968-72, Alderman for Prince Rupert 1972-74. *Parliament:* Elected 1974, defeated 1979. Parliamentary Secretary to Minister of Indian Affairs and Northern Development, Minister of State for Fitness and Amateur Sport. Privy Council, 1976. *Riding:* Skeena, B.C.

The minister of fisheries usually comes from the Atlantic region or British Columbia. Today care is also taken to include members from groups such as women or minority groups that have not always been represented in the past.

Sometimes it is not possible to meet all these needs from members of the House of Commons belonging to the governing party. For instance, during much of Pierre Trudeau's time as prime minister, the minister responsible for the Wheat Board was Senator Hazen Argue from Saskatchewan.

The prime minister must also keep party considerations in mind. Powerful and popular members of the party must be included even if they are rivals of the prime minister. Otherwise the prime minister may lose the loyalty of the party.

Cabinet Solidarity

The cabinet meets regularly to discuss important issues. These meetings are often stormy and full of harsh words. However, once a decision has been reached, *all ministers are expected to support it in public.* If a minister finds it impossible to support the prime minister or fellow cabinet members, that minister usually resigns. For example in 1963 Douglas Harkness resigned as minister of defence in John Diefenbaker's cabinet when the cabinet refused to arm Canadian Bomarc missiles with nuclear warheads.

A prime minister must balance several factors when choosing a cabinet minister. Ability, experience, ethnic or religious background, popularity, and regional origins are some important points to be considered.

Assume you are the prime minister. Choose one of the three candidates described here to be your **Minister of Finance**. Be prepared to explain your choice.

Eileen Dewar, 42, MP from Toronto.
Religion: Protestant (United).
Marital Status: Married with three children. Husband a financial adviser for several big corporations.
Education: degree from McGill University (Montreal) in business finance.
Work Experience: served as financial expert for corporations and government agencies.
Finances: worth several million dollars in stocks and bonds.
Standing in Party: little known; a relatively new MP; popular with female members of the party who are keen to see a woman in charge of such an important department.
Personality: quiet but firm; poor speaker but in private has a dry and witty sense of humour; well organized and excellent with statistics.

Armand Bolduc, 37, MP from Moncton.
Religion: Roman Catholic.
Marital Status: single; a swinging bachelor with many glamorous friends.
Education: Ph.D in Economics; studied at universities in Canada, England and the United States.
Work Experience: has done research for major corporations and labour unions; has taught economics at several universities across Canada.
Finances: only income is salary as an MP.
Standing in Party: seen as a leader by younger members; perceived as a bit "radical" by older members; MP for two years.
Personality: sincere, dedicated, witty; tends to be emotional; a free-thinking, independent type.

George Hornenuk, 51, MP from Calgary.
Religion: Eastern Orthodox.
Marital Status: separated; has four children who live with their mother.
Education: left high school after Grade 10 to support parents.
Work Experience: worked his way up from the bottom in the petroleum industry; built a giant oil company from scratch.
Finances: multi-millionaire.
Standing in Party: several years' experience as MP; liked by press but feared by some party members; controversial and outspoken about party policy.
Personality: tough, hardworking, energetic; excellent speaker but sometimes gets carried away; cares more for exciting ideas than dull statistics.

The Opposition

We tend to think of elections in terms of winners and losers. The "winners" are the members of the party with the largest number of seats in the House of Commons. They run the country. Their leader becomes prime minister, their leading members are appointed to the cabinet.

But what about members of the other parties? They are "losers" in the sense that they do not control the government. They are winners too, though, because each of them has won the election in his or her constituency and has a seat in the House of Commons.

MPs who belong to parties that came second or third in elections continue to play an important and effective role in our government. They form the opposition. In effect, they earn their salaries by criticizing the party in power.

The leader of the party with the second largest number of seats in the House of Commons becomes "the Leader of Her Majesty's Loyal Opposition". This honour and responsibility brings an extra salary and an official residence (Stornoway) in Ottawa.

The Leader of the Opposition's Job

The leader of the opposition must make sure that opposition members provide intelligent, effective criticism of government policy. Opposition MPs must be kept informed of what the government is doing, and they must decide how to respond. In some ways organizing the opposition can be nearly as hard as running the government. The leader must:

- appoint leading party members to monitor, or "shadow" specific government departments. Together, these opposition MPs form the "shadow cabinet"
- decide which questions should be asked, and by whom, during Question Period
- appoint members to the committees that examine proposed laws
- speak across the country at party rallies and conventions, and appear on TV to promote party policy
- keep the party machinery across the country rolling smoothly, encourage membership drives and fund-raising campaigns.

Members of other parties are also part of the opposition. Their power and importance depends on the number of seats they hold in the House of Commons.

Members of the opposition sit facing the government, on the other side of the House of Commons. The prime minister and the leader of the opposition sit directly opposite one another.

The Importance of the Opposition

The opposition plays a vital role in Canadian government. Without a spirited and well-informed opposition, the party in power would be free to make whatever laws it wanted. The opposition keeps the government party on its toes, presents alternative viewpoints, and sometimes forces changes in government policy. Occasionally an alert opposition will expose government errors, waste, or corruption.

When the opposition is at its best, it provides informed and intelligent criticism. It offers voters and the media an alternative to the party in power. Sensible criticism can bring about needed changes in proposed laws, or prevent the introduction of bad laws. Parliament can become the centre of reasoned and intelligent debate that is a credit to all Canadians.

When the opposition is weak or divided, it may criticize blindly. Opposition members may try to harrass and embarrass the governing party. There are times when debates in the House of Commons become trivial, bitter, and petty.

Sometimes it seems that the opposition is simply out to attack all government policies, good or bad. We should remember that members of the opposition do not have access to all the facts and ideas that lead the government to set these policies. Even so, insults are not valid substitutes for intelligent criticism.

A Motion of Non-Confidence

When the opposition wishes to highlight its criticism of the government, it proposes a motion of non-confidence. In effect, this means that the House of Commons must vote on whether the party in power should continue to govern. Opposition MPs usually support non-confidence motions; government MPs, who want to stay in power, usually vote against it. If a majority of MPs show that they no longer have confidence in the government, then the government must resign.

In a majority government, non-confidence motions can usually be easily outvoted. But non-confidence motions are very dangerous for minority governments. If the opposition parties unite, the government can be defeated, and forced to resign. This happened in 1979, when Joe Clark's minority government was brought down by a non-confidence motion supported by Liberals and New Democrats.

Leading the Opposition

Pierre Trudeau (L): Has been in parliament since 1965, PM since 1968, and was Leader of opposition for 9 months in 1979. Intended to resign, but on the defeat of the minority PC government Trudeau decided to stay on.

Joe Clark (PC): Has spent most of his life in politics. He is an experienced strategist and organizer. Has led the opposition since 1976, excepting for 9 months as PM in 1979. Skilled debater and effective critic.

Ed Broadbent (NDP) born 1936 in Oshawa, Ont. *Education:* University of Toronto, London School of Economics and Political Science (Eng.). *Career:* University professor, Professor of Political Science at York University 1965-68, Reserve officer R.C.A.F. *Parliament:* Elected 1968, re-elected 1972, 74, 78, 80. Chosen leader of New Democratic Party July 1975. *Riding:* Oshawa, Ont.

1. Name the present leader of the opposition in the federal government and your provincial government. Write to them both, asking for information on their careers. Find a newspaper or magazine article on each of them.
2. Examine recent statements by members of the opposition. Try to decide whether the statements are:
a) constructive suggestions to improve government policy
b) opposition for the sake of opposition
c) an alternative to the government's policy
3. Watch question period on your local television station. How would you describe the words and behaviour of the opposition? How did the government respond in your opinion?

The Senate

Not all members of the Parliament of Canada are elected. Members of the Canadian Senate are appointed. The Senate and the House of Commons are the two houses of Canada's Parliament. The Senate is sometimes called the Upper House.

The Senate shares power with the House of Commons. For example, all bills must be debated and passed in both houses before becoming law. But the House of Commons holds more power than the Senate because it is elected by the people of Canada.

Senators are appointed by the governor-general, who follows the advice of the prime minister and cabinet. Once appointed, senators hold office until the age of 75, when they must retire.

To be eligible for a seat in the Senate, you must be a Canadian citizen between 30 and 75 years of age, and own property worth at least $4000. In addition, you must reside in the province you are appointed to represent. These are the technical requirements. Theoretically, you must also have shown the prime minister that you will be able to play a useful role in helping to run the government.

In practice senators are often appointed for being loyal "party warhorses." This type of purely political appointment weakens the prestige of the Senate.

A Senator's Job

As a member of Canada's Upper House, it is the senator's duty to:
- represent the interests of his or her province in the federal Parliament
- give "sober second thought" to bills passed by the House of Commons
- delay, amend, or stop unwise and careless bills which are passed by the House of Commons
- introduce bills (Senators may not introduce bills that involve the raising of money. Only MPs, because they are the elected representatives of the Canadian people, have that power. Since most laws require the raising and spending of money, this greatly reduces the Senate's power).

Some Recent Senators

Thérèse Casgrain (NDP, Que.): born 1896, died 1981. *Career:* Early supporter of women's rights and civil liberties. Led the CCF in Quebec but failed to get a House of Commons seat. During WW II she opposed conscription and the internment of Japanese Canadians. *Senate:* appointed at 74, forced to retire at 75. One of few NDP members appointed to Senate. After retirement she actively continued to oppose the Quebec separatists to the end of her life.

David Croll (L, Ont.): born 1900 Russia, 1905 emigrated to Windsor, Ont., with his family. *Career:* Lawyer, Mayor of Windsor, MPP (minister of Public Works), MP for Toronto-Spadina. *Senate:* Appointed 1955. Has been a leading member of the Senate. Has led Senate committees on Aging and Poverty. He was successful in getting eligibility for Old Age Security pension reduced from 70 to 65 years of age.

Ernest Manning (SC, Alta.): born 1908 in Carnduff, Sask. *Career:* was a pioneer in the Social Credit movement led by "Bible" Bill Aberhart. He served as a Cabinet Minister in Aberhart's first Social Credit government in Alberta in 1935. He continues to work as an active Christian broadcaster. Serves as director of several Canadian companies. *Senate:* appointed 1970, after serving 25 years as Social Credit Premier of Alberta. Has co-authored numerous reports on Canadian energy problems.

Should the Senate be changed?

Not everyone is convinced that the Senate is a useful and necessary part of Canadian government. It has altered little since it was created in 1867. Now some people feel that it should be changed or even abolished. Read the following arguments and make up your own mind.

The Senate should be abolished because:
a) Senators are appointed, not elected, and therefore do not represent all Canadians. The Senate is undemocratic.
b) The House of Commons is all that is necessary to enact laws to govern Canada. The Senate rarely makes changes to laws. It's obvious that it does not perform any useful function.
c) Many Senators are appointed because they have done political favours for the party in power, and not because they are well suited to serve Canada.
d) Most Senators do very little work anyway, and it's difficult to control what they do or don't do.
e) The Senate is an unnecessary government expense.

You Reform the Senate

In recent years a wide range of suggestions for improving the Senate have been proposed. These include:
a) reducing the age for compulsory retirement to 65 or lower
b) limiting the time served in the Senate to 10 years
c) letting the provinces appoint half, or even all, of the Senators
d) appointing younger people
e) giving the Senate more specific power

The Senate is just fine the way it is because:
a) Two heads are better than one. By the time legislation has been debated in both the Commons and the Senate, it has been very carefully examined. The Senate can serve as a useful check on the House of Commons, and keep it on its toes.
b) Senators do valuable background research on government and social issues.
c) Senators can state their views freely because they don't have to worry about losing the next election if what they say is unpopular.
d) Many brilliant people who have much to offer their country do not want to run in elections. If they did run, they might not have the right sort of personality to get elected. Canada can use their skills and experience by appointing them to the Senate.
e) If excellent people are appointed, the Senate will do excellent work.

Working in small groups prepare your own suggestions for reform of the Senate and present them to the class. You will probably have to start by discussing just what you think is wrong with the Senate, and what you think its strengths are. Select the best of these suggestions. Perhaps you could send your list off to the prime minister, selected MPs and senators.

The Crown

Your Majesty

It often surprises Canadians to learn that the official head of state for Canada is not the prime minister. It is someone who does not even live in Canada: the king or queen of Britain. This is a reminder of the fact that Canada was once part of the far-flung British Empire. Although Canada is now an independent country, the monarch in England is still recognized as Canada's head of state.

Canada's form of government is known as a constitutional monarchy. This means that the monarch's power is limited by a series of laws and customs. The monarch has little power in Canada, or in Britain.

The monarch's role in Canadian government is said to be "symbolic." A symbol is something which stands for something else. For example, the Canadian flag is a symbol of Canada. The monarch, as head of state, is a personal symbol of the system of government that Canadians have chosen.

Symbols are more important for what they stand for than for what they are. So rather than talking about actual kings or queens, we use the term "the crown" to refer to the symbolic role of the monarch. In court cases, the crown attorneys represent the people of Canada as a whole. Publicly owned lands are known as crown lands. A crown appears on many government documents as a symbol of government authority.

The Crown is an idea more than a person and I want the Crown in Canada to represent everything that is best and most admired in the Canadian ideal.

Governor General Edward Schreyer

Lily Schreyer and Governor General Edward Schreyer

Your Excellency

The monarch is represented in Canada by the governor general. When Canada was still a group of British colonies, the governors actually ran the government. Today the governor general advises, but it is the prime minister who actually leads the nation.

The governor general is appointed by the king or queen on the advice of the Canadian prime minister. A great deal of care goes into the selection. Governors general usually serve terms of five to seven years.

In 1952 a Canadian-born governor general, Vincent Massey, was chosen for the first time. Until then governors general were sent by the monarch from Britain. After 1952 there was a pattern of alternating French and English Canadians in the post. Edward Schreyer was the first governor general to come from neither French nor English stock.

The Governor General's Job

The duties of the governor general are largely ceremonial. As head of state, the governor general:

● represents the crown in Canada
● is the symbol of national unity
● is the ceremonial and social leader of Canada
● is the official host for visiting heads of state from other countries
● acts as an impartial adviser to the prime minister, who must keep the governor general informed of political decisions
● signs all acts of parliament before they become law
● awards honours and medals such as the Order of Canada
● summons and dissolves parliament on the advice of the prime minister
● makes the "speech from the throne" which outlines government policy at the beginning of each session of parliament
● may travel abroad as an official representative of Canada

The governor general lives at Government House (also called Rideau Hall), in Ottawa, and has a summer residence in the citadel in Quebec City. Being governor general means long hours of work and travel, days and nights of receptions, tours of schools, hospitals, and factories, formal dinners, balls, and many thousands of handshakes. The governor general does not have the most powerful position in the country, but has the top ceremonial post. Officially, he or she is the most honoured person in Canada.

1. In August 1980 a nation-wide Gallup Poll found that 47% of Canadians approved of having the queen as Canada's head of state. 43% did not approve. 10% were undecided. What do you think? Take a poll in your class or school to find out what other students think.
2. What do you think are the important things to consider in choosing a governor general? If you had to choose a prominent Canadian to be governor general, how would you decide? Who would you choose?

Making a Law

All laws start with ideas about solving problems. Adults complain about the use of drugs by teenagers. Minorities demand an end to discrimination. Couples want fair family laws. City residents complain about high levels of noise and pollution. Military specialists want better equipment for the armed forces. Manufacturers want protection from foreign competition. Government workers want to change the way their departments operate. We all have problems, complaints, and issues that we want solved.

When we demand action from the government, we are asking for laws. Laws to prevent or stop this. Laws to provide the money to do that. Laws! Laws! Laws! Some people feel there are too many laws and want laws to end laws.

Laws are made at all three levels of government in Canada. At the federal level, law-making is the chief responsibility of Parliament.

Where do Laws Come From?

Pressure for new laws, or changes in existing laws, may come from newspaper editorials, opinion poll results, election promises, public demonstrations, the advice of respected experts, or the government's own policies. As the pressure builds for action, the law-making process begins.

When the prime minister and cabinet have decided a new law is required, public servants, lawyers, and other experts get to work on the exact details. The cabinet will look it over and perhaps make some changes. The minister whose department is most concerned will introduce the proposed law to parliament.

---

1. A Problem Arises

For example,
- price increases
- increased crimes of violence
- energy shortages
- pollution

2. Pressure Builds

Individuals or groups begin to demand action. This may take the form of:
- letters to the editor
- public protests
- television news stories
- pressure from opposition MPs
- advice from experts

The people express their views . . .

2. (cont'd)

. . . by the way they vote in elections.

3. The Prime Minister and Cabinet Act

Public servants are asked to
- study the problem,
- suggest possible solutions,
- draft a government "bill" to be presented to the House of Commons.

4. Debate in the Commons

A bill is given three "readings" in the House of Commons:
- At first reading, the bill is introduced.
- At second reading, the principle, or intent of the bill is approved. After second reading, the House "goes into committee" to study each part of the bill in detail. MPs, including the opposition, may introduce amendments that change or improve the bill.
- Third reading is of the bill including all the changes; if it is passed, it is then sent to the Senate.

At this stage the proposed law is called a *bill*. When it has been approved by all three divisions of parliament — the House of Commons, the Senate, and the Crown — it will become an *act of parliament*. Its provisions will then be *law* and binding on all Canadians and other people in the country.

Together we are Parliament
Queen Elizabeth II in the speech from the throne to the Senate and Commons of Canada, 1967

What would you like to pass a law about? Write your ideas down as a "bill." Read your bill to your classmates so that they know what it is about. Then read it again so that they can discuss it in detail.

Some students may be able to suggest improvements. On the other hand, others may completely disagree with your ideas. What are their criticisms? Are they valid? If so, should you scrap your bill, modify it, or start all over again?

Read your bill again, complete with any changes you have made. Then put it to a vote.

If you really feel strongly about your ideas, who should you approach? Do they come under federal, provincial, or municipal responsibilities?

Think hard: Is your law really workable in Canada today?

7. The Courts

Judges read the law carefully in order to pass judgement according to the exact meaning of the law.

9. Carrying It Out

Some laws directly affect all people in Canada, others affect only certain groups.
In either case, all people are responsible for the law. Obeying the law may mean:
- filling out forms to give the government certain information
- paying new taxes (or even getting a tax refund)
- changing methods of working or doing business
- paying stiffer (or lighter) penalties for certain crimes

5. Debate in the Senate

The bill goes through the same process of first, second, and third readings. The Senate takes a thorough look at the bill before giving its approval. If it makes changes in it, the House of Commons must approve the bill all over again or it is considered defeated. (Sometimes bills are introduced in the Senate and then go to the House of Commons for approval.)

6. Royal Assent

The governor general signs the bill. It is now an Act of Parliament, and its provisions are law.

8. Public Servants

Workers in departments that the law concerns, put it into practice and inform the people who need to be aware of it.

Serving the Public

The term *public servant* means exactly what it says: a person who serves the public. The people of Canada are the public. The government exists not only to lead and direct the public, but also to serve it. A public servant works for the government.

Many public servants live and work in the National Capital Region of Ottawa and Hull. (Hull is across the Ottawa River in the province of Quebec.) In fact, government is by far the biggest "industry" in the region. But there are public servants right across the country.

In big cities, public servants work in employment centres where people can get advice on looking for work and register for unemployment insurance benefits. Accountants, bookkeepers, and file clerks work in the district taxation offices, distribute forms, and explain them to taxpayers; another group looks after any local tax problems. Parole officers help former prison inmates adjust to life on the "outside." Inspectors check food for its quality and scales in supermarkets for accuracy in accordance with government measuring standards.

In smaller centres, there are also public servants.

They run the many weather reporting stations and they operate air traffic control towers at local airports. Federal meat inspectors check that meat is clean and fresh, and grade it according to rigid quality guidelines. In towns on the ocean or along the border with the United States, immigration and custom officers control entry and exit. Maintenance workers, forestry experts, and tour guides help run the national parks.

The federal government is trying to "decentralize" the public service. It is establishing the head offices of some government departments in regional centres across Canada. For example, the Department of Veterans' Affairs is run from Charlottetown, Prince Edward Island; and the Wheat Board operates from Winnipeg, Manitoba.

Canadian public servants also work in many foreign countries. Ambassadors and other diplomats try to maintain good relations with other governments. Trade consuls help Canadian companies deal with governments and companies in other countries to obtain contracts. Other workers help Canadian tourists with problems they meet when travelling abroad.

Who Becomes a Public Servant?

Most public servants are very little different from other workers. They are clerks, computer programmers, truck drivers, librarians, janitors, scientists, and nurses. But there is a special procedure in becoming a public servant.

The Public Service Commission holds examinations for job openings regularly in centres across Canada. The applicants with the highest and best results are hired regardless of their political beliefs or background. Promotions, too, are based on skills and experience.

A very small number of high-level public servants are chosen because they are supporters of the political party in power. The Cabinet appoints them because they are experts in all fields — administration, research, production. As they are friendly to the governing party, they can be relied on to carry out government policies. Usually these "political appointees" resign or are fired when a different party takes over the government.

Crown Corporations

The mail carrier is one worker that many people think of when they think about public servants. But mail carriers do not work for the government. They work for Canada Post, a crown corporation.

A crown corporation is simply a business owned and operated by the government. The people who work for crown corporations are not actually public servants. But it is their duty to work in the interests of all Canadians.

Discuss these letters to the editor. What do you think?

Dear editor:

In recent years the public service has mushroomed! The federal government alone employs about half a million people. They are paid from taxes--your taxes and mine.

If the public service just goes on growing, you can guess what will happen to those taxes. And I ask you: Do we get our money's worth? I doubt it. Public servants are inefficient, lazy, and overpaid. They have cushy jobs with guaranteed job security and one of the best pension schemes in the country.

Economists tell us that a large, expensive public service like ours in Canada causes inflation. I say we have to cut back.

Yours in frustration,

T. Payer

Dear editor:

Recent suggestions that the size of the public service should be reduced are unrealistic. Canadians expect the government to do more and more for them. The more tasks the government takes on, the larger and more expensive the public service must become.

Public servants are as hard working and efficient as any other group of workers. Because they work for the public, that is, you and me, they are easy targets for criticism. But the jobs they do are vital to our well-being and to the development of Canada.

I'd like to ask the complainers this: could they really do the jobs we expect better, faster, or more cheaply?

Yours sincerely,

J.Q. Public

Public servants and other people who work for the government often have the same job titles and do the same type of work as those in private industry.

Brainstorm to build up a list of occupations. Try to make it as broad and as long as possible — from actor to zoologist. Then go through the list and analyse each occupation. Could a person do this job for the government? Explain your reasons for thinking as you do.

The Courts

Who has to go to court? Most Canadians would answer, "People who break the law," and they will be thinking about criminals. But criminals are a very small proportion of the people who appear in court for one reason or another. Many people go voluntarily so that the court can help them with their problems.

People go to small claims court to collect unpaid bills, to get their money back on items that don't live up to the guarantee, or to decide who should pay for a fence between two properties. In small claims court you can plead your own case without a lawyer. The court can only deal with matters involving fairly small sums of money — the top limit differs from province to province.

Family courts, as the name suggests, deal with problems between husband and wife, parents and children. They can order a parent who has moved away from the family to help support the children. Juvenile courts, which deal with young people accused of crimes, work closely with family courts — usually juvenile court is a division of the family court system.

If a person dies without a will, or if the will is unclear, the property is handled by surrogate court.

Criminal Courts

People who are accused of minor offences such as some traffic violations are not given a full criminal trial. In fact, in many places they can be tried after supper in "night traffic court" without interrupting their daily routine.

It is easy to see that the dramatic trials we hear about on television or read about in our newspapers are only a small part of the work of the court system. Such trials are usually held in County or District Courts, which handle people accused of major crimes such as murder, armed robbery, fraud, assault, drug trafficking, or breaking and entering. These courts also hear "civil cases" where more important issues or larger sums of money are involved than can be handled by small claims courts.

There is something we should always remember when we hear that someone is on trial for a crime. This is that in Canada an accused person is considered innocent until proven guilty.

Appeals

In a criminal trial, evidence is presented by lawyers for the crown (that is the people of Canada) to show that a crime has been committed by the defendant. The defendant's lawyers' job is to prove that the defendant could not have committed the crime and to find holes in the Crown's evidence. The jury assesses the evidence to decide innocence or guilt. The judge's duty is to decide how the law applies to this case, and, if the defendant is declared guilty, to decide on the penalty.

> Find out more about juries. How are they chosen? In what kinds of cases are juries used? What are their duties? Do you know anyone who has served on a jury?

If either the crown or the defendant disagree with the decision, they have the right to appeal. (The crown's appeal is limited in certain ways.) The case will be heard again by a higher court.

The Supreme Court of Canada

When a court makes a decision, that decision is used by other judges and lawyers to help decide similar cases. The higher the court, the more influence the decision will have. The court of final appeal is the Supreme Court of Canada. A case appealed to the Supreme Court may often have important implications for all Canadians, because the court has the final decision on what the law really means and how it should be applied.

The nine judges of the Supreme Court are chosen from among the finest and most experienced judges in Canada. They are appointed by the governor general on the advice of the prime minister. One of their most important tasks is to interpret the Constitution Act.

The nation and system of government of Canada is based on the Constitution Act, 1867 (the BNA Act). Various changes and additions to the Act have been made over the years until the Constitution Act, 1982, which included the Charter of Rights and Freedoms. In the years to come, it will be the Supreme Court that decides what these rights and freedoms really mean. This may even mean declaring that a law passed by parliament or a provincial legislature goes against the constitution. In this case, the law is overturned.

Therefore in a sense, the nine judges of the Supreme Court are more powerful than the parliament of Canada. They guard the rights and freedoms assured us by our constitution.

The Planet Aurora

It is 400 years since young settlers were space-wrecked on Aurora. They named the planet after the ship that brought them. At first, they had thought they were alone on the planet and could govern it in their own way. However, they soon met the Aurorans, a group of humans who had been on Aurora too long to remember any other place of origin.

Some years later, ships from Earth did find the survivors of the spaceship *Aurora*. But by this time they had grown to love their planet. Their children knew it as home. So they sent messages to relatives and friends on Earth, but remained where they wanted to be — on Aurora.

They were soon joined by other settlers. At first people arrived singly or in small groups. But when times were hard on Earth, the tide of immigrants would rise to a flood. Occasionally, the system of government would have to be adjusted to meet changing times, attitudes, and conditions.

Now, 400 years later, the people of Aurora have learned a great deal. However, they sometimes disagree about what is best for the planet or for their particular region. Today delegates are gathering at First Touchdown, the planetary capital, to discuss the writing of a new constitution. They have a number of important concerns:

1. How much should Aurorans expect the government to do for them?
2. What are the rights of the individual and what are the rights or powers of the state of Aurora?
3. What checks and balances are needed to make sure that Aurora will have good, workable laws?
4. Should government leaders be chosen by political parties or in some other way?
5. Aurorans have disagreements over matters ranging from family affairs, through traffic problems and crime, to the powers of government. Who should they expect to help them settle such arguments?
6. Once they have written their new constitution, there will be debates about what was really intended and what it really means. Who should they ask to have the final word on such disputes?

Towards the Next Century
ADVANCE ORGANIZER

1

Canadians live in a world of continuous change. Every aspect of our lives is changing faster than at any other time in history. What the future will bring, we cannot know for sure. However, with our knowledge of the past as a guide we can at least try to make reasonable guesses, and consider some of the key issues that may face Canadians as they approach the twenty-first century.

2

Scientific discoveries and new machines have made great changes in our lives during the twentieth century. This technological revolution will certainly continue, doubtless at a faster and faster rate. We will face hard decisions about the use of new technologies. Machines should serve the needs of people, not disrupt society and bring hardship.

3

A growing technological society like Canada uses energy — lots of energy. As oil becomes more expensive and supplies are used up the search for other kinds of energy will become more important. The hunt for oil and gas will continue, but other forms of energy will be studied. The challenge will be to develop cheap, safe, reliable energy sources without poisoning the environment and bringing disruption to particular regions or groups of people.

Word List
Candu   identity   society
fibre optics   pluralistic   technology
gross national product silicon chip   Telidon

4

Our national identity is still evolving to reflect our changing society. Canadians of native ancestry are speaking out for their rights and traditions. English-speaking Canadians are becoming more aware of the concerns and aspirations of French Canadians. And Canadians of French and British ancestry have been joined over the years by people from many other lands. The contribution of all Canadians, new and old, will influence the kind of society that we know in future.

5

More and more, we live in an interdependent world. In an age of jet travel, intercontinental missiles and space satellites the safety and well being of Canadians is linked to that of all other people. War and peace, poverty and development, human rights, international trade, the uses of outer space, the fate of the world's oceans, these and many other questions will concern Canadians in the world community of the future.

6

History is like an unfinished journey leading from the past into the future. Canadians will face great challenges in a changing and uncertain world. The way ahead, however, is based on past events. Perhaps we can be inspired by the examples of Canadians who, through courage and determination in the face of adversity, have overcome great difficulties. With a reasoned pride in our past we can face the challenge of the twenty-first century.

The High Tech Revolution

High technology means many things — jet planes, space satellites, atomic reactors, lasers, and much more. Perhaps most of all in the future it will mean computers. Computers have already brought incredible changes to our lives but, according to many experts, "You ain't seen nothin' yet!" The real computer revolution is still to come.

The Computer Age

The first electronic computer, called ENIAC, began operating in 1945. It cost $13 million, weighed 30 t, covered 150 m² of floorspace, needed 19 000 vacuum tubes, and used as much energy as a railway locomotive. By the 1980s you could go to your nearest electronics store and buy a computer that cost less than $200, could be held in your hand, used the energy of a light bulb, and could perform more functions, faster and more accurately, than ENIAC.

This progress was made possible by improvements in the electronic components that are used to build computers. The heart of today's computer is the chip, a paper-thin slice of silicon, smaller than your fingernail, printed with hundreds of microscopic circuits and capable of performing thousands of complex operations in microseconds.

Applications for computer technology have

A computer chip can fit in the eye of a needle.

grown rapidly over the years. Early computers did just that — they made mathematical computations and recorded the results. As they improved, computers came to do many other things. Now, computer chips operate your pocket calculator, digital watch, clock radio, self-focusing camera, electronic games, and many household utensils. Combinations of chips are being used to make sophisticated office and industrial machines. Without them, the space program, with its many complex calculations, would be impossible.

Computers and Canada

Canada has been a leader in some areas of computer technology, such as fibre optics, communications satellites, the Telidon two-way television system, and digital communications. Many new industries have grown up. In the Ottawa area there were over 200

The "Canadarm" on the U.S. space shuttle. As high technology gets more expensive and more complicated, companies in many countries may work together on projects like the shuttle.

Canadian-owned high technology companies by the early 1980s. By 1990 it is expected that over 50 000 people will be employed in these industries in this part of the country alone.

On the other hand, Canada is weak in some areas. Even into the 1980s only a few companies are

Optical fibres made of glass use pulses of light instead of electricity to transmit data.

making computer chips in Canada. In 1980 Canada was spending a billion dollars a year to import computers from other countries. By 1985 this could grow to five billion, and some people are concerned that Canada might be falling behind in the race to develop new computer systems.

This Displayphone, which was developed in Canada, lets users transmit data as well as speak to each other.

The Information Revolution

What will happen in the field of high technology is anybody's guess. The trends to smaller, faster, and cheaper computers will doubtless continue. Chips may soon be made of a new material, gallium, which has been found to transmit electrical impulses two to five times faster than silicon. Engineers are exploring ways to make circuits even smaller and more compact — perhaps only a few molecules thick. Scientists keep looking for materials that will transmit signals even faster — perhaps at the speed of light.

Some people have predicted that the future will be known as the Information Age, when control of computers and the information that they can store, will be the key to power and progress. Already computers are being linked in networks that pass vast amounts of information back and forth between continents and across international boundaries. Computers will also affect our working lives. Computerized machines, such as word processors in offices and "robots" in factories, will take over many routine jobs now done by humans. This will create new jobs in the computer industries, and will help keep Canadian companies efficient in world markets, but some people are afraid that many jobs will be lost as people are replaced by computers.

This kind of assembly line may soon be obsolete. In the future, these snowmobiles may be made entirely by computerized "robots," without need for human workers.

No one can predict the future of the high technology revolution, but one thing seems certain — computers and related technology will affect virtually every aspect of our daily lives, and will be of vital importance to the security and prosperity of the country.

Energy and the Environment

Since 1973 the price of oil has escalated dramatically. From $3 a barrel in 1973, the world price rose to over $40 by the early 1980s, with further increases sure to come. For most Canadians the first concern was simply money — the extra dollars needed to fill up the car, heat the house, run their tractors, airplanes, or fishing boats. But people also began to realize that oil and natural gas are non-renewable resources, and that they are being used up very quickly in a crowded world.

Canada is luckier than most countries in having large reserves that supply much (though not all) of our needs. Canadians have also been sheltered from the worst price increases since most Canadian oil sold in Canada is kept below the world price level. But sooner or later the oil will run out, and what to do about energy is sure to be a key concern in years to come.

The NEP

On October 28, 1980 the federal government announced its National Energy Program. This massive plan has many objectives, including the following:
- to increase Canadian oil production so that by 1990 Canada will not have to use any imported oil
- to reduce oil consumption to 40% of national energy needs by developing alternate sources of energy
- to increase Canadian ownership and control of the oil industry to at least 50% by providing special incentives to Canadian-owned companies

From top left: the Syncrude tarsands project; an offshore drilling rig in the Atlantic; an artificial drilling island in the Beaufort Sea; the Cold Lake enhanced recovery project in Alberta, which is testing ways to increase the amount of oil that can be pumped from conventional oil wells.

Many large projects have been suggested, such as: the Syncrude and Alsands developments to extract oil from the Athabasca tar sands; oil drilling in the Beaufort Sea and on the Grand Banks of Newfoundland; pipelines through the Mackenzie Valley, and along the Alaska Highway. How successful have these megaprojects been? What else might be done to increase the supply of oil? Should the oil industry be left entirely to private companies? Should the government take over? Should private companies get help to reduce the financial risks of exploring for oil? Should we put more emphasis on conservation, and less on increasing production?

Alternate Energy Sources

No matter how much oil is found, sooner or later the supply will run out. Before this happens we must develop other energy sources to take the place of oil. In coming years there will be much discussion of coal, wood, natural gas, hydro-electricity, atomic power,

In years to come all houses may be designed like this one to use the sun's energy for heat.

tidal, wind, solar, and other kinds of power. In the future we may run our cars on things like hydrogen, gasohol, propane, or electricity.

Each energy source has advantages, each has drawbacks. Hydro-electricity is clean and renewable, but we are running out of good locations for dams, and the larger reservoirs needed for these projects may affect the environment. Electricity from nuclear reactors is clean and cheap, but people are concerned about the danger of radiation leaks and the disposal of nuclear waste. Canada has plenty of coal, but coal causes pollution and acid rain. What are the pros and cons of different energy sources? Do you think there will be just one solution, or perhaps many?

Whatever happens, the search for new sources of energy will be a constant concern. We will have to take into account all the factors such as cost, safety, pollution, efficiency, impact on the environment, and disruption of people's lives, before we make our decisions.

The Pickering nuclear generating station near Toronto uses the Candu reactor designed and built in Canada.

The Canadian Identity

Skaters enjoying a winter outing on the Rideau Canal in Ottawa — what could be more typically Canadian? But if these are typical Canadians, what would we expect them to be like? Blond hair or brown? Tall or short? White skin, black, yellow, or brown? As you can see, any attempt to choose one physical description for a typical Canadian would be difficult and misleading. Canadians come in all shapes, sizes, and colours.

To describe the culture and beliefs of a typical Canadian would be just as difficult. Most of these people probably speak English. But if they are representative of the country as a whole, every third person would speak French as his or her usual language. It is also possible that a few of our skaters speak other languages such as Italian, Vietnamese, Arabic, or many others from around the world. In religion, most of these Canadians would be Christians, but some would be Jewish, Muslim, Buddhist, Hindu, or other. Even among the Christians there would likely be a wide variety of Protestant, Catholic, and Orthodox believers.

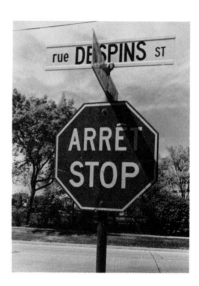

A Multicultural Experiment

Canadians have not one identity, but many. Canada is already a mixed, pluralistic society. Our future lies in a country where people speak different languages, follow different religions, and come from many racial

Some people, such as these Mennonites in Kitchener, Ontario, have come to Canada in order to preserve their beliefs and special way of life.

and cultural backgrounds. Most Canadians accept this and enjoy the chance to meet people of different cultures and languages. Some, however, do not.

In the past there has been prejudice against people of different races, languages, and cultures. French-speaking Canadians were sometimes denied the right to schooling in their own language. Japanese Canadians were unfairly treated during the Second World War. And the history of other countries has shown that it is not always easy for people of different races to live together peacefully. In a sense, Canada's future will be a great experiment to see if this kind of mixed society can survive and grow.

Positive Actions

Tolerance and respect for people's differences are important for society as a whole, but sometimes there are special groups that may need more than this.

Women have made great gains during the twentieth century, but still lag behind men in jobs and pay. Should governments pass laws to guarantee women equal pay and opportunities? Will women continue to gain freedom and power in years to come?

Handicapped people are another group facing special difficulties in our society. Are we prepared, for example, to spend extra money to allow people in wheelchairs to move freely in our cities? How much extra money are we prepared to spend to educate people with learning disabilities?

What about people with exceptional talents? Should we give special training and equipment to the best artists, athletes, scientists, and mathematicians to develop their talents?

Canada's native peoples face special difficulties and have concerns about preserving their traditions and way of life. Many native groups have land claims against Canada. How should these be settled? Should native people have special rights and privileges? Should economic development be slowed or stopped in the north to protect the traditional way of life of the Dene and Inuit?

Native workers in an oil company cafeteria at Norman Wells, N.W.T. Canada's native peoples face difficult choices as they try to adjust to modern conditions while preserving their separate identity.

Canada and the World Community

Whether we like it or not, Canada's future will be influenced by the rest of the world. Our planet is one interdependent whole; problems in one country may affect any other. More than ever, Canadians will have to be aware of, and take part in, the affairs of the global community.

War and Peace

Canada's new Leopard tanks.

The tanks in the picture are part of a large program to equip Canada's armed forces with new, modern weapons during the 1980s and 90s. We have promised to spend millions of dollars for new weapon systems during these years. Despite this, Canada's armed forces are very small compared to the world as a whole. It is estimated that by 1980 a million dollars a minute was being spent on arms around the world, and this is certain to increase. Does this incredible military buildup bring security, or does it increase the chances of war? Does the cost threaten the world economy and use up scarce resources? Would it be better to spend

this money on economic development and social services in a world where perhaps 1000 million people do not know how to read and write, 500 million do not have enough food to eat, and half a million children die each month from infectious diseases?

Perhaps the deadliest threat is nuclear war. In a full nuclear exchange between the U.S. and the U.S.S.R. it is estimated that 200 to 300 million people would die — and Canada would be right in the middle. Should Canada acquire nuclear weapons of its own? Should we encourage efforts to reduce or even ban them?

Another concern is nuclear proliferation. The short time since 1945 has seen nuclear weapons, or the ability to make them, spread from one country to more than a dozen, and this number is sure to grow. Canada has developed the Candu reactor for peaceful use, but should we continue to export it, if it is used by other countries to develop nuclear weapons? People are also concerned about what might happen if nuclear

Lester Pearson addresses the General Assembly during the Suez Crisis. Canada played a key role in creating the first UN peacekeeping force, and continues to take an active part in international affairs.

In the future, food may become the most precious resource in an overpopulated world.

weapons fall into the hands of international terrorists. What should Canadians do to help reduce international tensions, combat terrorism, and eliminate the causes of war?

Population, Development, and Trade

World population continues to grow. Every day there are 200 000 more people on Earth, over 700 million new people every year. Many of these people live in the developing countries in conditions of poverty, disease, and hunger. These nations will continue to fall behind the developed countries. Canada has a good record of assistance to developing countries, but we still spend less than 1% of our gross national product on aid. Should Canada spend more, or should we encourage businesses to build up these countries through private investment?

Despite its small population, Canada is a major trading nation. An open system of world trade is vital to our economy. However, unlike our major trading partners, the U.S., the Common Market, and Japan, Canada does not have a large domestic market. Our industries often face competition from mass-produced imports. Should we raise tariffs and/or put quotas on imports? Should we join the U.S. in a common market or economic union? Should we seek new markets in other countries?

The patterns of world trade will also be an issue with the developing countries. They claim that they must pay high prices for manufactured goods, but cannot get a fair price for their raw materials. Should Canada and the other rich nations agree to pay higher prices for these commodities in order to help poorer countries? In the hungry world of the future, perhaps the most important resource will be food. Should Canada concentrate on developing its agriculture? Will food perhaps be used as a weapon in times of famine and starvation?

The Unfinished Journey

When we think about the future, it is easy to get discouraged. The problems and dangers are all too obvious. Will there be war? Inflation? Pollution? Overpopulation? Separatism? Unemployment?

We should not forget, however, that Canadians have faced problems before. We have made mistakes. We have sometimes lost chances through timidity and hesitation. We have had our share of failures. But overall, Canadians have faced up to the challenges of the twentieth century with energy, courage and imagination.

When we think about the future we can look with pride to the achievements of the past. From a country of less than five and a half million in 1900, Canada has grown to a population of over 24 million. Working together, native-born Canadians and immigrants have built an open, democratic society with a high level of health care, education, economic opportunity and social justice for most people. From a land of fishermen, lumberjacks, small farmers, and shopkeepers, we have become the seventh largest industrial nation in the Western world. From a sheltered position in the British Empire, Canada has moved onto the world stage as a fully independent member of the international community.

When things get tough — and we can be certain that the future will have its share of dangers and difficulties — Canadians can also look to the examples of individuals who, through courage and determination, have made notable achievements in the face of adversity. There is no better example of this than Terry Fox, who raised millions of dollars for cancer research despite terrible hardship and a struggle with cancer that ended in death.

Terry Fox can be an inspiration for all Canadians as we continue our unfinished journey into the future.

Terry Fox

1958 — born in Winnipeg. Family moves to Port Coquitlam, B.C. where Terry grows up. Shows strong interest in athletics, works hard to excel.

1976 — enters Simon Fraser University, makes the Junior basketball squad.

1977 — right knee begins to hurt. Despite drugs, the pain continues. Cancer is diagnosed.

9 March 1977 — right leg amputated above knee. During recovery, must take drugs that make his hair fall out. "I got more upset over the loss of my hair than of my leg." Receives artificial leg after a few weeks, learns to walk, jog, play golf, drive a car. Returns to university, begins to run regularly, builds up physical and emotional strength.

1979 — has idea of running across Canada to raise money for cancer research. Cancer Society gives support.

12 April 1980 — dips artificial leg into the Atlantic Ocean at St. John's, Newfoundland and sets out for Victoria, B.C. on Marathon of Hope.

1 July 1980 — reaches Ottawa for Canada Day celebrations.

28 July 1980 — celebrates 22nd birthday at Gravenhurst, Ontario.

3 August 1980 — passes halfway mark at French River, Ontario.

29 August 1980 — approaching Thunder Bay, feels pain in chest.

30 August 1980 — chest pains increase. Runs for most of the day but finally collapses in exhaustion. Has reached 5340 km mark. Taken to Port Arthur General Hospital. Cancer of the lungs is diagnosed.

2 September 1980 — returns home for treatment.

19 September 1980 — invested as youngest Companion of the Order of Canada. Receives many other awards. Millions of dollars from across Canada pour into the Terry Fox Fund for cancer research.

February 1981 — cancer continues to spread. Doctors announce his condition is getting worse. Despite pain, continues to try to live as normal a life as possible.

June 1981 — enters hospital on the 19th and dies ten days later.

April 1982 — commemorative stamp issued in honour of Terry Fox and the Marathon of Hope.

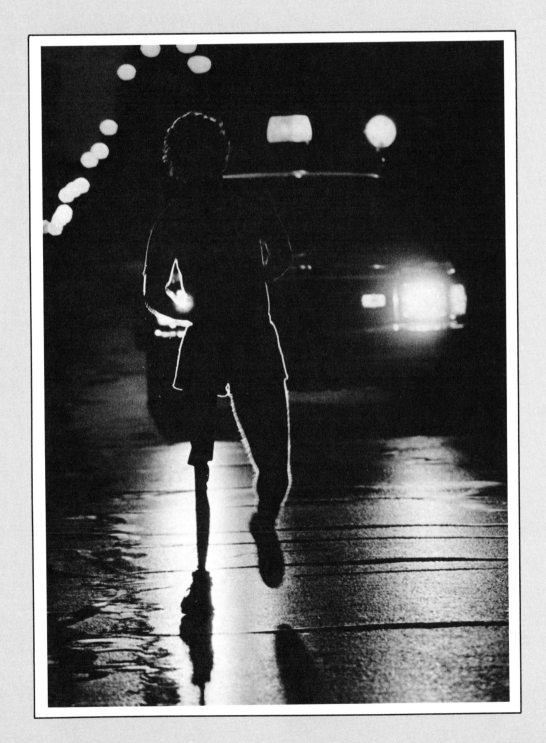

Glossary

abolish do away with.

abortion an early end to pregnancy, usually caused intentionally.

abuse 1) improper use; 2) ill-treatment.

ace a war pilot who has destroyed five or more enemy aircraft.

acid rain rain that has become an acid because it has absorbed chemicals in polluted air.

acquit declare that someone accused of a crime is innocent.

act a bill that has passed through both houses of parliament and become law; compare with *bill* and *law*.

advance move forward.

agitators people who try to excite others into action over social or political issues.

air raid bombing attack by enemy planes; **air raid warden** someone who organizes and protects people during air raids.

alcoholism disease resulting from drinking too much alcohol over a long period.

aliens people from other countries.

ally friend or helper; **Allies** nations that helped one another fight Germany and her supporters during the two world wars.

ambassador representative of a country's government in a foreign country.

amend change, improve.

amplification in radio, a device for increasing the volume of sound.

appeal to ask a higher court to reconsider a decision made by a lower court.

appeasement giving in to some of an enemy's demands in the hopes of keeping peace.

apprentice a worker who learns a trade or business on the job.

armaments weapons and military equipment.

armistice truce, the agreement to end a war.

arrogant proud, stand-offish.

artillery large guns; also army units who use them.

assassinate murder someone (usually a public figure) in a surprise attack.

assembly line a way of organizing workers so that each person does the same job over and over as the product moves through the factory.

astronaut space traveller.

atrocities terrible or cruel actions.

backlog a build-up which overloads the system and causes delay.

bail out to jump out of a plane with a parachute.

ballot voting paper showing the names of election candidates. The voter marks the ballot to indicate the choice of candidate.

ballot box sealed box in which voting papers are placed in elections.

ban forbid; stop.

bankrupt to have lost one's money in business; being unable to pay one's debts.

barbarous crude, savage-like.

batch group.

benzene chemical that burns easily.

beverage drink.

big business term used to describe the group of large companies that have a lot of power.

bill a proposal for a law; compare with *act* and *law*.

binder farm machine that cuts and ties grain.

biplane plane with two sets of wings, one above the other.

birth control use of methods or devices to prevent pregnancy.

black market unofficial (often illegal) system of buying and selling goods.

blockade using force to cut off supplies to an enemy.

bobbed (hair) cut short.

bolsheviks communists who took part in the Russian revolution.

bond a certificate which you buy, and can later cash at a profit.

boom grow rapidly, do well; **boomtown** fast-growing town.

bootlegging making and selling something (often liquor) illegally.

boycott avoid, refuse to deal with.

branch plant local factory owned by a company with its head office in another place or country.

brewer maker of beer or ale.

bribery use of gifts or money to buy favours.

buff fan.

bush pilot pilot who flies light planes to remote areas.

buggy light carriage.

bully beef canned beef.

by-election special vote called in a constituency between general elections to replace a representative who has resigned or died.

cabinet group of government members which advises the prime minister.

campaign presentation throughout the constituency, province, or country to convince electors to vote for a political party or its candidate.

Canadian shield vast rocky area in northeastern Canada that is rich in minerals.

Candu a special type of atomic reactor developed in Canada and used since 1962 to produce nuclear energy.

canvass door-to-door or telephone approach to voters to get their support for a party or a candidate.

capitalism economic system in which most businesses are owned by private individuals, not the government, and run to make a profit for their owners; compare with *communism*.

cash crop crop grown for sale rather than for use on the farm.

casualties soldiers who have been killed, injured, or taken prisoner.

centennial 100th anniversary celebration.

citizen a person who by birth or acceptance by the government has full rights and responsibilities in a country.

civilian a person who is not in the armed forces.

civil law laws about the property, rights, duties and responsibilities of individual citizens.

civil rights freedoms and privileges of citizens guaranteed by a country's constitution or charter of rights.

clique a group that sticks together and keeps outsiders out.

closure a rule in parliament that lets the government cut off debate and bring about a vote on a bill.

cockpit the part of a plane where the pilot sits.

colony a territory under the political control of another country; **colonial** someone from a colony.

combat fight, battle.

commerce buying and selling, especially between countries.

commonwealth a political association of a group of independent nations (including Canada) that used to be part of the British Empire.

communications the exchange of information and ideas.

communism economic and political system in which the state as a whole owns all property and runs business and industry for the common good, rather than for private profit. No opposition to the government is permitted; compare with *capitalism*.

company a firm or business.

competition contest; two or more businesses trying to sell the same things to the same people.

compromise splitting the difference; an agreement in which neither side gets everything it wants.

concentrate bring together.

concentration camp prison camps to hold large numbers of political enemies or unwanted people.

confederation the joining together of several political units into one large unit

or country; especially the Canadian Confederation.

conquer win or overcome, as in war.

conscription a system to make people join the armed forces.

conservation protecting, saving, and using wisely natural resources such as trees, lakes, wildlife, etc.

conspiracy a plot to do something evil.

constituency the parliamentary representative's home district, or the group of people in that district.

constitution the framework of rules and traditions which set out how something (such as a country) is run.

consumers people who buy things.

consumption the buying or using of goods.

contract formal agreement covering the purchase of goods or services or any other business deal.

convention 1) a meeting or conference; 2) accepted customs, rules, etc.

convict in a trial, declare someone guilty of a crime.

convoy a group (of ships) travelling with a protective escort.

corner the market to buy all supplies of something, so that you can sell it at a high price without competition.

corporation business, company.

corrupt dishonest.

coureur de bois "runner of the woods"; independent fur trader.

court of appeal a higher court that reconsiders the decisions made in trials.

criminal law laws about major crimes such as murder, robbery, arson and other dangerous actions.

crown (the) the symbol of the authority of the monarch.

crude oil oil before it has been refined and treated.

culture 1) way of life; 2) the learning and arts (including painting, music, literature, drama) of a nation.

Czar emperor of Russia.

dairy farm farm that keeps cattle to produce milk, not meat.

dam a barrier across a river to control the flow of water.

debt something (usually money) owed to someone else.

decade ten years.

decentralize reorganize so that things are run in local districts rather than from one central place.

delegate representative, someone who attends a meeting on other people's behalf; **delegation** a team of delegates.

demand how much people want something, combined with how much they can pay for it.

demilitarized area area that armed forces are not allowed to enter.

democracy system of government by the people or by representatives elected by the people. **democratic** of democracy.

demonstrate *1)* show; *2)* make a public protest (by marching, gathering with signs, etc.)

Dene "the people"; group of native Indian tribes now living in the Northwest Territories that is working to maintain their people's hunting and fishing areas and other traditional rights.

depression a period when business drops and there are few jobs.

deputy returning officer (DRO) — person responsible on election day for operating a polling station, counting the ballots, and sending results to the district returning officer.

descendants your children, their children, their children, and so on.

diabetes disease caused when the body fails to produce enough insulin to control blood sugar levels; **diabetic** a person suffering from diabetes.

dictator single ruler who holds all power and usually uses force to stay in power.

diplomat civil servant who looks after dealings between countries.

diplomatic relations official dealings between the governments of countries.

discrimination treating people differently on the basis of their sex, skin-colour, background, etc.

distribution of wealth the way money, property, and goods are divided up among people, called *unequal* when some people are much richer than others.

diversity variety.

dividend a payment that is a share of profit.

dock place where ships can load and unload cargoes.

dogfight fight in the air between planes.

donate give.

drifter a person drifting from place to place, usually looking for work.

drudgery very hard, dull, badly-paid work.

earnings wages.

economy all of the business, industry, trade, and financial affairs of a country.

elect choose someone by voting.

emigrate leave one country to live in another.

employee someone who works for someone else in return for pay.

employer someone who pays other people to work for her or him.

empire a group of countries under one government.

energy power to heat and light homes, run cars and factories, etc., such as oil, hydro-electricity, the sun's rays.

enumerators people who compile the list of eligible voters for municipal, provincial, and federal elections.

environment the natural world: the air, sea, countryside, lakes, rivers, etc.

equality the same rights and treatment for everybody.

equalization payments payments made by the federal government to the poorer provinces so that they can provide the same level of services to the people as the richer provinces.

era a certain period of time, for example, the rock'n roll era.

execute kill, put to death.

exploit (*n*) heroic act; (*v*) treat someone unfairly for your own gain; to put something to profitable use, e.g. iron ore.

explosive something which explodes powerfully and easily.

exposition (*Fr.*) exhibition, display; for example, Expo 67.

extremist someone who holds unreasonably strong views.

factory a centralized place where workers and machines make a product.

fallout radio-active dust that falls after a nuclear explosion.

family allowance "baby bonus"; money given by the government to help families support children under 16.

fascism a form of dictatorship backed up by secret police and the army based on nationalistic and racist theories.

federal national level of government in a country that has regional governments as well.

federalism a system of government in which some powers are held by the central government, while others are held by regional governments.

fibre optics a system using optical fibres — thin glass filaments that transmit impulses of light that are converted into computer code at the receiving end. More messages can be sent at one time by this method than can be sent over wires.

flapper a "modern" young woman of the 1920s.

fleet a group of ships.

foreclosure take over mortgaged property when payments have fallen behind.

forge furnace where metal can be heated and shaped.

foreign affairs government relations with other countries.

fortify make stronger.

free elections elections in which any candidate who wants may run and in which people are free to vote as they wish.

free trade buying and selling between countries without any tariffs or customs duties.

freight goods that are transported from one place to another.

front battleground; the line where opposing armies meet.

furrow groove dug by a plough as it is pulled through the ground.

fuse material that burns easily and is used to set off explosion.

futuristic suggesting styles, inventions, changes that may occur in the future.

general election an election held in every constituency across the country or province. General elections must be held at least every five years but may be called sooner if the government resigns or is defeated. They give voters the opportunity to show approval or disapproval of the government and to elect new members to parliament or the provincial legislative assembly.

generating station place where electric power is produced.

generation gap lack of understanding between people of different age groups.

geologist a scientist who studies rocks and the structure of the earth.

grain elevator a tall building where grain is stored.

granary a storehouse for grain.

gross national product (GNP) the total market value put on goods and services produced in one country within one year.

guarantee be responsible for, promise to protect.

hardtack hard, dry biscuit, rather like a dog biscuit.

heckler someone who interrupts with jeers and annoying questions during a public speech.

heritage culture, traditions, and learning handed down from the past.

holocaust total destruction, especially the Nazis' mass killing of Jews, gypsies, homosexuals, and others in World War II.

horsepower a unit used to measure work based on the amount of work a horse can do.

humanitarian showing kindness and concern for human beings.

ideal the way a person or group think things should be if the world were perfect.

identity distinctive character of a person or group.

ideology a strongly held system of beliefs about how the world should be run.

immigrant someone who comes to live in a new country.

immune free from, protected from disease.

imperialist someone who supports an empire, such as the British Empire, or would like to set one up.

implement tool.

import (*v*) to bring things into a country; (*n*) something which is brought into a country.

independent managing by oneself; free; not under another's control.

industrialization *1)* the growth of factories; *2)* the changes that occur when large factories take over from small workshops, stores, and farms.

industrial waste liquids and solids left over and usually thrown out when an industrial product is made.

industry business operation that makes a special product, whether it be cars and trucks or canned lobster.

inflation rise in prices.

insulin hormone produced naturally in most people to control blood sugar levels. Diabetics do not produce insulin and must receive it through injections or pills.

insurance an agreement where you make small payments to a private company or government agency in return for protection in a big emergency (such as losing your job, a car accident, sickness, or a fire in your home).

interest the money someone has to pay to make use of someone else's money, usually calculated as a percentage of the loan. **Interests** a group of people with a special concern for something, for example, farming interests.

interior inland area, far from the coast.

internal affairs anything that goes on strictly within one country.

invade to enter a region or country by force.

investor someone who puts money into a business in the hope of making a profit.

isolationism the political belief that the country should look after its own needs and not form ties with other countries.

job market the number and range of jobs available at any one time.

jockeying competing as in a horse race; trying to get into the best position.

jury a group of citizens chosen to hear evidence in a trial and to decide whether the accused person is innocent or guilty.

juvenile delinquency crimes and violence committed by people too young to be tried in a regular court.

Kaiser the emperor of Germany

kilt short, pleated skirt worn by some Scotsmen and as a uniform by some army regiments.

laissez faire economic theory that the government should not interfere with business or industry.

law rule; compare with *bill* and *act*.

legislature provincial parliament.

legendary famous.

liberation setting free.

lice small insects that live on the skin or in the hair of people or animals.

lieutenant governor the representative of the Queen and the Governor general in each province.

life span the length of time someone can be expected to live.

lime a type of white clay used in making plaster and cement.

livelihood the way people make their living.

locomotive train engine.

lord chancellor a very high-ranking British government official with important legal duties.

loyalty faithful support, especially for the government.

lumber sawed-up wood; **lumber-jack** someone who cuts down trees.

lure (*n*) pull, attraction; (*v*) attract, tempt.

majority more than half a group, especially more than half the members of parliament, as in *majority government*.

malfunctioning not working properly.

mammoth huge.

management 1) planning and directing; 2) the people in a business whose job is to plan and direct the operation.

mania great enthusiasm.

manifesto a statement of beliefs and policies by a political group.

manpower human strength; the number of people available to work.

manufacturer a person or company that makes a product on a large scale, usually in a factory.

margin a part payment to buy shares, the stock broker lending the remainder.

market any area where buying and selling is done on a regular basis.

marquis wheat a type of wheat, developed in Canada to grow well in the weather and soil conditions of the prairies.

mechanize to bring in machines to do a job that used to be done by hand.

medicare health care paid for by the government.

merge blend, come together.

military machine whole system of armies, ships, supplies, weapons, etc.

militia ordinary citizens trained to act as soldiers in an emergency.

mill a place where grain, etc. is ground up; any place that processes raw materials, e.g. a pulp and paper mill.

mine a place where coal, minerals, or ores are extracted from the ground.

minimum wage the amount set by law that is the least an employer is allowed to pay a worker.

minister a cabinet member who is responsible for a department, e.g. fisheries.

minority less than half of a group, especially less than half the members of parliament, as in minority government.

missionary someone who goes to a distant country to spread a religion.

mobilize set in motion; prepare for war.

morality ideas about right and wrong; standards of behaviour.

mortgage a contract in which money lent for the purchase of a house or other property on the understanding that the lender may take over the property if the loan is not repaid.

mosaic something that is made up of many separate, distinct pieces.

motto a special saying that goes with a coat of arms.

mount fix in place.

mower a machine for cutting hay, grass, etc.

multicultural including or representing many different cultures.

multiracial including or representing many different races.

municipal of a town or city.

munitions guns and ammunition.

nation a country or the people of a particular country; a group of people with a common origin and strong cultural ties, e.g. the Dene nation, the French-Canadian nation.

nationalize to place an industry or resource under government (as opposed to private) management by "buying it out" or, in some countries, simply taking it over.

naval connected with a navy.

Nazi (national socialist) supporter of an extreme type of fascism that dominated Germany from 1933 to 1945, under Adolf Hitler.

neutral not taking sides in a dispute or war.

nomadic leading a wandering life, with no fixed home.

no man's land the stretch of land between two opposing armies, which is controlled by neither.

nominate suggest a person to represent a political party in an election.

non-renewable resources natural materials, like oil and other minerals, that do not grow back after they have been used up.

non-white term used to refer to skin colour in mainly "white" societies.

nostalgia a longing for the past, often remembered as better or happier than it really was.

nourishment the food and drink necessary to stay strong and healthy.

nuclear power energy created when the central "nucleus" of an atom is split, or when atoms are fused.

observers people who study and analyse various current events, usually political.

occupied Europe the part of Europe under the control of Germany and its allies during World War II.

offset to balance or make up for weakness or strength.

oil refinery an industrial plant where crude oil is made into gasoline, heating oil, kerosene, solvents, etc.

oldtimer someone who has lived for a long time.

opposition members of parliament who do not belong to the governing party.

optimism a hopeful outlook, expecting the best.

orchard an area planted in fruit trees.

ore a rock or other natural substance that contains a metal.

output the amount of goods produced.

overproduce to produce more of something than you can sell.

pacifist someone who believes in solving all problems peacefully, and is especially opposed to war.

pancreas the gland in the body that produces insulin to control the blood sugar levels.

parachute a large, frameless umbrella used to slow the fall of a body through the air.

paralysed unable to move or act.

paratroopers soldiers brought in by aircraft who parachute into battle.

parched extremely dry.

partisans strong supporters; organized but unofficial army that fights to drive out a foreign invader who controls the country.

patriotism strong love and support for one's country.

pavilion a large tent or other structure used for displays at fairs or exhibitions.

pawns people who are used by others for selfish purposes.

peasants farm workers or farming families without very much money. Also used to mean poor, uneducated country people.

pension money paid regularly to certain people, e.g. the elderly, the disabled, the retired.

pessimism a hopeless outlook, expecting the worst.

phenomenon a remarkable event, occurrence, or object.

phonograph a record-player.

pick a pointed tool used for breaking rock or ground.

picric acid a chemical used in making explosives.

pioneer someone who settles in a new region, e.g. the prairies; someone who investigates a new field of research, e.g. nuclear medicine.

pith helmet a light fibre helmet worn for protection from the sun.

platform things that a political party or candidate promises to do when and if elected.

plead to argue a civil or criminal case in a court of law.

pledge a promise.

plough a tool for breaking up soil (so seeds can be planted).

pluralistic a society where various religions, ethnic, racial, and political groups live in the same community.

policy a plan of action, especially in government.

political concerned with ideas of government.

polling station temporary office set up for election day where people go to vote in municipal, provincial, or federal elections.

pollution the presence of damaging chemicals and other impurities in the air, land, or water.

poverty the state of having very few of life's necessities (food, shelter, clothing).

prejudice an opinion (usually bad) formed before one has had time to judge someone or something fairly.

primary industries industries that harvest natural resources, e.g. mining, farming, fishing, lumbering; compare with *secondary industries*.

privy council a committee of high government officials appointed to advise the monarch or the governor general.

processing treatment that turns raw materials into finished products.

profit gain; the amount by which the income from something exceeds the costs to make it.

profiteers people who try to make unfair profits by taking advantage of others' needs in time of war and disaster.

prohibition a total ban on making and selling alcohol.

propaganda a systematic plan to persuade people that one political outlook is better than all others, using radio, T.V., the press, and other means.

propeller a set of rotating blades that moves a boat or plane through water or air.

property any possession, such as jewels, house, land, or money.

prosecute to take legal action against someone for a crime or other wrongdoing.

prospector someone who searches for valuable mineral deposits.

prosperity well-being, wealth.

public service workers for the Canadian government.

pulp a soggy mixture of wood fibres used to make paper.

quintuplets five babies born to one mother at one time.

rabble-rouser someone who excites crowds in order to cause a riot.

racial connected with race, colour, or nationality.

racism prejudice or hatred based on race, colour, or nationality.

radiation the energy released during a nuclear reaction or explosion that can harm or change living tissue.

ration *(v)* to divide something scarce (such as food or gas) into equal portions; *(n)* a portion or allowance.

raw materials the unprocessed materials used to make finished products, e.g. wood for paper or furniture.

rebellion an organized attempt to overthrow a government.

reciprocity an agreement between two countries to allow imports and exports with few restrictions.

recreational facilities parks, swimming pools, community centres, etc. that are provided for pleasure and relaxation.

recruit *(v)* to enlist or hire people to join the army or navy; *(n)* a person who has just been hired in this way.

referendum a vote by all people to accept or reject a government proposal. Also called a *plebiscite*.

refinery see oil refinery.

reformers people who want to change society or government for the better.

refugees people who have had to leave their countries to escape cruel treatment because of political disagreement with the government, other dangers, or war.

relief money, food, or clothes provided to people in need. The modern equivalent of "relief" is "welfare."

renewable resources natural products, like lumber or fish, that can grow again as they are used.

representative someone chosen by a group of people to speak for them and make decisions on their behalf.

resistance organized secret groups working to throw out a foreign invader who controls the country, e.g. the French or Yugoslav resistance during World War II.

resource useful natural product such as oil, fish, iron ore, water, wood; **resource industry** industry that uses and depends on natural resources.

revitalization bringing back to life.

revolution the overthrow of a government by some of the people.

riding a political division (based on the number of residents) represented by a member of parliament or a member of the legislative assembly (see *constituency*).

rights the opportunities and standards of treatment that every human being should be able to claim.

riot wild, often violent outburst by a large group of people.

role a part someone plays and the duties it involves.

rural to do with the country, or farms; compare with *urban*.

sabotage deliberate damage, especially in war, to anything the enemy might use for military purposes.

sacrifice give up something of value (such as life or property) for someone else's sake.

sandbag a small sack filled with sand; used to build military defences or to hold back a flood.

sanitation clean, healthy habits and facilities like running water and proper waste disposal.

satellite a small body that revolves around a larger one, e.g. the moon, or a space station around the Earth.

scapegoat someone who is made to bear the blame for another person's mistakes or crimes.

schooner a type of sailing ship with two or more masts and sets of sails.

scrutineer party member who attends at election polling stations to see that no irregularities happen.

secondary industries industries that use natural products to manufacture things, such as cars and radios. Compare with *primary industries*.

security safety; the safe-keeping of a nation's secrets about defence or other matters.

seeder a farm machine for sowing seed.

self-government government of a region by the people who live there.

self-sufficient able to live and function without help from others.

Senate the second or "upper" branch of many legislatures, such as the Canadian Parliament or the U.S. Congress.

separatism movement to separate Quebec from the rest of Canada and give it political independence.

services industries or businesses that supply service (rather than things) such as dry cleaning and education.

settlers people who go to a new area and make their homes there; pioneers; colonists.

shares equal parts of the ownership of a business; people who buy these shares are called *shareholders*.

shell ammunition fired from large guns containing explosives, etc.

shingle a woman's short haircut shaped close to the head.

shrapnel pieces of metal hurled out in all directions by a special type of shell that explodes in the air or on impact.

shrivel dry out.

sickle a tool with a curved blade for cutting grass or grain.

silicon chip a tiny wafer with a greatly reduced photographic engraving of an electronic circuit on its surface. These chips are used to reduce the size and weight of the circuitry used in computers, thus increasing the variety and complexity of the jobs computers can do.

sit-in a lot of people sitting down in a public place to cause inconvenience, to demonstrate for a cause, such as civil rights, peace, etc.

skilled specially trained for certain types of work (plumbing, car maintenance, etc.)

slum area of a city where poor people live crowded together, often in unsanitary housing.

slump a period when business is poor and there are fewer jobs.

smelter a furnace in which metal ores are melted down to separate the metal from the rock, etc.

sniper someone who shoots from a hidden place.

social of or about human beings living together as a group.

socialism a political and economic system in which property and businesses are owned by the community rather than individuals, and all people share in both the work and the profits.

society *1)* all the people in a community or country; *2)* a group of people with similar interests, attitudes, or standards of living.

sod surface layer of earth containing grass and matted roots. **sodbuster** settler on the Prairies who broke up the sod in order to prepare the land for raising crops.

solidarity standing together; loyalty among people who have common problems or goals.

soup kitchen a place where soup or other food is served to the poor or homeless.

spearhead to lead an attack.

spiral winding or twisting round and round, like a spring.

spy someone who tries to find out another person's (or another country's) secrets.

stalemate a stage in an argument, war, or discussion when neither side is willing or able to make a move.

standard of living the level at which a person (or the average person in a group or country) lives, with respect to food, shelter, and the variety and quality of goods and services that can be expected.

state a nation (e.g. the state of Japan) or a political unit within a nation (e.g. the state of Kansas); the government of a nation.

status rank or position.

steampower energy produced by a steam engine.

stock market the buying and selling of stocks and shares; the stock exchange is where this takes place.

stocks see *shares*.

strike a refusal by the workers to continue working.

stumbling block an obstacle or problem in the way of getting things done.

subsoil the layer of earth which lies just under the surface or topsoil.

suburbs the outskirts or outlying districts of a city.

suffocate to die from lack of air or oxygen.

suicide the act of killing oneself.

supersonic faster than the speed of sound (some jet aircraft travel at supersonic speeds).

supertanker a huge ship designed to carry a large cargo of oil.

supply the money the government needs to run itself (run the Houses of Parliament, pay MPs salaries, and so on).

supreme court the highest, most authoritative law court in Canada; the "court of final appeal."

tank a huge armoured war vehicle designed to cross all sorts of rough territory.

tank traps obstacles (such as blocks of concrete placed close together) which tanks cannot pass.

tariff a special tax on imports and exports.

tarpaper strong paper coated with tar; used for roofing and insulation.

tax money paid to or collected by the government.

taxation the system of arranging and collecting taxes.

technology, technological use of up-to-date scientific know-how in industry and everyday life.

Telidon a two-way communication system developed in Canada using a combination of television and computers.

temperance *1)* refusal to use alcohol; *2)* use in moderation.

terrorism organized use of violence and illegal acts to create an atmosphere of great fear and to put pressure on the government.

thresher, threshing machine a machine for separating the edible part of a crop (the grain) from the plant stalks.

timber wood or trees.

TNT an explosive.

token something meaningless in itself which is meant to stand for something more important; a symbol.

tractor a powerful farm vehicle, often used for pulling other farm machinery.

traitor someone who does something to harm his or her own country, especially giving away its military or commercial secrets.

transcontinental spreading across a continent.

transistor a tiny device that controls electric current; used in many electric appliances, allowing them to be small.

transportation the means of moving lots of people or goods.

treadle a foot-operated lever that controls the part(s) of a machine that spins or turns.

treaty an agreement between two or more groups, which is supposed to solve their differences.

trench a long, narrow ditch dug in the ground.

trench warfare during World Wars I and II, soldiers dug trenches to camp in and walk along, so they couldn't be seen or shot at by the enemy.

triple three of something.

trestles and ties the wood pieces that form the roadbed for a railway; ties lie crosswise under the steel track; trestles support bridges.

unemployment being out of work; a shortage of jobs.

unions organizations of workers in the same trade or working in the same industry.

united joined, sharing beliefs; sticking together.

unskilled with no special skill or job training.

urban in or relating to cities.

ventilate introduce air to a place or space.

veto a legal and official refusal to allow a government bill or other proposal to take effect.

victim person harmed by a physical, economic, or political act.

visible minority group within a society that looks different because of skin colour, physical features, or clothing style.

voluntarily by one's own free choice; willingly.

volunteer one who offers to join the armed forces; one who works without pay for a service organization (Red Cross, political party, etc)

vote choose among political candidates in an election or between proposals in a meeting.

war effort the working together of armed forces, civilians, industry, and government when trying to win a war.

warehouse a building used for storing large quantities of materials.

welfare state a state in which the government provides services for the people, such as health care, unemployment payment, old-age pensions.

will a legal declaration in which a person says what is to be done with his or her property after death.

"wipers" during World War I soldiers' way of pronouncing Ypres, a Belgian placename.

witch-hunt an investigation of people, accusing them, with little evidence, of betraying the country; sometimes used to get rid of political opponents.

workforce all the workers of a nation.

zero hour the time set for an important event, such as an attack during war.

Index

Acknowledgements

Picture Credits: Illustrations are listed as they appear from top to bottom, in each column of the page. Unless otherwise identified, in the credits that follow, numbers preceded by C or PA refer to the Public Archives of Canada (PAC) collection. Provincial Archives and Tourist Bureaus are identified by the initial(s) of the province followed by S and T respectively, e.g. AA, NBT. Other abbreviations used include: BQT — Bureau du Québec à Toronto: CN — Canadian National; DND — Department of National Defence; GA — Glenbow-Alberta Institute; IO — Imperial Oil; JCTA — James Collection, City of Toronto Archives; MTL, Metro Toronto Library Board; NFA — National Film Archives; OFL — Ontario Federation of Labour; SHF — Sports Hall of Fame; TY — Toronto Telegram Archives, York University.

Original Art *(supervised by S. Rauchman):* David Partington, pp 34-35, 84-85, 178-179, 228-229; Scott Caple, pp 60-61, 120-121; Dan Kewley, pp 152-153, 203-204, 287 (bottom); Penny Moir, 285, 287 (top), 288, 292, 298, 299, 300, 303, 305, 306, 309, 317, 318-319.

Art Gallery *(compiled by S. Budd and S. Rauchman):* 4 Robert Stacey; 5 McMichael Canadian Collection; 6 Robarts Library; 7 Metro Toronto Library; 8 Glenbow-Alberta Institute, Robert Stacey; 9 Canadian War Museum; 10 Canadian War Museum, Robarts Library; 11 Canadian War Museum; 12 Robert Stacey; 13 Canadian Pacific; 14-15 Robarts Library; 16-17 Art Gallery of Ontario; 18-19 National Gallery of Canada; 20 Canadian War Museum; 21 Canadian War Museum; 24 Western Producer Prairie Books; 25 Toronto Dominion Bank Art Collection; 26 University of British Columbia; 27 Dr. Bernhard Cinader; 28 Arthur Horsfall; 29 Toronto Dominion Bank Art Collection; 30-31 Toronto Dominion Bank Art Collection; 32 compiled by Robert Read; 33 Kaj Pindal.

A New Century *(design-Budd):* 36 OA S15070, C16378; 37 SA A6187, PAC 49972; 38 C681, PAC; 39 MA AA; 40 SA, PA88422, PAC 10400; 41 MA, PA41785; 42 GA NA1366-8, PA38590; 43 Eaton Archives, GA NA3403-13; 44 PA11566, PA42438; 45 PA61772, C56688; 46 United Church Archives, PA69966; 47 OA S2903, MA, PA60732; 48 MA, Ontario Hydro; 49 MTL, OA S13722; 50 PA38622; 51 C56695, General Motors, JCTA 42, PA37798; 52 Canadian War Museum J29642-2; 53 C2082, C5110; 54 JCTA; 55 C15874, C17945; 57 MA, C27674; 59 PA16831, OA 9066#14.

Canada Goes to War *(design-Budd/Rauchman):* 62 MTL, C89316; 64 PA4910, JCTA; 65 JCTA, PAC 2468; 66 PA683, PA648; 67 PA1398, PA1679, PA518, PA3737; 68 PA5001; 69 PA1879, PA1110, PA1332; 70 PA1654, PA25148; 71 GA NA1258-2; 72 PA24363; 72-73 C19948; 73 JCTA 1782; 74 PA88504, PA42869; 75 JCTA, C95314, PA25180; 76 PA22784, PA156; 77 PA1368, PA4422; 78 C29484, C6859; 79 C12592, PA2318; 80 PA2946, JCTA, PA3270; 81 PA3842; 83 JCTA 4007, PA74, Glenbow NA2001-14, PA83986.

Boom and Bust *(design-Budd/Rauchman)* 86 JCTA 906, PA33971; 87 JCTA, nk; 88 C37275, C39556; 89 nk, C66639; 90 C21569, Catherine Lyle Cleverdon, 91 MIL, C54523; 92 C56167, PA24412; 93 JCTA 1028, Eaton Archives; 94 PA30308, CN, CN, Grant McConachie; 95 Ontario Hydro, PACT, General Motors, CN, CN, CN; 96 Eaton Archives; 97 PA74716, PA86257, PA83988; 98 NFA, NFA; 99 NFA, NFA; 100 SHF, MTL, PAC 50440, SHF; 101 C4752, SHF, PA50338, SHF; 102 PA86236; 103 MTL; 104 MTL, C29396; 105 C30811, GA NC6-12955B; 106 GA ND3-6742; 107 GA 2496-1, MA; 108 C13236; 109 C24840; 110 C9064; 111 PA37922; 112 MTL; 113 C9339, C19518; 114 all NFA; 115 NFA, NFA, PA49651; MTL; 117 C29449; Air Canada 9944, University of Toronto.

The World at War *(design-Budd/Rauchman):* 124 C24963, C16812; 125 C24954; 126 C24958; 127 Roderick Stewart; 128 DND/PAC PA 107907; 129 DND PL3053; 130 C29856; 131 C14160; 132 PA95708; 133 C33442, MTL; 134 C45026, C47402; 135 C46350, David Suzuki; 136 MA; 137 DND/PAC PA107903; 138 PA108273, PAC C79525; 139 DND/PAC PA107904, DND/PAC 37479; 140 C92393; 141 C29452, PAC C22001; 142 PA114482; 143 DND, PA107937; 144 DND GM2243; 145 PA113697, DND ANP36701; 146 Yad Vashem; 147 Toronto Sun Syndicate; 148 TY; 149 TY, TY, C3570; 150 C25, MTL, MTL; 151 C29854, C29857, C29588.

Midcentury *(design-Budd/Rauchman):* 154 TY; 155 C20049, C471; 156 C30760, DND/PAC PA107932, C56829; 157 C17219; 158 AA P2733, TY; 159 C47009; 160 Ontario Hydro; 160-1 *Map and graphs:* St. Lawrence Seaway Authority; 161 JCTA 2140; 162-4 all TY; 165 TY, PA120148; 166 PAC 80883; 167 PAC 15160, DND; 168 PA 117617; 169 PAC; 170-1 all NDP Archives; 172 MA, MTL; 173 TY, TY; 174 PAC 26756, PAC 30084; 175 Expo 67, TY; 177 QT, MA.

Creative Tensions *(design-Rauchman/Reid):* 180 PAC 27281; 181 PAC 112579; 182 IO/Kenneth Powell; 183-5 all OFL/Alan Pryde; 187 Employment and Immigration Canada 188 Shing Wah Daily News, AT, MT, OT, MT; 188-9 QT; 189 OT, QT, NBT, NT; 190 Dept. of Indian Affairs and Northern Development, 192 IO, IO; 193 IO, West Baffin Eskimo Co-operative; 194 Transair, OFL; 195 OFL; Ontario Ministry of Labour Women's Bureau; 196 MTL, Dick Flohill, Wally Ballach, MT, Alden Nowlan; 197 Stratford Festival; Dick Flohill; 198 SA 67-665-39, Prudential Life; 199 Toronto Blizzard; QT; Montreal Expos; D.J. Konihowski; 200 OFL/Alan Pryde, campaign button; 202 Petro-Canada.

Canada and the World *(design-Rauchman/Reid):* 206 United Nations Association of Canada; 207 both UNICEF; 209 PAC 77793; 210 DND 12C75-365; 211 DND REC76-106; Lockheed; 212 PAC 18846; 214 both UNICEF; 215 Ken Bell, Torstar; 216 TY, TY; 217 DND ME78-233, TY; 218 Torstar; 219 ROM; PAC 6440, PAC DC8162-21, BCT, TY, Torstar, Time; 220 U.S. Consulate in Toronto, PA 117602, Dept. of External Affairs; 221 BC Hydro; 223 Performing Rights Organization of Canada, Gord Marci, International

Management Group, CBC, National Ballet of Canada, CBS; 224 Torstar; 225 OFL/Alan Pryde.

One Nation or Two? *(design-Reid):* 230 QT; 231 NBT; 232 PAC; 233 MTL; 234 QT; 235 TY, PA 117531; 236-7 all TY; 238 BQT; 239 Torstar; 240 BQT, campaign buttons; 241 BQT, BQT; 242 TY; 243 MTL, BQT, BQT; 244 Ville de Montréal; 245 QT, QT, QT, Petro-Canada, Ville de Montréal, QT, QT, BQT.

Regional Report *(design-Rauchman):* 248 MA 73-5332; 249 QT; 250 MTL, Hudson's Bay Co.; 251 PA 116541, G.G. Graydon, Steven Bradley; 252 SA; 253 SA; 254 Picturesque Canada, BCT; 255 BCT, Rio Algom, BCT, BCT; 256-7 all BCT; 258 Picturesque Canada, AA; 259 AA, MT, SA R-A 9877 (5), AA; 260 SA; 261 IO; 262 BCT; 264 MTL, OT; 265 all OT; 266 Stelco; 267 OFL/Alan Pryde; 268 Picturesque Canada, Ville de Montréal; 269 QT, Denis Brodeur, Alcan, QT; 270 Techniques Audio-Visuelle; 271 QT, QT; 272 Picturesque Canada, NBT; 273 NBT, NBT, PEIT; 274 NBT; 275 PEIT; 276 George Draskoy; 277 Gulf Oil 15894-B; 278 BCT, AT, ST: 279 OT, QT, NST.

Government in Canada *(design-Reid):* 282 SA 67-665-39, TY, WJL Gibbon; 283 Office of the Speaker of the Senate, Cavouk of the Colonnade, Cavouk, OFL/Alan Pryde, SA 67-665-39; 285 Environment Canada, Ontario Ministry of the Environment, Toronto Dept. of Public Works; 290 Canadian Press; 291 Canadian Unity Information Office; 301 Andrews-Newton Photographers, Photo Features, Gaby; 302 Liberal Party of Canada, Progressive Conservative Party of Canada; 304 Jean-Marc Carisse, Flora MacDonald, M. Redford, J. Gregg Eligh; 307 Liberal Party, Progressive Conservative Party, Photo Features; 308 PAC 68509, Harold Clark, MTL; 310 Office of the Governor General; 311 Cavouk of the Colonnade; 313 Canadian Unity Information Office.

Towards the Next Century *(design-Gillen):* 319 NASA; 320 Northern Telecom 44633-2, NASA courtesy Spar Aerospace; 321 Northern Telecom, Northern Telecom, OT 6-J-0171; 322 IO 80 (57) 1406, IO 8-1068, IO 79 (3C) 104, IO 77-39; 323 Ontario Hydro 13A1283A, Ontario Hydro 12A1004; 324 OT79020001, MT OT77080518; 325 Ontario Hydro 7A19508, MT 68-1873, IO 80-1199; 326 DND 78-287, United Nations; 327 AT, CN 69799-4; 328 MTL; 329 Oakville Journal Record/Pete Martin.